*If you survey books on theology you will find very little written on the topic of how God will reward His people. This book demonstrates that this is a major theme in Scripture and that faithfulness in this life will determine rewards in the next. This sobering reality should motivate us to live each day for the glory of God lest we miss the greatest rewards when in the presence of Jesus. Read it, meditate on it and ask God to bring your life in line with eternal values.*

**Dr. Erwin W. Lutzer**
Pastor Emeritus
Moody Church Chicago

*The most important day in the Christian's future is the day we stand before our Lord at the Judgment Seat of Christ. What we enjoy for all eternity will be determined on that day. Kevin Kaufman's* **Investing in Eternity** *explores that day thoroughly and the need to prepare for it today.*

**Dr. Woodrow Kroll**
Creator of
The HELIOS Projects

*"***Investing in Eternity** *will challenge you. And it may change the way you understand God's purposes.** Kevin's research and analysis of God's eternal rewards are more complete than any I've seen. It's shocking how silent this mega-truth is in the church. I highly recommend you spend time with this book and let his work open your eyes and take you deeper into God's Word."*

**Jeff Anderson**
Author of Plastic Donuts and Divine Applause.

*"In* A Guide to Investing in Eternity*: God's Conditional Promise of Reward, Kevin W. Kaufman has performed an important service for the church in this exhaustive review of the Bible's "if this...then that" promises of God. The book is a readable, thought-provoking, and often insightful exposition of what those many verses teach.*

*Throughout, Kevin relates to 'people who are struggling with purpose in life.' Born of a long season of personal pain, Investing in Eternity is—as Kevin puts it— 'for all who desire more out of life, suffer in this life, feel listless or unfulfilled, are tired, experience little satisfaction in the successes of this life, and are curious about what lies beyond this life.'* Investing in Eternity *is biblically sound as well as thorough; broad as well as practical. Most importantly, it is a book of hope. I highly recommend it."*

**Dr. Ed Hoskins, MD, PhD**
Author – A Muslim's Heart (NavPress 2003) and A Muslim's Mind (Dawson Media 2011)

A Guide to

# Investing in Eternity

*God's Conditional Promise of Reward*

KEVIN W. KAUFMAN

WESTBOW
PRESS®
A DIVISION OF THOMAS NELSON
& ZONDERVAN

WestBow Press books may be ordered through booksellers or by contacting:

WestBow Press
A Division of Thomas Nelson & Zondervan
1663 Liberty Drive
Bloomington, IN 47403
www.westbowpress.com
1 (866) 928-1240

Unless stated otherwise, all Scripture quotations are taken from The Holy Bible, New International Version®, NIV® Copyright © 1973, 1978, 1984, 2011 by Biblica, Inc.® Used by permission. All rights reserved worldwide.

Scripture quotations marked NLT are taken from the Holy Bible, New Living Translation, Copyright © 1996, 2004, 2015 by Tyndale House Foundation. Used by permission of Tyndale House Publishers, Inc., Carol Stream, Illinois 60188. All rights reserved.

Scripture quotations marked KJV are taken from the King James Version.

Scripture quotations marked ESV taken from The Holy Bible, English Standard Version® (ESV®), Copyright © 2001 by Crossway, a publishing ministry of Good News Publishers. All rights reserved.

ISBN: 978-1-9736-8747-4 (sc)
ISBN: 978-1-9736-8746-7 (e)

Print information available on the last page.

WestBow Press rev. date: 4/11/2020

# About the Author

Kevin W. Kaufman is an entrepreneur, inventor, and writer living in West Lafayette, Indiana. He was most recently the president of the Foundation for Christian Stewardship, an affiliate of the National Christian Foundation. For twenty-seven years before heading this ministry, Kevin was a business owner while serving as a lay leader in his church.

A graduate of the Moody Bible Institute in Bible and theology, he received his BA in history and economics from Lawrence University in Appleton, Wisconsin.

Kevin and his supportive wife, Sandra, have three children: Rachel, Andrew, and Emma.

# Disclaimers

First, *Investing in Eternity* is not about how to go to heaven when you die. If you have yet to put your faith in Jesus, then please go to appendix 5 and learn of God's wonderful gift of salvation. God's rewards are for those who have already received that unmerited gift. So please consider accepting His gracious offer of forgiveness and salvation now, during, or after you read *Investing in Eternity.*

Second, this book does not advocate (because Scripture does not teach) a "prosperity gospel." The "health and wealth gospel" is worse than mistaken; they are evil. If you believe the Bible promises temporal rewards, please read appendix 1.

*Dedicated to my mother*
**Carolyn Gutwein Kaufman**
*through whom Jesus beautifully reveals His love.*

# Addendum

This book has been published in the midst of the coronavirus pandemic. Never has the world more needed the message of hope found in *Investing in Eternity*.

# Contents

# Acknowledgments

As the recently appointed president of the Foundation for Christian Stewardship, I began reading everything I could find concerning the biblical teaching of financial stewardship. I was particularly interested in what properly motivates faithfulness in financial matters. The idea that God promises to reward first caught my attention as I read Randy Alcorn's *Money, Possessions, and Eternity.* Alcorn pointed to the hope of rewards as a powerful biblical motivation for financial stewardship. He called the central driver of this incentive, "The Treasure Principle": "You can't take it with you, but you can send it on ahead" (Alcorn, 19).

"Hmm," I thought as I read, "I wonder if the Bible speaks of whole-life stewardship, too."

Once upon the scent of this doctrine, I hunted for verses that speak of it: to gather all I could find in the Bible that speak of rewards. Some of the verses I collected had been cited by Alcorn. Bruce Wilkinson's *A Life God Rewards* contained a treasury of Scripture references. John Piper writes of others in *Desiring God.* Woodrow Kroll's radio series (and the corresponding book) *Facing Your Final Job Review* aired at a most opportune time to encourage my quest. I have since read and recommend an earlier book by Dr. Kroll, *Tested by Fire,* published initially as *It Will Be Worth It All.* Dr. Erwin Lutzer's thought-provoking contribution to the subject is *Your Eternal Reward.*

Those and other writings reassured me that I had not "discovered" some new teaching of Scripture. (If I had, it would be suspect indeed!) I found that the doctrine of rewards has been taught from early in church history and across the theological spectrum, as you will see in quotes throughout *Investing in Eternity* and in appendix 6.

*Investing in Eternity,* however, is different from other books on the subject. As I explain, I consider *every* explicitly and implicitly conditional promise of blessing to speak of reward for faithfulness. I have attempted to identify all of them. There are hundreds of such promises, printed in appendix 7 and categorized in indexes 1–3. While the writings of others helped my understanding, it is Scripture that has convinced my heart of the truth and importance of God's promise to reward. My wonder at the extent of the Bible's teaching on the subject is matched only by my bewilderment that God's intent to reward is so seldom mentioned by Christians.

(Unless otherwise noted, Bible quotations are from the New International Version. Verses that do not speak of conditionality are bracketed {thus}.)

Kevin W. Kaufman

# Preface

*Everything is meaningless . . . completely meaningless . . .*
*So, I gave up in despair, questioning the value*
*of all my hard work in this world.*
{Eccles. 1:21, 2:20 NLT}

Nietzsche or Sartre could have said it no better. You may sigh in agreement with Solomon: "That's why we so much look forward to heaven, right?" I suppose . . . But melancholy musings on the meaninglessness of life expose a lingering question about the life to come. Like a pesky house mouse darting in and out of my peripheral view, it abruptly commands my attention and prompts a question.

### *"Why, God . . . ?"*

If all Your people will *equally experience heaven*, what is the purpose of this immeasurably-brief-as-compared-to-eternity life? If the only decision or action of eternal consequence is whether or not to accept God's gift of salvation, then what else, if anything, matters in this life? Why shouldn't I simply make myself comfortable to the end of my days—and then forever enjoy heaven?

I intend no insolence, Lord. I am merely echoing the psalmist: *"Remember how fleeting is my life. For what futility have you created all humanity!"* {Ps. 89:47}. It was Job's lament: *"My days are swifter than a runner; they fly away without a glimpse of joy"* {Job 9:25}. You pronounced it so Yourself through your prophet Isaiah, *"All people are like grass, and all their faithfulness is like the flowers of the field"* {Isa. 40:6}.

Theologian and scientist Blaise Pascal pondered the question.

When I consider the brief span of my life absorbed into the eternity which precedes and will succeed it—*memoria hospitis unius diei praetereuntis* (remembrance of a guest who tarried but a day)—the small space I occupy and which I see swallowed up in the infinite immensity of spaces of which I know nothing and which know nothing of me, I take fright and am amazed to see myself here rather than there: there is no reason for me to be here rather than there, now rather than then. (Blaise Pascal, *Pensées, 22*)

Our lives begin and end as a drop in a boundless ocean of time. Your purposes, Sovereign Lord, will be accomplished with or without my help. You are in no way dependent upon me, are you? People won't go to hell *because* I failed to tell them about Jesus, will they? If I am a spiritual slouch and forfeit something that You want for me in this life, I won't remember the loss when I get to heaven. A millennium of millennia from now, how I lived won't matter. Whether I sacrifice all or little to You, what I do in this life will be *"meaningless"* (Solomon's word).

If "1" represents my salvation and "$1^x$" represents my obedience, $1 \times 1^x = 1$, whether $x = 0$ or $1,000,000$. Either way, at my life's end, I will be happy and joy-filled in heaven for all of eternity. Bereft of defining axiom, life has no more point than Euclid would ascribe.

So, Lord, for the follower of Christ,

### *"What is the purpose of life?"*

**Perhaps my reader has a ready answer:**

*"Because God commands us to serve Him."* Yes, He does. But unless you believe our persistent efforts *preserve* our salvation, that doesn't answer the question.

*"Because this life will be better for you if you obey God."* It may be so. But what of the millions of Christians who have suffered (or are suffering) persecution, trials, or imminent death? In what sense is this life better for the person who forsakes all and picks up his cross to follow Jesus? What benefit accrues to one who boldly professes his faith and promptly has his head lopped off?

"*Because God uses us to spread the Good News of Jesus.*" Again, that's true; but it still doesn't answer my question. God doesn't *need* my efforts. Does He? Why does it matter whether or not I choose to participate in His work?

"*Because God chose you to do good works.*" Yes, but what is the big deal if I sit out one or two of His work assignments? I will enjoy heaven forever, won't I?

"*We can't fully understand His purposes.*" That is undoubtedly true. But one doesn't have to know everything about something to know something fundamental to it. Proficiency in trigonometry isn't necessary to the knowledge that one plus one equals two. A compass is not as helpful as Google Maps, but it will at least keep me from walking in circles. On this question, does God leave us wandering in the woods?

**Am I alone with my question?**

Perhaps you unconsciously ask it, too, but it has never surfaced in your conscious mind.

Perhaps you have had an easy life, so the question hasn't demanded attention.

Perhaps you think it is wrong to ask or even consider such a question.

Perhaps you have steadfastly ignored the question.

But you certainly know people who are struggling with the purpose of life, consciously or unconsciously. For example, I spoke recently with a follower of Jesus who has much pain in his life. When I asked how he was doing, he replied in despair, "You know when Paul says he would rather be away from his earthly body because then he would be at home with the Lord? Well, that is sounding pretty good to me, too." Paul wrote those words to encourage suffering people with the hope of heaven. But this man's tone of voice unmistakably communicated that he mostly wished himself *dead*!

Christians aren't alone in questioning the purpose of life. According to a recent poll, 89 percent of sixteen to twenty-nine-year-olds and 80 percent of all ages in the UK say life is meaningless (*The Sun News*, 2019). The world is weary of its shallow existence. The Oscar-winning song from the movie *A Star is Born* resonates in its heart.

Aren't you tired,
tryin' to fill that void?
Or do you need more?
(Lady Gaga, "Shallow")

The Bible tells Christians to be ready to give an answer to *everyone* (Christian and non-Christian alike) who asks about the hope that is in you. What "hope" are you prepared to share with people who question the point of life?

## Why I Wrote *Investing in Eternity*

What if the premise of the preface, the underlying
assumption of my question, is mistaken?
What if the Bible *does not teach* that all will
have the *same experience* of heaven?
What if God promises that *more* can be *gained* in and from this life?
What if that which you and I acquire will last forever?
That would be a rather big deal, wouldn't it?
Jesus said,

*Do not store up for yourselves **treasures** on earth,*
*where moth and rust destroy, and where thieves break in and steal.*
*But store up for yourselves **treasures** in heaven,*
*where moth and rust do not destroy, and where*
*thieves do not break in and steal.*
(Matt. 6:19-20)

I know a thing or two about storing-up "*treasures on earth.*" I spent nearly three decades in the business of storing grain. I also bought and sold the grain I stored. The goal, as with the trading of any commodity, was to buy low and sell high. But there were any number of variables in the marketplace, many of them (weather, for example) wholly out of my control, which made that endeavor particularly challenging.

The more grain I attracted from customers (primarily farmers), the more money I might make when I sold it and delivered it to buyers (usually by rail to poultry growers in the southern US). So, in addition to being competitive in my prices and service to both seller and buyer, acquiring and delivering higher volume required the risks of investments in storage bins and handling equipment and of borrowing to finance my purchases.

A single bin of grain can be worth millions of dollars, so I had to be careful to preserve the grain's quality between its acquisition and shipment. Its moisture content made grain prone to rotting in the bin, so it had to be precisely, mechanically dried. If inadequately protected (a leaking bin roof, for example) or otherwise poorly tended (such as allowing an insect infestation), financial disaster could result.

Furthermore, grain bins are not secure, like bank vaults. It is easy for thieves to *"break in and steal"* the grain's value from the bin, during its transit, or in the process of its payment. I had to continually convince financiers that I would be able to repay the multimillion-dollar loans with which I bought the grain. And in every transaction, I had to meet the exacting standards of government regulators to maintain my operating license.

There were many other risks, but I think you now understand my visceral appreciation for the perils of *"storing up treasures on earth."* But the most significant threat from the business's uncertainties and vicissitudes was to my emotional heart. During tough times, I worried—and felt guilty about my anxiety, as Jesus reminded me:

> *Who of you by worrying can add a single hour to his life?*
> *Since you cannot do this very little thing, why do you*
> *worry about the rest?* {vv. 25-26}

During times of plenty, I was satisfied with earthly riches, but I felt ashamed when Jesus compared me to the rich fool who said,

> *I will tear down my barns and build bigger ones, and there*
> *I will store my surplus grain. And I'll say to myself . . .*
> *"Take life easy; eat, drink and be merry."* {Luke 12:18-21}

Jesus said the man died that very night. His purpose had come to naught. Jesus concluded,

> *This is how it will be with whoever stores up things for*
> *themselves . . .*

I got the point. However—and this is the object of my story—during this long period of my life, I little understood nor appreciated the weight of what Jesus was talking about when he added . . .

### . . . but is not rich toward God.

I was oblivious to the alternative riches He offered. My understanding was simply this: By God's grace, I had come to know Jesus; with God's help, I am to live a God-honoring life, and then (whew, finally!) I will go to heaven. The end. And so (to change metaphors), I tossed aimlessly, frustratedly; year after year I rode the swells of fortune and misfortune. I had little idea how to actually *enjoy* the voyage; I looked forward only to someday reaching port. And I was clueless about the riches I might find when I eventually made landfall.

That trying season of life ended when I sold my grain business, and God set me on a new path— literally—on a walk home from church. As I prayed and worshiped God, I sensed His great desire for a closer relationship with me. In response, I said out loud, "Lord, I would do or endure *anything* to have *everything* You want for me." To my great surprise, God spoke to me. A single word. A question.

*"Anything?"* God asked. That word was as clear to my mind as if it had been spoken to my ears.

I stopped dead in my tracks. The question was not posited hypothetically: Somehow, I was convinced that if I replied, "Yes, anything," God would give me what I sought, but by means of more, and more challenging, trials. And I knew that if I answered, "No, not *anything*," God would withhold some of those trials—and the blessings they would have produced. It was as clear a choice as was the fork in the path on which I stood, frozen.

After pausing to ponder the implications of my response, I took a deep breath and said, "Yes, Lord. *Anything*." Then I continued walking, with conflicted excitement and a sense of foreboding.

As expected, more troubles have come. Many of them have been trials of physical pain. But the most difficult have pained me emotionally, as I've suffered with people whom I love deeply who are themselves profoundly hurting. (As some of you know, there is no more significant pain. I would tell you more about those struggles, but they are not mine alone to tell. Instead, perhaps you can fill in the blanks with your own bitter experiences.)

But, as I had been promised, those challenges have produced the blessing I sought from God. Now I also know a thing or two about "*storing up treasures in heaven.*" Because of the trials, my heart has become increasingly convinced of the promise of God's reward. As a result, I increasingly take Paul's words as my own.

> *Not that I have already obtained all this, or have already been made perfect, but I press on to take hold of that for which Christ Jesus took hold of me. Brothers, I do not consider myself yet to have taken hold of it. But one thing I do: Forgetting what is behind and straining toward what is ahead, I press on toward the goal to win the prize for which God has called me heavenward in Christ Jesus.* (Phil. 3:12-14)

When I wrote the above story, I was struck by the irony of my "new path" having begun on a physical path. Later, I came across the meaning of the place-name from which Abraham, and later Jacob, were called to go to Bethel, the "House of God." "*Paddan-aram*" is a combination of words from Akkadian and Hebrew that can be translated "path of rescue." What I have learned on my own "path of rescue" has become the content of *Investing in Eternity.*[1]

### God's promises are for you, too!

*Investing in Eternity* is for all who desire more out of life, suffer in this life, feel listless or unfulfilled, are tired, experience little satisfaction in the successes of this life, and are curious about what lies beyond this life. But it is also for all who are currently comfortable with their life's circumstances. Learn from my mistakes.

Whatever your prior understanding or experience of Christianity, if the Bible's commands have seemed as burdensome rules to you—or if you struggle with trusting God in the midst of intractable circumstances—then I hope you will seize upon God's great promises of blessing. As the implications of the Bible's teaching sink into your heart and mind, you will join me in my sense of urgency to take advantage of life's fleeting opportunity to gain for yourself something of immeasurable and eternal value.

Imagine you are looking through the window of an expensive jewelry store like Tiffany's. All of these treasures can be yours, too! God's promised reward will provoke a desire to do whatever it takes to have those riches and to share God's treasure with those around you.

You are in for a pleasant surprise! God's Word will inspire you to live a life of obedience and service that God rewards.

**Notes and Asides:**

*Some of the "Notes and Asides" in* <u>Investing in Eternity</u> *will expand on matters not understood or conceded by all of my readers. The rest should be read as you would watch extra features of a movie: as illustrative, maybe even fun, but not essential to the plot.*

[1] *In the gift shop at the Getty Museum in Los Angeles is a book written by the museum's benefactor, J. Paul Getty, entitled* <u>How to Be Rich</u>. *Like the man of whom Jesus spoke in Matthew 13, Getty found his fortune (of oil) in the ground. I hope Getty didn't give away his money "to be noticed by men." But if he did, then the title is a poignant juxtaposition of the earthly riches of which he wrote to the heavenly riches of which I write. I could have used Getty's book title* <u>How to Be Rich</u>, *with the subtitle* <u>In Heaven</u>!

# An Introduction to *Investing in Eternity*

*Investing in Eternity* is based upon this biblical premise:

> God conditionally promises to reward faithfulness to Him.

It is not the primary purpose of *Investing in Eternity* to prove that doctrine, the truth of which is taken as a given. Instead, we will address a question the many conditional promises provoke:

> **Why does the Bible contain so many promises to reward?**

The answer to that question is the thesis, the central message of *Investing in Eternity*:

> **The doctrine of rewards is an essential teaching of Scripture.**

*Investing in Eternity* establishes the *importance* of this doctrine to our walk with Christ. Without faith in God's promise to reward, it is impossible to please God (Heb. 11:6). *"He who has an ear, let him hear"* what Jesus has to say about the rewards that await those who overcome (Luke 8:18; Rev. 2:7, 11, 17, 29; 3:6, 9, 13). *"Carefully consider"* this teaching, Jesus warned, for *"with the measure you use, it will be measured to you—and even more"* (Mark 4:24). *"Reflect on what I am saying"* about the importance of God's reward, and *"the Lord will give you insight into all of this"* (2 Tim. 2:1-12).

Belief in God's promise to reward motivated the life of the Apostle Paul:

> I do all this for the sake of the gospel, that I may share in its blessings. Do you not know that in a race all the runners run, but only one gets the prize? Run in such a way as to get the prize. Everyone who competes in the

> *games goes into strict training. They do it to get a crown*
> *that will not last; but we do it to get a crown that will last*
> *forever.* (1 Cor. 9:22-25)

Life was not a game for Paul. He was not psyching himself up to run a 5K. By the time he wrote his next letter to the Corinthian church, he had five times received thirty-nine lashes with a whip. Three times he had been beaten with rods; once he had been stoned and left for dead. Under attack from pagan Gentiles, from his kinsman Jews, and from supposed believers in Christ, he was constantly on the move.

Driven from city after city, Paul faced dangers in transit from bandits, raging rivers, and stormy seas, which thrice left him shipwrecked and once set him adrift for a day and a night. He often worked without sleep; hungry and thirsty; cold and naked. And at the time he recounted those many ordeals, he had ten or so more years of harassment to endure before he finally was beheaded by Emperor Nero!

Why did Paul press on in the face of persistent opposition? Because he believed that living for Christ holds *"promise for both the present life and the life to come"* (1 Tim. 4:8). Paul—of all people—was not striving to earn his salvation.[1] Neither was he (metaphorically) running merely because he was commanded to do so by Jesus. He was passionate in his desire to gain something, wasn't he? What was Paul hoping to acquire in sprinting headlong into peril? God's reward. Take a glance at the verses quoted in appendix 7 and scan indexes 1–3. The teaching about God's intent to reward is found everywhere in Scripture. Those promises motivated Paul—and millions of other Christians since—to faithfully serve God and others.

(Note that appendix 7 represents less than one-third of the conditional verses I have found in Scripture. For the complete list, go to www.Investing-in-Eternity.org.)

Most of us are well acquainted with how people *should* live their lives. We are much less familiar with the biblical *reasons* to do so.[2] We know the answer to "What?" *Investing in Eternity* gives an answer to "Why? It reminds—and for some informs for the first time—of an important reason to live a life that is faithful to God: the Bible tells us that our experience of eternity depends upon the conduct of our lives.

Some of my readers do not accept the premise of *Investing in Eternity*, let alone the thesis. What follows aims to convince you of the truth of the premise as it simultaneously supports the thesis, because as I argue that the doctrine is *essential*, it should become clear that it is *true*. Other readers accept the premise that God rewards, but that belief has little impact on their lives. They don't consider the doctrine of rewards to be an essential teaching. *Investing in Eternity* will convince you to the contrary.

Our neglect of God's promise to reward is largely due to a simple hermeneutical error of omission: We do not see the "if you do this, then that will happen" (i.e., the conditional construction) of many biblical promises. Instead, we read the promises of God as if they are unconditional. So, while basking in the glorious promises of God's blessing in Isaiah 51:3-4, for example, we forget the condition for those blessings the prophet plainly sets forth in verse 1: "*Listen to me, you who pursue righteousness and who seek the LORD.*" We forget that it is only "*the righteous*" who "*will enjoy the fruit of their deeds* [their works, their actions]" (Isa. 3:10). The *fullness* of God's blessing (the "*reward*"; the "*recompense*") is always *conditional* (Isa. 40:10). It is dependent upon our voluntary response to God.

Furthermore, misconceptions about the nature of God's reward, and of God's purpose in promising it, keep our hearts and minds from even noticing them. Their beauty and power are hidden in plain sight, like in this picture of an old woman.[3]

Or maybe you see a picture of a *young* woman.

It is both, actually. Until your attention was directed to look for it, you likely would not have perceived the alternative view. That is what I hope to do in *Investing in Eternity*: direct your attention to the importance of a doctrine of Scripture that many of us have not noticed. It is not a new teaching, and— adequately understood—it may conflict with little or none of your current understanding. (Please re-read that sentence; it is an important point.) If you read Scripture looking for its teaching of God's conditional blessings (rewards), you will see it. You may come to wonder—as I did—how you ever *missed* it.

Still others ignore the implications of this teaching because the notion that God rewards is discouraging to them: "I am a loser. God will never reward me." For them, an offer of reward is an invitation to failure. They respond to "*Run to win!*" as I would to a solicitation to compete in a marathon, "Yeah, right. Like I'm going to do that. . . ." I address concerns about this doctrine throughout *Investing in Eternity*. But if your emotional objections are strong enough that they must be addressed before you continue reading, I invite you to turn to Appendix 2: Emotional and Theological Objections.

## The Method of *Investing in Eternity*

The truth and importance of this teaching is most clearly stated in the many verses that speak explicitly of reward, using the terms "reward," "wage," "crown," "prize," etc. But such words are only the most obvious references to rewards in the Bible. A more comprehensive understanding is found in a reading of the if-then promises of blessing found throughout Scripture.[4] The rewards and the conditions for receiving them are sometimes explicit statements, such as in Zechariah 3:7: "*If you will walk in my ways and keep my requirements, then . . . I will give you a place among these standing here.*"

More often, there is either an "if" condition or a "then" consequence. The conditional word "if" appears no less than 141 times in the Bible. Two hundred and fourteen times, the conditionality is signaled with "*anyone who,*" "*whoever,*" "*he who,*" "*all who,*" or "*the man who,*" etc.[5] "He who / God will" is a common construction. There are others referenced in index 1.

In addition, often both the "if" condition and "then" consequence are implicit. For example: "*the Lord heard Hezekiah and healed the people*" (2 Chron. 30:20). Many times, the writer speaks of "*our,*" "*my,*" or "*his*" faithfulness, which results or resulted in blessing. Sometimes the verse simply highlights the quality that warranted God's reward: "*the simplehearted,*" "*the humble,*" "*the good man.*" When the statement is retrospective, "since" replaces "if." Often the "then" result precedes the "if" condition. Dozens of times, the blessing is described as being "*according to*" what one has done. Often the lesson of Jesus's parables is simply and precisely this: if you do this, then that will happen.

There are a total of 169 words or phrases indicating "then" consequences, of which sixty-seven use the word "then." Adding the "if" conditions and the "then" consequences together, the Bible contains no less than **585 *such indicators of conditionality*** in the Bible.

The point of that recital of variations on a theme is this: every one of the conditional promises in the verses quoted could accurately be understood as "if this, then that" statements. As a can opener removes the lid from a can of peaches, that understanding opens a fully-stocked-pantry's-worth of sweet and refreshing promises.

For example, this verse from Luke 12,

> *I tell you, whoever acknowledges me before men, the Son of Man will also acknowledge him before the angels of God.* (v. 8)

. . . could accurately be understood as saying . . .

> I tell you, if anyone acknowledges me before men, then the Son of Man will also acknowledge him or her before the angels of God.

Likewise,

> *Blessed are the meek, for they will inherit the earth.* (Matt. 5:5)

. . . could be rendered . . .

If anyone is meek, then he or she will inherit the earth.

There are **seven hundred seventy-seven (777) descriptions of God's conditional rewards** in the verses referenced in *Investing in Eternity.* There may be others, but having looked long and hard for the last three or four, this seemed the perfect number of promises on which to end my search. You will find them referenced in Index 2: Index of Descriptions of Rewards.

The ubiquitous and unambiguous conditional promises of blessing in the Bible leave no doubt as to their meaning: We have been given an only-in-this-lifetime opportunity to *"lay up for yourselves treasure in heaven"* (Matt. 6:20). While some of the Bible's teaching can be reasonably debated, this crucial instruction is not one of them.

> *So be careful how you live. Don't live like fools, but like those who are wise. Make the most of every opportunity in these evil days. Don't act thoughtlessly, but understand what the Lord wants you to do.* {Eph. 5:15-17 NLT}

**The Scope of *Investing in Eternity***

The Bible speaks of two kinds of conditional rewards: *positive* rewards and *negative* rewards, otherwise known as *punishment*. We will address positive rewards—and will refer to them simply as "rewards"—though negative rewards are even more prevalent in Scripture than are positives rewards. The doctrine of rewards permeates Scripture. In fact,

> *Taking positive and negative rewards together, it can*
> *be reasonably asserted that the doctrine of rewards is*
> *one of the most discussed tenets of the Bible.*

Yet, sadly, it is the church's least discussed important doctrine.

*The opportunity*

*Investing in Eternity* focuses on the good blessings God wants to give us.

> *And we know that in all things God works for the good of*
> *those who love him, who have been called according to his*
> *purpose.* (Romans 8:28)

While much in the Bible describes that "good," I mostly reference verses in which the good *promise* of reward is proximate to the *means* of gaining it (those above-described if-then statements). I do so to establish the strongest biblical evidence for the conditional relationship between our faithfulness and our reward.

In these passages is a rich vein of biblical truth, with more to mine than I could ever exhaust. As John said in a different context, *"If every one of them were written down, I suppose that even the whole world would not have room for the books that would be written"* {John 21:25}. Human language has limitations in any event, so a deeper understanding of this doctrine comes by God's Spirit, which witnesses God's truth to our spirits.

The promises described in *Investing in Eternity* are for those who have put their faith and trust in Jesus (John 13:17-18). If you are not yet a follower of Christ, I hope you will get a taste of what God wants for you, which prompts you to go to appendix 5 and invite God into your life.

### The opportunity lost

While I have chosen to emphasize in *Investing in Eternity* the good things God wants for us in this life and at the Judgment Seat of Christ,[6] not all that happens there may be pleasant. Much of that review of our lives may feel like it did for Charles Dickens's Ebenezer Scrooge during his vision of the Ghost of Christmas Past in *A Christmas Carol*. We may plead with the Spirit, as Scrooge did, "Show me no more!" And the reply may be similar, "These are the shadows of things that have been. That they are what they are, do not blame me."

What will that Judgment be like?

> *For we must all appear before the judgment seat of Christ, that each one may receive what is due him for the things done while in the body, whether good or bad.* (2 Cor. 5:10)

> *If any man builds on this foundation using gold, silver, costly stones, wood, hay or straw, his work will be shown for what it is, because the Day will bring it to light. It will be revealed with fire, and the fire will test the quality of each man's work. If what he built survives, he will receive his reward. If it is burned up, he will suffer loss; he himself will be saved, but only as one escaping through the flames.* (1 Cor. 3:12-15)

Paul was well acquainted with God's use of *fire* in the Old Testament. In a display of His holiness, God delivered His Law on Mount Sinai with fire {Exod. 19:18}. When the Israelites complained about their hardships, "*fire from the LORD burned among them*" {Num. 11:1}. God judged Korah's rebellion with fire {Num. 16:35}. Paul's words echo those of Isaiah, "*Surely they are like stubble; the fire will burn them up*" {Isa. 47:14}. Paul speaks purposely of fire, four times in two verses! That's the kind of warning that sends people stampeding to the exits. And his warning was to Christians!

Do you think that because we are saved by grace our sin has no consequence before Holy God? Do you believe that the Old Testament warnings about sin have no relevance to you? Why would you think that? Paul warned the Corinthians that all Christians will stand before the Judgment Seat of Christ, where each will receive his reward ("*komizo*") "*for the things done while in the body, whether good or bad.*" In some measure, we all will *"suffer loss . . . by fire."* What loss? It will be the loss of what might have been, the *"gold, silver, costly stones"* that are the **rewards we might have had.**

Will that judgment be painful? *"Escaping through the flames"* sounds ominous to me. God is a holy God, just as He was in the Old Testament. And none of us will completely escape that Judgment, for none of us will have been entirely faithful to God. Yes, God is forgiving. There will be no perpetual shame or regret for our failures. But it does not follow that our sins are without eternal consequence. To believe to the contrary is to say that our choices in life really don't matter.

Yes, Jesus will wipe away every tear, but some of those tears will be shed at the revelation of rewards unearned. He will comfort us in that opportunity loss, but it will nevertheless be an eternal loss. Clearly, whatever else is implied, Paul is telling us that the less there is to burn, the better.

At the end of the book of Ezra is a long list of names of people who had privately sinned against God. Their disobedience has been part of God's public record for over 2,500 years. Jesus warned us,

> *There is nothing concealed that will not be disclosed or hidden that will not be made known. What you have said in the dark will be heard in the daylight, and what you have whispered in the ear in the inner rooms will be proclaimed from the roofs.* (Luke 12:2-3)

The "right to privacy" may or may not be a right in the US Constitution, but it clearly is not guaranteed in the Bible. We may be horrified at the thought of private, unconfessed sins made public; but why would we be less troubled at the idea that God knows our secrets? Is it because we treat God's grace like we use "incognito mode" on our browsers? "God doesn't see my sin because I'm covered by the blood of Jesus." Such an attitude cheapens the costly gift of God's grace: Jesus on the cross.

> Cheap grace is the preaching of forgiveness without requiring repentance, baptism without church discipline, Communion without confession, absolution without personal confession. Cheap grace is grace without

discipleship, grace without the cross, grace without Jesus Christ, living and incarnate. *(The Cost of Discipleship,* 5)

And though it is of great comfort that John tells us God will forgive us *"if we confess our sins"* (1 John 1:9), it would be wise to do so before we stand before Jesus on that Day of Judgment. We should humbly confess our sins daily, hourly, on the spot! And I am not speaking only of sins like angry words or visits to inappropriate websites; I am talking about those attitudes, preoccupations, habits, and motives that are not honoring to God.

We are only vaguely aware of many—perhaps most—of our sins. *"A person may think their own ways are right, but the Lord weighs the heart"* {Prov. 21:2}. So, we must ask God to reveal them to us, to show us not only when we have sinned but also the ways in which our *hearts* are sinful. I suggest the words of David for such a prayer: *"Search me, oh God, and show me if there is any wicked way in me!"* {Ps. 139:23-24}. And bathe yourself in God's Word,

> *For the word of God is alive and powerful. It is sharper than the sharpest two-edged sword, cutting between soul and spirit, between joint and marrow. It exposes our innermost thoughts and desires.* {Heb. 4:12 NLT}

And then confess what God reveals, now—before it is brought to light and burned up on the Day.

I will leave the warnings about the consequences of sin to Joel, Amos, Obadiah, Nahum, Habakkuk, Zephaniah, Haggai, Zechariah, Malachi, and others. As I said, our focus will be at the *good things* God wants to give us. I set before you the incredible opportunity to gain a harvest of blessing from God for having lived a life faithful to Him.

**What Awaits the Faithful**

No doubt you have been encouraged countless times by fellow believers to run your race to *"gain a crown"* and to *"win the prize"* only to then have the substance and nature of those rewards pronounced mysterious or unknowable.[7] It is true that much cannot be known about the prize that awaits us. As Solomon said, *"No one can fathom what God has done from beginning to end."* Our sounding line is not long enough to plumb the depths of God's wisdom. But Solomon also told us that God has *"set eternity in the human heart"* {Eccl. 3:11}. His Word reveals much to our minds, too. God has told us far more about what is in store than is commonly understood. The verses cited for *Investing in Eternity* are brimming with descriptions. To be sure, the *fullness* of God's reward is a mystery, but our glorious future is no mystery.

> *What no eye has seen, what no ear has heard, and what no human mind has conceived—the things God has prepared for those who love him—**these are the things God has revealed to us by his Spirit.*** (1 Cor. 2:9-10)

Furthermore, God gives us foretastes of that eternal life: the rewards often experienced in this life. They are like the sun peeking through the clouds on a dreary, overcast day. And they hearten and motivate us to have even more of what God wants for us.

God was gracious to once give me an extraordinary such foretaste. He spoke to me again a few years after that portentous conversation described earlier. I sat in the bleachers at my son's high school swim meet, feeling overwhelmed by life. Adding to my disquiet was the noise of my surroundings: the crowd, the crack of the starting gun, the splashing of the water, and the teams' shouts of encouragement to their teammates. The natatorium reverberated and amplified the sound into a cacophony that echoed the turmoil in my soul. In anguish, my heart cried out to God.

Again, unexpectedly and shockingly, God spoke to me, as He did to Elijah after the wind, the earthquake, and the fire. With a still, small voice, He said, *"I am pleased with you."*

As before, I heard His voice as clearly as if He were sitting next to me in a quiet room. The peace and satisfaction that settled upon me were like nothing I have ever experienced before or since. It is beyond description. Even now, years later, writing about that moment brings tears to my eyes. God had given me a taste and a foretaste of something so precious and profound it has never left me.

And my thirst for more of it has only grown. More than anything I can imagine or wish to have, I want more of that praise from God, to receive more "divine applause," as Jeff Anderson calls it in his book of that title.[8] I don't even want to contemplate that, because of my unfaithfulness, I might be *"disqualified for that prize"* (Paul's words in 1 Cor. 9:27). I want to forever know and enjoy His pleasure with me.

At 36,200 feet, the deepest place in the ocean is the "Challenger Deep," located beneath the Pacific Ocean at the end of the Mariana Trench. We are about to dive into the Bible's equivalent. To borrow another line from the Lady Gaga song quoted in the preface,

*"We're far from the shallow now."*

We will not all equally share in the riches of heaven. Our eternal future depends upon the conduct of our lives. So, I can do no other than obey God's command to . . .

*Tell the righteous it will be well with them, for*
*they will enjoy the fruit of their deeds.*
(Isa. 3:10)

**Notes and Asides:**

1  Other than in appendix 5, _Investing in Eternity_ does not describe how one becomes a Christian. The good works discussed in _Investing in Eternity_ are not required for salvation. As Luther explained in _The Bondage of the Will_, Scriptures teach that, apart from God's grace, we are incapable of holiness. Works in no way merit salvation, which is a gift of God's grace (Eph. 2:8-9; Rom. 4:1-5; Titus 3:5). How one becomes a child of God (and thereby becomes empowered to earn the rewards described in this book) is explained in Appendix 5: The Gift of God.

   For a discussion of the relationship of God's sovereignty and mankind's free will and of God's grace and our works, see Appendix 2: Common Emotional and Theological Objections.

2  A well-known radio personality and columnist recently said, "My philosophy of life is easily summarized: God wants us to be good. Period." He captured the essence of many Christians' incomplete view of what God wants for us. Do you doubt me? Then ask the next ten Christians you meet why they try to live in obedience to Christ. While at least some, I hope, will sincerely answer, "Because I love Jesus," I'd be surprised if even one speaks of their hope of God's reward for living a life that honors Him. I predict you will mostly hear some variation of, "Because we should," for that is what they are most often told from the pulpit.

   We will discuss God's larger plan in Chapter 4: Rewards Are Essential to God's Gracious Purpose and Goal.

3  W. E. Hill, Puck Magazine, 1915.

4  You will find many of these if-then verses reprinted and summarized in appendix 7. The complete list can be found at Investing-in-Eternity. org. It is my intent to have identified all of them in the Bible, but tell me of any you find at kevin.w.kaufman@gmail.com.

5  John Hill writes, "Every time we meet a promise that begins with the word, 'Whosoever', we can immediately say to ourselves, 'That means me'" (175).

6  I understand that this judgment, at the Judgment Seat of Christ, is where the lives of Christians will be evaluated. Those who have not placed their trust in Jesus will appear before the Great White Throne of Judgment. It is possible that these two judgments are two aspects of the same Judgment, but it would be a distinction without a meaningful

difference, for either way there will be a judgment of all people (John 5:29).

7   For as much understanding and encouragement as it brings, we might as well use the words of pagan Romans, "*Per angusta ad augusta!*" ("Through difficulties to honors!"), which appealed to Roman soldiers' desire for human glory in battle.

8   Jeff Anderson, *Divine Applause* (Colorado Springs, CO: Multnomah Books, 2015). It is a most encouraging read.

# Section 1 The Doctrine of Rewards Is Essential

This section establishes the biblical context of God's rewards.

In chapter 1, I will introduce the ideas that God's rewards are *essential* to God and to you, they are *of the essence* of God's purposes, they are *integral* to our love and gratitude, and they are *biblical*.

In chapter 2, we will see that God's rewards fulfill our deepest desires and they motivate and encourage our work for God.

Then, in chapters 3 and 4 we will see that rewards flow from God's character and are essential to God's purposes and goals in creating the world.

# Chapter 1  Overview: The Importance of God's Reward

Have you ever eaten a pomegranate, a fruit mentioned in the Bible? Did you know that it is by tradition consumed on Rosh Hashanah because it symbolizes fruitfulness? Also, it is said to have 613 seeds, which correspond to the 613 commandments of the Torah. The pomegranate is a sweet symbol of the sweetness of God's Word.

But if you have ever *peeled* a pomegranate, you also know that woven among the sweet and crunchy seeds is a bitter-tasting membrane. One must carefully pull the sweet fruit from that lining, or it will taste bitter. So it is with much of our understanding of God's purposes. We must carefully look through His Word and leave behind preconceptions that can make its sweet message taste bitter. It takes patience and prayer to separate the truth of God's Word from what is not true in our understanding of it. As with peeling a pomegranate, it is worth the effort because God's Word is sweet!

I make assertions later that assume you have read explanations in earlier pages; therefore, I suggest you proceed in chapter order. However, if you are especially curious about how I describe God's rewards, read Chapter 5: Overview of God's Rewards. I explain the relationship between our work and God's provision in Chapter 13: Overview of How to Gain God's Rewards. Read appendix 1 if you think rewards are material blessings in this life. I encourage you to reference the selected Scripture at the back of *Investing in Eternity* and reprinted in full at Investing-in-Eternity.org at any time. And since everything described herein is for followers of Jesus, go to Appendix 8: The Gift of God to learn how to become part of His family.

**Rewards Are Important to God.**

Ponder this question as you read *Investing in Eternity* and the verses from which it is drawn:

> *If rewards are not important **to God**, then why does He tell us of them throughout Scripture?*

Every book of the Bible speaks of rewards that are the consequences, good and bad, of our motives, thoughts, and actions. The doctrine permeates Scripture. If you take God's Word seriously, then you must settle on an answer to the above question. I beg you, please do not wait to discover the answer as you stand before the Judgment Seat of Christ!

There are several reasons why God wants us to know of His intent to reward. First, the Bible's teaching of reward reveals something important about who God is. God desires to demonstrate His love and holiness in His just rewards for both sinfulness and faithfulness. God wants us to know that He notices when we serve Him. He wants us to know that *"God is not unjust; he will not forget your work and the love you have shown him as you have helped his people and continue to help them. . . ."* (Heb. 6:10). Furthermore, God demonstrates His *love* in His promise to reward. (More on this in Chapter 3: Rewards Are Essential to God's Character.)

Second, rewards are important to God because He wants us to be *motivated and encouraged* by the promise of them. He told us of His desire and intent to reward so we would look forward to that reward with greater hope in, and love for, the God who promises it.

*Rewards are biblical.*

Many truths are so because God declared them to be so. For example, God said that eating the fruit of the Tree of the Knowledge of Good and Evil would result in death. And so it did. If you consider the Bible to be the inspired Word of God, then you must face this biblical fact: how you live your life *will* affect your and my eternal future because God declared that to be so. The Bible could not be more explicit on the matter.

And that fact has serious implications. If that claim is doubtful or even offensive to you, and if you are about to set *Investing in Eternity* aside, please, do this first: bookmark this page and then, for ten or fifteen minutes, peruse the Bible verses printed in the back. Especially notice the words that I have **bolded**. Then return to this overview.

Did you notice how many of the verses use the actual word "reward"? Did you see the pattern of "if this, then that"? Did you notice that the promised blessings are granted only on condition of obedience?

Spend as much time as you need in those verses. I would be happy if you never read what I wrote on the subject and instead read—and reread—the passages of Scripture reprinted in the back of this book. If you discover too late, at the end of time, that God indeed rewards, God is not likely to ask, "Didn't you read Kevin's book?" That's a silly thought, I know. But not so funny is the question He is more likely to ask: "Didn't you read *My Word* on the subject?"

Jesus might even apply what He said concerning the book of Revelation to the entirety of His Word:

> *I warn everyone who hears the words of the prophecy of this scroll: If anyone adds anything to them, God will add to that person the plagues described in this scroll. And if anyone takes words away from this scroll of prophecy, God will take away from that person any share in the tree of life and in the Holy City, which are described in this scroll.* (Rev. 22:18-19)

With those two verses much on my mind, I ask and give my own answers to a lot of important questions about the implications of the Scripture I cite. If you do not agree with my answers, then I urge you to have your own answers ready. Someday you, like I, will stand before Jesus and give an account for your life.

I have reprinted many verses on rewards in the last appendix for three reasons:

First, when one reads passages about rewards one after another, preconceived ideas are less likely to filter out the message. The reader is more alert to look for what otherwise might have been missed and to have an open mind to what God says in His Word. (The scriptural basis for the doctrine will be all the more apparent once you have highlighted words and phrases per my suggestions in appendix 3.)

Second, I reprint the verses, rather than merely refer to them, because it is easier for you to study the passages. I genuinely want you to read the

Scripture! I include as much of the context of the teaching as is practical, so you will see that this doctrine is not built upon texts ripped from their settings.

Third, I have tried to write nothing inconsistent with God's Word. If what I have to say is true, it is true because—and only because—of what the Scripture says. So I put the verses at the end of the book so that they literally "back" everything I say. Do you have doubts about my understanding of them? Great! I urge you to be like the Bereans of Acts 17, who *"examined the Scriptures every day to see if what Paul said was true."* If the Bereans thought it necessary to question the Apostle Paul, then there is no insult to this lowly writer if you critically examine the claims I make.

I sincerely hope you will find yourself using these passages of Scripture in your sermons (if you are a pastor), in your personal and small group Bible studies, and in your words and your writings of encouragement to fellow believers. Instead of merely saying, "Thank you!" or "God bless you," I hope you will find yourself saying, "God *will* bless you for your faithfulness!" and quoting one of the many promises of reward in God's Word! For, as Jesus said, *"Whoever practices and teaches these commands will be called great in the kingdom of heaven"* (Matt. 5:19).

You may be so taken with the Scripture on the subject that you won't even finish my book! That would be wonderful! But if you read the rest of my words, do so to compare your own understanding of Scripture with mine. If there is something that I say with which you disagree, let me know where you consider me in error.[1] You will be rewarded by God for your diligence!

Reactions to what I've said thus far likely range from "Amen!" to "Ahem . . ." To the latter, I hope to address your discomforts and objections throughout the book.[2] But as it is my purpose to emphasize the positive evidence of my thesis, I refer extended discussion of objections to appendix 2. Nevertheless, let's briefly address one obstacle to our understanding.

### Reward's counterfeits

One reason Christians especially avoid the word "reward" is that our thinking has been muddled by the world's use of it. As kids, we are told that Santa Claus will reward us with presents if we are good. Then, as adults, we are urged to reward *ourselves* for our hard work. "You deserve it," we are assured. We are invited to earn payback for using our credit cards. At the grocery store, the gas station, and in our email inboxes, such messages are everywhere. We are encouraged to earn rewards, even double rewards, for traveling, flying, staying in hotels, indeed, for making any purchase. A cellular phone company advertisement touts "Rewards brought to you by the belief project." ("The belief project"? *What's that?*) My favorite example is from the purveyor of essential oils: Essential Rewards. These uses of reward incentives lead us to think of rewards in crass commercial terms: transactional, coercive, and manipulative.

Come to think of it, isn't that the message of all advertising? Isn't it an appeal to our desires? "Buy my product or service, and you will be happy."[3] What does it tell us that the world spends billions of dollars on such incentives to motivate people to self-gratifying action? And, for that matter, what does it tell us that all the rest of the world's religions offer the reward of a blissful eternity in exchange for good works performed in this life?

Well, the Accuser,[4] the ruler of this world, knows how we were wired by God. He knows our God-given desires. And you bet he knows the Bible well. That's why he is so good at distorting its truth. The Evil One understands God's intent to reward—and he seeks to thwart it by offering alluring counterfeits of God's promise at every turn. He entices with zirconium because it *looks like* a diamond!

This world's "rewards" are shabby imitations of God's rewards. So, before you dismiss the teaching of rewards as gimmicky or selfish, you should be sure you understand what the Bible actually says about them. Lay aside the small-print rules for earning our *"Expiring Soon!"* earthly rewards and ignore the distortion of the truth in other religions, and pick up the unambiguous language of reward in this life and the next as taught in God's Word. As you do, I believe you will become more comfortable with this teaching—and you will find yourself seeking to earn a guaranteed treasure in heaven.

"Reward" was God's word before its meaning was corrupted by marketers and other religions, so let's rediscover its meaning! God's rewards don't expire. There are no blackout dates. They are real, and they are redeemable forever.

**Rewards Are Important to You.**

Likewise,

> *If rewards are not important **to you**, then why does God tell us of them throughout Scripture?*

Do you, a follower of Jesus, know where you will go when you die? No, I'm not talking about heaven. I mean, do you know that you will someday stand before Jesus at the Judgment Seat of Christ? There the lives of *Christians* will be judged by Jesus. It will be the "Final Exam" of your entire life. If you are a follower of Christ, you will pass; but will you pass with an "A+" or a "D-"? To the extent you are judged worthy, you will be rewarded (1 Cor. 3:13 and 2 Cor. 5:10).

That which the faithful are awarded will be of value *forever*. That means that faithfulness to God that produces those benefits has *immeasurable value*. This truth utterly changes one's perspective on the importance of this life. When we get to heaven, this life will not merely have ended without consequence. What we have done for God in our lives will have accomplished something of lasting value.

**Rewards are essential to our motivation and encouragement.**

Do you feel as if anything is at stake *for you* in your obedience (or lack of obedience) to God? Do you think that, in heaven, how you lived (or did not live) in faithfulness to God will produce any enduring consequences *for you*?

Are you offended by the questions? "This life isn't all about me. It's about serving God!" you might be thinking. But what if the Bible teaches—*and what if God wants you to know*—that how you conduct your life will have a significant and lasting impact upon the *quality* of your eternal existence? What if the Bible explains that those who serve God more fully in this life will have a better, fuller, more joyful, more glorious experience of heaven than will those who are less obedient to God in this life? Most importantly, what if a better experience of heaven is what God most wants for you?

To be sure, God loves us so much that He often blesses us in spite of ourselves {Isa. 45:5}. And no doubt many of my readers are experiencing the rewards of faithfulness discussed in this book, but you don't think of that joyful experience as a consequence of your obedience. So genuinely dedicated you are to God's work, and so grateful you are for the experience of God's love, you do not pause to consider that the one follows the other. The mere suggestion to do so may be abhorrent to you: "Why would I speak and think in terms of 'rewards'? Such selfish expectation would diminish my experience of God's love!"

We will consider at length the reasons that the prospect of God's reward enhances, not diminishes, the joys of serving Jesus. But for now, please consider this: Not everyone is *experiencing* the blessings of obedience as keenly as you are, either because of their own failings or because God, in His wisdom, is deferring them. Either way, for such people, *life is hard.* Such people need such encouragement! And, indeed, sometime in the future *you* may need such encouragement. Where will you find it?

You may quote Romans 8:28 liberally, but you may not much expand upon its meaning. What is the *"good"* that God promises? "Such is for *God* to decide," you sternly reply. Very true! Indeed, God has *already* decided—and He has told us plainly of His intentions. The Bible is full of descriptions of the good He will produce out of pain and suffering! He often calls them "rewards," but He more often uses a myriad of other words to convey His intent. If the church is not speaking openly and frankly of those rewards, then how are we to help people out of their despair if we neglect to refer to God's many promises to bring sweet fruit from those bitter circumstances?

Look again at the verses at the back and pick out three or four of the more poignant passages (e.g., Mark 4:24; Gal. 6:7-10; Eph. 6:7; 1 John 2:28). Ask yourself as you read them: What are the implications of this teaching for my eternal future? How would a belief that God rewards influence my life's decisions?

Suppose, by way of example, the winning prize for the Boston Marathon increased a thousand-fold, from its current $150,000 to $150 *million.* Would you be surprised if records were smashed in the next running of that race? I would be surprised if they were not! Even the most driven runners would likely push themselves even harder to win such a large prize.

Well, the prize God offers is of higher value than any prize this world could offer. In fact, the size of the award is immeasurable because the benefit of God's rewards will continue forever. His rewards never end! So the case *literally* cannot be overstated: whether or not you acknowledge it now, what you do (or don't do) in this life will matter to *you—forever.*

### Rewards are essential to gratitude and praise.

God's rewards enhance our gratitude and hence, our praise of God.[5] When we receive something from God for obedience, our response is and will be, "Thank you, Lord!" Our gratitude is the acknowledgment that everything He gives us, including His reward, is a gracious gift from God. He rewards so that our hearts might overflow with gratitude and praise for both His promise and provision, without which we would have no reward. Thanksgiving is always given to God for who God is or for what God has done, but never is it a "condition" for more blessing. That is because the praise of God is an end in itself.

We often and properly are encouraged to love God out of gratitude for what Jesus has already done for us. We are reminded of Romans 12:1: *"Therefore, I urge you, in view of God's mercy, to offer your bodies as a living sacrifice."* But this verse gives *a reason* to give our lives to God, *not the sole reason* to do so.

When we hear only that we should be grateful for what God has already done for us, that implies that God, like Master Bumble in *Oliver Twist*, is appalled at our outrageous hope for "More?!"—and He might just smack us with a blow for it! "After all that Jesus has done for you, how could you think of asking for more? You should serve Him out of your indebtedness." On the contrary, it is right and proper to want more of what God wants for you because *service* to God that results in *reward* from God produces more *praise* from His people. So, let us give thanks to the Lord, for *"He is good; his love endures forever!"*{1 Chron. 16:34}.[6]

### What does God have in store for you?

In a word, *treasure!*

I mentioned diamonds a moment ago. Have you ever seen the "Hope Diamond"? Not just a picture of it, but the real thing in the National Museum of Natural History in Washington, DC. I saw it many years ago on a high school field trip, and I'll never forget those 45.52 carats of pristine clarity, its "cushion antique cut," faceted girdle, and pavilion. It is stunning. To fully appreciate its blue beauty, one has to slowly walk around the brightly lit case in which it is displayed to be dazzled by the light reflected in its many facets (Smithsonian).

The Hope Diamond is an apt (and aptly named) metaphor for the reward that awaits the faithful in heaven. And the 360-degree view of it is analogous to our study of God's promised rewards in *Investing in Eternity*. Our rewards—the jewels and precious stones—will be uniquely cut for each of us and set in gold and silver crafted by God Himself. (You can be sure that God won't hand out costume jewelry!)

10

Yours may have the color and shape of what we will discuss. It may have characteristics only hinted at in the Bible. It will be personalized, rich with significance to each of us. Each of us will receive a unique reward because each has been given distinct personalities, gifting (*dynamin*, Matt. 25:15), and opportunities. And each of us will have qualified in our obedience for it in different ways.

### Our stories told

"For what is joy if it goes unrecorded, and what is love if it is not shared?" (*Call the Midwife*).[7]

The Hope Diamond also has a fascinating history about which the Smithsonian produced a documentary. It was likely mined in Golconda, India. A French merchant, Jean Baptiste Tavernier, purchased the then crudely cut $112^3/_{16}$-carat diamond in 1668 and sold it to King Louis XIV of France in 1668. Recut in 1673; sold to King Louis XV in 1749; taken from Louis XVI and Marie Antoinette during the French Revolution in 1791; stolen by the mob in 1792; acquired by the British king George IV in 1812; sold in 1830 to pay his debts; bought and sold several more times over the next 100 years, including by Henry Philip Hope, for whom it is now named. It was finally donated to the Smithsonian Museum on November 10, 1958, where it now can be enjoyed by all.

I recount that lengthy—though truncated—story of the Hope Diamond to illustrate this: Your diamond, your reward, will have a story, too, which will be the story of your life. At the Judgment Seat of Christ, Jesus will recount that story, His and others' roles in it, and how it affected the lives of those around you. You will see how—as with a diamond—God used the pressures of life to form your character. He will show you the imperfections in pieces he trimmed while cutting your diamond. And we will all listen with rapt attention. I so look forward to hearing your story told by Jesus!

My wife, Sandy, and I recently watched an inspiring documentary, *Billy Graham: An Extraordinary Journey*. It portrays the total devotion to Christ of one of history's most influential Christians. But Graham was not the star of the show. He was the supporting actor. The star was Jesus, who—with Billy's willing assent—lived His life through Billy. Everything Graham did lifted up Jesus. That brief review of his life is a mere foretaste of the millions of Director's-cut documentaries we will watch in heaven. I can't wait to celebrate such lives.

In the words of Bart Millard's song, "I can only imagine" what that Day will be like. But it is such fun to try! What I cannot imagine is that we will experience an eternity of bliss that is devoid of memories of this life. "My life passed before my eyes!" is a common experience in a brush with death. Do those memories die when we die? If our eternity isn't informed by our stories—if we will spend forever with heaven's equivalent of Alzheimer's—this life is meaningless.

Read the narrative of the Bible in the Old Testament, in the gospels, and in the book of Acts. Listen to the parables of Jesus. Clearly, God loves stories. He loves them because they are about people and their relationships, their motivations, and their moments of decision. And He wants to be part of those stories. God is no less interested in biography than are we when engrossed in *The Diary of Anne Frank* or *Churchill: A Life*. And someday Jesus, the master storyteller, will narrate it all in riveting detail, before all of heaven.[8]

God tells us that His and our story, like all good stories, will have an exciting climax: when Jesus returns to establish His Kingdom. And our individual stories will have their denouement (where the strands of the plot are drawn together, and matters are explained and resolved) at the Judgment Seat of Christ. After that, our stories will continue on the course that was set in this life.

It is an exciting hope, is it not? For as Paul tells the Corinthians,

> *He will bring to light what is hidden in darkness and will expose the motives of men's hearts.*

> *At that time each will receive his praise from God. (1 Cor. 4:5)*

Or in the words of another follower of Jesus, syndicated radio personality Paul Harvey, "And now, for the rest of the story!"

> ***It only matters if it matters forever.*** So, let us …
> *fix our eyes not on what is seen, but on what is unseen.*
> *For what is seen is temporary; but what is unseen is eternal.*
> *(2 Cor. 4:18)*

**Notes and Asides:**

1   *I can be reached at kevin.w.kaufman@gmail.com.*

2   *This is not to say all the world's appeals are to our sinful desires. For example, there is a long series of commercials produced by the Thai Life Insurance Company that appeals to our good desires with a message of hope that even the Heavenly Life Insurance Company could use.*

3   *In the witty musical, <u>1776</u>, the question of independence from England is put to Mr. Hopkins of Rhode Island. His response: "In all my years, I never seen heard nor smelled an issue that was so dangerous it couldn't be talked about!" (Hunt). I wish more Christians felt that way about the doctrine of rewards.*

4   *I refer here and elsewhere, of course, to Satan—which is Hebrew (שָׂטָן) for "accuser" or "adversary."*

5   *Only five times does the word "thanks" or "thanksgiving" appear in the hundreds of verses containing conditional promises—and none indicate thanksgiving as a condition of reward. There is no mention of "gratitude" in any of our verses. That is because thanksgiving and gratitude are not the means of gaining reward: they are an end in themselves.*

6   *You might express your gratitude in French,"<u>Je vous remercie</u>," since "<u>remercie</u>" is derived from the Latin "<u>re</u>," meaning "back," and "<u>merces</u>," meaning "wage."" <u>Je vous remercie, Roi Jésus</u> [King Jesus]! Thank you for paying the back wages of my sin on the cross and then for paying the wages You promised for my faithfulness!" Or, less formally, you might say, "<u>Je te remercie, Jésus, mon ami</u> [my friend]."*

     *It may surprise you to learn that the root of the English word "mercy" likewise has its derivation from the Latin word "<u>merces</u>," meaning a compassionate bestowal of a reward or wage.*

> *Mercy: late 12c., from Old French mercit, merci (9c.) "reward, gift; kindness, grace, pity," from Latin mercedem (nominative merces) "reward, wages, pay hire" (in Vulgar Latin "favor, pity"), from merx (genitive mercis) "wares, merchandise." In Church Latin (6c) applied to the heavenly reward of those who show kindness to the helpless. (<u>Online Etymology Dictionary</u>)*

[7]  *This beautiful line is from the BBC TV series <u>Call the Midwife</u> (season six, episode eight), which is based on the book of that title by Jennifer Worth. It is spoken as a voice-over by the main character of the series, Jenny, in retrospect of her life as a midwife in mid-twentieth-century England.*

[8]  *We forget over time what actually occurred, and—especially when the memories are emotional—we fill gaps in our memory with details that we did not experience. In heaven, our memories of the events of our lives will be accurate and complete.*

*Here I cross into reasonable speculation about events at the Judgment Seat. My imagination was inspired during a recent visit to the Museum of the Bible, where Sandy and I were treated to a drone-photographed 360-degree virtual reality tour of biblical sites. Wow! We felt like we were actually there! It is astounding to me that humans could have created such a realistic, virtual reality. Is the Creator of reality itself, from the quark to the quasar, capable of less?*

*So imagine that a 360-degree camera has been recording your entire life. (Might that be the "scroll of remembrance" of Malachi 3:16?) And imagine watching it—with Jesus offering director's commentary on the events of your life. He points out the moments when you were obedient, when you cried out to Him, when you persevered, and when you influenced someone to trust in Jesus. Can you imagine Jesus celebrating you?*

*Imagine Jesus explaining to you what He was doing behind the scenes to make those victories possible; how He arranged for people to be in the right place at the right time; how He prompted you to say or do just the right thing; how He emboldened you, and how faithfully you did your part at that moment. He'll show you why He allowed the painful events of your life, and you will see Him and His angels in this made-for-heaven video, standing beside you the whole time.*

*Discovering our individual human lineage has become a popular craze with the advent of DNA testing. Well, imagine watching the stories of your **spiritual** ancestors, back to the time of Jesus and beyond. And similarly, imagine Jesus occasionally hitting the pause button to explain the impact you had made upon specific people—and how what you did or said rippled through time—long after you died. Doesn't that sound exciting?*

14

*Like the virtual reality we witnessed, imagine that this review will feel like we are actually there, reliving what happened, but with the added insights and explanation that Jesus will provide. Imagine friends, family, and even strangers who were part of those stories, cheering as they look on!*

*Also at the Museum of the Bible, we saw videos and displays about people who—sometimes to their personal peril—were instrumental in the translation and transmittal of the Bible through the centuries. We rightly honor those people for their work and dedication. Will God do less for any of us?*

*Museums of our presidents describe the events of their lives from childhood, how they rose to prominence, and their setbacks and victories. These public shrines house historical documents—from treaties to diaries. There is a museum dedicated to Walt Disney in San Francisco. It contains original drawings of animations we all know and love. Millions of people visit such libraries every year. In heaven, will God be less interested in the events of our lives than we are interested in the creator of Mickey Mouse or the presidencies of FDR or Ronald Reagan?*

# Chapter 2  Rewards Are Essential to Our God-Given Desires

Rick Warren's *The Purpose Driven Life* has sold over a quarter of a billion copies and has been translated into eighty-five languages. The subtitle asks, "What on earth am I here for?" That question is an expression of the need identified by Maslow in his Hierarchy of Needs, which he called "self-actualization": to accomplish one's fullest potential (15). As with the Army's onetime marketing slogan, "Be all that you can be . . .", the appeal is to humanity's supreme desire: for purpose in life (US Army).

In Maslow's understanding, that purpose can only be fully realized once more basic needs and desires are met. The most basic of these are our physiological needs, followed—by order of importance—by our needs for physical and emotional safety, love, belonging, and esteem. Only having met each more fundamental need can one achieve "self-actualization."

There is truth in Maslow's portrayal. After the Fall, Adam and Eve would have to work for the satisfaction of needs and desires that had been met by God.

> *Cursed is the ground because of you; through painful toil you will eat food from it all the days of your life. It will produce thorns and thistles for you, and you will eat the plants of the field. By the sweat of your brow you will eat your food.* (Gen. 3:18)

Likewise, apart from God's provision, our emotional desires would only be met by our own devices, often with similar difficulty and disappointing results. But our problem is even more profound: Not only have we lost God's provision of our God-given desires, but our desires themselves have been corrupted. They lead us in the wrong direction, further into the desert toward the mirage of an oasis.

Thus is our predicament laconically lamented by Mick Jagger in the hit 1965 Rolling Stones song, which is number two on a list of *"Five Hundred Greatest Songs of All Time"* (Rolling Stone Magazine).

> I can't get no satisfaction
> I can't get no satisfaction
> Cause I try and I try, and I try and I try
> I can't get no, I can't get no.
> (Richards/Jagger)

Jagger admitted that "Satisfaction" was "my view of the world, my frustration with everything" (*Rolling Stone Magazine*). The number one song on that list, "Like A Rolling Stone" by Bob Dylan—released three months after "Satisfaction"—expresses similar disdain for the world's puerility. Bono still hasn't found what he's looking for. Such songs are the cry of a generation impatient for heaven on earth.

Most of us nevertheless persist in our pursuit of purpose in life. Like the boy in the old joke, we optimistically dig in the barn, convinced that "with all this manure, there *must* be a pony in here somewhere!" Well, put down your shovel and instead dig into God's Word. There you will find the difference between your sinful desires and your godly desires and where you will learn how to satisfy them.

## Essential to Our Desires

Unaware of or unmotivated by God's enticing promises, some of us persist in yielding to our ungodly desires, sometimes even abandoning ourselves to them. Others manage our passions through the practice of the cardinal virtue of temperance: moderation in all things. In Aristotle's term, we search for the "golden mean."

Many other Christians take another—seemingly more spiritual—approach of outright denial, avoidance, or suppression of our desires. It is that approach for which Paul criticized the Colossian church, with its legalistic rules: *"Do not handle! Do not taste! Do not touch!"* Such denial of needs and desires has *"the appearance of wisdom,"* but has *"no true value"*{Col. 2:20-23}.

Charles Finney, the great preacher of the Second Great Awakening, suggested that Christians empty themselves of all desires:

> Because they have no self-interest . . ., they have no appetite that must be gratified, no passion that must be catered for, none of these to contend for or hold on to. They are emptied out and every particle of self-value is gone entirely. (*The Oberlin Evangelist*, 194)

Maybe you agree with that statement. But is denying all self-interest, appetites, and passions what God calls us to do? Does it not depend upon what interests, appetites, and passions are being denied? Not all of our desires are bad. Many were given to us when we were created.

In fairness to Finney, I quoted him out of context to make my point. He was commenting on *"blessed are the poor in spirit"* in the Beatitudes (Matt. 5), where Jesus tells us how to satisfy a desire we all have—for true happiness. For Jesus—and for Finney—self-denial is not an end in itself; it is a means to the end of satisfying our genuine desires.

God does not call us to ignore our own self-interest. Instead, He calls us to *redirect and sanctify* our efforts for achieving it. Indeed, when exhortations to self-denial are unaccompanied by the promise of blessing, our teaching is little different than Buddhism or Stoicism, which encourages practitioners to find happiness in the denial of all passions. So we must be careful that our calls of submission to God are always accompanied by the promises of reward for obedience, lest we teach a false gospel.[1]

To speak and act as if we have no personal interest in the satisfaction of our needs and desires is—to put it charitably—foolish. As C. S. Lewis said in *The Four Loves*,

> It would be a bold and silly creature that came before its Creator with the boast, "I'm no beggar. I love you disinterestedly." (12)

More perniciously, your claim of disinterest in gaining something from God in your service to Him may be an expression of arrogance. As John Piper warned:

If you come to God dutifully offering Him the reward of your fellowship instead of thirsting after the reward of His fellowship, then you exalt yourself above God as His benefactor and belittle Him as a needy beneficiary—and that is evil. (111)

As we focus on God's promises to fulfill our true desires, we will increasingly find their fulfillment in Him in this life and in the life to come.

**Essential to Our Desire for Affirmation**

Maslow labeled another of our needs "esteem."

Discussing the end-of-the-universe scenario in an actor's most recent movie, Stephen Colbert asked his show's guest, "What do you think happens when we die, Keanu Reeves?" (Reeves). The audience laughed nervously at the unexpectedly deep question. The *John Wick* actor paused, exhaled, then delivered an answer that went viral on Twitter. "I know that the ones who love us will miss us." The audience sighed a collective "Aww."

Why would that be inspiring? When the universe ends, or for that matter a hundred years from now, who will care that any of us lived? Perhaps people will remember us—until *they* die. But let's be honest. How often do we go to the funeral or memorial service of a respected individual and think to ourselves, "Wow, I hope people say nice things like that about me at my funeral"? Is that what we live for—to be thought well of by people after we are dead? Wouldn't it be infinitely better to hear those words of praise in heaven from Jesus Himself, whether or not they are said of us at that same moment on earth?

Don't most of us have people's perceptions of us in mind when we post something on social media? Wouldn't we do better to be concerned with God's view of us—and with people's opinion of Jesus, whom we represent on earth? I am loath to admit it, but I even encounter this temptation at church when I lift my hands in praise during worship. I wonder to myself, am I raising them as a show of my godliness? Or, conversely, do I keep my arms down for fear of people's perceptions? Maybe I should discreetly hold my palms up at chest level, even though I really want to raise them high to heaven.

Jesus cautions us not to do our acts of righteousness with peoples' opinions of us in mind. *"If you do, you will have no reward from your father in heaven*" (Matt. 6:1). Such warnings keep me focused on God's assessment of me. God's promise to reward helps me to realign my thinking about my real value. Descriptions of those many affirmations are found in chapters 7–11.

## Essential to Our Desire for Encouragement

### Godly encouragement

What hope would you have offered to the man in the preface who wished himself dead? I said to him, "Be assured, my friend, that every breath God gives you is another opportunity to earn God's reward." To which he dolefully replied, "Oh, I hadn't considered that." Why hadn't he considered that? Because he is seldom reminded of that hope. He has forgotten the point of life's struggles. So he forgets what Paul said immediately after expressing his longing to be home with the Lord:

> *So whether we are here in this body or away from this body, our goal is to please him. For we must all stand before Christ to be judged. We will each receive whatever we deserve for the good or evil we have done in this earthly body.* (1 Cor. 5:10)

God could have kept secret His intent to reward, hiding His blessings behind His back as a surprise to be revealed at the end of time. His love and justice would have been satisfied just as well if He had waited until the final judgment to reveal His reward. God did not have to so much as hint that there is something to gain from faithful service. So why did He tell us of His intent?

Well, have you ever done something for someone who makes no acknowledgment of your efforts—not so much as a thank you? Does the lack of appreciation discourage you from doing more? It certainly isn't encouraging. Neither would we be encouraged in our work if God waited to tell us of his intent to reward.

Fortunately, God did tell us—over and over again in His Word—of His promise to reward. We must consider why He did so. In addition to what we learn about God through the knowledge of His rewards (discussed in the coming chapters), we must conclude that God intends for us to be motivated to gain the rewards He promises.

## Ungodly encouragement

Instead of that hopeful message, what we are often told is—essentially—the Nike tagline: "Just do it!"[2] No wonder many followers of Jesus assume that it is wrong to be motivated by reward! The sermons we hear give us not even this simple promise of Scripture as a closing statement to its list of commands:

> *For if you do these things . . you will receive a rich welcome into the eternal kingdom of our Lord and Savior Jesus Christ.* (2 Pet. 1:10-11)

In his book *Desiring God*, Piper recounts his own doubts about being motivated by a desire for God's blessing.

> I had a vague, pervasive notion that if I did something good because it would make me happy, I would ruin its goodness. I figured that the goodness of my moral action was lessened to the degree I was motivated by a desire for my own pleasure . . . To be motivated by a desire for happiness or pleasure when I volunteered for Christian service or went to church—that seemed selfish, utilitarian; mercenary. (18)

Randy Alcorn identifies the root of the problem:

> It is common to believe God is glorified when we think of him alone and that any motive besides love for God is inferior or unacceptable. Yet it is God in his Word who gives us other motives—love for people, fear of disobedience and hope of reward among them. These are not mixed motives, but multiple motives—all God-given. ("Eternal Perspectives Ministry website")

*Biblical examples of such encouragement*

Those who endure and serve faithfully look forward to hearing our Master say, *"Well done, good and faithful servant . . . Come and share your master's happiness!"* (Matt. 25:21, 23). They look forward to being called *"great in the kingdom of heaven"* (Matt. 5:19). They look forward to possessing those treasures they have *"stored up"* for themselves in heaven (Matt. 6:20).

Jesus tells us in the Sermon on the Mount (Matt. 5) to *"rejoice and be glad"* when we are persecuted for the sake of Jesus. (In a parallel passage in Luke 6 He tells us to *"leap for joy."*) Why? *"Because great is your reward in heaven"* (Matt. 5:12).

The *"because"* in that verse is the same Greek conjunction, *"hoti,"* used in the previous verses of the Beatitudes, where Jesus pronounces as *"blessed"* those who are poor, hungry, sorrowful, and hated for the sake of Christ. In each case, the hearer is encouraged to take heart because (*"hoti"*) the bitter circumstances will be turned upside down for those who serve God.

Jesus isn't speaking only to those who happen to be poor, hungry, etc. His words speak just as well to those who place themselves into difficult circumstances for the sake of Christ. The Sermon on the Mount, therefore, tells us more than how we should conduct our lives (with humility, mercy, purity, etc.); it also encourages us with promises of blessings—rewards— for so-living. The so-called "Beatitudes" might better be called the "Reason-to-Be-Attitudes."[3]

Was it not the prospect of reward that encouraged those in the "Hall of Faith" in Hebrews 11 to obey God? Abram left his home, inspired by his faith in God's promise of a better country. Moses abandoned the pleasures of Egypt because *"he was looking ahead to his reward"* (v. 26).

*Others were tortured and refused to be released . . ., faced jeers and flogging, while still others were chained and put into prison. They were stoned; they were sawed in two; they were put to death by the sword. They went about in sheepskins and goatskins, destitute, persecuted and mistreated.* (vv. 35b-37)

Why did they willingly endure all of that? It was not to gain heaven. These people well-understood that their salvation was a gracious gift of God. Instead, they entered into and endured pain and persecution so that they might *"gain a better resurrection"* (v. 35). Commenting on this passage, Bob Sorge writes,

> True faith understands . . . that God rewards us according to the intensity of our pursuit of Him. God chasers reveal their faith by the way they run. *Men and women of faith cannot be distracted or detoured from their objective because they firmly believe that God is going to reward their pursuit.* And they're right! (14, italics in the original)

These giants of faith believed, even though *"none of them received* [in their lifetime] *what had been promised"* (v. 39). They endured because they believed, like Abraham, that God *"rewards those who earnestly seek him"* (v. 6).

Will it be said of us as it was of them, *"The world was not worthy of them"*? (v. 38). If not, perhaps it is because we are too comfortable in this life to contemplate the coming of God's righteous judgment. So accustomed are we to seeking and having our reward in the here and now that we find little incentive in the prospect of God's prize in the life to come. Those men and women of old who trusted in God and looked forward to His reward, stand today before Him in glorious splendor. Will we someday stand with them? Don't you *want* to receive a reward such as theirs? Matthew Henry certainly did:

> It is an unspeakable comfort to industrious Christians, that they are working together with God, and he with them; that their Master's eye is upon them, and a witness to their sincerity: he sees in secret, and will reward openly. (Matt. 6:6) God now accepts their works, smiles upon them, and his Spirit speaks to them good words and comfortable words (Zech. 1:13) witnessing to their adoption. And this is very encouraging to God's servants. . . . The prospect of the recompense of reward, is in a special manner encouraging to us in our work, and makes it pleasant, and the little difficulties we meet within it to be as nothing. (257)

**Essential to Our Desire for Godly Motivation**

Consider what Jesus told the disciples after He demonstrated for them (by washing their feet) what it means to be a servant of others. He said, *"Now that you know these things, you will be blessed if you do them"* (John 13:17).

Why would Jesus tell His disciples that they would be blessed for their service to people if it was not His intent that they be motivated by the prospect of that blessing? You shrug, "It's nice to know that God will reward, but I don't give it much thought. I am not *motivated* by "rewards." I have other (implied: higher, more spiritual) motives." I urge you to humbly consider: what motivates you personally isn't the issue. The question is: What is God's design? Have you explored God's Word on the subject?

*Our motivation to love people*

The more we experience the love of God as expressed, among other ways, in His rewards for obedience motivated by love, the higher will be our capacity to love God and others. After all, you can't give what you don't already have. You can only love to the extent that you have experienced love yourself.

So love and rewards produce a reinforcing cycle: When God rewards, the recipient feels God's love and approval. The more that love and approval are experienced, the more one wants others to have it too. When you have experienced His love by being rewarded or when you anticipate His reward in heaven, it spills over onto those around you like water poured into a cup that is already full.

Therefore, love and obey God not merely because you *should* do so but also because in doing so you will experience the blessings of God's love (His reward), which you can then share with others and which will produce a greater experience of His blessings for you, giving you even more motivation to love. Repeat ad infinitum. You will see this relationship between love and rewards throughout *Investing in Eternity* because love is integral to the doctrine that God rewards.

## *Our motivation to serve and obey God*

Again, here is Paul on the subject:

> *But one thing I do: Forgetting what is behind and straining toward what is ahead, I press on toward the goal to win the prize for which God has called me heavenward in Christ Jesus.* (Phil. 3:13-14)

Paul was not aimless or lackadaisical in his living. He was unashamedly motivated by his desire to have something that he could only obtain by striving, working, and disciplining himself. He was driven by his desire to have the prize. That is because, as Robert Wilkin points out, Paul was competing for the *"brabeion,"* "an award for exceptional performance" (519).[4]

Paul knows that there is more than salvation at stake[5]—and he unashamedly wants it. Shouldn't we, too? Recently my Christian music station enticed its listeners to offer financial support with the mere chance of winning a Carribean cruise. God is far more generous: He offers the *certainty* of winning an eternal reward for sacrificial giving to Him.

*All of us who are mature should take such a view of things.* (Phil. 3:15)

Will you be given a prize in the end for your service to God, even if you believe that there is nothing to gain from that service? Yes, of course, you will; that is, if indeed your intent was to serve and honor God. However, your reward will be no greater for not having been motivated by the prospect of reward.

On the contrary, the opposite seems more likely. Just as even the most dedicated athlete would run faster at a marathon should the prize be increased a thousand-fold, so would even the most diligent of God's servants have a greater determination to serve God for knowing a reward of great value is at stake.[6]

## *Our motivation to forsake all for Christ*

In this book's touchstone passage, Jesus tells us to *"store up for yourselves treasures in heaven"* (Matt. 6:19-20). Paul reiterates that advice in his first letter to Timothy when he commends those who *"lay up treasure for themselves as a firm foundation for the coming age, so that they may*

A Guide to Investing in Eternity

*take hold of the life that is truly life*" (1 Tim. 6:19). Notice the distinction between taking hold of "life" and that which is "truly life." Paul is talking about gaining something more than a place in heaven.

Jesus also warned us not to "*store up for yourselves treasures on earth, where moths and vermin destroy, and where thieves break in and steal*" (Matt. 6:19). Echoing Jesus, Peter tells us that "*the present heavens and earth are reserved for fire, being kept for the Day of Judgment and destruction of the ungodly*" (2 Pet. 3:7). Paul describes the "*wrath being stored up*" (Rom. 2:5).

Those promises of reward and promises of wrath use a form of the Greek word "*thésaurizó,*" translated "*lay up,*" "*stored,*" and "*kept.*" It is the origin of our English word "thesaurus," which means "treasury" or "storehouse." We all are storing up either that which will rust and rot or that which will endure forever. I hope *Investing in Eternity* will encourage you to store up treasure in heaven.[7]

**Notes and Asides:**

[1] Tim Keller provides another example in his commentary on the Gospel of Mark, _Jesus the King_. Not only does Keller **not** talk about the treasures in heaven that Jesus offered to the rich man (discussed in chapter 16 of this book), this is what he says about the motivation that is self-interested:

> If I lead an unselfish life primarily to make myself happy, then I'm not leading an unselfish life. I'm not doing these acts of kindness for others; I'm ultimately doing them for myself. . . . which doesn't make sense. (164)

Whatever Keller actually believes about the doctrine of rewards, this statement seems to deny an essential reason for striving for them: because we want the blessing God wants for us. Perhaps I have misinterpreted what he was saying, but that very misunderstanding would make my point: I don't know what he thinks of the doctrine of rewards because he doesn't speak unambiguously about it.

I realize that one cannot say everything that is true about God and His purposes in every sermon or in every chapter one writes. But, in order not to leave a false impression, encouragement to seek the good things God wants for us must be a regular feature of every sermon or book that teaches us about God, even if that reference is in passing.

Here is an example of the practical effect of neglect of such assurances. After a church service one morning, I talked with a friend with whom I have been sharing the Gospel. He complained that the morning's sermon, which was on the topic of sacrifice, made God seem like a demanding despot who orders us to be His slaves. That narrative was consistent with his experience with his own, unloving father. So we must communicate clearly the good things God promises to give us, lest we inadvertently misrepresent God's heart.

[2] Nike derives its name from the Greek goddess of victory. A form of that name, _nikao_, is repeatedly used in the book of Revelation to describe the vanquishing of the enemies of God. The difference is that, for Nike, pride of accomplishment is the reward; for the Christian, the reward is winning a crown from Jesus.

27

<sup>3</sup> *Lord Acton observed something in the mid-nineteenth century for which history has provided innumerable examples: "Power corrupts. Absolute power corrupts absolutely." Research has confirmed that perceptions of personal powerlessness increases—and, conversely, that having a sense of one's own power reduces—one's capacity for empathy. It is not only that bad people come to be in positions of power: power itself tends to diminish one's compassion. Kind and generous people tend to be suffering servants and vice versa.*

*To the extent one works to accumulate money (which is a form of power) and position, one will tend to care less for people. That is why Jesus said of the rich ruler, "How hard it will be for those who are wealthy to enter the kingdom of God!" (Mark 10:23). And that is why it is a mercy to oneself to relinquish your grasp of things of this world, lest you become like Tolkien's Gollum.*

*Those who are in circumstances of vulnerability are more blessed because the sufferer is more likely to humble himself before God and more likely to care for others. That is what Paul meant when he said:*

> *My grace is sufficient for you, for my power is made perfect in weakness. Therefore I will boast all the more gladly about my weaknesses, so that Christ's power may rest on me. That is why, for Christ's sake, I delight in weaknesses, in insults, in hardships, in persecutions, in difficulties. For when I am weak, then I am strong. (1 Cor. 12:9-11)*

<sup>4</sup> *Happily, unlike in races such as the Boston Marathon, there isn't a single winner. Everyone can win the race of which Paul speaks. One person's gain is not another person's loss, because God will reward out of His infinite storehouse of treasure.*

<sup>5</sup> *You will find my personal story of salvation by Christ in Appendix 8: The Gift of God.*

<sup>6</sup> *A few years ago, our street was given an overhaul that required one lane to be closed to vehicles. For a year and a half, traffic was allowed to flow only in one direction: south. Many of our destinations (grocery store, Walmart, hardware store, pharmacy), however, lay to the north. So, for example, to get to our church a few blocks to the north we had to turn right onto our street, go south for a mile, then west for a quarter-mile, then back north a mile and a half, and then take a*

*winding street back east. A one-minute drive took six. And as is usual with inconvenient road projects, the progress was glacially slow. Often no workers were in sight even on sunny days. I grumbled, but I had no other option. So I turned south to go north.*

    *Such was my frustration with life before learning of God's intent to reward. I "went south to go north" because I didn't even know there was a better way to live.*

7   *Ironically, God's "thesaurus" will leave you at a loss for words!*

# Chapter 3  Rewards Are Essential to God's Character

In one of the many dramatic accounts in the book of Acts, Paul encountered a group of philosophers at a marketplace in Athens. They may have come to the market to pick up some feta for the wife, but when they got there, they did what Greek philosophers do: debate.

The marketplace was the social media of the day. Luke tells us, *"all the Athenians and the foreigners who lived there spent their time doing nothing but talking about and listening to the latest idea"* {Acts 17:16-34}. Thrown into that mix of assorted polytheists were God-fearing Jews who also lived in the city. And you think arguments get heated on Facebook!

One of the philosophers might have said something like this:

"You Jews say there is one god. And you say he is sovereign over all his creation. So tell me: Why did this god of yours create the universe and then populate it with gullible humans? ('Adam' and 'Eve,' right?) Was he bored? So he wrote a human drama for entertainment? Or was it a farce! Maybe we are no more than animals in his zoo! Perhaps he was lonely. Or maybe he suddenly realized his own strength, and he decided to make beings that would cower before him. If so, your god is an emotionally unstable, all-powerful megalomaniac!"

One of the Jews present objected, "But our God is compassionate, too!"

"Oh! So he is a *benevolent* dictator! For Zeus's sake, then why did He make them latently rebellious!? Why did He even make it possible for them to do and experience evil? Why did he give Adam and Eve a free will? Why did he not create them to always obey, if subservience is what He wanted?

"Because He wanted mankind to choose to obey Him," the Jew answered.

"So why did your 'sovereign' and 'benevolent' god decree that for them and all their progeny suffering and death would be the consequence of disobedience? If he is the compassionate god you say he is, then why didn't he give his flawed creation a do-over, or why didn't he simply zap your 'Adam and Eve' out of existence for disobeying Him—and just start over?"

As some of the crowd nodded in agreement and others pondered the barrage of questions, the philosopher thoughtfully stroked his beard and then added, "And didn't you mention the other day that your god is omniscient, too?

Hearing the Jew's reply in the affirmative, he drew a breath and said, "So, tell me if I'm getting this right: You are saying that a benevolent yet wrathful, demanding, and all-powerful god created *fallible* human beings that he knew, *in advance*, would all suffer and die *by his own decree.*"

"Am I missing something?"

(Silence.)

"Ha! I thought not. Your god is as narcissistic as Greek and Roman gods!"

You've got to admit: if that is all the Jews in our imaginary conversation had told the philosophers about God, the philosopher's reasoning would be sound. Credit the Greeks for this: they pushed relentlessly to the εἰς ἄτοπον ἀπαγωγή, the reductio ad absurdum, that is, the absurd logical conclusion. Modern philosophers adopt the same argument, though they mostly choose scientific materialism (an atheistic variant of pantheism) as their religion.

But the philosopher had indeed missed something in his analysis. His premise lacked two qualities of God's character: His love and His holiness. These two aspects of God's nature are crucial to our understanding of both God's purpose and of God's promise to reward.

31

**Essential to Our Understanding of God's Love**

In creating mankind, God set out to reveal His unchanging and unending love. He wanted to share with his creation that which the triune God had experienced for all of eternity. God, therefore, created us with emotions so that we could experience—feel—His love.[1]

God desires more than our experience of His love, however. That is because genuine love—in its very nature and essence—is intensely interested not only in its object's receipt of love but also in its object's return of love. In a word, God desires *relationship*.

The desire for a relationship is essential to God's love. He created mankind with the same desire. Even faltering humans who are "hopelessly in love" nevertheless hope that somehow, someday, their love will be returned. Genuine love always gives with the hope of having the satisfaction of its return from its object. That is what God's love wants of and for us. That is what God's love desires of and for us.[2]

Furthermore, God wants our exclusive love. He requires monogamy with Him because He knows what we truly want and need is that for which He created us: the satisfactions of relationship with Him. He is jealous of our love because He will be content with nothing less than the best for us.

And so, our loving God is persistent. He continually woos us into relationship with Him. He does not stop His displays of love after He has succeeded, any more than a loving husband stops offering gifts after he has won his bride. That is because God wants more than the restoration of our broken relationship with Him. He wants His and our relationship to flourish! He never becomes frustrated in that desire.[3]

In Sonnet VII, Hartley Coleridge asks, "Is love a fancy, or a feeling?"

No. It is immortal as immaculate Truth.
'Tis not a blossom shed as soon as youth drops from the stem of life.

God's love never relents: *"Love . . . bears all things, believes all things, hopes all things, endures all things"* {1 Cor. 13:7 NASB}.
God's love loves . . .

In barren regions, where no waters flow,
Nor rays of promise cheats the pensive gloom.
It is love's being yet it cannot die,

Nor will it change, though all be changed beside.

Therefore, God persists with enticements of blessing in hope we will fall even more in love with Him. As Tim Keller puts it in *Jesus the King,*

> God created us to invite us into the dance, to say: if you glorify me, if you center your life on me, if you find me beautiful for who I am in myself, then you will step into the dance, which is what you are made for. (10)[4]

God didn't only bring us to the dance: He wants to dance with us! He wants us to move with Him to the rhythm of the music. He leads us, but he doesn't force us to dance. He doesn't whirl us around like Donald O'Connor's mannequin in *Singing in the Rain,* he invites us to be His dance partner. Think instead: Fred Astaire and Ginger Rogers.

As often as not, we are unaware that Jesus stands before us in a humble bow, hand extended with an offer to dance. We are content to sip punch, listen to the band, and watch others on the floor. Or we tango with other people. But you will never have a better dance partner than Jesus.

## Essential to Our Understanding of God's Holiness

God is not only loving. He is also holy. Without an understanding of His holy character, our understanding of God's purpose is incomplete. It is like driving through the Grand Tetons with a patch over one eye: You see the mountains. You may appreciate their beauty. But the full effect of their majesty is diminished without the depth of perception two eyes enable. Let us take the patch off the other eye, as it were, to reveal a greater depth of God's character.

### *The Judge*

Holy God is the Great Judge, the standard against which all conduct, good and bad, is measured: *"The heavens proclaim his righteousness, for God himself is the judge"* {Ps. 50:6}. He is the sole and final arbiter of what is worthy of blessing (His rewards for righteousness) and punishment (which are His rewards for sin).

While human judgments are often unpredictable or based on flawed, man-made law, God's judgments are rooted in His own holy character. God exercises judgment as naturally as you and I breathe because that is who God is, and that is what God does. *"He is the LORD our God; his judgments are in all the earth"* {Ps. 105:7.}

Since judgment flows from God's essential, holy character, the blessing, and punishment that result are woven into the very fabric of His moral universe. To ignore God's judgment is as foolish and perilous as denying or ignoring the law of gravity as you stand at the edge of the Grand Canyon. Conduct and attitudes consistent with His righteous character will be rewarded with good things, just as surely as behavior and attitudes inconsistent with who He is will be rewarded with punishment.

That is because blessings and punishments are two sides of the same moral coin. (An even better metaphor is a watch battery, with its positive and negative sides.) Blessing and punishment naturally and inevitably follow His judgment upon good and evil. God will no more fail to reward faithfulness than He will fail to punish wickedness. God's holy character guarantees it.

### The judgment

This truth is most starkly seen in those many Scriptures in which promises of reward for faithful service are proximate to promises of punishment for not serving God. We see this contrast of outcomes clearly, for example, in Deuteronomy 30.

> *See, I set before you today life and prosperity, death and destruction.* (v. 15)

> *This day I call heaven and earth as witnesses against you that I have set before you life and death, blessings and curses.* (v. 19)

> *Joshua reminds the people of God at the end of his life,*

> *You know with all your heart and soul that not one of all the good promises the LORD your God gave you has failed. Every promise has been fulfilled; not one has failed.* (Josh. 23:14)

But Joshua continues with a warning: violate the covenant of the Lord by serving other gods and . . .

*just as every good promise of the LORD your God has come true, so the LORD will bring on you all the evil he has threatened, until he has destroyed you from this good land he has given you.* (Josh. 23:15-16)

Solomon often wrote of blessing and punishment in the same sentence:

*If the righteous receive their due on the earth, how much more the ungodly and the sinner!* (Prov. 11:17)

*He who scorns instruction will pay for it, but he who respects a command is rewarded.* (Prov. 13:13)

*To the man who pleases him, God gives wisdom, knowledge and happiness, but to the sinner he gives the task of gathering and storing up wealth to hand it over to the one who pleases God.* (Eccl. 2:26)

Jesus did not change the rules laid down in the Old Testament. He repeatedly taught about reward and punishment in contrast to each other:

*Whoever finds his life will lose it, and whoever loses his life for my sake will find it.* (Matt. 10:39; see also Matt. 16:25)

*Whoever has will be given more; whoever does not have, even what he has will be taken from him.* (Mark 4:25; see also Luke 19:26; Matt. 25:29)

*For everyone who exalts himself will be humbled, and he who humbles himself will be exalted.* (Luke 14:11; see also Luke 18:14)

When God judges, He does not merely declare this to be good and that to be bad; He pronounces a consequence of the attitudes and actions He has judged. Does a human judge say to the murderer, "I find you guilty!

You are now free to go"? Does he withhold the financial settlement from a winning plaintiff? Of course not. As with a human court, God decrees consequences for behavior. The prophecy in Revelation will come to pass.

> *The time has come for judging the dead, and for rewarding your servants the prophets and your saints and those who reverence your name, both small and great—and for destroying those who destroy the earth.* (Rev. 11:18)

So intertwined is the judgment of both righteousness and sin that often the same phrase is used to describe both the results of sin and the results of faithfulness. Warning about the consequences of sin, Solomon asks in Proverbs 24:12, *"Will He not give to each person according to what he has done?"* On the other hand, that same phrase—*"give to each person according to what he has done"*—in Psalm 62:12 is encouraging to those who are faithful. Therefore, one phrase is used to convey both truths: God's judgments will fall upon the one who does evil and upon the one who does good, *"according to what he has done."*

Likewise, the words used to describe rewards for both sin and faithfulness are often the same Greek and Hebrew words. Index 1, under "Nature of Rewards," lists multiple examples of words that are variously translated "reward," "payment," "compensation," "wages," etc. to describe both the punishments that accrue to our sin and the blessings that accrue to our faithfulness.

So in these juxtapositions of positive and negative rewards, we have a stereo understanding of God's holy character, which will produce both punishment of sin and reward for righteousness. To emphasize God's judgment of sin to the exclusion of His judgment of righteous behavior—or, conversely, to speak of His blessings without speaking of His judgment—distorts our understanding of God. God is the *"righteous judge"* of evil (Ps. 7:11) and of good (Ps. 58:11). As I said, they are the two sides of a watch battery. God will judge because He is the Judge of the earth (Ps. 82:8; 94:2).

## Essential to Our Understanding of God's Coexistent Love and Holiness

How can God pass judgment on people He loves? Like these circles, His love and justice seem at odds with each other.[5]

### Opposed to each other

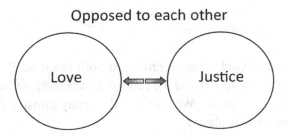

*As seen in Jesus*

Followers of Jesus understand that the synthesis of this seeming incompatibility of God's love and justice had its demonstration first and powerfully on the cross. Suspended between heaven and earth, the love and the justice of God were on display for the world to behold: God's love provided a substitute. His own Son suffered the just punishment for our sins. As a result, all children of Adam who are born again in Jesus—this time as a child of God—escape God's judgment.[6]

Jesus's obedience produced something more than the hope of our salvation, however. His obedience also resulted in His being *"crowned with glory and honor"* (Heb. 2:9). As a result of Jesus's obedience to the Father, God rewarded Jesus with the honor and position that is His due. Jesus *"humbled Himself, and became obedient to death, even death on a cross!"* {Phil. 2:8}. As a result, *"God exalted him to the highest place and gave him the name that is above every name"* (v. 9). God *"seated him at his right hand in the heavenly realms, far above all rule and authority, power and dominion"*{Eph. 1:20-21}.

In this way, therefore, God's love and justice merged in a second way: they produced a reward from the Father of glory and honor for the Son. So, like the circles below, God's love and justice overlap both on the cross and on the throne on which Jesus is now seated.

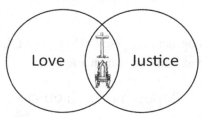

Overlapping each other

God's love and God's justice produced both the reward for sin (our punishment borne by Jesus) and the reward for obedience (the honor and glory bestowed upon Jesus). We will spend eternity praising God for His love and justice thus displayed.

### As seen in our reward

Hard though it is to imagine, this story gets even better! Paul tells us that we can *share* in Christ's glory (Rom. 8:17)! He tells the Thessalonians that those who *"stand firm and hold to the teachings"* will *"share in the glory of our Lord Jesus Christ"* (2 Thess. 2:14-15).

Ponder those promises for a moment. For my part, I can't read them without tearing up. It is an unfathomable truth: Unworthy though I am, God invites me to share in the glory which He has bestowed upon His own Son! Just as God's love and justice made my salvation possible through the obedience of Jesus, God's love and justice make it possible for me to share in the reward bestowed upon Jesus! Jesus endured the cross so that we could sit on a throne next to Him!

### The required condition

But notice the qualifiers in those two passages:

> *If indeed we share* in Christ's sufferings . . .
> *That you might share* in the glory . . .
> *stand firm and hold to the teachings.*

Glory will not be shared without the sort of sacrifice that earned Jesus His place on the throne of heaven: obedience to the point of death. Our reward—if we are to have it—will be the product of faithful and sacrificial living in obedience to God, just as it was for Jesus. The extent to which we share Christ's glory depends upon the conduct of our lives. We will not all have the same experience of heaven. God's love and justice guarantee that it will be so.

God's holy and loving character produces God's rewards. You will see further evidence of that truth throughout *Investing in Eternity*.

## Notes and Asides:

[1] *God created mankind in His likeness; so we are similar in important respects to our Creator, though different in many others. One of those similarities is our emotional desires, which mirror His own. But our satisfaction, along with our spiritual and physical needs, were created as utterly dependent upon God. Then, for reasons I will discuss in a moment, God gave Adam and Eve, and later all of us, the choice of where to find the satisfaction of those needs and desires.*

*You would think the choice of obedience to God would have been easy for Adam and Eve. After all, God gave them those needs and desires so they would come to Him for the "water of life"{Rev. 22:1} that would slake their thirst. Adam and Eve had no unmet needs or godly desires in the Garden.*

*Despite their personal experience with God, they were tempted by their desire for more than God had given them, which, as even the evil tempter would backhandedly acknowledge, was everything—but for the fruit of one tree.*

*Engaging her God-given senses and appealing to her desire, the tempter pointed out to Eve that the fruit looked good to eat, so it must be "good" to eat it. Then she listened without objection to the tempter's insinuation that God must be keeping the highest of satisfactions from her. When she touched the fruit—mistakenly thinking that doing so was prohibited—she did not die, thereby confirming her growing suspicion that God was a liar.*

*The pièce de résistance was a poison covered with a sweet sauce of truth and double half-truth. As Eve held—and no doubt smelled—the fruit in her hand, he enticed her with the promise that, if she tasted the sweet fruit, she would have the sweet knowledge of good and of evil.*

*That "knowledge" for which the Tree was named, is "yada," in Hebrew, that we will discuss in the next chapter. It is an experiential knowledge. Therefore, part of the lie was cruelly and ironically true, first because Eve already had experiential knowledge of the "Good": the God who loved her. And, truly, what she, and then Adam, would experientially know from tasting the fruit was Evil itself. The lie was that such knowledge, like the fruit itself, would be sweet.*

*And then came the tempter's second half-truth. For having eaten the fruit, they would indeed become like God in one respect:*

they would know the difference between pure Good and pure Evil. The tempter's lie of omission was that only God can have ongoing experiential knowledge of both good and evil. For the rest of us, the latter extinguishes the former. In mankind's saddest moment, their experiential knowledge of God's goodness died. Henceforth it would be only a faded memory. It survives as our conscience (Rom. 2:14-15).

In disobeying God, Adam and Eve had voluntarily broken their relationship with God. They were cast from the Garden of fellowship with God. Their innocence was transformed into shame. Suddenly, all their needs were no longer met by God. They would live only by hard work. They would suffer pain. And they were left at the mercy of their desires, which were now even more prone to seek their satisfaction apart from God. And then they, like their relationship with God, would die.

2   New Testament writers referred to this relationship between God and His people with the Greek word "ecclesia." That word, translated to the English as the "Church" of God, originally described the sort of assembly in Athens we just discussed. Human "ecclesia" is transformed into God's "ecclesia" by relationship with God.

As the essence of the word "church" has eroded in common understanding by divisions within God's family and for its use to designate a place as much as a relationship, I will refer mostly to "God's family" to emphasize the relationship between God and His people that characterizes God's true Church.

One biblical description of this goal, that of being "united with Christ," does not appear in our collection of verses of conditional promises. Nevertheless, such unity is an expression of the highest form of relationship found throughout the New Testament.

Not surprisingly, the Evil One has set before the world an analogous counterfeit: the hope of achieving "singularity." That is the technological end at which mankind achieves godlike powers of knowledge to produce a utopia. Singularity is the Hegalian goal of "transhumanism," which advocates for a rational, human-centric end to evil. According to this view, once mankind has learned to achieve immortality and mastery of the universe through science and technology, there will be no unmet needs or wants, and people will live in perfect harmony with one another. As an official at a major university told me, "We will take the next step in human evolution."

*In ages past, mankind looked to celestial gods to achieve fulfillment and happiness, but those gods have been replaced with the terrestrial god of science.*

*Transhumanist hope rests upon the lie that mankind's problems are caused by a scarcity of knowledge and resources. Of course, nothing in the human experience would indicate that humanity would be content in achieving such a state of knowledge and power. Mankind's boast is that of the first rebel against God, the Accuser, "I will ascend to the heavens; I will raise my throne above the stars of God; I will sit enthroned on the mount of assembly" {Isa. 14:13}.*

3    *When our love is of God, we too love people, even when our love isn't accepted and returned. And our greatest desire is that others also would know the purest of love, which is God's love. While we often give up on that hope when it is disappointed, God never gives up in His pursuit.*

4    *Keller attributes the "dance" metaphor to C. S. Lewis in* Mere Christianity. *In the context of describing the trinity and our relationship to it, Lewis writes,*

> *And that, by the way, is perhaps the most important difference between Christianity and all other religions: that in Christianity God is not a static thing—not even a person—but a dynamic, pulsating activity, a life, almost a kind of drama. Almost, if you will not think me irreverent, a kind of dance. The union between the Father and Son is such a live, concrete thing that this union itself is also a Person. I know this is almost inconceivable but look at it thus. You know that among human beings, when they get together in a family, or a club, or a trade union, people talk about the "spirit" of that family, or club, or trade union. They talk about its "spirit" because the individual members, when they are together, do really develop particular ways of talking and behaving which they would not have if they were apart. (151)*

*Keller continues the thought with a quote from Cornelius Plantinga,*

> *The persons within God exalt each other, commune with each other, and defer to one another . . . Each divine person harbors the others at the center of his being. In constant movement of overture and acceptance, each person envelops and encircles*

42

the others... God's interior life [therefore] overflows with regard for others. (22–23)

5    There is a theological asymmetry in juxtaposing God's justice and God's love, the former being an expression of God's holy and/or righteous character and the latter being of the essence of His character. However, in my experience, people speak of God's justice versus His love rather than God's holiness versus His love, so, with apologies to theologians, I put the contrast in everyday language. Indeed, I eschew erudition in Investing in Eternity for, as C. S. Lewis said, "Any fool can write learned language. The vernacular is the real test. If you can't turn your faith into it, then either you don't understand it or you don't believe it" (Version Vernacular, 143).

6    "For God was pleased to have all his fullness dwell in him, and through him to reconcile to himself all things, whether things on earth or things in heaven, by making peace through his blood, shed on the cross. Once you were alienated from God and were enemies in your minds because of your evil behavior. But now he has reconciled you by Christ's physical body through death to present you holy in his sight, without blemish and free from accusation—if you continue in your faith, established and firm, and do not move from the hope held out in the gospel. This is the gospel that you heard and that has been proclaimed to every creature under heaven, and of which I, Paul, have become a servant" (Col. 1:19-23).

# Chapter 4  Rewards Are Essential
## to God's Purpose and Goal

### Essential to Our Understanding of God's Grace

Quantum physics grapples with something Albert Einstein called the "duality paradox." Contrary to reason, every particle or quantum entity may be partly described in terms of both particles and waves. How can that be? No one knows.

> It seems as though we must use sometimes the one theory and sometimes the other, while at times we may use either. We are faced with a new kind of difficulty. We have two contradictory pictures of reality; separately neither of them fully explains the phenomena of light, but together they do. (Einstein, quoted by Kossack, 57)

Many Christians perceive an analogous theological "duality paradox." They see "two contradictory pictures of reality" in the efficacy of God's grace and our good works. But there is no incongruity between the two: God's grace provides a means of salvation, and God's grace offers a means of reward for obedience to God: "Neither of them fully explains the phenomena [of God's grace], but together they do." The former gives us our place in heaven. The latter offers the rewards of heaven.

Rewards are expressions of God's grace. They are of the essence of God's character. So this teaching is not optional or relatively unimportant as compared to other doctrines of Scripture. Peter, for example, tells us explicitly that rewards are integral to God's plan for us.

*Be like-minded, be sympathetic, love one another; be compassionate and humble. Do not repay evil with evil or insult with insult. On the contrary, repay evil with blessing, because to this you were called so that you may inherit a blessing.* (1 Pet. 3:8-9)

Living one's life without an understanding of God's intent to reward is like watching a 3-D movie without the 3-D glasses: not only is the visual impact absent, but the video is distorted because it was made for viewing through the glasses. Likewise, an understanding of this teaching is crucial to a full and integrated understanding of God's grace, as this graphic illustrates.

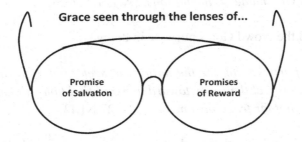

Here we see the distinction between the *manifestation* of the grace of God that saves us and *another manifestation* of the same grace of God that makes available to us the rewards of heaven. These are the "lenses" through which we will see God's purpose and goal.

We will put on those "3-D glasses" and see the "third dimension" as we continue in this chapter. We will see that God's rewards complete God's grace. In offering them, God has graciously provided both the opportunity and means by which we can gain something through our service to Him. To the extent that our contribution honors God, we will forever benefit.

Our foundation is laid *"by the grace of God."* But *"each one should be careful how he builds,"* for,

*If any man builds on this foundation using gold, silver, costly stones, wood, hay or straw, his work will be shown for what it is, because the Day will bring it to light. If what he has built survives, he will receive his reward.* (1 Cor. 3:11-14)[1]

**Essential to Our Understanding of God's Purpose in Creation**

When the Apostle Paul entered the discussion in Athens (in the previous chapter), he affirmed that the philosophers were on the right track, but they had a faulty understanding of God and God's purpose in creating the universe and the people in it. Unlike the Greek and Roman gods, He did not do so out of self-centered need.

> *The God who made the world and everything in it is the Lord of heaven and earth. [He] is not served by human hands, as if he needed anything. Rather, he himself gives everyone life and breath and everything else. From one man God made all the nations.* {Acts 17:24-26}

Then he told the crowd God's purpose in doing so.

> *His purpose was for the nations to seek after God and perhaps feel their way toward him and find him—though he is not far from any one of us.* {v. 27 NLT}

Was Paul implying that God stands—as it were—just behind us, but out of view? Why does He not tap us on the shoulder and say, "Here I am!"? He does so—but only after we have cried out to Him.

> *Then you will call, and the LORD will answer; you will cry for help, and he will say: Here am I.* (Isa. 58:9)

God doesn't force our notice of Him because God is not interested in merely having his existence known. He wanted far more when He created us. What was it?

*Relationship created*

We see the answer first hinted in Genesis. Having created Adam, God then created Eve so that Adam would not be alone. Then we see it in procreation set in the context of committed, monogamous marriage. And we see it in that which God promised and then delivered to Abraham, the "*Father of*

*Many*" {Gen. 17:5}: a child who would be the patriarch of a multitude of descendants. Clearly, God intended to create a human family.

But it was not God's goal merely to create human offspring (as Paul calls mankind, quoting Greek poets). "Human family" was only God's earthly metaphor for the family-like relationship He desires to have with His creation and between members of His creation.[2]

The quality of the relationship God sought is—and of necessity must be—entered into voluntarily. So God gave His human creations, Adam and Eve, the freedom to choose to stay in their relationship with God. To keep it, they had only to fulfill their part in two conditions essential to any good relationship:

- Both parties must be trustworthy, since no one trusts—or would be expected to trust—the untrustworthy.
- Both parties must willingly give their trust since no one can be forced into a trusting relationship with another.

### Relationship destroyed

Adam and Eve chose badly.[3] The distrust of God that led them to eat of the fruit severed their relationship with God. For while God is always trustworthy, they were not. And while God is always willing to have a relationship, they were not.

### Relationship restored

Was God's purpose thwarted? No, because in His sovereignty, God both anticipated the breach and used it for His purposes. Though our God and Creator owed mankind nothing, He set about to prove His love and trustworthiness to His creation. He did so over and over for His people in the Old Testament.

More importantly, because of His great love, God promised to unilaterally heal the fissure in the relationship caused by Adam and Eve's sin. He hinted at His intent to do so on the very day of the Fall, when He foretold that the serpent would someday strike His heel, but that He would crush the serpent's head. He gave a further—huge—clue when He provided the substitute for Abraham's sacrifice that we'll discuss in a moment. And in His Law God required that innocent animal blood be shed as a covering—a foreshadow of the remedy—for their sin {Rom. 3:25; Heb. 10:4}.

Then God made good on that promise. In space and time, God did what He had purposed to do before space and time existed: God demonstrated His love when He took upon Himself the penalty He had established for disobedience. He sent His Son, Jesus, to be crucified as the God-demanded sacrifice that would satisfy the God-declared penalty for our sin {2 Cor. 5:21}. God the Father personally experienced evil when Jesus suffered and died. At an inestimable personal cost, He severed His relationship with His own Son so that we could have our relationship with Him restored.

That three-day break in His relationship with Jesus was "temporary" to our time-bound understanding. But God doesn't exist in time. As the Creator of time, He exists beyond its constraints. He has no beginning and no end; He is the Alpha and the Omega. So, after Jesus had entered time and space as a human, died and rose from the dead, the triune God didn't sigh with relief and say, "I'm glad that's over!" God's experience of evil is in His being, in His consciousness, in a dimension of time and timelessness that we cannot comprehend. That is significant because it means God experientially knew the pain of Jesus's death when He spoke the first words of creation and set in motion the events to follow. So the cross was not Plan B. It was Plan A from the beginning.

Why did He do that? Because God wanted to have a loving relationship with us so much that He was willing to die for it. That was the whole point of creation. God's love is not passive about or disinterested in our response to Him. The lover of our souls has a powerful desire to have His love returned. God did not need mankind; He *wanted* mankind. He therefore *"demonstrated His love while we were still sinners"* {Rom. 5:8}. As I said, He determined to do so before He created us.

**Essential to Our Understanding of God's Goal**

That is not the end of the story, however. God never intended only to make possible the *restoration* of His broken relationship with mankind. His desire is to *re-create* it into something infinitely better than the original. And, as with the original, that re-created relationship requires ongoing trust and trustworthiness on the part of both parties.

### Re-creation begins with Abraham

### The conditional promise

The Lord said to Abram,

> Go from your country, your people and your father's household to the land I will show you. I will make you into a great nation, and I will bless you; I will make your name great, and you will be a blessing. I will bless those who bless you, and whoever curses you I will curse; and all peoples on earth will be blessed through you. (Gen. 12:2)

Notice the repeated "*I will*" is preceded by the command to "*Go.*" Abram would only be blessed if He obeyed God. And so he did, even when God gave him this shocking command:

> Take your son, your only son, whom you love—Isaac— and go to the region of Moriah. Sacrifice him there as a burnt offering on a mountain I will show you. . . . [So] Abraham bound his son Isaac and laid him on the altar, on top of the wood. Then he reached out his hand and took the knife to slay his son. (Gen. 22:2, 9-10)

For a moment, the Greek philosopher appears to have been right in his assessment of God's capricious character. But Abraham had come to know and trust God, so he believed God's promise to give his son Isaac countless descendants. He knew that couldn't happen if Isaac were dead. Therefore, as he raised his knife over Isaac, he was confident that God would either raise Isaac from the dead or He would provide a substitute for the sacrifice he was about to make. Sure enough . . .

> The angel of the Lord called out to him from heaven, "Abraham! Abraham! . . . Do not lay a hand on the boy," he said. "Do not do anything to him. Now I know that you fear God, because you have not withheld from me your son, your only son." (vv. 11-12)

49

God had again vindicated Abraham's faith in Him! (And in the process reiterated His intent to provide His own Son as the sacrifice.) But, wait . . . God said, *"Now I know . . ."* I thought God knows everything! Why did He put Abraham through that dreadful ordeal?

Because a relationship can only be everything it can be when there is total and unreserved trust in each other's character and intentions. Such trust must be demonstrated. It must be proven by actions. God had repeatedly shown His trustworthiness to Abraham. But God did not *experientially* know Abraham's complete and unreserved trust until he demonstrated it by his willingness to sacrifice his son.[4]

We have that understanding of God because the Hebrew word for *"know"* in that verse is a form of the Hebrew *"yada,"* which speaks of "experiential knowledge." It is knowledge of the heart, not of the head. The same word is used in the Bible to describe marital sexual relations—the consummate expression of human relationship that reflects the *"yada"* God wants to have of us and us of Him.

Just as Abraham had not experienced God's love until God demonstrated it, God does not *experience* our trust until we demonstrate it. That is what God called all the descendants of Abraham to do, over and over in the Old Testament. That is what God calls us to do.[5]

### The fulfillment

Abraham believed God—which is to say that he believed God's conditional promises of blessing. After he demonstrated that belief in God's trustworthy character, God swore by Himself to fulfill the promise that had years earlier enticed Abram to leave Ur of the Chaldees for the Promised Land.

> *I swear by myself, declares the Lord, that **because you have done this** and have not withheld your son, your only son, I will surely bless you and make your descendants as numerous as the stars in the sky and as the sand on the seashore. Your descendants will take possession of the cities of their enemies, and through your offspring all nations on earth will be blessed, **because you have obeyed me**.* (Gen. 22:16-18; Heb. 6:15)

Abraham may have thought God was merely waxing poetic. He had no idea how many would be his descendants! Through his offspring *"all nations on earth"* would be blessed—because Abraham had fully trusted God's promise. While God had initiated the relationship with Abram, and Abram had positively responded to God in the past, the fullest measure of blessings God promised him was dependent upon Abraham's demonstration of complete trust in God.

Many of Abraham's descendants did not respond to God as he had. They forfeited the promised blessings as a result. But, many others did; among them one of Israel's kings:

> *Hezekiah trusted in the Lord, the God of Israel.... He held fast to the Lord and did not stop following him; he kept the commands the Lord had given Moses. And the Lord was with him; he was successful in whatever he undertook.* (2 Kings 18:5-6)

## Re-creation continues in Abraham's spiritual descendants

### The promise

As with Abraham's physical descendants, so it is with his spiritual descendants. If we are to have all the blessings that God wants for us, we must prove ourselves faithful (1 Cor. 4:2). We must give everything dear to us; we must make **ourselves** a living sacrifice {Rom. 12:1}. When we do, we will fully know God and we will be fully known by God.

Many of my readers believe in Jesus. Your relationship with God has been restored. But that knowledge of God, glorious though it is, is only the beginning of the relationship God wants with you.

### The fulfillment

Having put on the "3-D glasses," with its twin lenses of **saving** and **rewarding** grace, we see God's great goal: relationship between God and man that is both **our** reward and **God's** reward.

51

## God's Great Goal

God's conditional promises of blessing and our continued faith and obedience are essential to growing (<<< >>>) our relationship with God. We enter that relationship by trusting in Jesus. We expand that relationship by increasingly trusting in Him. And notice the "Us" in the graphic. Our faith and obedience in response to God's promises to reward also expand relationships with the other members of His family.

You may have wondered: If mankind lived in perfect harmony with God before the Fall and that relationship will be fully restored for His people when Christ returns, what will have been accomplished in our experience of evil in the meantime? If human history is about the restoration of our relationships with God and people—about "Paradise Lost" and "Paradise Regained"[6]—what was God's purpose in allowing a painful detour into sin?

It is for this: Just as our memory of God's goodness remained after the Fall {Rom. 2:15},[7] a God-filtered memory of our experience of Evil's evilness—like the scars on Jesus's body—will remain after our resurrection {John 20:20; 1 Cor. 13:12}. That memory will be devoid of the experience of pain {Rev. 21:4}, but it will be fully aware of what God accomplished through that pain {Joel 2:27; Phil. 1:12}. Because we will have that memory of Evil, we will forever possess the knowledge of the *difference* between God's goodness and Evil's evilness.

As a result, for all of eternity, followers of Christ will never again want to experience Evil. We will have been inoculated against the disease of sin. God will have used mankind's rebellion against Him for the "*good*" of those who love Him (Rom. 8:28). There will be no repeat of Adam and Eve's bad choice, for we will freely and forever choose to stay in a loving relationship with our good God. And we will praise Him forever for having made that possible.

God will have produced an even better relationship than that which He

52

and His human creations enjoyed before the Fall. He will not have merely restored it; He will have re-created it, in a New Heaven and a New Earth populated by people born to the New Adam, Jesus {2 Pet. 3:7-13; Rom. 5:18-19}.

*The prize to be won*

That brings us to the climactic point of this chapter as it relates to God's reward:

In the hereafter, those who most faithfully served Christ in this life will have the strongest memories of their struggle against Evil and of God's provision in this life.[8] Thus:

Those who are *"rooted and established in love"* will forever and more fully
*"know ["gnōseōs"] the love that surpasses knowledge ["hyperballousan gnōseōs"],"*
experience *"how wide and long and high and deep is the love of Christ,"* and
be *"filled to the measure of all the fullness ["plērōma,"* the superabundance] *of God."*
(Eph. 3:17-19)

This was God's purpose in creating the world;
this was God's purpose in allowing sin to enter it;
this was God's purpose in sacrificing His own Son to redeem it;
this was God's purpose in enticing with promises
of reward into a deeper trust of Him:
That we—and our God—may together and forever
experience the "superabundance" of
*loving relationship.*

*Such will be God's great reward for His love.*
*And such will be our great reward for returning His love.*

**Notes and Asides:**

[1]  *The Greek word translated "reward" could also be translated "wage,"*
*"salary," "compensation," making it clear that such payments are*
*earned for performance. "By the grace of God . . . he will receive his*
*reward" (vv. 10, 14). This passage is one of the clearest indicators in*
*Scripture that not all will have that reward even though they will go*
*to heaven, for it ends with: "If* [his life's labor] *is burned up, he will*
*suffer loss; he himself will be saved, but only as one escaping through*
*the flames" (v. 15).*

  *"A good deed has God for its debtor, just as also an Evil One;*
*for a judge is the rewarder in every case" (658). That quote from*
*Tertullian, the Father of Western Theology, is from the third century*
*AD. By the time of the Reformation, 1,300 years later, the doctrine*
*of rewards had become conflated with the doctrine of salvation by*
*grace and thoroughly corrupted by the Roman church. The Reformers*
*rightly rebelled. It seems, however, that now the pendulum has swung*
*too far in the opposite direction. Many modern Protestants cringe at*
*the thought of "earning" anything from God. Romans 6:23—"For the*
*wages of sin is death, but the gift of God is eternal life in Christ Jesus*
*our Lord"—needlessly creates a cognitive dissonance in our minds.*
*Just as our salvation is dependent upon God's gracious provision, so*
*our reward is dependent upon God's gracious provision.*

  *R. C. Sproul, a Reformed theologian himself, correctly observed*
*that we owe much of our misunderstanding about rewards . . .*

> *. . . to the Protestant emphasis on the doctrine of justification by*
> *faith alone. We hammer away at that doctrine . . . to the extent*
> *that people conclude good works are insignificant and have no*
> *bearing at all upon the Christian's future life. (Now That's a*
> *Good Question)*

> *The Reformers are not to blame for that error, however; for they taught*
> *the doctrine of rewards.*

> *Now when Christ says: make to yourselves friends, lay up for*
> *yourselves treasures, and the like, you see that He means:*
> *do good, and it will follow of itself without your seeking, that*

54

*you will have friends, find treasures in heaven, and receive a reward. (Luther, 3:10-11)*

> *We should regard as above all controversy the teaching of Scripture that, just as God, variously distributing his gifts to the saints in this world, beams upon them unequally, so there will not be an equal measure of glory in heaven, where God shall crown his own gifts . . . Nothing is clearer than that a reward is promised to good works, in order to support the weakness of our flesh by some comfort . . . (Calvin, 1005)*

> *We teach that good works are meritorious – not for the forgiveness of sins, grace, or justification (for we obtain these only by faith) but for other physical and spiritual rewards in this life and in that which is to come. (Melanchthon, 175)*

*The doctrine of rewards was affirmed in the Westminster Confession of 1646, Chapter 16:6:*

> *Being accepted through Christ, their good works also accepted in him, not as though they were in this life wholly unblameable and unreproved in God's sight; but that he, looking upon them in his Son, is pleased to accept and reward that which is sincere, although accompanied with many weaknesses and imperfections.*

2  *The "perhaps" in Paul's statement is telling, for it indicates that God knew that not all would seek Him and find Him. That raises the question: If it is the will of a sovereign God that people find Him, why do some **not** find Him? Of course, the answer to that question is much debated and the various conclusions concerning it have led to great division in the Church of God. Some emphasize God's sovereignty. Others emphasize man's free will. Many, frustrated by the seeming contradiction, tend toward agnosticism on the matter. My own understanding is somewhere in between.*

*My epistemology is this: We were created in God's image, with "eternity set in our hearts" {Eccl. 3:11; Rom. 2:15}. And followers of Christ have been given His Spirit, the Counselor who, among other things, informs our understanding. While our comprehension of God is infinitely limited, we have been given rudimentary intellectual and*

55

spiritual knowledge sufficient to the understanding of the essence of His character and purposes. I believe that limited understanding extends to His grant of free will (i.e., of choice).

### Free will

Choice—by definition—must have at least two potentially attractive options, or it is—literally—no choice. As Justin Martyr said:

> If the human race does not have the power of a freely deliberated choice in fleeing evil and choosing good, then men are not accountable for their actions. (53)

Mankind must have been given such a real choice by God, for had He not then God would have created defective humans, which is inconceivable. The sovereign and sole Creator of mankind, the originator of mankind's very soul, by definition and design, would be responsible for Adam's and Eve's bad choice—for their sin—and, by extension, for the sin of all mankind. Of course, that is impossible, since such an action would be against God's own character.

### God's sovereignty

God is sovereign, which means He can and will always only do that which comports with His character. Without diminishing His attributes, our sovereign God can voluntarily delegate some of His sovereign control to the humans He created in His own image. He did so—in a way limited in scope—by giving Adam and Eve a choice: to trust or not to trust Him. Doing so was no more a diminution of His sovereignty than my headship of my home is diminished for allowing my kids to move freely in it.

### God's purpose in the granting of free will

The grant of free will and the sinful exercise of it notwithstanding, God's sovereign purpose was nevertheless accomplished: for it was God's sovereign will to demonstrate aspects of His character in the process. Among them are His love and holiness, the light of which can only be fully appreciated by humanity in contrast to the darkness of evil. So, despite the choice that Adam and Eve made, God's sovereign will is accomplished.

### Relevance to the doctrine of rewards

*Fortunately, a complete understanding of the nature of our free will is not required for an understanding of God's rewards. All we need to know is this: God gave mankind the ability to choose, mankind chose badly, and then God provided humanity with the means—Jesus's sacrifice—by which mankind's ability to choose well might be restored and empowered—by His Spirit—and further motivated—by the promise of reward—to do God's will. Such is my understanding of Philippians 2:13, "For it is God who works in you to will and to act in order to fulfill his good purpose."*

*His work in us must be understood as cooperative, not as coercive. If that is not so, then all the conditional promises in the Bible and discussed in <u>Investing in Eternity</u> would lose their plain meaning: freedom of choice between options, with the consequence of that choice to follow. Vast swaths of God's Word would thus be—at best— meaningless to our understanding. Worse, they would implicate God of false pretense, for He would be speaking as if the hearers have a choice when, in fact, they do not.*

*If that understanding is wrong: if God alone is responsible for Christians' godly behavior and we have no choice in our obedience after we become followers of Jesus, then how do we explain our frequent failure to do so?*

[3] *The effects of the denigration of family, marriage, sexual liberation, and the radical redefinition of sexual identity are chronicled in <u>Primal Screams: How the Sexual Revolution Created Identity Politics</u> by Mary Eberstadt.*

> *Systemwide familial dislocations are now having repercussions at every stage of human life, as shown by new data about the steep rise in psychiatric problems among American teenagers and young adults; decades of empirical evidence about the harms of fatherless homes (a literature as well-known as it is stoutly ignored); the "loneliness studies" now proliferating in sociology; spotlighting the increased isolation of the elderly in every Western nation; and troubling new evidence of the human costs of new techniques for making babies, such as anonymous sperm donation. (209)*

*The secular psychiatrist Bessel Van Der Kolk agrees, at least with regard to human relationships:*

> *Our culture teaches us to focus on personal uniqueness, but at a deeper level we barely exist as individual organisms. Our brains are built to help us function as members of a tribe. We are part of that tribe even when we are ourselves, whether listening to music (that other people created), watching a basketball game on television (our own muscles tensing as the players run and jump) or preparing a spreadsheet for a sales meeting (anticipating the boss's reactions.) Most of our energy is devoted to connecting with others. (80)*

*Eberstadt explains why our Western society has moved from healthy associations with people into a hateful tribalism and identity politics. Echoing and updating Allan Bloom in* The Closing of the American Mind, *Eberstadt blames the sexual revolution—widespread abortion, divorce, cohabitation, and redefinition of sexual identity—for the breakdown of the most fundamental of relationships, the family, where people learn to love and trust. As functional families become increasingly less common, people lose their sense of who they are, so they seek it in identity politics.*

> *Many people today are claiming to be victims because they* are *victims—not so much of the "ism" they point to as oppressors, but because the human animal has been selected for familiar forms of socialization* that for many people no longer exist. (209, emphasis in original)

[4] *Though Jesus Himself never sinned, He was a descendant of sinful Adam, and therefore, Jesus was born willingly under the curse of death decreed by God for Adam's disobedience. Because He was without sin, His blood was the acceptable substitute for God's final judgment of our sins that the blood of innocent lambs had heretofore forestalled. Having accepted Jesus's sacrifice, God raised Jesus from the dead with a body that that did not originate from Adam. We need only to confess our sinfulness to God and claim Jesus as our sacrifice of atonement for it. Then we, too, will someday receive resurrected bodies.*

⁵  *Here again, we come against the limit of our understanding of the infinity of "time" in which God lives. God always "knew" Abraham would be faithful because Abraham was faithful—in a moment in time. I put "time" and "knew" in quotation marks because we can think only in terms of time—before, present, and after. God is not bound by time. And yet He entered time and space in the person of Jesus. Such knowledge is too deep for me; it is beyond my understanding {Ps. 139:1-6}.*

*God's foreknowledge (again, a time-referential word) does not require one to believe that God **determined** what Abraham would do in time. Our inability to see reality from God's eternal perspective makes such matters as the doctrine of election impossible to comprehend.*

⁶  *If that had been God's only goal, as John Milton's book title implies, the purpose of the human experience would boil down to this: when Good God wins over Evil, Evil will be judged, mankind will have witnessed that victory, and followers of Christ will cheer it forever. God will have vindicated His good character, and His people will praise Him forever. That will be part of the glorious outcome; however, God has more in mind.*

⁷  *Paul tells us in Romans 1:20, "For since the creation of the world God's invisible qualities—his eternal power and divine nature—have been clearly seen, being understood from what has been made, so that people are without excuse." No doubt Paul had studied Aristotle, the 4ᵗʰ century BC, Greek philosopher who—employing logical syllogism— came as close as any non-Jew to understanding God and his purposes. (See especially his Metaphysics.) One of the most manifest natural signs of God's plan, power, and provision is the sun. It reliably rises daily and gives life to all living things. Its setting is an allegory of the darkness of sin and death—the absence of goodness and light. And since at least the sixth century BC, with the observations of the Greek philosopher Anaxagoras, it was understood that the moon's light was reflective of the sun's light. Thus, the moon is an allegory of our human conscience: our innate understanding of right and wrong, reflecting the light of God's moral character.*

⁸  *In his book, The Final Destiny of the Servant Kings, Joseph Dillow argues persuasively that "not all believers are disciples."*

*When Jesus calls a man to become a disciple, He is not asking him to accept the free gift of eternal life. Instead, He is asking those who have already believed to accept the stringent commands of discipleship. If being a disciple is a condition for becoming a Christian, why does Jesus exhort those who are already Christians to become disciples (Luke 14:26, 33)? (362)*

*Dillow makes other points too lengthy to recount here. But if my reader does not see the distinction, I suggest you read his book.*

# Section 2 Descriptions of God's Reward

There are many descriptions in God's Word of God's rewards, some of which are experienced in this life and most of which we will experience in the life to come. We will explore them in chapters 5–12.

Read this section as you would window-shop on Park Avenue in New York City. Allow yourself to dream of having what you see on display in those exclusive shops. But rather than yearn for the beauty of things of this earth, long for these beautiful treasures of heaven. They can be yours!

To remind you, the content of this book is driven by the content of the if-then promises in the verses printed at the back of the book and quoted in full at Investing-in-Eternity.org. A glance at index 2 will demonstrate the ubiquity of these promises in Scripture. Those descriptions notwithstanding, keep in mind that often the rewards in this section, *Descriptions of God's Rewards*, and the means of acquiring them in the next section, *How God's Rewards are Gained*, are one and the same. Therefore, there is a blend of content between this and the next section of the book.

There is a similar overlap in content in the individual chapters within each of the two sections: the *rewards'* descriptions overlap with each other, and the *means* of their acquisition overlap with each other. This book does not so much describe God's rewards (plural) as it describes God's Reward (singular). And the means (plural) by which they are earned are all manifestations of a singular means: faithfulness to God.

So, just as facets of the Hope Diamond are repeated around its circumference, each new facet in the coming chapters will have previous facets in view as well. In the end, we will have observed the whole.

# Chapter 5  Overview of God's Rewards

My brother Steve was born with Down's syndrome. Like many people with that condition, Steve was joyful and gregarious—except during one dark period in his life . . .

As his four younger siblings progressed through school, college, and—one by one—got married, Steve noticed that he wasn't advancing in life. He was mentally disabled; he wasn't stupid. I became painfully aware one memorable day of Steve's increasing consciousness of his condition. He had said something to which I replied, "Oh, Steve. You dummy." Of course, I meant no insult. I spoke in the same joking way I might have to any of my siblings. But Steve heard it otherwise. I looked to see his head in his hands. He was *sobbing*.

Steve understood that he was . . . *different*. He knew that being "special" was not very special. He was smart enough to know he wasn't intellectually smart. And as that realization grew, so did a root of bitterness. The enemy seized upon his vulnerability. Though he was in his thirties, Steve began to behave like a rebellious teen. For months he became sulky and defiant against his parents, with whom he lived. He stopped doing routine chores. Worse, he spoke disparagingly of Jesus. He refused to go to church. He even burned his Bible. Mom and Dad were gravely concerned and earnestly prayed for God's intervention.

Then, miraculously, one morning Steve awoke wholly transformed. His countenance was full of joy. Over and over, he exclaimed, "I saw Jesus!" "I saw Jesus!" "I saw Jesus!"

The Lord had revealed Himself to my brother in a dream that night. The bitterness and anger had been replaced with peace and hope. He began regularly reminding people of the imminent return of Jesus. "It could be today!" he would say, with confidence and excitement. Stevo could not wait to see Jesus again! (My dear brother finally met Jesus face to face some thirty years later.)

That longing to see Jesus is at the heart of *Investing in Eternity.*

**"Where Will Your Dreams Take You?"**

That was the question atop a brochure I picked up at the bank one day. Below were pictures of exotic and alluring destinations. One was of elephants on an African plain, suggesting the excitement of a safari; another offered the beauty of snorkeling in crystalline waters; a third beckoned to the serenity of a floating-above-it-all, hot-air-balloon flight. "Now you can redeem Gold Standard Reward Bonus Points for those dream-come-true life experiences!" the brochure promised.

"Where will your dreams take you?" It's a great question. Indeed, your hopes and dreams *will* take you somewhere—though not perhaps where you expect. Your hopes and dreams will determine how you conduct your life. As Jesus said,

> *Where your treasure is, there your heart will be also.*
> (Luke 12:34)

Scott Hafemann elaborates on this passage:

> Whatever we hope for inevitably determines how we live. The object of our hope determines the contours of our conduct. This is a universal principle of human nature. Even at the trivial level, hope is what motivates us. . . . Our treasure becomes our hope. In turn, our hope determines how we act, since we always spend our lives on whatever we think will make us happy. As a result, life is one long "treasure hunt" in search of the things we hope will meet our needs. . . . Notice that Jesus does not say that we should give up wanting treasure. The issue is what that treasure is–God or the world." (168–70)

As discussed earlier, we do nothing in this life in which we are genuinely disinterested. We all are driven by desires we seek to fulfill. Even a Buddhist's self-denial has a self-promoting end: to be happy (by avoiding desire). The question isn't *whether* we all seek our happiness. *We all do.* The question is how you and I will go about finding our own happiness and self-interest. Will it be our way, or God's way?

What are *your* dreams? Are they of earthly comforts and pleasures? Then I urge you to heed Jesus:

> *Sell your possessions and give to the poor. Provide purses for yourselves that will not wear out, a treasure in heaven that will not be exhausted, where no thief comes near and no moth destroys.* (Luke 12:33)

What is the *"treasure in heaven"* that we will provide for ourselves by giving everything to God and others? No book could fully answer that question, both because the treasure is richer than could ever be described and because each individual will experience it differently. But we can at least begin to grasp what God has in store for us.

**God's Reward Is God Himself**

In Genesis 15, God tells Abram. *"Do not be afraid, Abram. I am your shield, your very great reward"* (v. 1). We better understand what Abram could not have fully understood: that the blessing God promised Abram in return for his faith and obedience was God Himself, incarnate in Christ Jesus. Jesus prayed in John 17:3,

> *Now this is eternal life: that they may know you, the only true God, and Jesus Christ, whom you have sent.*

Eternal life is to . . .

> *. . . know Christ and the power of his resurrection and the fellowship of sharing in his sufferings.* (Phil. 3:10)

Our reward is—and forever will be—God Himself: Father, Son, and Holy Spirit. To be with God, in relationship unspoiled by sin and its consequences, to be in His loving embrace, to know His love to our core (1 Pet. 1:8), and to rest forever in His sweet presence (Ps. 16:11)—these blessings are immeasurable, and they will be enjoyed by all of God's people, but only to the extent of our love and obedience in this life.

Jesus, our betrothed, also joyfully awaits *His* reward—His bride—as she walks down the aisle toward Him!

> *Listen, daughter, and pay careful attention:*
> *Forget your people and your father's house.*
> *Let the king be enthralled by your beauty;*
> *honor him, for he is your lord.*
> *All glorious is the princess within her chamber;*
> *her gown is interwoven with gold.*
> *In embroidered garments she is led to the king;*
> *her virgin companions follow her.*
> *those brought to be with her.*
> *Led in with joy and gladness,*
> *they enter the palace of the king.*
> {Ps. 45:10-15}

And like the steadily processing bride who can't wait to reach her beloved at the altar, the closer we get to our Beloved, the more we can't wait to be with Him. I've seen such yearning in my dear mother as she ages into her nineties. Her longing grows as she gets closer to Him, both in spirit and in time. She has *"longed for His appearing"* most of her life (2 Tim. 4:8). "I just can't wait to see Jesus," she sighs.

So great has been her devotion to Him that my mom also has more to look forward to than most of us do. That is because, upon such ardent lovers, God will shower His wedding gifts.

> *I clothed you with an embroidered dress and put leather*
> *sandals on you. I dressed you in fine linen and covered*
> *you with costly garments. I adorned you with jewelry: I*
> *put bracelets on your arms and a necklace around your*
> *neck, and I put a ring on your nose, earrings on your ears*
> *and a beautiful crown on your head.* (Ezek. 16:10-12)

The beauty and costliness of a groom's gifts are expressions of his love for his pure and faithful bride. The bride cherishes the gifts—not the objects themselves, but as expressions of love from her loving and beloved husband. Likewise, our experience of receiving God's rewards will be rapturous because they are God's everlasting expression of love toward us.

Of course, God loves every one of us, the entire Church, which is His bride. We, on the other hand, return that love to varying degrees. Like a bride looking forward to her wedding day, the *faithful* bride will have prepared herself for her grand wedding of the Lamb. But there is one thing for which she won't have to shop because the *"fine linen, bright and clear"* that the faithful bride wears will have been given to her by God because of her *"righteous acts."* By her faithfulness to her betrothed, she will have *"made herself ready"* (Rev. 19:7-8).

The Bible has a myriad of descriptions of the *"fine linen"* that awaits the faithful. In index 2, I have listed, by keyword and phrase, the Bible's descriptions of those rewards. It is a long list! There are *hundreds* of characterizations in the Bible of the ways God will express His love in His rewards. Keep in mind as you read the chapters in this section that every description of what awaits the faithful bride has, at its heart, God Himself. Everything God gives us draws us closer to Him.

## God's Reward Is People We Love

Chapter 9 discusses this reward at length, but you will also find it throughout the book. That is because the reward of *people* is intrinsic to other rewards from God. It is at the core of what God wants for us: to forever experience the fullness of relationship—not only with Himself but also with others.

## God's Reward Is Earned

Question 63 of the Heidelberg Catechism asks the question, "How can our good works be said to merit nothing when God promises to reward them in this life and the next?" The answer the catechism gives is: "This reward is not earned; it is a gift of grace." Respectfully, that response is only half right. Rewards are both a gift of grace and they are earned.[1]

Most of us have earned a paycheck. When you received your check, you may have been grateful that you had a job. You may have been thankful that you had that particular job. You may even have thought to yourself, "I can't believe I actually get paid to do this!" However, did you tell your boss to keep the money? "I don't deserve this. Please take it back." I didn't think so. Why? Because you earned it! You worked hard for that wage. You gave of your time and your energy. You literally gave of yourself in exchange for that paycheck. That was part of the deal, wasn't it?

Now consider the words God uses to describe what He intends to give the faithful. The Greek words often translated "reward" could as well be translated "wage," "repayment," "compensation," "a restoring of what was given," "what is due," "a price paid for services," "a payment on a contract," "a salary," or "a fare." The words connote the return of something due or a consequence of actions performed. In many instances, those words are used instead of the word "reward" in Bible translations.

The Hebrew words used in the Old Testament that are often translated "reward" have the same meaning as the Greek words: "repayment," "recompensation," "requital," "a fee for hire and wage." The English word "reward" often used to translate the Greek and Hebrew is appropriate: it is from the Middle English and means "to look back at," "regard," or "compensate."

One hundred and seven times the Bible uses words in the original Greek and Hebrew that are translated with the word "reward" or a similar term.[2] That number does not include the six hundred-seven descriptions of rewards that use different words. The sheer quantity of the Bible's teaching is staggering, especially considering how seldom we hear this doctrine taught. Over and over again, God uses the language of reward to describe His intent. Anyone who wishes in good conscience to dispense with this teaching is going to have to deal with that pesky word "reward" and its siblings!

*If these words do not carry their obvious meaning, then I beg you to tell me: What do they mean?*

In addition to the biblical language of "rewards," further evidence that rewards are earned is found in the language of "crowns." The Greek word for crown is *"stephanos."* Paul encourages us to run to win the prize, the victor's crown: the *"stephanos"* (1 Cor. 9:25; 2 Tim. 2:5). The *stephanos* of righteousness will be awarded (paid, yielded) to those *"who have longed for his appearing"* (2 Tim. 4:8). James says that the man who perseveres under trial will *"receive the stephanos* of life that God has promised to those who love him" (James 1:12). Peter assures faithful shepherds of God's flock that they will receive (be compensated with) a *"stephanos* of glory . . ."* (1 Pet. 5:4). Jesus promises a *stephanos* of life to those who are faithful *"even to the point of death"* (Rev. 2:10). Each of these crowns is awarded to people for their love and faithfulness. The award of each is *conditional*: only those who have *earned* these crowns will wear them (and have them to cast at the feet of Jesus).

Why does the thought of *earning* a reward (wage, award, compensation, repayment) make some of us feel uncomfortable? I propose that the underlying reasons are honorable: We want to lift up Jesus. We want to acknowledge His power and grace in our lives, as well as His greatness and our unworthiness. We want to remember that it is only by His work in our lives that we can do anything of value. Those are good and proper desires. But without minimizing those appropriate sentiments, the Bible straightforwardly tells us that, despite our feelings of unworthiness, God— also because of His boundless grace—intends to repay us for our service to Him.

> *I the LORD search the heart and examine the mind, to reward a man according to his conduct, according to what his deeds deserve.* (Jer. 17:10)

> *Whatever you do,* Paul tells us, *work at it with all your heart, as working for the Lord, not for men, since you know that you will receive an inheritance from the Lord as a reward.* (Col. 3:23)

## God's Reward Is Conditional

To repeat, the passages I reference in *Investing in Eternity* all contain "if" and/or "then" words and phrases that support the premise that *rewards are conditional,* based upon our faithfulness.

### The "if" condition:

There are no less than 416 total instances of an "if" (indicators of a condition for reward) in the verses selected for *Investing in Eternity.* Blessings accrue only to those who meet the condition. (These are listed in index 1.) Every "if" condition is followed by the act(s) of faithfulness that is required to meet the condition. (These are listed in index 3.)

## The "then" consequence:

There are no less than 169 total instances of a "then" (indicators of a consequence of reward) in the verses selected for *Investing in Eternity*. Every satisfied "then" condition is followed by a reward. (These are listed in index 2.)[3]

Some verses have *both* an "if" and "then." Many have *either* an "if," with the "then" implied, *or* a "then," with the "if" implied. (Often, both the "if" *and* "then" are implied in the Bible. *Investing in Eternity* only references such verses when they are in proximity to expressly conditional promises.)

By these various methods of speaking, implicitly or explicitly, the message of the passages or verses is: "If you do (this or that) good deed or act of obedience, then you will receive (this or that) reward."[4]

## Proportional to our performance

> The glory of the saints above will be in some proportion to their eminency in holiness and good works here. Christ will reward all according to their works. (*The Works of Jonathan Edwards*, 342)

The rewards God gives are not only dependent on whether we trust, serve and obey God; they are also *proportional* to our trust, service, and obedience. Look at the many verses that tell us our reward will be *"according to what is done"* (including Ps. 62:12; Prov. 24:12; Matt. 16:27; Rom. 2:6; Rev. 22:12).[5] We will be judged *"according to our deeds"* (Rev. 2:23). God will judge each of you *"according to his own ways"* {Ezek. 33:20; 7:27; 18:30, 24:14}. Our reward, Paul tells us, will be based on each person's labor (1 Cor. 3:8). His most faithful will receive in abundance (Matt. 25:29). To those who love their enemies and do good to them, the *"reward will be great"* (Luke 6:35). Anyone who leaves family, security, or comfort will receive *"a hundred times as much"* in return (Matt. 19:29; Mark 10:30; see also Mark 4:8, 20; Luke 8:8).

Of course, Jesus was speaking figuratively when He said *"a hundred times"*: His reward is immeasurable because it is eternal. David tells us several times in Psalm 112 that the benefits of a faithful and righteous life will continue forever. Jesus tells us that the treasures we lay up in heaven *"will not wear out"* nor *"be exhausted."* Paul tells us in 2 Corinthians 4:18 that what we endure in this life will earn for us an *"eternal weight of glory."* So it is actually more accurate to say that our rewards are *exponential* to our service! God won't just pay us back. He will return to us infinitely more than we gave to Him!

### For even the smallest acts of obedience

Jesus told us that He will reward us for something as seemingly insignificant as the offer of a cup of water. Water costs little or nothing. Giving it requires only our small effort and time to acquire it and bring it to the thirsty person. Yet Jesus says that when we offer it in His name, we earn a *great* reward (Matt. 10:42; Mark 9:41; quoting Prov. 25:21). Jesus was teaching us in this mundane, everyday example that he notices even the smallest acts of faithfulness. He assures us that, for even such a simple gesture, one *"will not lose his reward."*

In a seeming paradox, it is sometimes the very smallness of our contribution that makes it so valuable, because God glorifies Himself all the more when He uses an apparently insignificant act of obedience and does a great work through it. God takes our loaves and fishes, as it were, and multiplies them by the thousands.

Consider Gideon in chapters 6–8 of the book of Judges. God commanded—or did He taunt?—Gideon to *"go in the strength you have and save Israel out of Midian's hands."* *"But Lord,"* Gideon asked, *"how can I save Israel? My clan is the weakest in Manasseh, and I am the least in my family."* Gideon didn't mention that he was currently hiding in fear from the Midianites. God had indeed chosen an improbable leader.

The Lord answered, *"I will be with you, and you will strike down all the Midianites together."* So Gideon mustered an army that God promptly pared to three hundred men. Why did He reduce the size of Gideon's army? *"In order that Israel may not boast against me that her own strength has saved her . . ."* Gideon and his men, by an unlikely scheme devised by God, routed the Midianites.

Though—or even because—Gideon had little to offer, God chose to use him. God intended to do (as the expression goes) "the heavy lifting," but He didn't tell Gideon to step aside and watch Him work. He gave Gideon a small but *significant* role. God brought glory to Himself in the very smallness of Gideon's actions. As a result of God's plan and Gideon's obedience, Israel enjoyed peace for the remaining years of Gideon's life.

In the same way, God's grace is magnified in our feeblest efforts. Rather than denigrate our contribution with false and misguided humility, we do well to recognize that God offers us a meaningful role in His work. However seemingly trivial, our part is so significant to God that He will repay us for our effort. (More on this in Chapter 13: Overview of How to Gain God's Rewards.)

**God's Reward Is Experienced**

While our emotions were profoundly corrupted by the Fall, our ability to experience emotions is of God. We were created in God's image, so we should expect that feelings will be part of our eternal existence because *God is emotional.*

Now you may be getting emotional about what I just wrote! "What do you mean, God is emotional!? How can you ascribe emotions to God?" Because God ascribes emotions to Himself: love, hatred (of sin and evil), anger, grief, compassion, indignation, abhorrence, patience, long-suffering, joy, and every other good affection and emotion are attributed to God in the Bible.

Our understanding of how these emotions are experienced by God is—to say the least—limited, but, as Charles Finney wrote,

> [God] must feel, or he is not virtuous. Virtue cannot consist
> in the mere abstractions of the intellect, but belongs to the
> heart. And an intellect without moral feeling cannot be
> virtuous. (*The Affections and Emotions of God*, 169)

Our discomfort with emotion is born of our everyday experience of emotions perverted by sin. Our experience is often of volatile and destructive impulses. We have so little control over our feelings. We are well aware of how fleeting and shallow they can be. They are unreliable, and they can be dangerous! Our emotions are often provoked by our circumstances. We often wrestle with anger, bitterness, and fear.

And even granting that God bestows pleasant emotions, it is often difficult to distinguish between a godly emotion and a pleasant emotion produced by our own pride or an agreeable situation. It is understandable if we play it safe by keeping emotions in check or by having as little to do with them as possible.

But it does not follow that godly and enjoyable feelings are not to be sought. Rather than deny or ignore our emotional needs and desires, we do better to find their satisfaction from God. We put to death that which belongs to our sinful nature (Col. 3:5), including our unruly emotions, and seek to experience God-given emotions to their fullest.

And we have this hope—a pleasant emotion!—that whatever our imperfect experience in this life, our experience of God in heaven will be forever free of the corruption of sin. Our emotions will be redeemed. We will be finally and forever free to fully *enjoy* God. Those godly emotions will be a part of our reward, to be experienced in proportion to our faithfulness to God in this life. It is therefore good and right to seek godly emotional satisfaction now and to be encouraged—another godly emotion—by the promise that, if we are faithful, we will experience the fullness of emotional satisfaction in the life to come.

And lest you fear that seeking our own emotional enjoyment is sinful—that it sets the satisfaction of our own desires above the interest of glorifying God—consider this question: When are you most happy with someone you love? Is it not when he or she is likewise most happy with you? Are you not most delighted with that person when he or she is most greatly delighted with you? Isn't the father most satisfied when his little girl climbs onto his lap and says, "I love you, Daddy?" So it is with our loving heavenly Father. God is most glorified when we search for—and find in Him—the satisfaction of our deepest emotional needs.

Ponder for a moment what we have seen thus far. The stakes are infinitely high. Our faithfulness to God, from the smallest to the greatest, will be rewarded—forever. There is literally no limit to the blessings God will bestow upon those—and only upon those—who love and serve Him. And you have this life and this life alone in which to earn that which God has promised.

That is stunning! We serve a kind and gracious God! We do not deserve such outrageous and lavish generosity. But God said it, so I will claim His promises.

I would be a fool not to want God's rewards.

## Notes and Asides:

[1]  *As we discussed in chapter 4, the two are not mutually exclusive. Read three of the passages the catechism offers—Matthew 5:12, Hebrews 11:6, 2 Timothy 4:7-8—all of which I cite in this book in support of the doctrine of rewards. Then read my discussion of the fourth passage— from Luke 17—in appendix 2 under "We are not worthy of anything from God!"*

[2]  *You will find references to these verses listed in index 1, with the Greek and Hebrew words and their definitions. The index is mostly if-then statements of positive rewards. There are other such conditional promises of negative rewards (punishments) listed (always in juxtaposition to positive rewards) and many more in the rest of the Bible not listed.*

[3]  *My accounting may not be 100 percent accurate. But, as Paul said, "No matter how many promises God has made, they are 'Yes' in Christ" (2 Cor. 1:20).*

[4]  *The doctrine of rewards is not only found in the Old Testament; it is reiterated throughout the New Testament. The density of conditional promises in the New Testament is approximately 8 percent greater than that in the Old Testament.*

[5]  *Would it be just of God to give to two people the same reward if one of them lived his or her life in exceptional service to God and the other did not?*

# Chapter 6 The Reward of
# Experiencing God's Pleasure

One Thanksgiving, my daughter and I made pumpkin pie. It was beautiful when it came out of the oven. It had that characteristic orange-brown hue. The crust was golden. It had the aroma of freshly baked pumpkin pie. But, when we bit into it, we realized that this was *not* my mom's pumpkin pie. It tasted bitter! Uuuugh! We had forgotten to add the sugar!

We leave the "sugar" out of our biblical teaching when we ignore the doctrine of rewards. Even if the other ingredients of our teaching are correctly measured, our "recipe" for godly living is incomplete and, consequently, not sweet as God intends. Indeed, for those who need encouragement, what we *don't say* sometimes communicates as much as what we *do say*. The missing reference to God's reward makes the message *bitter*. God's Word, and our experience of relationship with God, doesn't "taste" as it did to the psalmist: *"How sweet are your words to my taste, sweeter than honey to my mouth!"* (Ps. 19:10; 119:103).

Just as sugar sits in our cupboards, the Bible's cabinets are full of sweeteners:

*Gladness, rejoicing, pleasures, security, steadfastness,
pleasantness, peace, enjoyment, happiness, satisfaction, delight,
joy, hope,[1] comfort, renewal, thanksgiving, glory, fellowship*

Each of these is a pleasant emotion; each of them is *"sweet to the soul"* (Prov. 16:24; 24:14). These emotions will be part of our everlasting experience of God. Godly emotions are not separate from, or tangential to, our experience of God. They are not "whipped cream" to optionally spoon onto the otherwise bitter pie. They are to be blended into our *experience of God*. (Find a complete list of biblical references to these rewards in index 2.)

Having been created in the image of God, we were created to experience those sweet emotions. David tells us in Psalm 16 where we will find real satisfaction for our souls.

> *I have set the LORD always before me.*
> *Because he is at my right hand, I will not be shaken.*
> *Therefore my heart is glad and my tongue rejoices;*
> *my body also will rest secure . . .*
> *You have made known to me the path of life;*
> *you will fill me with joy in your presence,*
> *with eternal pleasures at your right hand.*

David chose to keep the Lord "*before* [him]," "*at his right hand*," so he could stay "*in* [the Lord's] *presence*." As a result ("*therefore*"), his heart was glad, and his voice expressed rejoicing. Indeed, his entire body felt secure and at peace. God overwhelmed David with joy when he was in God's presence.

To be in and to enjoy the intimacy of God's presence is, and forever will be, our great reward. When we delight ourselves in the Lord, He gives us the desires of our hearts (Ps. 37:4). The word "*heart*" appears 118 times in our collection of verses on reward 725 times in the NIV. This is no mere transaction; this is the blissful experience of a loving relationship.

**The Pursuit of Godly Pleasures**

If you are of at least a certain age, you may remember waiting at a rail crossing as a child and looking forward to seeing the caboose with its friendly, waving conductor. Well, I'm sorry to tell you if you haven't already noticed that there is no longer such an expectation to enjoy. Railroads have dropped cabooses as an unnecessary expense. Now the only satisfaction one has for having waited at a crossing is that, when the wait is over, you can finally be on your way.

We have been correctly taught that feelings are the "caboose" behind the "engine" of biblical fact and "coal car" of faith. But, like the railroads, many live as if the "caboose" of feelings is unnecessary to the Christian walk. We imply in our teaching that, as long as our mind's understanding is in order, we have all we need.

Of course, we are not expressly told to unhitch our feelings. But we are seldom reminded that it is good to seek the fulfillment of our emotional desires in God. We are told how we should feel: gratitude, joy, happiness, and so on. We are exhorted, for example, to be a cheerful giver, without being told why and how to be so.

Or worse, we are told our desires are wicked. Many of us, therefore, trudge along, content—or not—to do our duty, Spock-like, without the hope of ultimately enjoying rewards. Or we seek satisfaction in the wrong places. C. S. Lewis noticed our tendency to downplay our deepest emotional longings. In his insightful essay *The Weight of Glory*, he wrote:

> The New Testament has lots to say about self-denial, but not about self-denial as an end in itself. We are told to deny ourselves and to take up our crosses in order that we may follow Christ; and *nearly every description of what we shall ultimately find if we do so contains an appeal to desire.* (25, emphasis added)

The "desire" of which Lewis speaks is for—among other things—those longings deep within our souls for wholeness, peace, love, and the other pleasant emotions promised in Scripture and listed earlier in the chapter. Lewis suggests why Christians in the Western world suppress their yearnings.

> If there lurks in most modern minds the notion that to desire our own good and earnestly to hope for the enjoyment of it is a bad thing, I submit that this notion has crept in from Kant and the Stoics and is no part of the Christian faith. Indeed, if we consider the unblushing promises of reward and the staggering nature of the rewards promised in the Gospels, it would seem that Our Lord finds our desires not too strong, but too weak. (26)

Perhaps Lewis had read Matthew Henry:

> You have got a notion it may be, and are confirmed in it by the common cry of the multitude, that religion is a sour melancholy thing, that it is to bid farewell to all pleasure

and delight and to spend your days in grief and your years in sighing . . . (233).

Again, Christians are rightly wary of seeking the fulfillment of their desires, for they are well acquainted with the temptation to fill them apart from God's provision. So they settle for Christian Stoicism. They deny their longings and do their duty without passion, all the while believing that they are especially virtuous in doing so!

Think of people you consider to be committed followers of Jesus. Are they joyful? At peace? Happy? Patient? Why is that? Because such feelings are the fruit of the Spirit—and that fruit is sweet and satisfying. Is it not God's great desire that we experience such emotions?

And if our experience of pleasant emotions is independent of our response to God, then why does God not give us that fruit—always? Is it not clear that we are the impediment to our enjoyment of the fruit of the Spirit, not God? As James said, *"You do not have because you do not ask God"* (James 4:2).

We are often told that it is our *duty* to please God. Once in a while, it is suggested that it is a pleasure to please God. Seldom are we assured that it is proper to desire and to strive for the pleasure of pleasing God. We are exhorted like children to "Eat your peas!" How much better to invite with this: "The peas are sweet! Try them!" If we were more often reminded that God wants us to do everything in our power, and by His power, to experience His pleasure, to know that He is pleased with us and to find satisfaction in that pleasure, we might strive harder to attain it.

Instead, we are mostly told that "He is God, and He deserves it!" And He does deserve it. With or without a benefit to us, we should serve God in this life. He created us to do good works (Eph. 2:10). If God had not promised to give us anything in return for our service, it would be our duty and privilege to serve Him anyway.

But God *does* promise to reward us. As Randy Alcorn points out, "Rewards are His idea, not ours" (*Treasure Principle*, 41). God delights to reward![2] Therefore, our good works are not an end in themselves; they are service to God that we render (by the power of His Spirit) *in exchange* for what He wants for us and promises to give us when we are faithful. Our good works are our love-offerings to Him. His rewards are His love-gift back to us.

Our reward is not diminished for having had the expectation of experiencing His pleasure. On the contrary, the hope of His reward spurs us on to please Him all the more. God wants us to please Him so that we will know the pleasure of pleasing Him.

> Now it is here demonstrated by Eternal Truth itself, that *it is our interest to be religious*; and therefore religion deserves to be called wisdom, *because it teaches us to do well for ourselves.* And it is certain, that the way to be happy, that is, perfectly holy, hereafter, is to be holy, that is, truly happy, now. (*The Miscellaneous Works*, 2, emphasis in original)

"True piety has true pleasure in it," Matthew Henry concludes. How could it be selfish to want to experience—as the title of the essay puts it—the "Pleasantness of a Religious Life"? Is the gift of fresh-picked wildflowers diminished because the little girl who offers them hopes to get a loving hug from her mom in return? Of course not! On the contrary, the little girl demonstrates her love as she reaches for the thank you from her mother. And her loving mother is delighted to give her that hug.

Consider the boy who obediently does his chores. Is the value of his service discounted because doing the work is a condition for receiving an allowance? Not at all. His father could have merely ordered the boy to mow the lawn. Instead, he promises the boy something in return. As he works to earn the allowance, the boy expresses trust that his father will uphold his end of the bargain. His expectation of payment affirms his belief in his dad's good character. It does not even cross his mind that he might not be paid. For his part, the good father delights in the boy's trust and in the work the boy does. And he delights to pronounce the job, "Well done!" and to pay his son the promised allowance.

At the heart of the reward in those two examples is a loving relationship between parent and child. While the give-and-take involves a transaction, it is no mere transaction. In the parent-child relationship we have with God, we need not fear it becoming merely a transaction because God Himself is the reward. God gives more of Himself as we give more of ourselves to Him.

**The Chief End of Man**

John Piper laid the groundwork for my understanding of the Bible's teaching on rewards. He considered the first question of the Westminster Shorter Catechism, "What is the chief end of man?" The catechism asks for a single response ("What is the . . .") and then pronounces two: "To glorify God and enjoy him forever." He playfully voiced his complaint with the catechism's answer:

> "And"? Like ham and eggs? Sometimes you glorify God and sometimes you enjoy him? Sometimes he gets glory, sometimes you get joy? "And" is a very ambiguous word! Just how do these two things relate to each other? (17)

"Exactly!" I thought as I read Piper's question. To such a profound question, one expects an unambiguous, "unified theory" of mankind's purpose. So, Piper offered a simple remedy to the problem: a one-word (plus one verb-form change) change to the answer.

> The chief end of man is to glorify God *by* enjoying Him forever. (18)

> Darby Livingston puts it this way,

> "God is most glorified in us when we are most satisfied in Him." (26)

Here is the connection of this insight to the matter of rewards: It is in the caldera of this brief and often difficult life, when we are tempted to turn to the things of this world for our comfort and sustenance, we can learn to seek the enjoyment of pleasing God instead. God is glorified as we make it our highest aspiration to enjoy His pleasure. As we "*make it our goal to please Him,*" we find our reward in our joyful experience of having pleased God (2 Cor. 5:9).

Our delight in pleasing God will become a harvest of delight, kept in the storehouse of heaven for our eternal feasting. The extent to which we will "glorify God by enjoying Him forever" in heaven will be in proportion to our desire to "glorify God by enjoying Him" in this life. If we go to heaven a pauper in our enjoyment of God, then we will be poorer for all of eternity. If, on the other hand, we are rich in this life in desiring above all else to enjoy "*the surpassing greatness of knowing Christ*" (Phil. 3:8), then we will be filled forever with "*joy in* [God's] *presence and eternal pleasures at* [His] *right hand*" (Ps. 16:11).

It is here that we can most clearly see how personal and utterly non-transactional the nature of God's reward is. Our reward for eternity will be the fulfillment of those deepest, God-given desires for which we longed in this life, when life was hard, and the way was uncertain, and when we had only our faith in God's goodness and intent to reward to propel us forward.

Yes, heaven will be satisfying for all who gain it, but some will find heaven more satisfying than others. In His usual pithy and poetic way, Jesus taught:

> With the measure you use, it will be measured to you—and
> even more. (Mark 4:24; Luke 6:38)

R. C. Sproul paraphrases Jesus in this way,

> Everybody's cup in heaven is full; but not everybody
> in heaven has the same size cup. (*Now That's a Good
> Question*, 287)[3]

J. I. Packer concurred,

> There will be different degrees of blessedness and reward
> in heaven. All will be blessed up to the limit of what they
> can receive, but capacities will vary just as they do in this
> world. (264)

Our eternal emotional capacities are determined by how we conduct ourselves in this life.

So, let us pray the words of the hymn:

> Fill my cup Lord, I lift it up, Lord!
> Come and quench this thirsting of my soul;
> Bread of heaven, feed me till I want no more.

Fill my cup, fill it up and make me whole!
(Blanchard)

## The Example of Marriage

I sometimes buy flowers for my wife. When I give them to her, I hope that she will throw her arms around me and give me a big kiss! To be honest, I sometimes even hope my gift will lead to a romantic evening. I want her to know that I love her, and *I want to know that she loves me back*. I want to feel her love in response to mine. Do you think me *selfish* in that desire?

When I say to my wife, "I love you," I don't expect her to respond, "Well, you ought to love me! I'm your wife, after all, and a pretty good one at that. In fact, I'm a better wife than you deserve! You are only doing your duty in loving me because you made a commitment to me at our wedding and because the Bible says you should love your wife."

My wife is undoubtedly better than I deserve, and the Bible does indeed tell me to love my wife. And I did vow to commit myself to her. No matter her response to me, I love her and try to treat her with respect. But you know what? It sure is nice when she expresses love to me in return.

Isn't that as it should be? Wasn't marriage designed by God to be a reciprocal relationship? Isn't reciprocity essential to the nature of a healthy marriage—from the smallest interaction to its consummate expression? Marriage is only fully satisfying when it is so. It is a failed marriage in which love only ever flows in one direction, where one always gives, and the other only receives.

### *Our marriage to Christ*

Likewise, when we bring gifts of service to God, He doesn't respond, "That is the least you can do for me since I gave my Son for you. You owe me big time!" God is entirely within His rights to speak thus to us. He did make an unfathomable sacrifice on our behalf. We should be willing to give everything out of gratitude for His great gift of salvation. But what sort of relationship would it be with God if we never sensed His ongoing pleasure with us and if we never experienced His love in return for our expressions of love to Him? It would be, as with a one-sided marriage, something considerably less than fully satisfying.

Fortunately, God's Word is filled with promises of gifts of love and delight and comfort and hope and peace for those who demonstrate their love for Him in their offerings of worship and sacrifices of service. We are His bride! He shows us His love as plainly as a good husband shows his devotion to his wife: *"As the bridegroom rejoices over the bride, so shall your God rejoice over you"* (Isa. 62:5).

Bernard of Clairvaux, the twelfth-century French monk, describes the rapture that awaits the faithful bride of Christ.

> Dearest indeed, who are intoxicated with love. Intoxicated indeed, who deserve to be present at the wedding feast of the Lord, eating and drinking at his table in his kingdom, when he takes his Church to him in glory, without blemish or wrinkle or any defect. Then will he intoxicate his dearest ones with the *torrent of his delight*, for in the most passionate and most chaste embrace of Bridegroom and Bride, the rush of the river makes glad the city of God. I think this is no other than what the Son of God, who waits on us as he goes, promised . . . Here is fullness without disgust, insatiable curiosity that is not restless, an eternal and endless desire that knows no lack, and last, that sober intoxication that does not come from drinking too much, that is no reeking of wine but a burning of God. (199, emphasis added)

If the passion in that passage is uncomfortably romantic for you, steer clear of that great allegory of God's love for His bride, the Song of Solomon, on which St. Bernard's sermon was based! The King James Version speaks of a husband "knowing his wife" to describe sexual relations. The "knowing" is the word *"yada"* in Hebrew we discussed earlier. It is in "knowing" one's partner in the fullest, experiential sense that marriage is complete, not only physically but also emotionally. Love in marriage illustrates what I think is the most easily understood form of God's reward: *Our faithfulness to God yields the emotional satisfactions of a loving relationship.* Our reward is to know the pleasure of the embrace of our loving God.

## A Share of the Master's Happiness

In one of Jesus's parables, the master invites his faithful servants to *"share in your master's happiness"* (Matt. 25:21, 23). This was an invitation to a special closeness of relationship with the master. The master had elevated them from a position of humble servant to that of beloved family. Now, because of their faithfulness, everything that brought their master joy and happiness would be *shared* with them. That is astonishing!

> *Rejoice and be glad, because great is your reward in heaven.* (Matt. 5:11)

> *Rejoice in that day and leap for joy, because great is your reward in heaven.* (Luke 6:23)

> So, *"Let us rejoice and be glad!"* (Rev. 19:7)[4]

## Duty as Simultaneous Reward

David tells us that the Lord will repay each man *"for his righteousness,"* while the author of Hebrews tells us that someday we will reap a harvest *"of righteousness"* (1 Sam. 26:23; 2 Sam. 22:21-25; Heb. 12:11). Peter, quoting Leviticus, commands us to *"Be holy, because I am holy"* (Lev. 11:44; 1 Pet. 1:16), even as the faithful are promised that their reward will be to *"share in His holiness"* (Heb. 12:10). Righteousness and righteous living, therefore, is both its own reward and a reward to come.

We may not even have to wait for the reward, for it comes simultaneously with the work. Take, for example, the fruit of the Spirit: love, joy, peace, patience, kindness, goodness, faithfulness, gentleness, and self-control (Gal. 5:22-23). These qualities are both that which we strive to exhibit in this life and that which we enjoy as our reward. In his delightfully titled essay *The Pleasantness of a Religious Life Displayed, Proved and Recommended to the Consideration of Every One, Particularly of the Young*, Matthew Henry discusses a dozen such "pleasures of religion." He then asks . . .

> . . . *whether religion be not a pleasant thing, indeed, when even the duties of it themselves are so much the delights of*

*it: and whether we do not serve a good master, who has thus*
*made our work its own wages, and has graciously provided*
*two heavens for those that never deserved one.* (240)

Another Brit, Olympic runner Eric Liddell, expressed that sentiment succinctly: "When I run, I feel God's pleasure" (*Chariots of Fire*).

## A Godly Worldview

If we fail to see this simple truth, it may be because we are accustomed to viewing the world in crass, commercial terms. G. K. Chesterton spoke of our suspicions in his autobiography,

> The [modern cynic] always imagines that there is an element of corruption, in his own cynical manner, about the idea of reward, about the position of the child who can say, as in Stevenson's verses, "Every day when I've been good, I get an orange after food." To the man made ignorant by experience this always appears as a vulgar bribe to the child. . . . But it does not seem like that to the child. . . . For the child is not a Manichee. He does not think that good things are in their nature separate from being good . . . He has the ordinary selfish obstacles and misunderstandings; but he does not, in his heart, regard it as odd that his parents would be good to him, to the extent of an orange . . . He has no sense of being corrupted. It is only we, who have eaten the forbidden apple (or orange) who think of pleasure as a bribe. (52–53)

That point was beautifully illustrated for me. A friend of mine relocated his office, rendering obsolete thousands of brochures on which his old business address was printed. He showed me several rolls of stickers printed with the new address and asked if my young daughter, Emma, would be interested in affixing them to the brochures on the top of the old address.

When I proposed the project to Emma and told her she would be paid, she immediately asked, "How much?!" I said I did not know, but I was sure it would be fair and, knowing the man, probably generous. Her dad's assurance was all she needed. She immediately threw herself at the task. At regular intervals, she proudly pointed to the growing stack of completed brochures: "Look how many I've done, Daddy!" She trusted without hesitation my guarantee of fair payment, and she delighted in hearing her father's sincere praise for her work. I was—as the expression goes—in Daddy heaven.

God wants us to come to him in that way: giving to Him with *every valid and unassuming expectation* of receiving in return as from a kind and loving Parent: *"The kingdom of God belongs to such as these"* (Matt. 19:14; Mark 10:14; Luke 18:16).

**"Ask and It Will Be Given to You."**

One day my mother called me with a question: "Do you ever pray for joy, Kevin?" I considered the question and had to admit that I seldom do. "You should try it," she said.

Later in the day, on my way to the store, I was thinking about what mom had said. I realized that often I *want* to be grumpy about life's circumstances. I don't *want* to feel joy! At other times, I don't feel deserving of joy, or that God would not give me joy merely for the asking. Nevertheless, I love and respect my dear mother, so I prayed, "Lord, please give me joy."

Almost immediately after my prayer, a song called "Let It Move" began to play on my car's radio. It was by the group "For King and Country," whom I'd heard interviewed a couple weeks earlier. "What do we want to be the central message of the album?" they asked themselves. It would be about joy, they decided. They even entitled the album "joy." [*sic*]. The song that played on the radio is one of the most joyful songs you will ever hear. It repeatedly declares, "I choose joy!" And it ends with words I sang as a child: "I need the joy, joy, joy, joy down in my heart. I need the joy, joy, joy, joy down in my heart to stay." I sat in the car until the song's end, soaking in the joy with which God had just doused me in response to my prayer. Then, I walked—joyfully!—into the store.

But God wasn't finished answering my prayer. Once inside, I struck up a conversation with an older gentleman. His name was Jim, and he loved to talk. But though he nattered on and on, I couldn't help but be absorbed in what he said because he was so—you guessed it—*joyful!* He told me about the family tobacco farm on which he had grown up in eastern Kentucky. I learned about his children, his eight siblings, and his father, who was *murdered* when he was eleven. He told me about his thirty-seven operations. "I've twice had my throat cut by a woman," he said with a wink, pointing to surgery scars on his neck.

His manifest joy prompted me to ask, "Are you a follower of Jesus?" "Oh, my, yes!" he said, without hesitation. He then told me all about the church in which he'd grown up and about his baptism. He would still be talking—and blocking other shoppers in the aisle—if I hadn't had to move on.

God had answered my prayer for something He wants for all of us: the fruit of the Spirit. The first four fruit of the Spirit—Love, *Joy*, Peace, and Patience—are emotions, are they not? To be sure, these emotions find expression in actions as well as in feelings. Nevertheless, the fruit of the Holy Spirit are experienced. These are gifts of the Spirit that God wants us to enjoy in this life. Those pleasant emotions will be part of God's eternal reward, too.

(By the way, you should have heard my mom's joy when I told her that story!)

We laid an essential foundation of understanding in this chapter because all of the remaining rewards have elements of the experience of God's pleasure. One such reward, the subject of the next chapter, is that of experiencing God's approval. That commendation, as well as our other rewards, are and will be, experienced emotionally. At its most fundamental, visceral level, God's reward will be the experience of—to use Bernard of Clairvaux's phrase—"the torrent of His delight."

## Notes and Asides:

[1]  *The one emotion in this list that will not be experienced in heaven (or at least not in the way we do now) is hope. Hope is a reward we receive in this life for our trust in God. In heaven, our "faith will become sight," and we will have no more reason to hope. We will have all for which we hoped, to lack nevermore the gladness and rejoicing for which we longed. Hope is one of this life's great rewards because hope, resting on pillars of faith, is a bridge to the life to come.*

[2]  *"The reward is given, not because the works themselves, due to their intrinsic value, impose an obligation on God to reward them, but because God in his grace offered such a reward as part of an agreement" (R. C. Sproul, <u>What is Reformed Theology</u>?, 169).*

[3]  *In <u>Paradiso</u>, Dante asks Piccarda how she feels about her lower rank than that of others in heaven:*

> *Yet inform me, ye, who here are happy,*
> *Long ye for a higher place*
> *More to behold, and more in love to dwell?*

*While everyone will be happy in heaven, some will be happier than others. (See the Beatitudes in Matthew 5, for example.) How can one be happy in heaven when aware that one might have been happier? The answer:*

> *Brother! our will*
> *Is in composure settled by the power*
> *Of charity, who makes us will alone*
> *What we possess, and nought beyond desire. (Canto 3)*

*But that raises yet another, more puzzling question. If we all will be content with our station in heaven, then what difference will our faith and obedience in this life make to our eternal existence? Well, everyone enjoys beautiful sunsets, but some people are enraptured by them. Many of us like art and music, but some of us revel in it. We all like a delicious meal, but some are content with McDonald's hamburgers and others seek the delights of tender veal in a red wine sauce studded with mushrooms. Likewise, some will more thoroughly relish the beauty and* satisfactions of heaven—because they have trained their passions for them in this life. Those supplemental pleasures will be palpable.

The greatest of these enjoyments will be our proximity to God. While everyone will be close to God in heaven—and thus happy, some will be closer to God than others—even as they were in this life.

I understand if you are wary of emotions. I am typical of many—especially males—who are distrustful of feelings. Men tend to be more at ease with logic and order. Emotions are "wild" and alogical. Since our pastors and theologians are most often men, that may explain why we hear so little about the rewards of emotional enjoyment. We are told much about propositional truth from our pulpits, but we hear little about the satisfaction that we find in the arms of Jesus.

Even when we experience them, the pleasant emotions arise without an awareness that the feelings are a result of our faithfulness, or that more of those pleasant emotions are appropriately sought. Or, sadly, we don't speak of pleasant, godly emotions because we do not often experience them, so we do not encourage one another to seek them.

I am not suggesting that our pastors should literally follow David's example of "danc[ing] before the Lord with all his might, wearing a priestly garment." But hopefully, our example will have the same effect: "So David and all the people of Israel brought up the Ark of the Lord with shouts of joy and the blowing of rams' horns" (2 Sam. 6:14-15). Do we have less to celebrate?

# Chapter 7  The Reward of Commendation

At the gym recently, I overheard a man tell of an exploratory visit he and his father had made to a retirement facility. Since the father was in relatively good health, they inquired first about the apartments and amenities of independent living. The father then asked, "So, what do you have for me when I can no longer manage on my own?" "You would then move to assisted living," the facility representative replied. "And then . . . ?" "Skilled nursing." "And then . . . ?" The representative demurred, so the father lightheartedly answered his own question: "The next move would be to Crown Hill Cemetery, right?"

The men chuckled nervously at the punch line. But I wanted to suggest one more "And then . . . ?" For those who love and serve Jesus in this life, the next step after the Crown Hill Cemetery will be the Crown of Righteousness. That crown will not be given to everyone who merely trusts in Jesus for salvation. Paul tells Timothy it will be *"awarded"* to all who, among other things, *"have longed for his appearance"* (2 Tim. 4:6-8).

## A Rich Welcome

Peter encourages us to *"make every effort to add to our faith, . . . goodness, . . . knowledge, . . . self-control, . . . perseverance, . . . godliness, . . . brotherly kindness, . . . and love." "For if you do these things,"* he writes, *"you will receive a rich welcome into the eternal kingdom of our Lord and Savior Jesus Christ"* (2 Pet. 1:5-11). The condition for receiving a *"rich welcome"*—as opposed to an unremarkable welcome—is unmistakable. It is required that *"every effort"* be put forth to receive an extraordinary greeting upon your entry into the Kingdom. A commendation from Christ Jesus awaits those, *and only those*, who have served God.

**Praise from God**

Paul echoes the lessons of Jesus's parables in his first letter to the Corinthians:

> *Those who have been given a trust must prove faithful. . . .*
> *Wait till the Lord comes. He will bring to light what is hidden*
> *in darkness and will expose the motives of men's hearts. At*
> *that time each will receive his praise from God.* (1 Cor. 4:1-5)

Similarly, in his next letter, Paul writes,

> *For it is not the one who commends himself who is approved,*
> *but the one whom the Lord commends.* (2 Cor. 10:18)

For his part, Paul cares only about the evaluation of his life and ministry that will count for eternity. He brushes aside the judgment of any human or human court. In the end, even Paul's own assessment of himself accounts for nothing to him. *"It is the Lord who judges me,"* Paul concludes (1 Cor. 4:4). Keep in mind that this is the same Paul who wrote so often and eloquently of grace. Why, then, does Paul write to *Christians* about hidden motives and the judgment of God? Because a response of obedience is required to receive praise from God.

That is not at odds with Paul's doctrine of grace; it is complementary to it. While we can do nothing of genuine value on our own strength, Scripture is clear that God often gives us a choice whether to allow or not to allow Him to work in and through us. Paul, like the servants of Jesus's parable, fully expected that, if he were found faithful in that with which he had been entrusted, he would *"receive his praise from God."* Paul's familiarity with his own potential for sin kept even him from predicting that he would ultimately receive a reward of praise from God, but he trusted in God's promise to commend him if he indeed lived faithfully to the end. He believed, as did his fellow apostle, that if you *"Humble* [yourself] *before the Lord, he will exalt you"* (James 4:10). Paul's life goal was to someday be exalted by God.

**Glory and Honor**

This teaching was not new. Quoting both David and Solomon (Ps. 62:12; Prov. 24:12), Paul tells us, *"God 'will give to each person according to what he has done.' To those who by persistence in doing good seek glory, honor, and immortality, he will give eternal life"* (Rom. 2:6-7).

Look carefully at what Paul says in that Romans passage. It is to those who *seek* glory and honor that God gives eternal life. Since this is the same Paul who tells us in Ephesians 2:8-9, among other places, that we are saved by grace, not by works, we must consider the *"eternal life"* of which he speaks to be an enhancement to that which all followers of Jesus receive by His grace. There is something extra to be had *"by persistence in doing good"*; namely, *"glory and honor."* Paul repeats himself a couple verses later: there will be trouble and distress for those who do evil, but *"glory, honor, and peace for everyone who does good"* (Eph. 2:10).[1]

If this is offensive to one's understanding of grace, consider that grace and merit for good deeds are not mutually exclusive. The doctrine of rewards actually resolves a seeming dissonance between grace and merit. No one is justified (i.e., declared righteous) due to his or her good works (Rom. 4:4-8, Eph. 2:8-9); however, good works *"accompany salvation"* (Heb. 6:9, Eph. 2:10). *"Faith by itself, if it is not accompanied by action, is dead"* {James 2:17}. As we will discuss later, the works we do can only be performed by God's grace and provision, but it does not follow that there is no effort required of us and that there is no reward for service rendered to God. Grace makes that effort both productive and rewarding.

> *Instead of their shame my people will receive a double portion, and instead of disgrace they will rejoice in their inheritance; and so they will inherit a double portion in their land, and everlasting joy will be theirs.* (Isa. 61:7)

**Our Stories Told**

Over two dozen times in the books of 1 Kings and 2 Kings the question is asked, *"As for the other events of* [one of the kings of Judah or Israel], *are they not written in the book of the annals of the kings . . . ?"* As far as I know, the *"annals of the kings"* have been lost to this world, but that doesn't matter because God has a first edition copy. The deeds of these kings are recorded in heaven, along with all the deeds and events of our lives.

God has a reason for recording what we do. Those records will be placed into evidence someday when, as Paul reminded the Corinthians, we *"all must appear before the judgment seat of Christ"* (2 Cor. 5:10). Dr. Woodrow Kroll points out, "The word 'appear' does not merely mean to 'show up.' We will not just put in an appearance at the judgment seat. This word more strictly means 'made visible'" (*Tested by Fire*, 49). Think of "appearing" before a human court when an important matter is at issue. The word "appear" can also be translated "made known," "made manifest," "revealed." Paul uses a related word in 1 Corinthians 3:13 when he tells that each man's work *"will be shown* [revealed, made manifest, made outwardly obvious] *for what it is . . ."* The core character of our being will be exposed as our work is made apparent before all people. The Judgment Seat of Christ will be an x-ray of the soul!

For a few dollars, one can buy a device that sits on your counter and listens to everything you say—and responds when you call out "Siri!" or "Alexa!"[2] Is it a surprise that God could listen to and record our every thought, motive, word, or action? Jesus said,

*There is nothing concealed that will not be disclosed, or hidden that will not be made known.* (Matt. 10:26)

All will be *"brought out into the open"* (Luke 8:17). A word study of *"eyes of the Lord"* in Scripture produces a long list of verses such as this: *"the eyes of the LORD are everywhere, keeping watch on the wicked and the good"* {Prov. 15:3}.

Likewise, Paul wrote that the Lord *"will bring to light what is hidden in darkness and will expose the motives of men's hearts"* (1 Cor. 4:5). Like it or not, your life will be publicly examined. Dietrich Bonhoeffer well understood this.

That is how God made things to be, before whom everything hidden is already revealed. God wants to show us what is hidden. God will make it visible. *Being revealed in public is the reward ordained by God for hiddenness.* The question is only *where and from whom* people receive this reward of public recognition. (*Discipleship*, 151, emphasis added)

Charles Spurgeon, the influential British preacher who lived not long before Bonhoeffer, stated his understanding of Matthew 10:26 in loving, familial terms:

He will reward you, reward you openly, reward you as a Father rewards a child, reward you as one who saw what you did, and knew that you did it wholly unto him. (72)

## Biblical Examples of Commendation

### For faith

According to a recent poll, about 80 percent of Americans believe there is a God. (Pew) Belief is not the same as faith, however. Faith does not merely believe in God's existence; it trusts God to—among other things—make good on His promises. Trust is an expectation based upon experience, an extrapolation of future actions from past performance. If someone has proven himself trustworthy, you trust (i.e., put your faith in) him. You do not generally trust a stranger about whose character you know little.

And so it is with our faith in God. We trust in God because He has demonstrated His trustworthiness in the biblical account, in church history, in our lives, and in the lives of those around us. We believe what He says He will do because of what He has already done. We have faith, therefore, in His promises for the future, including His promises to reward us, because of His faithfulness in the past. Such was the expectation of the people of God in Hebrews 11.

That chapter is referred to as the quintessential biblical passage on the subject of faith, but it might more accurately be described as about the *results* of faith and faithfulness. It describes what faith produces: God's reward. The subjects of Hebrews 11 had faith in a God who "*rewards those who earnestly seek him.*" Indeed, we are told that it is impossible to please God without faith in a God who rewards (Heb. 11:6).

What reward did these people of faith receive? Among other things, they were commended by God. Abel "*was commended as a righteous man, when God spoke well of his offerings*" (v. 4). Enoch was "*commended as*

94

*one who pleased God*" (v. 5). All of those who endured persecution and suffering—most of them unnamed—were commended for their faith in God's promises. The commendation, the "Well done!" from God, was a part of their reward.

### For a job well done

Have you ever been praised by a recognized authority, like your boss or a public official? Or a community organization or church for which you performed service? Perhaps you have received praise from someone for whom you have great respect, like a favorite teacher or an esteemed colleague. Such recognition feels good, doesn't it?

But don't you agree that the most satisfying praise is that which is bestowed sincerely and earnestly by someone you greatly love: your mother or father, your spouse, or a dear friend? Our satisfaction in being praised depends not only upon who gives it but also upon the value *we* place upon that person's opinion. You feel praised to the extent you want that person to be pleased with you. As Faramir said to Sam Gamgee in *The Lord of the Rings: The Two Towers*, "The praise of the praiseworthy is above all rewards" (368).

Ask yourself: How much do I look forward to hearing Jesus praise me?

In Matthew 25:14-30, Jesus tells of a man who entrusted property to the care of his three servants as he was about to go on a journey. Two of the servants immediately set about to invest what they had been given. Then, at his return, they presented the master with the property and its earnings.

The two faithful servants in the story could hardly wait to present their earnings to the master. "See, I have gained five more!" said the one, and "I have gained two more!" said the other. They were delighted to place at the master's feet the fruit of their labor. It pleased them greatly to please their master! They were not disappointed in his response: the master enthusiastically pronounced the servants' accomplishments "Well done!"

### For righteous character

The servants had done well, but, more profoundly, in their actions, they had demonstrated their good and faithful character. They were pronounced *"good and faithful."*

Like the servants in this parable, you and I have been entrusted with varying measures of His resources. You have been given financial means, relationships, experiences, education, abilities, positions, and opportunities. More importantly, you have been given the inestimably valuable gift of the knowledge of God, revealed in His Word and by the indwelling of His Spirit. By that Spirit, you have the power to use these gifts to further God's purposes.

Faithful stewards are aware that Jesus, the Master, has given us these resources to steward on His behalf. They anticipate the Day He will return and "*settle accounts,*" when he assesses the stewardship of treasures entrusted to our care. Therefore, they go "*at once*" and "*put his money to work.*"

A wicked servant, such as the one in this parable, completely misjudges the master's intentions. He does not expect the master to repay his servants for faithful stewardship. On the contrary, he says, "*I knew that you are a hard man, harvesting where you have not sown and gathering where you have not scattered seed*" (v. 24). In other words, the wicked servant expects the master to keep everything for himself and to give nothing in return. He does not expect to share in the bounty he might produce, so he makes nothing of the talents he has been given. Instead, he buries them.

The wicked servant in the parable might have pleaded ignorance, for the master had not explicitly told the servants of his intent to pay them for their labors. However, he had as much reason as the other two servants to know the master's good character and intentions. The wicked servant should have known that the master would not take advantage of his servants.

You and I, on the other hand, have a weaker excuse than the wicked servant for neglecting our whole-life-stewardship opportunities. In this story and throughout His Word, God has made clear His promise to repay faithful service. We have been told that a day of accounting is coming. Our sin is even worse than that of the wicked servant if we fail to trust His promise to reward our faithfulness over that which He has made us His stewards.

Suppose a wealthy man gave you $1 million and says, "This money is for you to spend as you wish. It is yours." (This represents our salvation in the illustration.) But suppose He added, "Furthermore, I will reimburse you $100 for every dollar of this money you spend to promote my good name, to serve my interests and to invite others to share in your bounty."

What would be your response to such a proposition? "Oh, that is just too generous! I cannot accept it!" I think you would not be so foolish. You would be grateful beyond expression for the man's initial, unconditional generosity (the $1 million) *and* for his conditional generosity (the potential of an additional $100 million).

Isn't that the message of the parable of the talents in Matthew 25 and of the minas in Luke 19? Isn't that what Jesus meant when he said to his disciples that everyone who leaves family and security will receive 100 times as much in return? Do you or I deserve that? No! Will those who leave behind all that is dear to them be grateful when they receive the hundredfold reward? Of course, they will. Would it be selfish of them to sacrifice everything in order to obtain the promised reward?

These parables teach that what you do in this life matters to your future. Whether or not you eventually hear, *"Well done, good and faithful servant! Come and share your master's happiness!"* depends upon whether or not you have invested God's resources for the benefit of God's Kingdom. Your willingness to make such investments depends in no small part upon your trust in God's promise to reward faithfulness.

One might wonder, "But what is one moment of commendation as compared to a lifetime of sacrifice. Is it really worth it? So, I get to heaven, Jesus slaps me on the back, and says, "Good job." And then . . . that's it?" Well, what if that "moment" of commendation never ended? What if, for your faithfulness in this life, you will forever experience an extra measure of God's approval? What if that commendation rang in your heart for all of eternity? Would it not then be worth the cost, any cost?

### For godly motivations

This doctrine was not academic for the theologian Bonhoeffer. His belief in rewards no doubt bolstered his resistance to the Nazis and sustained him until his death by hanging in the Flossenbürg concentration camp. He was *"not afraid of those who kill the body but cannot kill the soul"* (Matt. 10:28). Bonhoeffer had counted "the cost of discipleship" and had considered it worth its weight in gold. Listen to what he wrote in his book of that title published in 1937, eight years before his death and by which time Bonhoeffer was alert to the growing danger of Nazism. Speaking of obedient followers of Jesus, and perhaps with a sense of what the future held for him, he said,

These meek strangers are bound to provoke the world to insult, violence and slander . . . while Jesus calls them blessed, the world cries: "Away with them, away with them!" Yes, but whither? To the kingdom of heaven. "Rejoice and be exceeding glad: for great is your reward in heaven." (Dietrich Bonhoeffer Works)

What a glorious display of faith in God's promises!

King David anticipated that final examination of his life: *"The LORD rewards every man for his righteousness and faithfulness"* (1 Sam. 26:23). He expressed a similar certainty in Psalm 58:11, *"Surely the righteous still are rewarded; surely there is a God who judges the earth."*

Sometimes amid our struggles, we have doubts that our faithfulness to God will ultimately matter. We relate to the lament of Isaiah, *"I have labored to no purpose; I have spent my strength in vain and for nothing."* Even prophets of God sometimes felt demoralized! Isaiah did not despair, however, for he found hope in the promise that *"what is due me is in the LORD's hand, and my reward is with my God"* (Isa. 49:4).

Similarly, Jeremiah acknowledges of God that *"your eyes are open to all the ways of men; you reward everyone according to his conduct and as his deeds deserve"* (Jer. 32:19).

Paul warns us that *"we will all stand before God's judgment seat"* (Rom. 14:10), but he also encourages us that *"the Lord will reward everyone for whatever good he does. . ."* (Eph. 6:8). Peter calls us to be holy *"since you call on a Father who judges each man's work impartially, live your lives as strangers here in reverent fear"* (1 Pet. 1:17). Like Peter, John cautions us to *"not lose what you have worked for, but that you may be rewarded fully"* (2 John 8).

We have just read the words of David, Isaiah, Jeremiah, Jesus, Paul, Peter, and John. Each one encourages us—or warns us—that God is going to judge all of mankind and *"reward everyone for whatever good he does."* It is just for God to do so. While we get to heaven for no more than faith in Jesus, He will nevertheless reward according to His righteous judgment.

*Do not be deceived: God cannot be mocked. A man reaps what he sows. The one who sows to please his sinful nature, from that nature will reap destruction; the one who sows to please the Spirit, from the Spirit will reap eternal life.* (Gal. 6:7-8)

Do you honestly expect to receive commendation from God if you don't seek to please Him?

It is difficult to imagine the experience of this recognition from God, but it is important to try. So if you are where no one will hear you, speak aloud those words that you so much want to hear from Jesus someday, *"Well done, my good and faithful servant"* (Matt. 25:22).

Now make it personal. Speak again what your heart most desires to hear, but this time insert your name into the statement: *"Well done, _____, my good and faithful servant."*

Since in humility and timidity, you probably whispered the words, say it yet again, loudly, and with the enthusiasm with which you hope to hear Jesus speak it to you. Don't hold back, for there is no presumption intended in anticipating those blessed words—only hope that, by God's grace, by the power of His Holy Spirit, and as a result of your faithful service to God, you will be worthy of hearing that wonderful commendation from the lips of your Master.

*"If you do these things,"* you will hear His praise. (John 13:17).

**Notes and Asides:**

[1]   *See footnotes 2–4 at the end of chapter 16 for a discussion of the meaning of "eternal life." It is richer than what you might think.*

[2]   *Alexa may know less about you than the manufacturer of your late-model car. In fact, what your car's maker knows about you may be surpassed only by your own Maker. Consider: it may know how much you weigh (belt/airbag sensors in the seats), your favorite radio stations and music, and all of the contacts in your phone (through the Bluetooth connection). It knows whether you are cautious or reckless (onboard speed records); whether you are courteous (turn signals), rude (long and frequent honking), or impatient (jackrabbit starts and frequent tailgating, from the RPM gauge and the car's radar); whether you are mindful of your surroundings (sudden, frequent, and hard braking); and whether you are attentive to your vehicle's condition (and thus perhaps to other aspects of your life, from your tires' pressure gages). It knows where you live, work, stop for fast food, shop for groceries, bank, where your kids attend school, what social activities you engage in, your visits to the doctor and pharmacy (and thus something about your health), and your beliefs, from whether or where you go to church (all from GPS records).*

   *One estimate puts the value of such data at $750 billion per year worldwide by 2030 (when most all vehicles will be thus equipped). It may or may not be used to your and my benefit, but it is valuable to someone. So, I ask again, is God less capable of knowing all this and more about you? And is He less interested in you than is Toyota or Ford?*

# Chapter 8  The Reward of Honor

While we will lay our crowns at the feet of Jesus in praise of His grace, that doesn't mean that He won't tell us to pick them up and wear them. Those crowns will be His visible proclamation that the wearers lived faithfully for Him. You will wear yours publicly—if you have been given one—because it will please the Father to honor you—*before others*—for your faithfulness.

That God will commend our faithfulness (the subject of the previous chapter) is not an especially difficult concept for the mind to understand, even though it is impossible to anticipate the fullness of the experience. Harder to grasp, however, is the biblical teaching that His praise will be made publicly. This biblical teaching is contrary to our usual expectations.

Or is it?

## Honor of this World

Staff Sergeant Roy Benavidez's ordeal began at Loc Ninh, a Green Beret outpost near the Cambodian border. It was 1:30 p.m., May 2, 1968. Suddenly, someone screamed over the shortwave radio, "Get us out of here!" The cry for help was coming from a twelve-member reconnaissance team that had come under intense enemy fire. Benavidez volunteered so quickly to join in the extraction that he didn't have time to grab his M-16. "I'm coming with you," he informed the helicopter crew.

From the time Sergeant Benavidez jumped from that helicopter into a hail of bullets, medic bag in hand, until he had retrieved the last fallen comrade and was finally pulled aboard a helicopter, he sustained seven major gunshot wounds (one through his back exiting just beneath his heart) and twenty-eight shrapnel wounds and had both arms slashed by bayonets. His right lung was destroyed. He had injuries to his mouth and the back of his head from being clubbed with a rifle butt. It took him almost a year to recover from his injuries. For having thus risked his life to save his fellow soldiers, Sergeant Benavidez was awarded the Medal of Honor, our country's highest military award.[1]

Did you know that every Medal of Honor winner, whatever his rank, is saluted by everyone else in the military, no matter their rank or branch of service? A four-star general (even a five-star general, in time of war) salutes a lowly private who wears the Medal of Honor. Do they do so reluctantly? No, indeed! They are delighted to honor the person who distinguished himself with valor.

Would anyone begrudge the award of the Medal of Honor to Staff Sergeant Roy Benavidez? Is anyone not inspired by such selfless acts of courage? Wouldn't all of us like to shake his hand? Isn't that what the Medal of Honor is about: public recognition of sacrifice and service?

**Honor from God**

Of course, our hero didn't act heroically in order to be honored. He acted selflessly. How could it be right to strive for and to even look forward to that public commendation by God? Wouldn't that negate the selflessness of the act?

Let's begin our look at this unanticipated, seemingly contradictory biblical concept with a fascinating story from Mark 10:35-45 (and its parallel passage in Matt. 20). James and John (and their assertive mother) ask Jesus to grant them the highest positions of honor in His kingdom: the seats to the right and left of Jesus's throne. Can you believe their audacity?! What made them think they had the right to ask for such an honor? No wonder the other disciples were indignant upon hearing of their request! How utterly selfish and self-seeking of them, the others must have thought.

Notice, first, that Jesus did not deny such positions exist in heaven. That is because God's idea of fair is not that everyone's experience of heaven will be the same. Jesus was no proto-socialist. He definitely did *not* teach a heavenly egalitarianism in which everyone will be equal in honor and rank. Quite the contrary, Jesus explains to James and John that "*these places belong to those for whom they have been prepared*" (v. 39). So, not only are there such positions of honor and authority in heaven, God already knows who will fill them.

Shockingly, however, Jesus did not rebuke James and John for asking for those positions of honor and authority. Rather than scold them, Jesus described how they could have them—first by implication and then more explicitly in the ensuing discussion with the rest of the disciples. He asks James and John, "Are you willing *to do whatever it takes* to have those seats of honor? Are you willing to give up your lives to qualify for the position you seek?" (paraphrase of v. 45; see also Matt. 20:28). So we see that the honors James and John want are not granted merely for the asking or assigned arbitrarily by God; they are bestowed by the Father upon those who sacrifice their lives—just as Jesus would sacrifice His life. In short, the honors are based upon *performance.*

### Why should that surprise us?

As we discussed in chapter 3, at this very moment, Jesus is being praised by all of heaven for what he *did.* He is seated on that very throne, the seats to the left and right of which James and John sought to occupy. Jesus sits upon that throne—as King of all the earth—because he is *worthy.* He is worthy, not only because He is God's Son, but because He gave His life in obedience to the Father and he trusted God to raise Him from the dead. Even as you read these words, angels are singing, *"Worthy is the Lamb who was slain!"* {Rev. 5:12}. Jesus is—and forever will be—praised for his obedience to the Father, obedience to the point of death.

Jesus was telling James and John—and by extension, He was telling us—that they would *share in that glory* by sacrificing their lives as He did: for *"drinking of the cup"* of which Jesus drank and for being *"baptized with the baptism"* (Mark 10:38) in which Jesus was baptized. While we may get to heaven with a lukewarm devotion to Christ (1 Cor. 3:15), there is so much more to gain! We will actually *"share in his glory . . . if indeed we share in his sufferings"* (Rom. 8:17).

Conversely, our refusal to follow Jesus's example will disqualify us from this great honor. Why would it be otherwise? As Jesus taught, the servant is no greater than his master. What arrogance or flaw of doctrine makes us think that we will have all that the Father gave to the Son—and all that God would like to give to us—without living the sort of sacrificial life that Jesus led?

*"Whoever wants to become great among you . . ."*

Jesus then turns to the rest of the disciples and makes explicit the promise of honor that was implied in His conversation with James and John. Again, rather than reproach James and John for their desire for positions of honor, Jesus tells the disciples that the rank they seek is available to all, to *"whoever wants to become great among you"* (Matt. 20:26). He then goes on to tell them what to do to achieve that greatness.

Of course, the means of greatness, and the nature of the greatness itself is much different than—and seemingly contradictory to—what the disciples expected, but (and this is my point) Jesus validates the *desire* to achieve greatness in the Kingdom. Jesus encourages this desire to be honored by God and (as we will examine in greater detail later) to have the authority in heaven that comes with sitting on the thrones to the left and right of Jesus.

This is not an isolated passage. Whoever *"practices and teaches"* God's commands, Jesus says in the Sermon on the Mount, *"will be called great in the kingdom of heaven"* (Matt. 5:19). Such people will be called great by God the Father: *"My father will honor the one who serves me"* (John 12:26). And they will be honored by Jesus: *"The Son of Man will acknowledge him . . ."* (Luke 12:8). Why would Jesus say that if He didn't want us to *want* to be great, honored, and acknowledged in the Kingdom of heaven?

Sadly, some of you are told that what you do is of no real value anyway: "Any 'good work' you do isn't even measurable on God's yardstick." In a misapplication of Scripture, we are told that "[our] *righteousness is as filthy rags"* {Isa. 64:6}. While there is a degree of truth in those reminders, they are only part of the truth. Our offerings are indeed paltry, but they are nevertheless profoundly valued by God and, by God's promise, worthy of reward.

Jesus tells us in Matthew 6 not to do our works before men to be noticed by men. But He is not telling us to never do good works in public view. Such a command would render much of our work impossible to do. He is talking about who we consider to be our "audience" as we do those good works. He is telling us that an award of lasting value will come from the Father, not from people. So the pure motive is not uninterested in the personal outcome: the pure motivation is the one that seeks only what God offers in return for service.

Commenting on this passage, N. T. Wright concedes our discomfort with this notion:

> Many people imagine that [Jesus] is asking us to do everything with no thought of reward, and are then rather shocked when he repeats, three times, his belief that our heavenly father will repay us. Clearly, Jesus is not so bothered about the notion of disinterested behavior or "altruism," as we sometimes are. (53)

How could it be wrong to seek God's praise and affirmation for service to Him? Indeed, it is sinful *not* to do so.

## Honor Granted Publicly

But Father and Son are not alone in attendance when the faithful are honored. Honor is, by definition, bestowed by someone in the presence of others. By its nature, honor is "honorable" because it is given by someone who is great, upon one who is being proclaimed great—in the presence of others. If it is a private affair, it is no great honor.

Before whom will the faithful *"be called great in the kingdom of heaven"*? Some part of the honor will be presented before angels: *"I tell you, whoever acknowledges me before men . . . will be acknowledged before the angels of God"* (Matt. 10:32). Not having met an angel (as far as I know), I have trouble comprehending the greatness of this honor. I can only begin to imagine what it will be like to hear God speak words of commendation—if I am to have any—before those creatures of unimaginable beauty, power, and purity.

But God also will bestow honor upon the faithful before all the people of God in heaven. Those who delight in God's commands *"will be lifted high in honor"* (Ps. 112:9). In Luke 14:10, Jesus told his disciples, *"You will be honored in the presence of all your fellow guests"* (Luke 9:46-48). Luke records an argument among the disciples as to who is the greatest. Once again, Jesus does not reprimand the disciples. He does not tell them it is wrong to desire to be the greatest. Instead, he explains how to achieve genuine greatness.

Later we will examine more fully Jesus's teaching about how to attain a place of honor. (In what may have seemed a paradox to the disciples, Jesus explains that it is through humility.) But for now, the point is this: there is a place of honor to be occupied, and that place of honor will be bestowed upon the worthy *"in the presence of all your fellow guests."* As David put it, *"How great is your goodness, which you have stored up for those who fear you, which you bestow **in the sight of men** on those who take refuge in you"* (Ps. 31:19).

*For making ourselves "last"*

In Matthew 19:30, Jesus picked up this theme in a way that was characteristically disruptive of the conventional wisdom of His day. Jesus says, *"But many who are first will be last, and many who are last will be first."* He says something similar in Mark 10:31, Luke 13:30, and Matthew 20:16.[2]

The privileged expected they had special favor with God that would place them in front of the line, ahead of regular people and certainly ahead of sinners such as tax collectors and former prostitutes. The *"first"* will not be those who expect to receive a high honor in the kingdom by virtue of their lineage, position, or place of birth. (Prideful Pharisees or those Jews who thought themselves better than the Gentiles, for example.)

You will find a helpful discussion of this saying of Jesus in *Your Eternal Reward* by Erwin Lutzer. He concludes that the attitude Jesus is critiquing is the same as that of the elder brother in the parable of the lost son found in Luke 15:11-32. The elder son was representative of those sons of Abraham who felt an entitlement to the Kingdom (136). (Which raises the question: Who are there "elder sons" of our day? Are they perhaps Christians who feel an entitlement to the riches of heaven simply for being a child of God?)

Lutzer's understanding is consistent with two parables in the following chapter of Matthew. In the parable of the two sons in Matt. 21:28-32, Jesus concludes with this: *"I tell you the truth, the tax collectors and the prostitutes are entering the kingdom of God ahead of you."* Jesus concludes the parable of the tenants in Matt. 21:33-43, *"Therefore I tell you that the kingdom of God will be taken away from you and given to a people who will produce its fruit. . . .When the chief priests and the Pharisees heard Jesus' parables, they knew he was talking about them."* They were not pleased with what they heard.

The message is similar in a humorous story in Luke 14:7-14.[3] Jesus— noticing that some guests had chosen for themselves seats of honor at the table—warned his disciples against such presumption, for they might be humiliated when the host asks them to move aside for one more worthy. Jesus was immersed in the writings of Scripture, so His poetically poignant prophecy was a summary of the words of Solomon,

> Do not exalt yourself in the king's presence, and do not claim a place among his great men; it is better for him to say to you, "Come up here," than for him to humiliate you before his nobles. (Prov. 25:6-7)

The implication in the story, in fact, is that the presumption itself disqualifies one from the honor. Unexpectedly, it is humility—the very sense of unworthiness—that makes one worthy. The last—that is, the one who positions himself in the last place—will be placed at the head of the table by God Himself.

### A warning to us as well

As I pictured the scene at the table Jesus described, my laugh should have been a nervous one. I wonder—and now that I have spent time pondering it, I fear to discover—the extent to which my heart presumes I will have a seat of honor in heaven. It is one thing—a good thing!—to hope for and strive for the honor that God will give to the faithful. It is quite another to *presume* the honor.

We will discuss in later chapters how we can make ourselves "last." But what does it mean to be "first"? In what sense will those who humbly and obediently serve God be first? In the context of each of the passages quoted, it is clear that to be made "first" is to be given honor (and, as we will see in a moment, authority) in the presence of others: *"For everyone who exalts himself will be humbled, and he who humbles himself will be exalted"* (Luke 14:11). The Greek word (*"hupsoo"*) translated "exalted" means to "lift up or to elevate." Those who humble themselves will be *"raised up"* by God before others.

Jesus used the same language to contrast the tax collector who humbled himself before God and to the Pharisee who made an impressive and public spectacle of himself (Luke 18:10-14). As Jesus said of the *"hypocrites who love to pray standing in the synagogues and on the street corners to be seen by men, I tell you the truth, they have received their reward* [of honor before men] *in full"* (Matt. 6:5). *"For everyone who exalts himself will be humbled, and he who humbles himself will be exalted"* (Luke 18:14).

### For seeking honor from God

So those who honor God will be honored by God in the presence of others. What is more, Paul encouraged the Romans to seek such glory and honor. It is good and right to *want* (to *"seek"*) to have glory and honor bestowed upon us by God. It is appropriate to do good work to gain glory and honor from God. And, lest we forget the main point of this section, the honor and glory we rightly seek are that which is given by God before others.

Peter, writing to followers of Jesus who are enduring persecution, encourages them with these words,

> So when your faith remains strong through many trials, it will bring **you** much praise and glory and honor on the day when Jesus Christ is revealed to the whole world. (1 Pet. 1:6-7 NLT)

Why are we told these things if we are not to act upon them?

We are not Stoics! Endurance is not an end in itself; it is a means to an end. By faith in God's promises, we endure and persevere through trials to gain something. That something is, among other things, "praise, glory, and honor." If we endure, Jesus will crown us! If we submit to God, He will lift us up, honor us, and shower us with praise and glory in His time.

### Honor That is Eternal

Does God's reward of praise just . . . *end* . . . after it is bestowed? Not according to the psalmist:

> A *righteous man will be remembered forever.* (Ps. 112:6)

You probably think there is no way you will ever occupy one of those two seats next to the throne of Jesus. Don't be too hasty to rule yourself out. Consider some heavenly math: What is an infinite number divided by a finite number? It is an infinite number, is it not? Well, our time in heaven will be unlimited, and the number of heaven's residents will be finite.

Therefore, for any one person in heaven, there will be an endless amount of time to do any given heavenly activity, including the occupation of the seats to the left and right of Jesus. So you could well sit at the right or left of Jesus—if you qualify. It is an exciting thought, isn't it?[4]

## Honor's Foretaste

Here is an earthly illustration of the honor God bestows—and will bestow—upon the faithful:

Early in a service at church, a member of the congregation, Mike, was honored for many years leading "Helping Hands," a ministry of practical assistance to needy and vulnerable people in the congregation and the community. People came forward to share their experiences of God's love through Mike's ministry: a disabled man who had needed a ramp down his home's steps; a struggling mother abandoned by her husband and dealing with a clogged sink; an elderly gentleman with a tree branch that had fallen across his driveway; a woman with multiple home repair needs whose husband had died of cancer.

The sermon that followed was on 1 Peter 5:1-6. Having discussed its commands, the pastor pointed out that when Jesus returns, those who have served *"willingly, as God wants you to . . . will receive the crown of glory that will never fade away."* That *"crown of glory"* will be akin to the honor we gave earlier to Mike. But that was a mere foretaste of what awaits him—and anyone like him—in heaven.

> *"For if you humble yourself under God's mighty hand,"* then *"God will lift you up in due time"* too (1 Pet. 5:6). Jesus will tell details of His provision in those acts of service of which even those involved were unaware. And He will speak of those who were touched by that service, indirectly a hundred years later, as the effects of that service rippled across time. And He will explain to us that He did not need our service to these people. Instead, He wanted to *share with us* His joy in meeting their needs.

The pastor spent much of the rest of his sermon elaborating on those promises of honor and praise from God. For he understands that for his congregation to be most willing to do what God commands them to do, they must look forward with hope and expectation of having God's honor and praise for doing it.

How will it feel to publicly receive God's praise? Will you feel pride? No. Indeed, for the first time in your life, you won't even be tempted with pride. On the contrary, you will feel a profound sense of humility and gratitude, far beyond that which you have ever known.

You will understand that you did something genuinely worthy of God's praise, but you will *equally* appreciate that it was only by God's grace and power that you were able to do it. You will know—you will utterly know—both the **vanishing smallness and the weighty significance** of your contribution to His purposes. As St. Chrysostom understands God to say to us:

> You are bound to me by innumerable favors, and now I ask
> you to make some return. Not that I demand it as my due.
> I reward you as though you were acting out of generosity.
> *For your trifling gestures, I am giving you a kingdom.*
> (Walsh, 601, emphasis added.)

In all of this, you will know God's pleasure, overwhelmingly and eternally. You will be unable to speak but in songs of praise to God. And who will be most gratified and glorified when you receive His praise? God Himself. That God's praise *for* His people will result in the great and eternal praise *of* God is one of the reasons God promises to reward.

## Notes and Asides:

[1] *This is an abridged version of that remarkable story. For more on Staff Sergeant Benavidez and others like him, go to www.history.army.mil.*

[2] *This parable of the workers called at different times of the day (Matt. 20) is sometimes cited as evidence that all will receive the same "wage" in heaven. If Jesus was teaching that all Christians receive the same wage, then he was talking in this instance about the "wage" of heaven itself, not of "wages" in heaven. In other words, heaven is for anyone who answers the Landlord of heaven's call to work in His earthly vineyard, no matter when he or she is called to it. It is not necessary to have spent one's entire life in service to Jesus to go to heaven because works are not required for salvation. Only the answer to Jesus's call to humble ourselves before Him will give us entry into heaven. (See appendix 2 for more on this parable under the objection, "Jesus taught we will all receive the same wages in heaven.")*

*But, with Jesus's summary statement ("the last will be first, and the first will be last"), the lesson of the parable is also the same as that of the story of the rich man and the ensuing conversation with His disciples (discussed at greater length in chapter 16): the wages in heaven for our labors might be different than we expected.*

[3] *Not that Jesus thought the scene was funny. It just strikes me so. But that prompts an intriguing question about humor in heaven. Most, if not all, humor makes fun of human foibles. Even our laughter at animal behavior is anthropomorphic. So, if we laugh in heaven, what will provoke it, if not our sin nature? (I suppose there might be puns in heaven. But surely they will be forbidden, for it is generally observed that puns provoke laughter mostly from the punster and groaning from everyone else. . ..)*

*I think that in heaven we will laugh at events from our lives. We will laugh at ourselves. Some of those episodes may not have been funny to us at the time, but Jesus will scrub them of the embarrassment and pain, and we will laugh at them. The memories will remind us of our human frailty, of God's love and provision, and of the people we enjoyed in this life.*

*I often chuckle with my mom and sibs at the memory of this or that which my late brother Steve did or said. As I wrote in chapter 5, Stevo had Down syndrome. And he was most beloved by everyone who knew him. But he had some quirks. (Don't we all?)*

*One Sunday, Steve sat in his usual spot at church: on the front row, next to the center aisle on the right side. The sermon went long. Mom and Dad, sitting a few rows back, noticed his increasingly impatient fidgeting. He occasionally glanced back at them with an eye roll. Finally, Steve could endure no more. While the preacher was still speaking, Steve did what some of us have been tempted to do in similar circumstances: He stood up— and walked down the middle aisle toward the back of the sanctuary. Pausing at the pew where his parents sat, he pointed at his watch and said, loudly enough for all to hear, "It's late!"*

*That is but one of dozens of poignant and funny things Steve said and did. He was irreproachably honest about how he felt, even if his frank expressions were impolitic. We often mimic his distinctive voice as we speak his signature phrases at moments he would have said them. ("That's gross!" "Here we go again . . ." "Are you serious?") We smirk as we remember him asking another disabled person he had just met, "Are you special, too?" Or when my cousin, in an adjoining bathroom stall, heard Steve say with his characteristic stutter, "Uh oh. N, n, n, no toilet paper." Or the time the pastor asked for prayer requests during the service and Steve raised his hand, "Um, I, I, I have one. M, m, mom and Dad had a fight."*

*And as we remember those incidents in heaven, there is no doubt the biggest guffaws will come from Stevo himself. (Wait 'til you hear his beautiful laugh!) As with all of us, there will be no shame in those memories. As we laugh at our idiosyncrasies and weaknesses, we will all the more appreciate what Jesus did for us and we will grow to know each other better. Those delightful moments—and others we don't even remember—have made us love our dear brother more every time we recount them to one another. They reveal the Stevo we were privileged to have in our family. We miss him so much.*

⁴ *I wonder, too, what other activities we will engage in the New Heaven and New Earth. Some of my golf-playing friends can't wait to hit the golf courses. If indeed there are such in heaven, no doubt those courses, like all of re-creation (pun intended), will be stunning. But what fun would it be if all in the foursome shot an eighteen every*

outing?! The first few times in doing so would be exciting, but would I be still hitting the links after a thousand rounds?

So much of our human activity—even our fun activities—involve (hopefully friendly and honest) competition, either against an opponent or against the clock. Humans compete; it's what they do: as siblings and students; socially and professionally; at work and at play. As we watched a documentary about Mario Andretti, Sandy asked, "So, when was the first auto race?" I replied that I don't know, but it was probably shortly after the second car's manufacture.

What will "amuse" us if there is no opponent and no clock? I hope I will (finally) be able to play the piano! Will I have to learn it? (If so, it's good that heaven is eternal.) Will I have any sense of accomplishment in doing so? Or will I suddenly acquire the ability?

These whimsies about heaven have a point: While the Bible tells us much about what awaits us, it is impossible for us, from our earthbound vantage point, to fully appreciate how different the life to come will be from, and yet familiar to, our current experience. But His promise of reward in heaven sparks curiosity in me about the nature of what He has in store for us. And that, in turn, prompts a growing desire to do whatever it takes to have all of its riches, whatever they are—to, as Lewis put it, "Come further up and come further in!" (The Last Battle, 148).

A respected radio Bible teacher once fielded a question from a listener about heaven. He ended his comments with this: "I think we think too much about heaven." Later I suggested to the teacher that, if anything, we speak far too little of it, quoting Paul:

> Since, then, you have been raised with Christ, set your hearts
> on things above, where Christ is, seated at the right hand of
> God. Set your minds on things above, not on earthly things.
> (Col. 3:1-4)

The teacher replied that he was referring to questions on matters about which the Bible does not speak. I agree with him: we can get caught up in trivial discussions about what awaits us. However, when we seldom talk of what the Bible does say about heaven, we leave the impression that our experience of heaven is unrelated to our life on this earth. We should always be thinking about heaven. Heaven is our eternal destiny, and its quality will be affected by the way we live our lives.

113

# Chapter 9 The Reward of People

Son Jong Nam was personally acquainted with the brutality of the Pyongyang regime long before he had crossed from China back into his native country of North Korea. As the Associated Press reported in 1997, his wife, who was eight months pregnant, had been arrested for allegedly saying Kim Jong Il had ruined the economy and caused mass famine. To gain her confession, her interrogators kicked her in the belly, causing her baby to be stillborn. Upon her release, Son and his family had fled to China, where his wife soon thereafter died of cancer.

While in China, Son became a committed follower of Jesus, and he enthusiastically shared his faith. As a result, he was arrested in 2001 by Chinese authorities for proselytizing and was deported to North Korea, where he was immediately imprisoned and tortured with beatings and electric shocks. Upon his release in 2004, he sneaked back into China to briefly see his daughter, but he soon voluntarily returned to North Korea to share the Gospel, carrying with him Bibles and cassettes. Son was again arrested and imprisoned, tortured, and finally killed.

Will it not seem right and proper to you if Son Jong Nam is especially honored by God for his faith and sacrifice? Conversely, would it not seem unfair to you if those who, unlike Son Jong Nam, had made no particular sacrifice in their lives nevertheless received the same praise from God as those who gave their lives entirely to God's service?

If so, then your heart is in tune with God's, because God will indeed honor those who sacrifice themselves for the sake of His Kingdom. Jesus said, *"Whoever loses their life for me, will find it . . .For the Son of Man . . . will reward each person according to what he has done"* (Matt. 16:25-27). (See also Mark 8:34-35; Luke 9:23-24.) *"The Father,"* Jesus said, *"will honor the one who serves me"* (John 12:25-26).

Son Jong Nam is but one of tens of millions of martyrs in the history of the church. Won't you be delighted to hear God's praise of these people for giving their all to Jesus?

## Reward of Loved Ones

If we will glory in the honor bestowed upon people like Son whom we didn't even know in this life, how much more will we glory in the honor bestowed by God upon those we loved in this life? Think of someone who is a hero of faith to you. Not Billy Graham or Mother Teresa, but someone you know personally who endures suffering with grace, who loves and serves the unlovable, or who lives a simple life in order to give more generously to Kingdom work. Now compare that person's commitment and service to God to your own. While stipulating that only God knows the heart, do you think that you and your spiritual hero are deserving of the same richness of eternal existence?

Imagine how it will feel to witness God's praise of someone you led to Christ; of a person you discipled; of a child you raised to know Jesus; of a spouse you loved into the Kingdom; of a neighbor for whom you prayed; and of people who, influenced by your words and example, gave themselves to faithful service. How wonderful it will be to hear these people praised by God Himself! Imagine the fruit of *your* labor, your "*joy, and crown*," being honored by God {Phil. 4:1}!

Your joy on their behalf will be beyond description. And it will be eternal. You will feel for them what God feels for them. You will be delighted that the entire world knows about the faithfulness of your brother or sister in Christ. Those who participated in the discipleship or encouragement of others will glory in the praise God gives people into whose lives they ministered.

Those whose loads you bear
are the crowns you will wear.

These people are now—and forever will be—your reward for service. You "*will glory*" in them "*in the presence of our Lord Jesus when he comes.*" They will be your "*glory and joy*" when they are honored before God (1 Thess. 2:19). Together you will praise God for all of eternity.

**Reward in this Life**

My wife and I have had a singular foretaste of this reward as adoptive parents. Our first and tepid steps in the process that brought Emma into our lives were prompted by a miscarriage. The grief at our loss was compounded when good friends of ours announced they were unexpectedly (and not excitedly) expecting a baby, the due date of which was the same as that of the baby we had lost to miscarriage! We questioned God. How could He take from us a child we so much wanted and give to another couple a child they did not seek? And why did He rub salt into our wounds with that coincidence of due dates?

Around the time of these events, my brother and his wife returned from China with an adopted child. Sandy and I wondered if God would have us follow their example. So, using my brother's contacts, we warily inquired into a Chinese adoption. Filled with apprehension, we began the process which finally produced the phone call we eagerly awaited. We had a referral! My hand shook as I took notes with Sandy excitedly looking over my shoulder: it was for a girl of about ten months from the southern coastal city of Yangjiang. And she was born on September 26th.

As I wrote the date of birth, my wife gasped. I had not noticed something that was immediately apparent to Sandy: Our Chinese baby had been *born* on the due date of both the baby we had lost to miscarriage and of our friend's baby. The statistical odds of a coincidence of three dates is 1 in 133,225. But that such coincidence would have *significance* to us is of incalculable odds. In His grace, God confirmed His sovereign will in our lives, even in taking from us the baby we had so much wanted. He had a plan in mind all along.

A week before our scheduled departure for China, a thunderstorm tore a plastic tarp that protected a pile of corn worth $1 million. Doused by torrential rain, the grain was in danger of rotting. I was terrified of the potential financial consequences—including that we would be unable to go through with the adoption of our little girl.

I couldn't sleep the night of the storm. After an hour of tossing and turning in gut-wrenching anxiety, God spoke to me—sternly. As I recorded the next day in a letter to our daughter-to-be, God told me, "Stop worrying! I have commissioned you to get Emma, Kevin! Nothing will prevent it. I want her for my own. I have *chosen* Emma. She is mine."[1]

Fast forward to the eve of the tenth anniversary of Emma's adoption.

Out of the blue and with an air of nonchalance—but veiled excitement—she announced, "I became a Christian the other night, Daddy." My eyes widened. "What? When? What happened?!" I stammered. "A few nights ago, when I was afraid and alone in bed," she said. "I prayed that God would help me sleep. And then . . . I went to sleep." That was it. Just a simple answered prayer. But Jesus had met Emma in that moment.

Clearly, God had begun something in her. Sandy and I exchanged smiles when we heard Emma happily singing, "Our God Is an Awesome God" as she prepared for bed. Later, when Sandy returned from turning off Emma's bedside light, she told me that Emma had been reading her Bible. The next day Emma said, "You know, Daddy, the Bible says *a lot* about rewards!" (That's my girl!) Not only had she been reading from Matthew— in which Jesus indeed does speak a lot about rewards—but also she had *highlighted* passages with a marker!

Later she produced her sermon notes from the previous Sunday. The bulletin's note page was *full*—and with small print—with such as: "We Become What We Worship," "Whatever controls my life controls my heart," below which was a list of possible usurpers of God's controlling influence: "Success, appreciation, confidence in skill, beauty, brains; ministry." "God strips our idols from us." "God forgives." The page was *covered.* (Her notes were far better than mine!) And she was only eleven years old! We were overjoyed!

People have often told us how selfless we were in giving Emma a home. But she has given us so much love and joy in return, we have not the slightest sense of having made any sacrifice. Besides, the chief inducement to adopt was the longing left unfulfilled at the death of our child—not some altruistic desire to give a home to an orphan. Furthermore, our fearful hesitation needlessly delayed—to over a year—a process that could have been completed in six months. God graciously took our weakness of faith—and the extra time thereby required— into account and, despite our hesitancy, gave us precisely the little girl He had planned for us all along.

Those confessions of our smallness of faith notwithstanding, do you know what? We were obedient to God when we took the first, faltering step, and then the next and the next—until finally, we got Emma. And what we received in return for our obedience is . . . well, it is immeasurably and indescribably beautiful. What we did is hardly to be compared to our reward. And now that she has come to know Jesus, we will enjoy that reward, our joy and crown, which is our dear, sweet Emma—*forever*![2]

**Reward to Come**

But I am not yet satisfied with my reward. I am "greedy" for more! I want even greater things to come of Sandy's and my small but significant acts of faithfulness. I wish more for Emma than what she already has in her possession: the gift of heaven. I want her to someday know the exceeding joy of hearing God's praise for a life she lived well. *I want to experience the joy of hearing God's praise of Emma.*

We all will enjoy forever the people for whom we had a part in bringing into the Kingdom of God, but our rejoicing will be magnified beyond description—our *"joy will be complete"* (John 15:11)—when the people whom we love are honored and praised by God for their faithful service to Him.

> Just as *"if one part* [of the body] *suffers, every part suffers with it,"* so, too, *"if one part is honored, every part* [of the body] *rejoices with it."* {1 Cor. 12:26}

God's public praise of the faithful will be no mere formal ceremony with polite clapping. There will be no program bulletin by which to anticipate the ceremony's interminable end. There will be no yawning or glancing at the clock, as at an earthly ceremony. There will be no envy of those who are honored. There will be no thoughts of recipients' undeservedness. No one will preen before the cameras or seek to upstage and impress the crowd.

This awards ceremony will be unlike any you have witnessed. It will be a riot of celebration! All of heaven will reverberate with praise! It will ring with great shouts and music and singing and dancing as we all celebrate one another and applaud God's marvelous work through us. The *"doorposts and thresholds"* of heaven will shake (Isa. 6:4)!

You will hear God's praise for your own spiritual ancestors, *"God's fellow workers,"* some of whom planted and others who watered the seeds of the Gospel (1 Cor. 3:8-9). You will hear God's praise for their labor and for their sacrifices even to death, as they passed the words of life from generation to generation until, centuries later, you heard and accepted the Good News of Jesus. Likewise, they will rejoice to hear God's praise of their own spiritual descendants. Finally, and gloriously, *"the sower and the reaper* [will be] *glad together"* (John 4:36).

For eon upon eon, you will hear riveting stories of the struggles and triumphs of people you never knew, from other lands and from centuries past and future. Jesus, the master storyteller, will recount details of God's provision about which even those present were unaware.[3]

## Reward of Being God's Reward

Lest you think living one's life in order to receive such praise is sinfully self-centered, please consider this: Of all those who assemble to hear of your faithfulness, who do you think will be the most pleased that His people are being honored? Will it not be God Himself?

- God the Father, who gave His Son that we might be reconciled to Him, will be pleased that His faithful are praised, even as any father delights to publicly praise his children.
- God the Son, whose great love compelled Him to give His life for you. If Jesus still weeps—as He did at the death of Lazarus—then surely He will cry with joy when His beloved servants are honored.
- God the Holy Spirit, who comforted us, instructed us, and empowered us to do that for which God now—before all of heaven—displays His great pleasure.

Jesus will glory in *His reward* for *His faithfulness* to the Father. The Son will finally have His reward: His people; His redeemed; His treasured possession, given to Him because of the Father's great love for Him {John 17}. The Son will forever glory in the praise of those faithful whom He loves and for whom He died. *Our reward will be Jesus's reward.*

When God praises you, He will bring praise unto Himself. Therefore, to seek honor from *God* is to seek to glorify *God.* Our eternal reward of praise *from* God will produce eternal praise *of* God.

## Notes and Asides

1    *Years later, Emma experienced deep-seated feelings of abandonment not uncommon in adopted children. As Sandy and I prayed for her, I opened my YouVersion app devotional plan to the topic of fear and anxiety to find a Scripture with which to encourage her. The app suggested a verse in Isaiah which began, appropriately, "So, do not fear, for I am with you . . ." Curious as to what the "So" referred, I read the previous verse. To my jaw-dropping amazement, it reiterated what God had told me those many years earlier as we contemplated our journey to China:*

> *I took you from the ends of the earth, from its farthest corners*
> *I called you. I said, "You are my servant"; I have chosen you*
> *and have not rejected you. (Isa. 41:9)*

2    *What might you hear on that Day? Well, some of it might be from the people in assembly. If God gives us the opportunity to speak up, my daughter may recount this text conversation while she babysat the neighbor's kids.*

> *Emma: How, how did you do it???? ☺*
> *Me: What?*
> *Emma: Putting kids to bed is actually torture*
> *Emma: Like . . . oh . . . My . . . goodness!*
> *Me: ☺*
> *Emma: Just, HOW! ALL OF MY ENERGY IS LIKE DISSIPATED*
> *Emma: Like. Ugh*
> *Me: It's not so bad when you love them . . .*
> *Emma: That's true, but like still it's exhausting no matter what,*
>     *even when you do love them*
> *Emma: Thank you for raising me and taking care of me and*
>     *loving me.*
> *Emma: This experience just made me really see how much effort*
>     *goes into even the littlest things in the daily life of a kid.*
> *Emma: Idk why but I'm feeling super sentimental.*
> *Me: Take whatever we gave to you, Emma, multiply it times 100,*
>     *and that's how much we got back.*
> *Emma: I might cry*
> *Emma: I love you and mom so much!*

Me: *Love you more . . .*
Emma: *No, wrong. I love you more.*

3    *Have you seen the movie,* <u>Rudy</u>*? It is based on the true story of Daniel "Rudy" Ruettiger, who, by sheer willpower, became a valued member of the Notre Dame football team. Since he was not a good enough student to be included in the game squad, he labored on the second team— against the first team during practice. He relentlessly pushed them to excellence. His determination won the hearts of his fellow teammates. The entire university became aware of Rudy's indispensability to the football program when the school newspaper wrote an article about him. In appreciation for Rudy's inspiration to the team, its players insisted that the coach allow him to lead them onto the field for the last game of the year—Rudy's senior year.*

*In the final seconds, Rudy was finally given a chance to play. It was a real-life Hollywood ending: He **sacked** the opponent's quarterback! The crowd roared! "Rudy! Rudy! Rudy!" they chanted. His teammates were so excited for him that they carried him off the field—an honor no one has received in the forty-four years since.*

*Intelligence and giftedness are not requirements for the earning of God's reward. God looks for grit and persistence.*

*By the way, do you know who was most proud of Rudy? His father, a diehard Notre Dame fan who had come to see his son play. And so is our heavenly Father proud of you when you seek to please Him.*

# Chapter 10 The Reward of Vindication

It is a tried and true plot in movies: Against all the odds, and through relentless striving, the protagonist wins in the end. *Rocky, Hoosiers, The Karate Kid*; these movies were great commercial successes because people love underdog movies. Many of us feel like the underdog; we identify with his struggles or persecution. We want the protagonist to win because we also hope to win in life! And we love to see the antagonist get his due. Our hearts yearn for vindication!

Jesus loves that storyline, too! As we've seen on several occasions, he said the *"first will be last, and the last will be first."* Jesus prayed the Psalms, which often speak to that theme.

> *You have delivered me from the attacks of the people; you have made me the head of nations. People I did not know now serve me.* {Ps. 18:43}

> *You give us victory over our enemies, you put our adversaries to shame.* {Ps. 44:6-8}

> *They have greatly oppressed me from my youth, but they have not gained the victory over me.* {Ps. 129:2}

**God's Reward of Vindication**

I remember my confusion when first introduced to the notion that God will vindicate <u>Himself,</u> in N. T. Wright's *The New Testament and the People of God.* "What?" I thought. "To vindicate oneself is to offer evidence that exonerates from charges or accusations. God is God! He doesn't have to prove Himself to anyone! Why would He even dignify any accusation with a response?" It is true: God does not *have* to prove anything to anyone. But God will vindicate Himself. He will do so—for our benefit.

To "vindicate" is to judge between two parties. In that judgment, one is demonstrated to be, and then is pronounced to be, right or innocent of the charges made against him. The other is proved and pronounced wrong or guilty. More definitively than a jury merely deciding the prosecution was mistaken and the accused is "Not guilty," the accused is wholly exonerated by the judge and pronounced innocent of all charges!

So, God, the Great Judge, will someday vindicate Himself of the charges unjustly made against Him. He will finally and forever silence the accusations of the Accuser. The whole world will know that God was right (righteous in all His ways), and the Accuser was wrong (evil in all his ways). The accused will be vindicated and rewarded with praise. The Accuser and those who followed the Accuser will be proven and pronounced "Guilty!" and receive their just reward of punishment.

Finally, as at the end of a cinematic legal drama about an underdog, it will be declared, "Court dismissed!" Or, in Jesus's words, "It is finished!" The beginning of that end was on the cross when Jesus spoke those blessed words {John 19:28}. That is the reason the cross was such a glorious victory! But it "ain't over till it's over," as they say. There is much yet to be done before the final victory. The outcome is a foregone conclusion, as was the end of World War II in Europe after the success of the Normandy invasion. But our sacrifice of service is still required until the war finally ends, as it was for the thousands of soldiers who lost their lives at the Battle of the Bulge and the Battle of Berlin. The end of the Great War between God and the Accuser will come at the Great White Throne of Judgment (of the wicked), and at the Judgment Seat of Christ (where the faithful followers of Christ will be rewarded).

> *I will deal with them according to their conduct, and by their own standards, I will judge them. Then they will know that I am the LORD.* (Ezek. 7:27)

> *O house of Israel, you say, "I will judge each of you according to his own ways."* (Ezek. 33:20)

> *I will make known my holy name among my people Israel. I will no longer let my holy name be profaned, and **the nations will know that I the LORD am the Holy One in Israel**.* (Ezek. 39:7)

In that emphasized phrase from Ezekiel 39:7, we see that in doing so God will have finally and completely vindicated Himself before the whole world. (God's vindication of Himself is a theme of Ezekiel, with the phrase translated *"they will know"* followed by some variation of *"I am the Lord"* appearing thirty-four times!)

God is not always quick—from our perspective—to establish His justice and power. Often, He waits much longer to vindicate Himself—and our faith—than we think necessary. Not until God had, for example, allowed His people to suffer at the hands of Pharaoh did He allow Pharaoh to finally release His people. God even hardened Pharaoh's heart to prevent him from yielding to Him sooner, so that *"the Egyptians will know that I am the LORD when I stretch out my hand against Egypt and bring the Israelites out of it"* (Exod. 7:5).

In each plague, God demonstrated his power over the gods of Egypt, right up through the last plague, which struck Pharaoh himself and shattered his claim of deity. God waited to deliver His people so He would be all the more decisively vindicated before the Egyptians and—just as importantly—before the Israelites whom God had freed.

So it is with all of human history. The vindication will come in its time, after God has accomplished all His purposes: *"Let justice roll on like a river, righteousness like a never-failing stream!"* {Amos 5:24}. Or as Winnie-the Pooh paraphrased Amos, "Rivers know this: there is no hurry. We shall get there someday" (Milne, 92).

**Our Reward of Vindication**

*For the LORD will vindicate his people and have compassion on his servants.* (Ps. 135:14)

In vindicating Himself, God will vindicate all those who put their trust in Him. First and most importantly, God will vindicate His own Son Jesus for His obedience to the Father. His sacrifice will be seen, finally and fully, by the whole world, as the glorious victory that it is.

God will also vindicate the trust His people placed in Him, His promises, and His Son. That vindication, to the extent we deserve it, will be our reward. Those who—against the tides of culture or persecution or deprivation—relied on God's promises (i.e., all those who patiently awaited the Day of Judgment for vindication by God) will hear it spoken of them, as it was to Jesus: this, too, is my faithful servant, in whom I am well pleased. Job learned the sweetness of that vindication. Even though Job was in fact a righteous man (God Himself had pronounced him so), when he suffered physically he was falsely accused of having brought his suffering upon himself. He was reproached not merely by his so-called friends but by the Accuser. Our ultimate Accuser is always the Evil One, for we don't *"wrestle against flesh and blood"* but *"against the spiritual forces of evil in the heavenly realms"* {Eph. 6:12}. Thus, God's and our vindication is ultimately over the Accuser and his legions. Sweet indeed will be that victory!

In the depths of his pain, Job's faith faltered a bit. (Who could blame him?) But, in his heart of hearts, Job trusted God to ultimately vindicate his righteousness. He knew that his accuser, Elihu, was unwittingly correct: eventually and inevitably,

> *God repays a man for what he has done. He brings upon*
> *him what his conduct deserves. It is unthinkable that God*
> *would do wrong, that the Almighty would pervert justice.*
> (Job 34:11-12)[1]

Speaking through the prophet Malachi, God recounted charges brought against Him by His own people:

> *You say, "It is futile to serve God. What did we gain*
> *by carrying out his requirements and going about like*
> *mourners before the LORD Almighty? . . . Certainly*
> *evildoers prosper, and even when they put God to the*
> *test, they get away with it."* (Mal. 3:14)

They won't get away with it![2] And there is much to be gained for *"carrying out His requirements."* A *"scroll of remembrance,"* to be read at the end of time, has been prepared *"concerning those who feared the Lord and honored His name"* (Mal.3:16-18). God will read that scroll and make good on his promise to vindicate. In doing so, God will vindicate Himself.

David prayed,

*Vindicate me, O LORD, for I have led a blameless life; I have trusted in the LORD without wavering.* (Ps. 26:1) . . . *Surely there is a God who judges the earth.* (Ps. 58:10-11)

*May those who delight in my vindication shout for joy and gladness; may they always say, The LORD be exalted, who delights in the well-being of his servant.* (Ps. 35:27)

David lived in faith that

*. . . the LORD will vindicate his people and have compassion on his servants.* (Ps. 135:14)

David believed that

*He who has clean hands and a pure heart. . . will receive blessing from the Lord and vindication from God our Savior.* (Ps. 24:4-5)

David's petition in Psalm 35:24, "*Vindicate me in your righteousness, O LORD my God; do not let them gloat over me,*" prayed by Jesus and by generations of followers of Jesus, will finally and forever be answered. The time of gloating for the Evil One and all who follow him will end—once and for all—when God publicly vindicates His own. Sin and evil will have been dealt the ultimate blow. The last word will have been spoken.

*This is the heritage of the servants of the LORD, and this is their vindication from me, declares the LORD.* (Isa. 54:17)

When God proclaims his vindication to all of heaven, He will have satisfied the debt He obligated Himself to pay when He promised to reward {2 Tim. 2:9}. To the extent you patiently endured ridicule or shame or persecution or hardship—and to the extent that in the midst of it you "*humbled yourself under his almighty hand,*" trusting in him to "*lift you up at the proper time*" (1 Pet. 5:6)—God will vindicate Himself as He rewards you with His vindication.

126

*Therefore, my dear brothers, stand firm. Let nothing move you. Always give yourselves fully to the work of the Lord, because you know that your labor in the Lord is not in vain.* (1 Cor. 15:58)

## Look Back

One reason we know God will vindicate Himself and us someday is that He has done so in the past. Here is what God said to the people of Israel as they were poised to enter the Promised Land:

*Remember today that your children were not the ones who saw and experienced the discipline of the Lord your God: his majesty, his mighty hand, his outstretched arm; the signs he performed and the things he did in the heart of Egypt, both to Pharaoh king of Egypt and to his whole country; what he did to the Egyptian army, to its horses and chariots, how he overwhelmed them with the waters of the Red Sea as they were pursuing you, and how the Lord brought lasting ruin on them. It was not your children who saw what he did for you in the wilderness . . ., it was your own eyes that saw all these great things the Lord has done.* {Deut. 11:1-7}

Over and over again in the Bible, God tells His people to remember, recall, bring to mind, what He did for them in the past, so that they will know He can be trusted in the present. Not looking back to what God has done will deliver the same fate to you as that of those Israelites who doubted God: They were not allowed into the Promised Land. They died in the wilderness.

When you doubt that God will vindicate you, look back at what He has done for His people in the Bible, for you, and for others. Share your experiences of God's goodness with others, and vice versa, that we all will have greater hope in God's goodness.

Notice that God says, *"It was not your children who saw what he did for you in the wilderness . . . it was your own eyes that saw all these great things the Lord has done."* Why did He say that? God understands that some people have seen more evidence of God's work than others. Some

127

people have had many recent occasions to see God's provision in their lives. Such blessing comes with a heavy responsibility, however. We, like the adults to whom God spoke at the Jordan River's edge, were commanded to "*remember*" and act on those firsthand memories.

On the other hand, many of us look back at our lives and see less evidence of God's work. (The children of those who were delivered from Egypt, for instance. Job is an even better example.) Sometimes when we look back, all we see are the painful circumstances of our lives. So how are these weary souls encouraged by remembering?

Such people can only trust the promises of what is to come. They, more than most, draw courage in the hope that God will deliver on his promises. Theirs is a prospective look-back. They look forward to the day when they will finally turn around and look back; when God vindicates their faith as He shows them what He accomplished in and through their struggles. Frankly, I expect those who have suffered—either in situations beyond their control or because they chose to follow God into painful places—will end up with the lion's share of God's rewards.

We began this chapter with the idea of "underdog." Hollywood uses that storyline because they recognize our deep desire for vindication. Their stories give us hope that we will win in this life. But let us find our encouragement not in things of this world but in the hope of our ultimate vindication from God.

That God will vindicate Himself and His faithful people is **central** to God's purposes—not peripheral or tangential to them. God created the universe and the people in it that all might know His true character. Therefore, as God vindicates Himself and publicly vindicates His faithful followers, God will finally and definitively establish His trustworthiness, for He will have made good on His promise to reward both sin and faithfulness.

For that vindication we will praise Him for all of eternity. That is why it is essential for us to seek and to work for the rewards that God promises so that—*all the more*—God will be glorified when He makes good on His promises.

*Notes and Asides:*

1  *Through spoken by one of Job's "friends" as an accusation, that verse is the central message of the book of Job: God is just and He will vindicate and repay us for our faithfulness to Him. Job's vindication came in his lifetime (Job 42:7-17). But many of the righteous must wait in hope for their vindication at the Judgment Seat of Christ. They will be rewarded for their patient faith. As James said, "You have heard of Job's perseverance and have seen what the Lord finally brought about" (James 5:11).*

*Most often, however, our teachers summarize the book with this:"God is God and you are not. Get used to it!" That certainly is true; but if that is the only message heard in the pews, then God is not properly portrayed as the compassionate God of the Bible who promises to someday vindicate the righteous. Thus, the image of God's character is perverted, as it was in the Greek philosopher's conclusion in chapter 3.*

2  *Our general expectation is that those pronounced guilty are not followers of Christ. But what if the vindication, for example, is of destructive gossip perpetrated by a Christian? Perhaps Jesus will simply pronounce the victim righteous. But it seems more likely that the vindication will be like that in the book of Job, where Job's accusers, Eliphaz the Temanite, Bildad the Shuhite, and Zophar the Naamathite, are called to account by name.*

129

# Chapter 11  The Reward of
# Authority and Responsibility

In chapter 7, we discussed the master's commendation in the parable of the talents in Matthew 25. The obedient servants received more than the master's praise, however.

> [Since] *you have been faithful with a few things, I will put you in charge of many things.* (Matt. 5:21, 23)

We find a similar teaching in Luke 19:11-27, in which the master entrusts his servants with one mina each. The two servants who had been faithful with the master's possessions were first commended by the master, and then they were given responsibility proportional to their opportunity for, and success in, increasing the master's wealth. The one who earned ten minas was put in charge of ten cities. The one who earned five minas was put in charge of five cities.

**Responsibility**

What does it mean to be put in charge of "cities"? Will some rule over others in heaven? Will there actually be a hierarchy? Such would not comport with the supposition that heaven is an egalitarian place. What are the *"many things"* over which the faithful will be placed in charge? What sort of *"things"* could possibly need looking after in heaven? Will someone be the plant manager of Royal Crown Manufacturing? Will another be appointed head of the Department of Golden Streets and Sanitation? That's preposterous, I know, but what is Jesus telling us?

A clue to the answer is found in Matthew 24:45-47, the chapter before the parable of the talents. (See also Luke 19:11-26.) Jesus speaks of a servant

130

*"whom the master has put in charge of the servants in his household to give them their food at the proper time."* Jesus continues,

> *It will be good for that servant whose master finds him doing so when he returns. I tell you the truth, he will put him in charge of all my possessions.* (vv. 46-47)

Now, when Jesus says, *"I tell you the truth"*—as he does over four dozen times in the gospels—we do well to pay attention. Seven times in our collection of verses, Jesus says, *"I tell you the truth"* about rewards for obedience (Matt. 10:42, 19:28, 24:47; Luke 18:29; Mark 9:41; 10:29; John 12:24). Jesus says that those who are faithful in looking after the needs of *"the servants in his household"* will be put in charge of all his possessions. Possessions? What does God possess that is of such great value that He will entrust it only to those who have demonstrated faithfulness? Is it not His people? Look at how God describes His people in the Bible.

> *And the LORD has declared this day that you are his people, his treasured possession . . .* (Deut. 26:18)

> *The LORD your God has chosen you out of all the peoples on the face of the earth to be his people, his treasured possession.* (Deut. 7:6) (See also Exod. 14:2; 19:5; Ps. 135:4; Mal. 3:17)

God's people are not merely His possessions; they are His *"treasured"* possessions, *"a chosen people, a royal priesthood, a holy nation, a people belonging to God"* (1 Pet. 2:9). Such precious treasure is kept safe and well-guarded by God. God will only entrust their care to those who have demonstrated their trustworthiness in doing so.

So, for the servant who is faithful to look after the needs of God's most valuable possessions, the servants of God's household, the reward is *even more* responsibility in looking after His household. Those who lovingly and with humility serve God's people in this life will be given a treasure of *people* to serve—forever.

Now that seems a dubious reward, doesn't it? Serving people is hard work. It takes effort to sacrifice one's own desires and time. It takes energy and dedication. It takes humility and patience. A respite from serving people seems more appropriate as a reward for serving people! "Now you are telling me that my *eternal reward* is more of the same?" you ask.

Well, not exactly. Those whom we serve in heaven will no longer be a burden because all of us will be free of sin and sin's consequences. What will be left to do is that which made the service rewarding even in this life: being a conduit of God's love, or, as Peter puts it, *"faithfully administering God's grace . . ."* (1 Pet. 4:10).

It is hard to imagine what it will be like to serve people in heaven when that service no longer involves helping them in their weakness and struggle. But we do get glimpses of such service as we lead others into the presence of God in prayer; as we encourage them; as we display Christ in our actions; as we lead in Bible study, in worship, and in song; as we sing for God before others; and as we proclaim God's goodness and mercy. When we perform such service in this life, we experience a unique sense of fulfillment: of being a means—a channel—of God's grace. Anyone who has had that experience understands what I am talking about.[1]

Those who are practiced in leading others into worship and praise of God—in whatever manner—will be given the responsibility of leading *"cities"* filled with people in praise and worship of God, as *"every creature in heaven and on earth and under the earth and on the sea, and all that is in them"* sing: *"To him who sits on the throne and to the Lamb be praise and honor and glory and power, forever and ever!"* (Rev. 5:13).

As I said earlier, there will be a finite number of people to serve in heaven, and there will be an infinite amount of time for leading those people in praise of God; therefore, there is no limit to the opportunity the faithful will have to enjoy this reward of glorious responsibility. All who are faithful will have an eternity of time to lead heaven's hosts in their endless worship of God.

## Authority

While in exile in Babylon, Daniel was given authority of position in the kingdom of his captors. But he answered to a higher authority—and his loyalty to that Authority landed him in the lion's den. His offense? Praying to God. Daniel was dedicated to prayer. And God heard and answered his prayers.

*While I was speaking and praying, confessing my sin and the sin of my people Israel and making my request to the Lord my God for his holy hill—while I was still in prayer, Gabriel, the man I had seen in the earlier vision, came to me in swift flight about the time of the evening sacrifice. He instructed me and said to me, "Daniel, I have now come to give you insight and understanding. As soon as you began to pray, a word went out, which I have come to tell you, **for you are highly esteemed**."* (Dan. 9:20-23)[2]

But God did not always answer Daniel's prayers so quickly.

*At that time I, Daniel, mourned for three weeks. I ate no choice food; no meat or wine touched my lips; and I used no lotions at all until the three weeks were over. On the twenty-fourth day of the first month, as I was standing on the bank of the great river, the Tigris, I looked up and there before me was [a divine being].*

*He said, "Daniel, **you who are highly esteemed**, consider carefully the words I am about to speak to you, and stand up, for I have now been sent to you." "Do not be afraid, Daniel. Since the first day that you set your mind to gain understanding and to humble yourself before your God, your words were heard, and I have come in response to them. But the prince of the Persian kingdom resisted me twenty-one days. Then Michael, one of the chief princes, came to help me, because I was detained there with the king of Persia."*

*"Do not be afraid, **you who are highly esteemed**," he said. "Peace! Be strong now; be strong." When he spoke to me, I was strengthened and said, "Speak, my lord, since you have given me strength."* {Dan. 10:2-19, selected verses}

As in chapter 9, the divine being told Daniel—twice—that he was *"highly esteemed."* By whom was Daniel held in high regard? By no less than God Himself. Pause and think about that. Daniel's faith impresses the

Creator of the Universe! Why was Daniel esteemed? Because he earnestly and regularly submitted himself to God in prayer. As a result, God gave him strength and encouragement.

This passage also gives us a glimpse at a dimension of which we are only vaguely aware—of spiritual forces of good and evil. How could a divine being acting on God's behalf be hindered in his purpose by the demon that ruled Persia? The cosmic struggle between God and the Accuser is impossible for us to understand, but clearly, the battle is real. The enemy is potent {cf. 1 Thess. 2:18}.

And notice that while the agent of God fought the powers of darkness, Daniel persisted in prayer and fasting. In doing so, Daniel participated unaware in that celestial battle. Daniel exercised authority over spiritual forces through three weeks of prayer and fasting.

*"Jesus Himself would often slip away to the wilderness and pray"* {Luke 5:16}. Why would Jesus pray? He is God the Son, a member of the Trinity. But He is also a man. There is much that we do not understand about the incarnation, but Jesus, like Daniel, needed—and wanted—to be in the Father's presence in prayer. Jesus gained His strength to fight the Evil One through prayer. Do we need the power of prayer in our lives less than Jesus did?

I have heard it suggested that the Accuser has a custom-designed program of destruction for each of us. That may be true. It makes sense that he and his army would study me to know my weaknesses and hit me where I am most vulnerable. That's why Peter warns us to *"Be alert. Your enemy the devil prowls around like a hungry lion looking for someone to devour"* (1 Pet. 5:8).

Fortunately, our army's Commander has a plan, too. When Messiah Jesus came, His followers expected that He would overthrow the Romans and establish an earthly kingdom. But Christ's Kingdom will accomplish far more: the eventual destruction of the real enemy of mankind. We are invited to share in that overthrow of evil, but . . .

> *The weapons we fight with are not the weapons of the world. On the contrary, they have divine power to demolish strongholds. We demolish arguments and every pretension that sets itself up against the knowledge of God, and we take captive every thought to make it obedient to Christ.*
> (2 Cor. 10:4-5)

The strongholds of which Paul wrote were those of the devil and his demons. We have been given authority over those forces of darkness.

> *That power is the same as the mighty strength he exerted when he raised Christ from the dead and seated him at his right hand in the heavenly realms, far above all rule and authority, power and dominion, and every name that is invoked, not only in the present age but also in the one to come.* (Eph. 1:19b-21)

We share this *"incomparably great power"* (v. 19a) with Jesus in this life and—to the extent we exercise it in this life—in the life to come. This life's battles earn us a share in His Kingdom Authority, in this life and the next. Our reward is and will be to rule with Him.

> God has the power to overcome Satan without the cooperation of his church through prayer and faith, but if he did it without her it would deprive her of enforcement practice and rob her of the strength she would gain in overcoming. (Billheimer, 100)

> *Submit yourselves therefore to God. Resist the devil, and he will flee from you. Draw near to God, and he will draw near to you.* (James 4:7-8)

As in any battle, there will be casualties. While the Evil One cannot destroy the soul, he can kill the body. He killed Jesus, and he has slaughtered countless Christians throughout history. Most of us in the West will never know physical persecution.[3] But all around us is sin and evil to fight and to conquer. Our way is easy because we have taken too many pains to avoid pain. We have not yet joined the battle. Our lukewarm faith makes us unworthy of the Evil One's attention. But to those who engage the enemy and overcome, authority will be given in the life to come. Jesus will invite the faithful to share in His rule!

> *To him who overcomes and does my will to the end, I will give authority over the nations.* (Rev. 2:26)

135

> *To him who overcomes, I will give the right to sit with me on my throne, just as I overcame and sat down with my Father on his throne.* (Rev. 3:21)

That authority will be exercised on behalf of the Servant King, Jesus, by those who have demonstrated faithfulness as a humble servant in this life. It will be given only to *"him who overcomes."* That authority is both earned and exercised in ways that are different from those of the world.

> *You know that those who are regarded as rulers of the Gentiles lord it over them, and their high officials exercise authority over them. Not so with you. Instead, whoever wants to become great among you must be your servant, and whoever wants to be first must be slave of all. For even the Son of Man did not come to be served, **but to serve,** and to give his life as a ransom for many.* (Mark 10:42-45; Matt. 20:24-28)

God's reward of authority and responsibility is counterintuitive and countercultural because our thinking is backward. *"The last will be first,"* remember? Those who are *first* in heaven will have received God's reward for making themselves the *least* in this life. Humility is not inconsistent with greatness. On the contrary: humble service to God and people is the means to greatness in God's Kingdom.

> *Truly I tell you, at the renewal of all things, when the Son of Man sits on his glorious throne, you who have followed me will also sit on twelve thrones, judging the twelve tribes of Israel.* (Matt. 19:28)[4]

Do you think that overcoming and following Jesus means merely claiming Jesus as your Savior? Then why did Jesus say, *"Whoever does not bear his own cross and come after me cannot be my disciple"* (Luke 14:27)? One is saved by trusting in Jesus, but one is not a true disciple without a sacrifice of one's life, even as Jesus did.

The *"twelve tribes of Israel"* that genuine followers of Jesus will rule are all children of God: Jews and Gentiles who have been grafted into the Jewish nation. Those who have followed Christ's example of sacrifice will share His leadership of the inhabitants of heaven. It is difficult to comprehend the governance of His Kingdom because it will be unlike any in this world, where ruling requires obedience by pain of sanction. But in Christ's Kingdom, all (i.e., the twelve tribes) will be willing subjects and some of those people (those who sacrificed themselves in this life) will have positions of authority over others.

> *If you will walk in my ways and keep my requirements, then you will govern my house and have charge of my courts, and I will give you a place among these standing here.* (Zech. 3:7)

We can only have a vision of such leadership by God's Spirit and as we practice it in this life. So my prayer is that of Paul:

> *I pray that the eyes of your heart may be enlightened in order that you may know the hope to which he has called you, the riches of his glorious inheritance in his holy people.* (Eph. 1:18-19)

This great and unending privilege to serve God by leading others is one of God's great rewards.

**Notes and Asides:**

[1]  *It has been my great privilege to lead others in singing praises to God as a worship leader. It is a joy that—for me—is like no other. And yet, when I stand before a congregation, I am keenly aware of limitations that dampen my experience: First is ordinary self-consciousness: I'm in front of a lot of people I know—singing! Second, I am mindful of the sound of my voice, the notes I am singing, the rhythms, the words I am saying—and of my mistakes. But to the extent that I am not distracted by those self-centered concerns, I run into another barrier: when I am in unfettered worship of God, I literally cannot sing! I get choked up. The beauty of being in God's presence overwhelms me—especially if I raise my hands toward heaven as I sing.*

*I've dealt with a physical impediment to singing, too: a deviated septum in my nose, recently surgically removed. My doctor told me that after the surgery I will inhale and think to myself, "So this is how breathing is supposed to feel!" He is right! I wish I'd had the problem fixed years ago. And singing is almost effortless, now that the obstruction in my nose is gone. I feel like I've died and gone to heaven.*

*Someday, all such hindrances to praising God will vanish. I will be free to let my heart soar, to revel in glorifying God, and—I fervently hope—to lead others in doing so. What will it be like to be completely emptied of myself and given wholly over to God? I can begin to imagine when I lead in worship. Maybe God will let me sing a solo in heaven! And maybe—finally!—I'll be able to break into the third octave above middle C!*

[2]  *The "holy hill" for which Daniel prayed was Jerusalem, to which Daniel and his people longed to return. God had warned the children of Israel by his prophets that they would suffer captivity by the Babylonians for seventy years because of their sin. (At the Museum of the Bible, you can look upon actual spearheads used against the Israelites during the siege that resulted in the destruction of Jerusalem and of Solomon's Temple.) Daniel longed for the return to the Promised Land, even as we yearn for the return of Jesus and the establishment of His Kingdom.*

[3]  *I recommend* Tortured for Christ, *the cinematic retelling of the testimony of "Voice of the Martyrs" founder Pastor Richard Wurmbrand, based upon the book by that title. It is a sobering yet beautiful portrayal*

*of Christ's love in response to hatred from the Evil One. As I say elsewhere in <u>Investing in Eternity</u>, persecution is the experience of one in three Christians in the world. We may never be called to endure such oppression, but someday your children or grandchildren may be. It is for us to set the example of sacrificial living for them—and teach them of God's promises to reward—that they might be better prepared if or when it comes.*

4  *There are at least twenty-four thrones in heaven besides that on which Jesus sits. See Revelation 11:16 and 19:4.*

# Chapter 12  The Reward of Suffering with Christ

All the rewards we have discussed to this point are clearly experienced as pleasant emotions. This last one is not obviously so. It may seem more appropriately addressed as a grim *means* of gaining a reward from Christ, to be discussed in the next section of the book. Suffering hardly presents itself as a *reward*.

To be sure, faithfully suffering for Christ leads to God's reward. All that God allows into our lives, including suffering, results in something "*good*" for those who love Him (Rom. 8:28). For example, suffering produces a refinement of our character.

> *We also glory in our sufferings, because we know that suffering produces perseverance; perseverance, character; and character, hope.* (Rom. 5:10)

> *Therefore I am well content with weaknesses, with insults, with distresses, with persecutions, with difficulties, for Christ's sake; for when I am weak, then I am strong.* (1 Cor. 12:10)

Part of that reward for suffering is the opportunity it affords to comfort others who also suffer. For when people we love suffer as we have suffered,

> *we will be able to give them the same comfort God has given us. For the more we suffer for Christ, the more God will shower us with his comfort through Christ . . .* [and] *when we ourselves are comforted, we will certainly comfort you.* (2 Cor. 1:4, 7 NLT)

People who have not suffered simply cannot comprehend the pain of people who do. Neither can they as fully experience the joy of sharing the burdens of others.

So, suffering produces blessings to come. But more than other rewards from God, suffering is also a reward in itself. As such, this reward serves as a fitting transition to the next section, *How God's Rewards Are Gained.*

## Joy at the Prospect of Reward

Much of the reward we experience *during suffering* is at the *prospect* of the reward that will come as a result—when we trust that *"weeping may spend the night, but there is joy in the morning"* {Ps. 30:5}. The anticipation of joy is the reward of faith in God's promises.

Jesus modeled this for us when He endured the cross because of *"the joy set before him"* {Heb. 2:12}. Luke tells us, *"The apostles left the Sanhedrin, rejoicing because they had been counted worthy of suffering disgrace for the name of Christ"* (Acts 5:41). Peter writes, *"Rejoice inasmuch as you participate in the sufferings of Christ, so that you may be overjoyed when his glory is revealed"* (1 Pet. 4:13).

Paul encouraged the Roman church on the eve of intense persecution from the Romans:

> Now if we are children, then we are heirs—heirs of God and
> co-heirs with Christ, if indeed we share in his sufferings in
> order that we may also share in his glory. I consider that
> our present sufferings are not worth comparing with the
> glory that will be revealed in us. (Rom. 8:17-18)

Jesus taught us in the Sermon on the Mount that we can have happiness now—in the midst of suffering—as we look forward to our reward.

> Happy are you when people insult you and persecute you
> and tell all kinds of evil lies against you because you are
> my followers. Be happy and glad, for a great reward is
> kept for you in heaven. (Matt. 5:11-12 GNT)

Peter must have been taking notes on the sermon that day because he echoed Jesus.

> *In this you greatly rejoice, though now for a little while*
> *you may have had to suffer grief in all kinds of trials.*
> *These have come so that your faith—of greater worth than*
> *gold, which perishes even though refined by fire—may be*
> *proved genuine and may result in praise, glory and honor*
> *when Jesus Christ is revealed.* (1 Pet. 1:6-7)

*"In this you greatly rejoice"* is in the present. The joy Jesus and the apostles experienced in present suffering was a foretaste and an expectation of the joy to come. Much of that rejoicing is at the prospect of the *"praise, glory and honor"* to be bestowed in heaven upon Jesus *and* upon those whose faith was proved genuine.[1]

## The present experience of joy

"But, how can I rejoice during suffering—at the prospect of something I have not yet experienced? Can a caterpillar imagine himself a butterfly? I may take some small consolation in the hope that my pain will produce something good, but in the meantime, *it hurts*! I may see a speck of sky blue from where I sit at the bottom of my mile-deep well of sorrow, but meanwhile, I am sitting in the dark, cold, wet, and alone. I am supposed to be happy about that?! Am I called to be a masochist?"

Not at all. Because the joy of which Jesus and the apostles spoke isn't *merely* prospective. It isn't only the hope of something to look forward to as a reward for suffering, to only be experienced in the future. It is a reward itself, experienced in the moment we suffer. Look again at what Peter wrote: *"Rejoice inasmuch as you participate in the sufferings of Christ, so that you may be overjoyed when his glory is **revealed**."* He continues, *"If you are insulted because of the name of Christ, **you are blessed** . . ."* (1 Pet. 4:13-14).

The complete revelation (unveiling, uncovering) of Christ's glory will come in the future. But the Greek word *"apokalypsei"* translated "revealed" is in a form that does not bind it to a particular tense. Peter speaks of when Christ's glory *is* revealed, not *will be* revealed. So it speaks not only of the future revelation of Christ and the reward that He will bestow at that time: it is a revelation of Jesus that comes during suffering—in the moment it is experienced. Peter rejoiced *during* painful circumstances. In suffering, *"you are blessed."*[2]

Likewise, Paul wrote to the Colossians, "I rejoice *in* my suffering . . ." (Col. 1:24). And to the Corinthians,

> *We always carry around in our body the death of Jesus,*
> *so that the life of Jesus may also be revealed in our body.*
> *For we who are alive are always being given over to death*
> *for Jesus' sake, so that his life may also be revealed in our*
> *mortal body.* (1 Cor. 4:10-11)

Jesus is *"revealed"* in our suffering? To whom? To those around us, but also to the suffering person himself *"in our mortal body."* So Christ is revealed to us—in this life—during suffering!

## Suffering with Christ

But what does that mean? Perhaps this will illustrate.

*Henry V* is my favorite of Shakespeare's plays. Henry's climactic speech on St. Crispin's Day—as his vastly outnumbered troops were about to go into battle—is my favorite scene. And these are my favorite lines from that speech.

> We few, we happy few,
> we band of brothers;
> For he today that sheds his blood with me
> Shall be my brother.

The shared experience of an epic battle—the mortal dangers; the shared sense of never feeling more alive; the trust of each other with their very lives; participation in a story that will be recounted through the ages—creates an unbreakable bond amongst the "band of brothers."

This is what it is like to share in Christ's suffering. Christ's glory is revealed as we share the experience of suffering *with* Jesus. We share His rejection. We share His experience of the ugliness of sin. We share the love that made Him take the curse of sin upon Himself. And we share His work as we complete *"what is lacking in Christ's afflictions"* (Col. 1:24). In that sharing, God transforms pain into glory.[3]

> *For it has been granted to you on behalf of Christ not only*
> *to believe in him, but also to suffer for him.* {Phil 1:29}

Jesus cannot empathize with our experience of sin because He never sinned, but he does empathize with our weakness because He suffered weakness too.

> *This High Priest of ours understands our weaknesses, for*
> *he faced all of the same testings we do, yet he did not sin.*
> (Heb. 4:15 NLT)

But this is no mere sharing of similar—but distinctly different—experiences. It is not as if Jesus says, "Yes, my child, I went through that, too, back in the day. I can relate." Remember how Jesus mourned with those who mourned the death of Lazarus? He knew He was about to raise Lazarus from the dead, yet *"Jesus wept"* {John 11:35}. Why? He wept—*"was deeply moved and troubled"*—because those He loved were suffering the painful effects of sin and death.

Jesus suffers with us as we experience pain. Why can I say that? Because He lives inside of us.[4] He is no neutral observer of our pain who commiserates with "There, there . . ." He hurts—in real time—with us {2 Cor. 13:5}. He loves us, so how could He not hurt with us? Jesus not only endured the physical and emotional pain of the cross but also He continues to endure—through and with us—the suffering of mankind's rejection and rebellion. Our reward is to share—to suffer—that pain with Christ.

In such moments, we not only *endure* suffering, we *embrace* it. Suffering doesn't only produce a *"good" for us,* it becomes a *"good" in us,* as we share Christ's work of suffering. As Paul wrote,

> *I want to know Christ and the power of his resurrection*
> *and the fellowship of sharing in his sufferings, becoming*
> *like him in his death.* (Phil. 3:10)

Someone once verbally attacked me with a ferocity that I felt as if the Accuser himself was speaking the lies through him. My instinct was to flee, but I sensed God telling me to stay. For three hours, he accused and slandered. Many of the accusations were about real sins I had committed many years ago and which I had long ago confessed to God and those affected. Others were of more recent sins, likewise true and likewise confessed. But most were lies and distortions of the truth.

As the vicious accusations poured out, hour after hour, my armor held. Not one—not one—penetrated my heart! Not one provoked a defensive response. No word of protestation came from my lips. Not only did I remain silent . . . I was not even inclined to speak. (If you know me, you know how uncharacteristic that is of me.)

Instead, I just stood there and observed with amazement—as if from afar—what God was doing in and for me. As the enemy raged, I realized that he was powerless. All he had to hurl at me were lies and half-truths—and they bounced off like arrows off a shield.

Jesus showed me that I was experiencing what He endured when He was falsely accused. He too had been mocked. He also suffered lies from the father of lies. And, most importantly, He revealed to my heart that, since God loves me and the Accuser hates anyone who trusts in God, all the lies being spoken to me in that moment were directed ultimately at Him. I have never been so aware of what was happening.

Then, miraculously, I felt an intense love for my human attacker. I could see the ugliness of his enslavement. I had compassion for him. My heart prayed, *"Forgive them, for they know not what they do."* I wanted deliverance for my attacker. And God assured me it would happen. In His time, and after more such attacks, He would rescue him. This was but a battle in a war that Christ has already won. And I had participated in that battle. It was nothing short of glorious.

My suffering was transformed into joy as the Spirit of God revealed to my spirit that I was suffering with Jesus! I didn't merely share a common circumstance of Christ's life. I shared my experience *with* Him as I felt His presence in me, suffering with me. As Paul put it, I experienced *"fellowship"* with Christ. 24/365, God suffers the attacks of the Evil One upon His beloved people. He often doesn't deliver us from our suffering in this life *so that* He can meet us *in His suffering.*

So suffering is both a reward of fellowship with Christ and a means to other rewards for faithfulness.

*If when you do what is right and suffer for it and you*
*patiently endure it, this finds favor with God. (1 Pet. 1:22)*

We will share that fellowship with Christ for all of eternity—to the extent we enter the battle. Do you remember when I said this back in chapter 4?

> Just as our memory of God's goodness remained after the Fall {Rom. 2:15},[7] a God-filtered memory of our experience of Evil's evilness will remain after our resurrection {John 20:20; 1 Cor. 13:12}. That memory will be devoid of the experience of pain {Rev. 21:4}, but it will be fully aware of what God accomplished through that pain {Joel 2:27; Phil. 1:12}. Because we will have that memory of Evil, we will forever possess the knowledge of the *difference* between God's goodness and Evil's evilness.
>
> As a result, for all of eternity, followers of Christ will never again want to experience Evil. We will have been inoculated against the disease of sin. God will have used mankind's rebellion against Him for the "good" of those who love Him (Rom. 8:28). There will be no repeat of Adam and Eve's bad choice, for we will freely and forever choose to stay in a loving relationship with our good God. And we will praise Him forever for having made that possible.

Those who fought life's battles with Jesus will share in God's glorious victories over sin and evil in this life and the next. Believe me, you will not want to be like the men of whom Henry V spoke at the end of his speech:

> And gentlemen in England now a-bed
> Shall think themselves accursed they were not here,
> And hold their manhood's cheap whiles any speaks
> That fought with us upon Saint Crispin's day.

## Join the Battle

Not everyone is called to share the glory of wielding a sword on the front lines of that battle, though all of us must stand ready and willing to do so. Some are called to serve in other ways. What are your Commander's specific orders, soldier?

As you pray for them, don't forget that you have a standing order: Love people. It's a hard post. We know that our love of God is *always* reciprocated. When we love God, He is always ready to accept it, to give it back to us, to comfort us; to affirm us. As with love between a husband and wife, that reciprocity is what makes loving God so satisfying.

But people, to say the least, are not as dependable as God. When we love people with a godly, "*phileo*" love, we sometimes find that love unreturned or rejected. They may even hate us in return. In rejecting our love, they reject us. And as a man from Nazareth (the '70s rock band, that is) sang of rejection, "Love hurts." It hurts Jesus too.[5]

Sometimes our love of people produces a harvest of blessings. At other times it produces a harvest of pain that is transformed by God into a gloriously deepened relationship with Jesus. Either way, we are rewarded for our faithfulness. So, love! Love boldly. Love well! Even if it hurts!

Where are *your* opportunities to show love to people?

Is your boss unreasonably demanding? Do you wish you could find other work, but for whatever reason, you can't or shouldn't? If God wants you to be in this job, with this boss, and for this season, then—to the extent that you faithfully execute that God-given assignment, endure humiliation, show kindness when none is returned, and do so out of a desire to be faithful to God—rest assured, God notices. So,

> *Obey your earthly masters with respect and fear, and*
> *with sincerity of heart, just as you would obey Christ . . .*
> *because you know that the Lord will reward everyone for*
> *whatever good he does.* (Eph. 6:5-8)

Do you have children for whom you have lovingly toiled only to have them turn their back on you, curse you and your God, and pursue a life of sin? There is nothing more painful to endure than the waywardness of a child. Paul ached so much for his Jewish family that, if it were possible, he would have given himself up for their sake to eternal damnation. When you cry out before God on your child's behalf with tears and sorrow, you share in Christ's suffering.

For all of your efforts, does your spouse not return your love? Does he not show kindness and understanding? Does he not model Christ's headship? Does your wife not meet your desire for intimacy? To the extent you love your spouse as Jesus loves the Church, to the extent that you relinquish your rights and demands, to the extent you endure the ache of loneliness and sadness for the sake of Jesus, to the extent that you suffer in intercession on behalf of your spouse, you suffer with Christ.

> Do you experience sadness for being childless or unmarried?
> Do you wrestle with emotional or spiritual weaknesses?
> Do you have a vulnerability to depression or anxiety?
> Do you have intractable disabilities or pain?
> Do you feel alone and friendless?
> Do you struggle financially?

In what ways are *you* suffering? Are you sharing your pain with Jesus? Are you bringing those trials or heartaches before the Father in prayer? Is it your desire to be faithful to God in the midst of the trials? If so, then rejoice! You are experiencing the joy of suffering with Christ!

> It is in the quiet crucible of your personal private sufferings
> that your noblest dreams are born and God's greatest gifts are given
> in compensation for what you've been through.
> (Wintley Phipps)

**Notes and Asides:**

1    *See chapters 7–9 for an explanation of why the "glory, honor and praise" are bestowed both on Jesus and on His faithful followers.*

2    *While it probably originated as a substitute for exclamations of "Good God," "Good grief!"—an expression that predates Charles Schulz's Charlie Brown—would be suitably used to express an understanding that grief and pain can be "good."*

3    *It is as if God, unlike the frustrated alchemist, actually transforms lead into gold.*

4    *The Greek word for "in" (ἐν) is the same word used to describe Mary "being with" (i.e., pregnant with) the Christ child (Matt. 1:18 and other verses). Jesus (in the person of the Holy Spirit) is **in** us.*

   *Given the nature of love and this example of it in particular, it seems the doctrine of God's impassibility is an impossibility, at least as it relates to the pain of love's rejection. Much of our own emotionally painful suffering is **for** Christ, but how could that suffering be **with** Christ if He doesn't likewise suffer?*

   *When God decided to join Himself to that race in the person of Jesus, Sovereign God voluntarily allowed Himself to feel the pain inherent to love's rejection. No doubt God's pain is incomprehensible to us, but that doesn't mean that He does not feel it. I believe, therefore, that the doctrine of God's impassibility diminishes our understanding of God's love.*

5    *Love can hurt so much that it overwhelms any pleasure in the promise of God's reward for loving people. I have wondered: How can I take comfort in the knowledge that God rewards my love when a person I love is apart from God and, worse, that they may never come to know Him? It is simply too painful! The answer to that dilemma is beyond my understanding, as is my comprehension of how God Himself can "endure" (if that is the right word) the pain of His rejected love. Nevertheless, it is in those moments I most fully share in Christ's suffering—and that is glorious.*

# Section 3  How God's Rewards Are Gained

What I have said in this and previous chapters about the nature of rewards are, at best, introductions to what is in store for the servants of God. Inevitably, my words and ideas will fall short—because what we are attempting to anticipate is the experience of heaven itself. Our understanding of the infinite is—to infinitely understate the matter—limited: *"For now, we see only a reflection as in a mirror; then we shall see face to face. Now I know in part; then I shall know fully, even as I am fully known"* {1 Cor. 3:12}.

So, while we have examined some broad and crucial aspects of the Bible's teaching on rewards (some of which have been sorely neglected in the Church's teaching), I make no pretense at having exhausted the riches of God's promises. Indeed, we have barely scratched the surface: *"Such knowledge is too wonderful for me, too lofty for me to attain"* {Ps. 139:6}.

Nevertheless (to quote Paul again) there is a level of understanding that we can have because . . .

> *What no eye has seen, what no ear has heard, and what no*
> *human mind has conceived—the things God has prepared*
> *for those who love him—these are the things God has*
> *revealed to us by his Spirit. The Spirit searches all things,*
> *even the deep things of God.* (1 Cor. 2:9-10)

Those words of Paul remind me of something Job said. With great determination, a man digs deep for buried treasure! *"But where,"* Job asks, *"can wisdom be found? Where does understanding dwell?"*

> *There is a mine for silver and a place where gold is*
> *refined.*

151

> *Man searches the farthest recesses for ore in the blackest darkness.*
>
> *Far from where people dwell he cuts a shaft; far from men he dangles and sways.*
>
> *Sapphires come from its rocks and its dust contains nuggets of gold.*
>
> *Man's hand assaults the flinty rock and lays bare the roots of the mountains.*
>
> *He tunnels through the rock; his eyes see all its treasures.* {Job 28, selected verses}

That passage's message is that wisdom and understanding are found in the same way that Job's miner finds his treasure: *by digging.* By digging into God's Word, that is: *"You look for it as for silver and search for it as for hidden treasure"* (Prov. 2:4).

We find this treasure among the "rocks" of our ignorance and "dust" of our muddled thinking. Uncut precious stones are not easily identified by the untrained eye. Gold and silver, until it is separated from minerals surrounding it, is often hard to see. (That's why 49ers *panned* for gold.) Furthermore, we labor in what feels like *"the blackest darkness"* of understanding.

So, if a greater appreciation of the *"treasures of wisdom and knowledge"* concerning God's rewards has heretofore been elusive to us, it may be because we have not been trained in the art and craft of wisdom's mining. We may not know what the treasure looks like and how to find it! I hope that—for having seen the treasure dug from its buried setting in the previous section—you will have a keener eye for the gold, silver, and costly stones of God's rewards.

God has "buried" great wisdom and understanding in His Word on the subject of rewards. There is truth everywhere to be mined! I hope that what you have read thus far about the nature of God's rewards has excited you to dig even more into His Word to find a fuller and richer understanding of God's intent to reward. I pray that you will become a "miner" of the treasure that God wants for you, now and for all of eternity.

And I pray that you will *"lay up for yourself"* vast quantities of that *"treasure in heaven"* (Matt. 6:20, 19:21; Mark 10:21; Luke 12:33, 18:22; 1 Tim. 6:19) so that you *"may have the full riches of complete understanding, in order that* [you] *may know the mystery of God, namely, Christ, in whom are hidden all the treasures of wisdom and knowledge*" (Col. 2:2-3).

This section of the book is a miner's guide for digging this buried treasure. We will delve into the Bible's teaching about how you can discover and have God's promised treasures:

Chapter 13 is an overview of how God's rewards are earned.

Chapters 14–16 explain that rewards are earned by obeying the First and Second Great Commandments.

# Chapter 13  Overview of How to Gain God's Rewards

There is little you can do to earn God's reward.

"What?!" you may be exclaiming. "So, what is the point of this book?"

I said there is *little* you can do; I did not say that there is *nothing* you can do. Neither did I suggest that what you do is of small effect. On the contrary, what you do will affect how you spend eternity! Let me explain.

**"For When I Am Weak, Then I Am Strong."**

That statement of Paul from 2 Corinthians 12:10 was amusingly illustrated for my one day. As I drove toward one of my grain elevators, the crossing of the facility's rail sidetrack, the warning lights were flashing, and the crossbars were down. As a loaded railcar slowly passed, I could see that it was not being moved by an engine, but by Jimmy, my hardworking employee. Throwing his considerable strength and determination into the effort, he was pushing it along the track. But how could the exertions of even a powerful man like Jimmy move a railcar weighing 100 tons!

I smiled with amusement at the seeming impossibility, because I had worked with a civil engineer on the design of that rail sidetrack. It was installed with a grade, an incline, so that gravity does most of the work. Appearances of superhuman strength notwithstanding—by design—all that is required is that the railcar be given a push to overcome the last bit of inertial and frictional resistance.

Now, let me ask a philosophical question of you: Who moved the railcar? Was it the man who pushed or the engineer who designed the track to make use of the law of gravity?

The answer is both, isn't it? Without the engineer's design, there is no way on earth the man could have moved such a weight. On the other hand—and likewise, by the design of the engineer—the car would not

155

have moved but for the will and effort of the man. The engineer could have designed the track with a grade steep enough that no human push was required, but, to suit his purposes, he built into the system the requirement of human will and effort.

## The Universe's Great Engineer

Likewise, God, the "Great Engineer," has designed the moral universe—the rail track in our illustration—in comportment with the law of His character. By His plan and preparation—the death and resurrection of Jesus and the provision of His Holy Spirit—He made it possible to move that which, in our own strength, is an impossibly heavy load—to do God's will.

By this design, God has allowed us to meaningfully participate in His work. Our work is of utter insignificance *as compared to* the great work God has done through Christ and continues to do by His Spirit. (That is why I began this chapter with this: "There is little you can do to earn God's reward.") To infinitely extend the analogy: We push against not one, but an infinite number of railcars. The load we push against is immeasurably heavy. And yet, by God's design, our efforts move it. By "*his power that is at work within us,*" God can do "*immeasurably more than all we ask or imagine*" {Eph. 3:20}.

None of which implies that our work is not "work." By definition, "work" and "labor"—words often used in Scripture—takes deliberate exertion. As we just discussed, God adds the increase; nevertheless, we are called to "*work at it with all your heart, as working for the Lord*" (Col. 3:23) and to work until you have the rest of death. We are not called to simply make ourselves available to God's purposes and then wait until He, like some celestial puppeteer, makes us do it. It takes "*try-oomph*" to triumph!

Jesus, Paul, Peter, and the author of Hebrews each tell us multiple times and in various ways to make "*every effort*" to do this and that for the Lord (Luke 13:24; John 5:44; Rom. 14:19; 1 Cor. 15:58; Eph. 4:3; Heb. 4:11; 12:14; 2 Pet. 1:5, 15; 3:14; and more). "*It is God who works in you to will and to act in order to fulfill his good purpose,*" but, as Paul tells us in the same verse, it is for us to "*continue to work out our salvation with fear and trembling*" (Phil. 2:12). What, after all, is an effort that takes no. . . *effort*?

So, how are we to reconcile the seeming conflict between God's sovereign will and our own free will? With this axiom:

> **By God's design,**
> **our effort generally is a necessary**
> **—though infinitely insufficient—**
> **condition for God's work in and through us.**

Not *by* our efforts, but *with* our efforts, God's work is done. To be sure, there are exceptions to that rule. Our sovereign God can and often does act unilaterally, sometimes using us despite ourselves. But if Christians do not—at least sometimes—have a choice in our obedience, why would God not always make us do His will? Is this to be our understanding of sanctification: God *occasionally* makes us—against our stubborn will— to do His will? Have we no choice in the matter? Why then wouldn't He wholly sanctify us—immediately?

He doesn't do so because the slow and painful process of sanctification advances God's ultimate goal: a greater relationship with us. As we discussed earlier, a relationship is something one willingly enters into. One can be commanded or forced to obey, but one cannot be commanded or forced—against his or her will—into a loving relationship. God always does His part, but we must respond if the relationship is to thrive.

It is true that, in any given instance, we do not know whether our God-honoring actions are of God's unilateral doing or of our volitional cooperation with Him. Therefore, like Paul, I will leave it to God to tell me at the Bema on which occasions He worked *despite* me and on which occasions I voluntarily *cooperated* in His work.

> *Therefore judge nothing before the appointed time; wait*
> *till the Lord comes. He will bring to light what is hidden*
> *in darkness and will expose the motives of men's hearts.*
> *At that time each will receive his praise from God.* (1 Cor.
> 4:3-5)

So, in the meantime, given our intrinsically limited perspective—and the enormity of what is at stake—that uncertainty is all the more reason to **proceed in every situation** as if we have been given a choice by God to obey. For as Peter warned Christians,

> *Since you call on a Father who judges each man's work*
> *impartially, live your lives as strangers here in reverent*
> *fear.* (1 Pet. 1:17)

Do I really want to risk standing before Jesus someday and have Him ask me, for example, why I did not publicly claim Him as my Lord that day at the office when He had given me the perfect opportunity to do so? Am I going to reply, "Well, gee, I was waiting on You to *make* me do it!" I don't think so.

To repeat, our labor will only be productive when we work *"as to the Lord"* and as we are empowered by the Spirit, but that does not mean that no effort, no work, no labor, is required of us. While God does not need our efforts, our efforts are not superfluous to God's work. Like that of the boy with the loaves and fishes, our contribution is slight; but whatever our small part, God makes use of it and multiplies it to His ends. God does not patronize us for the seeming smallness of our efforts. Instead, He pays us back with far more than we gave. Our sovereign God can—and does—use us utterly despite ourselves and without our voluntary cooperation. But, to accomplish His purpose of growing our relationship, He gives us a part in His work.

**How Much Effort Is Required?**

The man in my story leaned hard into the railcar, putting all his strength into the effort. But God may not always ask that much of you or me. Whether to all the more display His greatness or because of His understanding of our weakness, He may at times require no more effort than my hand's touch, or that I lean into the "railcar." In that case, God will not have asked me to *do* something, but to *stop doing* something. Such exertion is not an effort as much as it is a ceasing of effort—a "letting go." (I don't know about you, but I find that sometimes is life's most demanding "work.")

On the other hand, God may ask you to walk to certain death, even as our Lord did. Jesus said that anyone who would follow Him must take up his cross (Matt. 16:24). Jesus told His disciples, *"No servant is greater than his master. If they persecuted me, they will persecute you also"* (John 15:20). Jesus has called us to a life of self-denial and self-sacrifice, such as He lived. Millions of followers of Jesus have answered that call over the centuries, to the point of death.

Jesus said his yoke is easy and His burden is light: he did not say that there is no yoke and there is no burden to bear. Our work is a small exertion as compared to the immensity of the task; nevertheless, what we are called to do is *work*. The burden of enduring the cross was bearable for Jesus because of *"the joy set before him"* (Heb. 12:2), but He nevertheless sweated drops of blood in the Garden of Gethsemane for even contemplating what He was about to do. Jesus collapsed under the weight of His cross as He carried it to Calvary. Our yoke is lightened at the prospect of gaining a *victor's* crown, but we—like Jesus—might first be asked to wear a painful crown of *thorns*.

Whatever effort God calls us to expend, our exertion will have a real and lasting effect because—and only because—of God's preparation (Eph. 2:10) and empowerment (1 Thess. 1:4-6); but God often leaves it to the individual to choose whether to participate. It is for the choice to honor and serve God that we will be forever rewarded (Deut. 30:19). Paul tells us in 1 Corinthians 3:11, *"No one can lay any foundation other than the one already laid, which is Jesus Christ."* Nevertheless, he also says *"each will be rewarded according to his own labor"* (v. 8).

Peter tells us God's *"divine power has given us everything we need for life and godliness through our knowledge of him who called us by his own glory and goodness."* In the next verse, however, he encourages us to *"make every effort to add to your faith . . ."* If you do these things, *"you will receive a rich welcome into the eternal kingdom of our Lord and Savior Jesus Christ"* (2 Pet. 1:5-11).

The author of Hebrews speaks of God's faithful people as *"land that drinks in the rain often falling on it and that produces a crop useful to those for whom it is farmed . . . But the land that produces thorns and thistles is worthless and is in danger of being cursed"* (Heb. 6:7-8). Without God's provision, no crop will grow, but the land in the writer's illustration isn't passive in the process. The *"land"* (you and me) must actively *"drink in the rain often falling on it"* and produce a *"useful"* crop, not *"thorns and thistles."*

The Bible often uses analogies that communicated to an agrarian society. Here is a nonagricultural illustration of what the writer of Hebrews was saying, found in a modern medical device: the BiPAP machine. I use this device to treat my sleep apnea. The word "apnea," comes from Greek *"apnous,"* which means "breathless." Without the help of the BiPAP machine, I am *"apnous"* (I literally stop breathing) during my sleep. The machine pushes air into my nostrils, helping my body to overcome the obstructions in my nasal passages that prevent my breathing.

Unlike the related CPAP (continuous positive airway pressure) machine, the BiPAP (bilevel positive airway pressure) machine does not continuously force air into me. It only pushes when I begin—almost imperceptibly—to draw breath; it waits until I start to breathe, and only then does it push air, thereby empowering my breathing. Likewise, God helps us in our spiritual sleep apnea, but He often empowers us—breathes into us—*only as we draw upon that power.* God does not always force Himself upon us. He often works in and through us as we come to Him for that which allows us to do His will.

This is a particularly appropriate analogy because the Bible often speaks of moving air (wind or breath) as a metaphor for the work of the Spirit of God. The word "spirit" is from the Latin *"spirare,"* meaning "to breathe." The Greek word from which our English is translated, *"pneúma,"* likewise means "wind" or "breath." Those words are undoubtedly accurate translations of Jesus's Aramaic in John 20:22, when He breathed on His disciples and said, *"Receive the Holy Spirit,"* using the word *"ruach,"* meaning "wind." So, Jesus "breathed" the Holy Spirit upon them. But He didn't force the Spirit into them. He told them to *"receive,"* or to "take" (*"qabal"* in Aramaic), the Holy Spirit. So, it remained for the disciples—and for us—to draw the Spirit into our being and thus allow His power to work in us. *By God's design*, it is a *joint effort*. As Paul said,

> *That's what I'm working for. I work hard with all*
> *of Christ's strength.* {Col. 1:29 NIRV}

### "So How Do I Earn God's Reward?"

I'm so glad you asked! That's what we will discuss in the next chapters! The answer is simple—if not always easy to do. Do that which you were exhorted to do in last Sunday's sermon and in this morning's reading of God's Word. Do what the Spirit prompts you to do during your next interaction with someone. Do what you feel led to do during prayer. In short: do anything the Spirit of God calls you to do and the Bible teaches you to do.

You earn God's promised reward by pleasing God and conforming to His will. How that plays out in your life is unique to you, your circumstances, your gifting, your weaknesses, and your opportunities. Everyone is called to live a life which, by the power of the Spirit, meets the calling and challenges set before him or her. That looks different for everyone.

Those differences notwithstanding, not surprisingly, there is a familiar theme in our collection of verses: we earn God's reward by fulfilling the First and Second Great Commandments, recorded first—and several times—in Deuteronomy and Leviticus and then reiterated by Jesus in the gospels.

> *Teacher, the expert in the law asked, which is the greatest commandment in the Law? Jesus replied, Love the Lord your God with all your heart and with all your soul and with all your mind." This is the first and greatest commandment. And the second is like it: "Love your neighbor as yourself." All the Law and the Prophets hang on these two commandments.* (Matt. 22:36-40; Mark 12:29-31; Luke 10:27-29)

The love commanded for God and neighbor is not just an emotion, as the ensuing parable of the Good Samaritan makes clear. True love *acts* in the interest of God and of others, usually at some expense of sacrifice to the giver. This is the sort of sacrificial love required of anyone who wishes to receive God's reward.

We fulfill the First Great Commandment, which is to love God, in two ways:

- By *being* what He wants us to be.
- By *doing* what He wants us to do.

Being and doing are inseparable, with the latter naturally flowing out of the former. What we do reflects what we are. Being what God wants us to be inevitably leads to godly actions {Matt. 7:16-20}. Furthermore, the "being" and the "doing" are often indistinguishable from one another. As Peter admonished us, *"Be holy in all you do"* (1 Pet. 1:15). We expand on both of these in the next two chapters.

We fulfill the Second Great Commandment, which is to love our neighbor, by treating people as God would have us treat them. What that means is the subject of chapter 16.

As with this entire book, what follows is drawn from the if-then verses on rewards collected for this book—unless bracketed {thus}. It barely scratches the surface of what they instruct us to do. Of course, the rest of the Bible has *even more* to say on the matter!

And as I will continue to point out, many of the means for achieving rewards are themselves rewards, for in them we enjoy the experience of sharing in the very character of God.

In light of the doctrine of rewards, the derisive mock, "Too heavenly minded to be any earthly good" is a non sequitur! Being heavenly minded is—in no small measure—to look forward to one's reward (as described in chapters 5–12), which are *earned doing good while on this earth* (discussed in chapters 13–16). The more mindful of God's rewards one is, the more earthly good one will seek to do.

And remember, Jesus will take note when you do:

> *I know your deeds, your love and faith, your service and perseverance, and that you are now doing more than you did at first.* (Rev. 2:19)

> *Then all will know that I am he who searches hearts and minds, and I will repay each of you according to your deeds.* (v. 23)

Let's now look more in-depth into how to earn God's reward.

## Notes and Asides:

1   *Appropriately, the railcar in my illustration was filled with "a harvest" of grain (Gal. 6:9)!*

# Chapter 14   Rewards for Loving God in Our Being

*"Love the Lord your God with all your heart and*
*with all your soul and with all your mind."*
(Matt. 22:37)

We demonstrate our love for God when we *are* what He wants us to be and—in the next chapter—when we *do* what He wants us to do. The verses cited in *Investing in Eternity* call us 1) to be holy, 2) to be of pure motive, 3) to be prayerful, and 4) to be trusting of God.

**Be Holy**

The man of God, according to Paul, is the one who flees from all manner of sin and instead pursues "righteousness, godliness, faith, love, endurance, and gentleness" (1 Tim. 6:11-12). Those who receive their reward will have exhibited the fruit of the Spirit in their lives (2 Pet. 1:5-7); {Gal. 5:22}. Furthermore, those who bear the fruit of the Spirit will have their reward— in part—in the sweetness of that very fruit.

Jesus described those who will be blessed as those who are poor in spirit, meek, mournful over sin and its evil impact on people, and merciful and hungry for God and the things of God (Matt. 5; Luke 6). He promised, *"To him who is thirsty* [for righteousness] *I will give to drink without cost from the spring of the water of life"* (Rev. 21:6).

God commands us to be holy, even as He is holy (1 Pet. 1:15-16); {Lev. 11:44, 45; 19:2; 20:7; etc.}. He calls us to be humble and ready to serve others (Luke 14:7-14; 18:9-14; 1 Pet. 5:6), to love people (1 Tim. 6:11; Heb. 6:10), to be patient (Heb. 6:12), and to be self-controlled (1 Pet. 1:13).

We are so often reminded that our sin is forgiven that it might feel as if our sin—especially our private sin when committed in moderation—is of no great consequence. While we may not consciously—as Paul put it in Romans 6:1—"*sin that grace may abound*," with the assurance that God's grace *does* abound, we consider our sin as no big deal. "Since Jesus already died and rose again that I can be forgiven, what practical difference does a little self-indulgence (etc.) make? It has been covered by the blood of Jesus." There are few, I suppose, who would state the matter that crassly, but I suggest that—consciously or unconsciously—the thought is in the minds of many of us.

But the Bible teaches that what we do in this life really does matter. Yes, the sins of those who have trusted in Jesus are indeed forgiven when confessed {1 John 1:9}. They are put away as far as "*the east is from the west*" {Ps. 103:12}, but it does not follow that there are no lasting ill-effects to the individual for having sinned. Even if there are no apparent consequences in this life for a particular "small" sin, at the very least, the transgression will have prevented the sinner—in the moment of its committal and in its aftermath—from doing the will of the Father. Each sin will keep the sinner from affording for himself a reward for obedience.

"For our deeds do not pass away as they seem to," warned Bernard of Clairvaux, the twelfth-century monk:

On the contrary, every deed done in this life is the seed of a harvest to be reaped in eternity . . . He who bears this in mind will never think sin a trifle, because he will look to the future harvest rather than what he sows. (21)

So, being holy is not just what we are *supposed* to do: being holy will reap a harvest of blessing in this life and the next. And holiness is not only a means to reward. Holiness, like all of the good character God produces in us, is a reward in itself. As Paul instructed Timothy,

Godliness has value for all things, holding promise for both the present life and the life to come. (1 Tim. 4:8)

**Be of Pure Motive**

Jesus warned to "*be careful not to do your 'acts of righteousness' before men, to be seen by them. If you do, you will have no reward from your*

*Father in heaven*" (Matt. 6:1). Instead, He says, when you give to the poor, pray, or fast, do so quietly without seeking recognition from men and "*your Father, who sees what is done in secret, will reward you*" (Matt. 6:4). The issue is not about *whether* we should seek rewards for our acts of righteousness: the question is from *whom* we will seek the rewards. If our desire is to be honored by people, then our reward—such as it is—will have been enjoyed in full here on earth (Matt. 6:1-18).

So, it is not our deeds alone that are accounted for by God: He searches the heart and mind to discern our motive. Solomon understood that God "*weighs the heart*" (Prov. 24:12). God knows our hearts much better than we do. That is why David prayed that God would examine his heart and tell him if there was any wicked way in him (Ps. 51). God tells us through the prophet Jeremiah, "*I the LORD search the heart and examine the mind, to reward a man according to his conduct, according to what his deeds deserve*" (Jer. 17:10). Jesus, the Lord in Jeremiah's prophecy, repeats Himself with similar words in Revelation, "*I am he who searches hearts and minds, and I will repay each of you according to your deeds*" (Rev. 2:23).

Paul understood that only God can probe the deepest intents of the heart. He instructed the Corinthians,

> *Therefore judge nothing before the appointed time; wait till the Lord comes. He will bring to light what is hidden in darkness and will expose the motives of men's hearts. At that time each will receive his praise from God.* (1 Cor. 4:5)

Each one's work . . .

> *. . . will be shown for what it is, because the Day will bring it to light. It will be revealed with fire, and the fire will test the quality of each man's work. If what he has built survives, he will receive his reward.*" (1 Cor. 3:12-15)[1]

What "*quality*" of the work is being tested? What distinguishes "*gold, silver, and costly stones*" from "*wood, hay, and straw*" (v. 12)? Our motivation. What is at stake? Our reward.

Of course, to advance His Kingdom our sovereign God can make use of anyone or anything He chooses. So, what we do may advance God's purposes—and yet yield no reward because of improper motivation. If we do the work to bring glory to ourselves, we should not expect to benefit from our labor *"since He knows the secrets of the heart"* {Ps. 44:21}.

## Be Prayerful

There is no intrinsic power in prayer as such. On the contrary, prayer is an acknowledgment of our need; our helplessness. If he chose, he could act arbitrarily without regard to our prayers, or lack thereof. All power originates in God and belongs to Him alone.

> *He ordained prayer not primarily as a means of getting things done for Himself, but as part of the apprenticeship program for training the church for her royal duties which will follow the Marriage Supper of the Lamb. Unless she understands this and enters into sincere cooperation with God's plan of prayer, the power needed to overcome and bind Satan on earth will not be realized.* (Billheimer, 100, emphasis in original)

On their journey to the Promised Land, the Israelites encountered the Amalekites, who were intent on the destruction of God's people (Exod. 17:8-13). As Joshua led the army against them, Moses stood on a hill where all—including the Amalekites—could see him standing *"with the staff of God"* in his hands. As long as Moses held the staff over his head during the battle as a sign of God's power, the Israelites prevailed. When he grew tired, Aaron and Hur stood to his right and left holding up his hands. The Israelites prevailed because Moses, Aaron, and Hur persisted in prayer and in reminding the warriors on both sides of the conflict that God would give the Israelites the victory.

We, too, have an enemy intent on our destruction. When we encounter evil, it is our impulse to react in our own strength. We form our battle plans and sharpen our swords, and then—with a quick prayer that God will bless our efforts—we rush headlong into the fight. That's why Paul talked so often about prayer, encouraging us to *"strive together";* to be *"always laboring earnestly"* in prayer. {Col. 4:12; Rom. 15:30 NASB}.

God doesn't need our prayers to accomplish His work: He invites us to participate in His work through prayer. In the words of Christian rapper NF, our response to that invitation often is:

> "Leave me alone God, I'll call you when I need you."
> Which is funny, 'cause everyone will sleep in the pews
> Then blame God for our problems, like He is sleeping on you.
> We turn our backs on Him, what do you expect Him to do?
> It's hard to answer prayers when nobody's praying to you!

Without continual prayer, we will no more win our spiritual battles than would have the children of Israel that day against the Amalekites. To state the obverse of 1 John 4:4, greater is he who is in the *world*—unless the Lord is fighting within and for us. As we go into battle, we and others had better be praying because, without persistent prayer, we will lose.

Genuine prayer is an attitude as much as it is an activity. It is a state of being punctuated by moments of doing.[2] That is what Paul is saying when he tells us to *"pray without ceasing"* {1 Thess. 5:17}. Our prayers come from hearts that are continually set on God.

We go in prayer to be with God.

> *But when you pray, go into your room, close the door and pray to your Father, who is unseen. Then your Father, who sees what is done in secret, will reward you.* (Matt. 6:18)

We go in humility.

> *If my people, who will humble themselves and pray and seek my face and turn from their wicked ways, then I will hear from heaven.* (2 Chron. 7:14)

We go in faith that God listens.

> *Then you will call upon me and come and pray to me, and I will listen to you. You will seek me and find me when you seek me with all your heart.* (Jer. 29:12-13)

We go in desperate need.

*Then you will call, and the LORD will answer; you will cry*
*for help, and he will say: Here am I.* (Isa. 58:9)

*The Israelites groaned in their slavery and cried out,*
*and their cry for help because of their slavery went up*
*to God. God heard their groaning, and he remembered*
*his covenant with Abraham, with Isaac, and with Jacob.*
(Exod. 2:23)

Prayer is an attitude often born, as is a baby, in suffering and distress. So, cry out to God! He hears you! But be prepared: even if you pray in this way, the trials may continue—or even intensify—because God uses trials to strengthen your faith in Him. Just keep on praying. God will honor the prayers of a humble heart that desires to do His will.

*"You will seek me and find me when you seek me with all*
*your heart. I will be found by you," declares the LORD.*
(Jer. 29:10)

And the pain you prayerfully suffer need not be your own: through prayer, you can enter into, experience, and share in the suffering of anyone God has laid upon your heart. But whether for yourself or on behalf of someone else, God listens. And He will reward the trust that brought you to Him.

*When every day is just another struggle and*
*every choice is an act of war.*
*Gotta pray, gotta press on to the prize worth fighting for.*
*When it feels like I'll never make it; When*
*my heart's crying out for more.*
*Gotta pray, gotta press on, to the prize worth fighting for.*
*The battle rages on, but Your promise keeps me strong.*
*I know I'll win this race with Your unfailing grace.*
*Your love is my reward.*
*(Jamie Kimmett)*

## Be Trusting in God

Perhaps you have noticed that the ancient practice of meditation is all the rage. And for a good reason: it works. It reduces anxiety, lowers stress, lengthens attention span, and generally fosters mental health and focus. Also known as mindfulness or contemplation (the word "meditation" is from the Latin *"meditatum,"* which means "to ponder"), the practice is a central feature of Buddhism, Islam, and Christianity.

For the Buddhist, meditation is the means of stilling the mind by laying aside all thought and desire. Similarly, in Islam, the more one practices meditation, the closer he will come to attaining Fanaa, the annihilation of self. For the Christian, the goal of meditation is precisely the opposite: it is to find completeness in—and oneness with—God. That communion begins in God's Word:

> *I have more insight than all my teachers, for I meditate on your statutes.* (Ps. 119:99)

> *Do not let this Book of the Law depart from your mouth; meditate on it day and night, so that you may be careful to do everything written in it. Then you will be prosperous and successful.* (Josh. 1:8)

Let your minds *"dwell on"* whatever is *"true,"* *"honorable,"* *"right,"* *"pure,"* *"lovely,"* and of *"good repute"* {Phil. 4:8}.

As we meditate on God and His Word, we increasingly trust in God, and we lean less upon ourselves and our own wisdom and means (Prov. 3:5-6). We rest in Him. We wait upon Him. We seek His will, not our own, because we trust Him, even when we don't understand His ways. To trust in God is to *"fix our eyes not on what is seen, but on what is unseen"* (1 Cor. 2:9; 2 Cor. 4:18). People who trust in God have set their *"hope fully on the grace to be given you when Jesus Christ is revealed"* (1 Pet. 1:13).

Trusting in God is foundational to other godly states of being. When we trust in God, we are, as David said, *"like a weaned child with its mother"* (Ps. 131:2). We feel safe and secure in spite of circumstances. Trust in God leads to hope, as we claim the promises in God's Word concerning our future. Once again, we see that the means to our reward is also a reward itself.

Trust in God leads us to lay aside sinful means of providing for our happiness. Trusting in God means seeking His Kingdom and depending upon His provision—not putting our hope in wealth (human provision, which is uncertain and temporary) or human wisdom, but in God, who provides us with everything we need (1 Tim. 6:17; Matt. 6:19-34). If our hearts are unsatisfied it is because of this: *"When you ask, you do not receive, because you ask with wrong motives, that you may spend what you get on your pleasures"* (James 4:2-3).

Unfortunately, I am often unaware of my distrust of God. I wish a buzzer would go off to alert me! Actually, there is one reliable indicator: anxiety. It is like the automatic lane-detection device on my car that beeps whenever I have crossed a line.

On the other hand, I often don't feel anxiety because—like these World War 2 pilots— I feel in control of my life.

*According to the 1945 report "Men Under Stress," the mortality rate for dogfighters was among the highest in the military; the pilots knew that half of them would be killed in action. Yet fighter pilots also enjoyed wildly high job satisfaction, with 93 percent of them claiming to be happy with their assignments. And why should they be so content? Because fighter pilots felt they were in complete control of their fate. They could maneuver however they liked through a huge airspace, and they believed, to a man, that their piloting skill would determine their survival, not luck.* (Clark)[2]

Do you feel in control of your destiny? Are you confident that your skill in navigating your life will guarantee your survival? Is it possible that your sense of security is—like that of the pilots—illusionary, self-reliant, prideful? Might you not go down in flames today?

Self-reliance is a celebrated virtue in our culture. The "self-made man," a term coined in 1832 by Senator Henry Clay, is the one who strives for the "American Dream" as articulated by Benjamin Franklin and as enshrined in the Declaration of Independence. Former slave Frederick Douglass extolled those for whom success lies within themselves. Men like Andrew Carnegie and John D. Rockefeller epitomize the rags-to-riches ethos of our nation's founding.

The exuberant optimism of the eighteenth and nineteenth centuries collapsed into the chaos of the twentieth century: the Great Depression, two World Wars, the Cold War, the Korean War, Vietnam. In this century, we face a new assortment of terrifying uncertainties: terrorism, pandemics, artificial intelligence, robots replacing jobs, personal data collection and breaches, de facto social credit scores, increasing disparity between the haves and have-nots, and the breakdown of the family. For good reason, many of us are fearful of the future. We are not in control of many of the events of our lives. And we certainly are not in control of the world around us. So, how are we to be free from anxiety?

We can have the confidence of those World War II pilots because we do have control over something far more consequential and everlasting than life itself. We have been given control—by God—over the quality of our eternal existence. We can choose now to trust a loving God who promises to forever bless us for trusting Him. We can trust that He will transform everything that happens in our lives—even the harsh and unexpected things—into something good (Rom. 8:28). While God is our pilot, we are His co-pilot; so He often gives us the plane's yoke. We must firmly grasp that yoke with our right hand of *faith* and our left hand of *obedience*.

Anxiety is the mirror opposite of trust in God. It is the go-to response when confronted with uncertainty. But don't despair at your lack of faith. Remember that He is continually stretching our faith in Him. A lesson learned leads to yet another test so that you will,

*Increasingly learn,*
*To increasingly turn*
*To God*
*With all your life's concern.*

The process of strengthening our faith is hard work. Faith must be exercised like a muscle. And the stronger we become, the more weight He will load onto the bar to make our faith even stronger. Our faith grows as we persist in our efforts to gain God's blessings. Consider the story in Genesis 32 of Jacob wrestling with God throughout the night. Jacob said to the Lord, "*I will not let you go unless you bless me*" (v. 26). That was an audacious demand of God, was it not? But listen to God's response.

*"What is your name?" "Jacob," he answered. Then the man said, "Your name will no longer be Jacob* [supplanter], *but Israel* [one who has prevailed with God], *because you have struggled with God and with humans and have overcome." * (vv. 27-28)

God was reminding Jacob that he was a deceiver and thief of his brother's birthright. But since Jacob was not content with who he was and had, he contended with God to gain what God was promised. He would not have worked and struggled for that blessing if he had not believed—if he had not been utterly convinced—that God *could* and *would* reward him for his persistence. He will reward you, too—if you persist in faith.

God is not reluctant to give us what we want from Him, but He makes us work for it because it is only in striving that we will have the richest of God's blessing: a deeper relationship with Him. We will have it only as we persist in trusting God's promise to reward.

### Notes and Asides:

1    *Lest anyone think Paul is talking about how one enters into heaven, he adds that though one suffers a loss of reward when his life's labors are burned up,"he himself will be saved, but only as one escaping through the flames" (1 Cor. 3:15).*

2    *Max Lucado quotes Clark in his excellent book, <u>Anxious for Nothing</u> (Nashville: HarperCollins, 2017).*

# Chapter 15  Rewards for Loving God in Our Doing

Scripture that promises rewards also tells us what to *do* to receive them: 1) serve and obey Him, 2) endure trials, and 3) persevere until the end.

## Seek God's Will

We know we are to do God's will. But even when we are *willing* to do it, we are often clueless of His will in any given circumstance of life.

Have you ever been to an escape room with your friends or family? It is a setting for a game of mystery—a whodunit. Participants are introduced to the story, instructed to search the theme-furnished room or rooms for prearranged clues, and given a limited time to solve the mystery. One clue might be hidden, for example, in a vase, which leads to the page of a book, which has seemingly random words circled, which can be ordered to form a sentence, which . . . You get the idea. It's like a treasure hunt. There might even be parallel threads, which, when both solved, lead to a third thread, etc. And be aware that there are false clues hidden in the room as well!

There is an added sense of urgency because, in the limited time you are given, you must solve the mystery to obtain the key to the locked door that prevents your "escape" from the room. If your team solves the mystery in less time than any group before you, your names and game time go to the top of a public list of winners for all subsequent players to try to best! The game is all the more enjoyable because it is a group effort. And though you have a common goal, there is also a friendly intra-team competition to find and decipher the next clue.

Sometimes it feels like God has placed us in an escape room, doesn't it? We can't get out of life's problematic circumstances until we've figured out the mystery. As most of us know, that game isn't always fun. But searching for the clues gives us hope. Many of them are in God's Word. Most of them come by God's Spirit in prayer. Hymns and worship songs are always a good place to look. We pick up some from conversations or books we read. (This one, perhaps.) Others come (keep your eyes open!) in the most unexpected events of life. I've even seen them delivered in dreams. Of all these clues, a proper understanding of them is essential. He gives us that understanding when we seek it from His Spirit.

Even better, we are not playing the "game" alone. We have teammates who likewise have an interest in discovering the outcome of *"God's mystery, that is, Christ Himself"* (Col. 2:2). But to find many of the clues, we have to be looking and listening for them. We know we'll solve the mystery of God's purpose for us if we do—because Jesus promised this: *"Ask and it will be given to you; seek and you will find; knock and the door will be opened to you"* (Matt. 7:7 and Luke 13:9; see also Deut. 4:8).

As for those annoying "false clues," I have a little trick for recognizing them. Having observed myself over the years, I have learned to start with the assumption that my first impulse generally will be to do what I want to do, not what God wants me to do. So, when I have an urge or inclination (a clue) to do something, I ask God to reveal my true motives in wanting or not wanting to do it. Very often, He reveals it to be a false clue: my motives are self-centered: fear, selfishness, avarice, whatever. But the great part of this simple test is that the correct course is then often evident to me: it is the exact opposite of what I had wanted to do! The false clue (my wrong motives) is thereby transformed by God into a useful clue!

Why would that surprise me? I know God makes *all things*, even my sinful impulses, work for my good when I love Jesus enough to ask for His help. And as I grow in Christ, I will increasingly experience joy in God's assurance that my motives are increasingly honoring of Him.

**Serve and Obey God**

God's dealing with Abraham and his family is one of our first clues. God told Jacob to go to Bethel (which means "House of God"), settle there, and make an altar to God.[1] We are called to the same, but with a difference; we already live in the house of God {1 Cor. 6:19} and the sacrifice we are to make is of ourselves {Rom. 21:1}. An altar was a place of violent death. Throats were cut, and blood gushed. God calls all of us to just as ruthlessly *"put to death the deeds of the flesh."*

Jesus perfectly lived such a life of sacrifice. He held back nothing, as Paul tells us in this beautiful passage from Paul's letter to the Philippians:

> *Christ Jesus, "being in very nature God, did not consider equality with God something to be grasped, but made himself nothing, taking the very nature of a servant, being made in human likeness. And being found in appearance as a man, he humbled himself and became obedient to death—even death on a cross!"* {Phil. 2:5-8}

If we are to share in Christ's glory, then anything that we could choose to use for our personal advantage: our abilities, our wealth, our education, our position, must be subjected to Christ's purposes. Even intrinsically wholesome pleasures in life, such as our comforts, privacy, conveniences, alone time must be seen, by comparison, as worthless and expendable as filthy scraps of garbage, if we are to have a resurrection to power and glory (Phil. 3:7-14). All that you sacrifice in this life, from small to great, is worthy of compensation.

Here's some food for thought: *"The hardworking farmer will share in the fruit of his labor"* (2 Tim. 2:6), Paul encourages Timothy. To the Galatians, he wrote, *"The one who sows to please the Spirit, from the Spirit will reap eternal life"* (Gal. 6:8). The endeavor is often a group effort: Paul reminds us that, while one plants and one waters, each will receive his reward according to his own contribution (1 Cor. 3:5). The message is unmistakable: what we sow, we will reap.[2]

In the Parable of the sower (the explanation of which is found in Matt. 13:18-23, Mark 4:14-20; Luke 8:11-15, Jesus changes the metaphor slightly, portraying God as the sower and us as the soil. He says that the seed (the Word), which falls on good soil (the man who accepts the Word) will produce a crop yielding *"thirty, sixty or even a hundred times what is sown."* Similarly, the writer of Hebrews speaks of the good soil, which produces *"a crop useful to those for whom it is farmed, receives the blessings of God"* (Heb. 6:7).

**Endure Trials**

Contemplating the verses on reward I'd collected, I was struck by how many of them promised a reward for enduring trials. If you check *index*

*3,* you'll see that there are about as many verses promising rewards for endurance and perseverance in trials as there are verses about otherwise earning rewards by serving and obeying God.

On further reflection, I could see why this would be so. Remember, I chose the verses in *Investing in Eternity* because they make either an explicit or implicit connection between our faithfulness and our reward. It is not surprising, therefore, that admonitions to endure and persevere amid the trials so often experienced by God's people would be accompanied by promises of reward. It is in the fiery ordeal that we most need the encouragement of God's promises of reward.

Paul, no stranger to persecution himself, wrote these words of encouragement to the Corinthians,

> *We are hard pressed on every side, but not crushed; perplexed, but not in despair; persecuted, but not abandoned; struck down, but not destroyed.* (2 Cor. 4:8)

Why were they not crushed, despairing, or destroyed? Because they knew that their *"light and momentary troubles"* (!) were *"achieving for* [them] *an eternal glory that far outweighs them all"* (2 Cor. 4:17). God allows trials into our lives for the same reason a loving father doesn't shield his son from all of life's difficulties: He knows the struggles will prepare him for manhood, just as they prepare us for heaven. (Heb. 12:7, 11)

> *So do not throw away your confidence; it will be richly rewarded.* (Heb. 10:35)

Other writers in the Bible also encourage persistence in the face of trial:

> *Blessed is the man who perseveres under trial, because when he has stood the test, he will receive the crown of life that God has promised to those who love him.* (James 1:12)

> *In this you greatly rejoice, though now for a little while you may have had to suffer grief in all kinds of trials. These have come so that your faith—of greater worth than gold, which perishes even though refined by fire—may be*

*proved genuine and may result in praise, glory and honor when Jesus Christ is revealed.* (1 Pet. 1:6-7)

*But even if you should suffer for what is right, you are blessed.* (1 Pet. 3:14)

*And the God of all grace, who called you to his eternal glory in Christ, after you have suffered a little while, will himself restore you and make you strong, firm and steadfast.* (1 Pet. 5:10)

These words were written to reassure people enduring trials and persecution that God would reward them for their sacrifice. These faithful people of God desperately needed such encouragement—and not only they but also the millions of Christian martyrs who have suffered and will have suffered, from the first century until Christ's return. These dear brothers and sisters in Christ relied upon (and will have relied upon) God's promises of reward. That is why there are so many verses urging steadfastness of faith in the face of trials accompanied by promises of reward for doing so: God wants His beloved children to know that He sees their suffering and that He will set things to right in the end.

Herein is a hint as to why we tend to ignore the doctrine of rewards: we don't face persecution in the midst of which we would find comfort in God's promises of reward. The threats we face—in the West anyway— are seldom existential; they are more often small risks to our comforts and securities. Our most significant concerns are about our next vacation ("Should I buy travel insurance?") or to our retirement ("Will I have enough?"). Our "suffering" is a loss to our investment portfolio. Sadly, to the extent we seek these things instead of seeking first the Kingdom of God, *"we have our reward in full"* (Matt. 6:5), such as it is.

Not that there is anything intrinsically wrong with seeking to provide for our material needs and securities. There is nothing wrong with having money set aside for a rainy day, with insurance against protracted illness or disability, with retirement accounts and investments. But the potential problem they create is what is referred to by economists as a "moral hazard." A moral hazard exists when someone behaves differently for being insulated from risk than he would have acted for having been exposed to the risk.

The *spiritual,* moral hazard is that we find ourselves depending on those measures we have taken to insulate ourselves from risk of harm, instead of depending upon God for our provision. We spend God's resources to hedge ourselves against 'acts of God.'

I do not presume to tell anyone how best to avoid this spiritual, moral hazard. I don't feel very confident in my own financial decisions in this regard. But it is a question we all should continually put before God in prayer. To the extent we trust in God to deliver us from the unknown and unexpected, we will be rewarded.

Many of us genuinely suffer through little or no fault of our own. Illness, heartache, death, estrangement from children or spouse, unforeseen financial hardship, emotional depression: it may not always seem that these are sufferings for the sake of Christ; nevertheless, when you endure such trials with faith in God and hope in His provision and care, you too will be rewarded.

**Persevere until the End**

Paul wrote to the Corinthians that he disciplines himself and makes himself as a slave *"so that after I have preached to others, I myself will not be disqualified for the prize"* (1 Cor. 9:27).[3]

That verse is disquieting. If Paul, the handpicked apostle of Jesus who taught us so much about God's plan and purposes, seriously considered that he could be disqualified from the prize (which this writer understands as his reward in—not of—heaven), then how much more am I at risk of losing my reward?

Paul might well have had Moses in mind as he wrote. After all Moses had done for God, after all of his (sometimes reluctant) obedience, after all he endured in leading the people of God across the wilderness, after the grumbling to which he listened, after all the patience he usually exhibited, after all the despair he felt at the peoples' disobedience, to the point of wishing he were dead . . . after all of this, and for a seemingly small act of disobedience, Moses was not allowed into the Promised Land.

Of course, Moses wasn't disqualified from heaven. We know, too, from his presence at the Transfiguration, that he did not lose his high position in heaven. But Moses suffered a real loss for having disobeyed God by angrily striking—rather than speaking to—the rock {Num. 10:11-12}. He was not allowed to share in the consummation of his ministry: he was disqualified from entry into the Promised Land to which he had led God's people.

Consider someone else of lesser stature, Uzzah, who reached out to stabilize the Ark of God when it was in danger of falling from the cart that carried it {2 Sam. 6:6-7}. His actions were against God's command not to touch the Ark. God killed Uzzah for his *"irreverent act."* "What?! God *killed* Uzzah?" Even David was angry with God for executing such a severe punishment! "Come on, Lord!" David may have said. "It was such a small sin—a mistake, really! He was only trying to keep Your Ark from falling! He was attempting to serve You!"

What we learn from these stories is this: while God will reward our service, we must offer it in godly fear and humility, being scrupulous in our obedience to the end, lest we too are disqualified from the prize. God forgives our sins, it is true, but we should not take His promise of reward (not to mention our sin) lightly.

*You need to persevere so that, when you have done the will of God, you will receive what he has promised.* (Heb. 10:36)

Jesus promised, *"Be faithful, even to the point of death, and I will give you the crown of life"* (Rev. 2:10). Do we think that if you give little to God, Jesus is going to say, "Ah, that's OK. I didn't really mean all that about 'losing out.' Here's your crown anyway."

What of those who sacrificed their lives to the point of death, or to a life of service to the poor, or to a tribe in South America, or to voluntary poverty for the sake of the Kingdom? What of the faithful in *Foxe's Book of Martyrs*, or the millions of other Christian martyrs in Church history, or the millions of Christians today suffering persecution in, for example, China or the Middle East? According to a recent report, one in three Christians in the world suffer overt persecution (Cranmer). Will God cheapen their reward by giving the same crown to those who have not in some way sacrificed themselves?

*Do not be deceived: God cannot be mocked. A man reaps what he sows.* (Gal. 6:7)

Jesus tells us, over and over in Revelation, that the promises are only to those who overcome.

> *He who overcomes will, like them, be dressed in white. I will never blot out his name from the book of life, but will acknowledge his name before my Father and his angels.* (Rev. 3:5)

> *I am coming soon. Hold on to what you have, so that no one will take your crown. Him who overcomes I will make a pillar in the temple of my God.* (Rev. 3:11-12)

> *He who overcomes will inherit all this, and I will be his God and he will be my son.* (Rev. 21:7)

Not until the end of his life was even Paul confident to declare, *"I have fought the good fight, I have finished the race, I have kept the faith"* (2 Tim. 4:7). So, don't quit! Go! Go! The race isn't over yet! The whole world does not yet know that Jesus is Lord of all!

Those are just a few of the Bible's "clues" to know and to do God's will in our doing. There are thousands more of them in the Bible. Just be sure to have the Holy Spirit on your team as you search for them. He is *really good* at the game of life. With His help, you will win, I guarantee. He knows best how to find what we are really looking for: *God's reward.*

***Notes and Asides:***

¹    When God told Jacob to go to Bethel, he was living in an area in Mesopotamia where Abraham was born and where his brother Nahor lived. The place-name was "<u>Paddan-aram</u>." This combination of words from Akkadian and Hebrew can be translated "path of rescue." It is the place where Abram stayed and built an altar on his way to Egypt and on his return. It was where Jacob, fleeing from the wrath of his brother Esau, fell asleep on a stone and dreamt of a ladder stretching between heaven and Earth and thronging with angels; and where God stood at the top of the ladder and promised Jacob the land of Canaan. Bethel was in the land that God had promised to Abraham. Bethel was the destination of the "path of rescue"—the place of worship and sacrifice to God.

²    Of course, we all sow and reap both good and evil.

David tells us that in keeping the righteous statutes of the Lord is great reward (Ps. 19:7-11). He sang this psalm of praise to God when the Lord had delivered him from His enemies and from the hand of Saul:

> The LORD has dealt with me according to my righteousness;
> according to the cleanness of my hands he has rewarded me.
> For I have kept the ways of the LORD; I have not done evil
> by turning from my God. His laws are before me; I have not
> turned away from his decrees. I have been blameless before
> him and have kept myself from sin. The LORD has rewarded
> me according to my righteousness, according to the cleanness
> of my hands in his sight. (Ps. 18:9-24)

Contrast that passage to another psalm of David, likely written after his spectacularly murderous and adulterous failure, in which David is praising God for His forgiveness of sin. He says that the Lord . . .

> does not treat us as our sins deserve
> or repay us according to our iniquities.
> For as high as the heavens are above the earth,
> so great is his love for those who fear him;
> far as the east is from the west,

*so far has he removed our transgressions from us.*
*As a father has compassion on his children,*
*so the LORD has compassion on those who fear him;*
*he knows how we are formed,*
*he remembers that we are dust.*
*{Ps. 103:11-14}*

    *In Psalm 18, David praises God for giving him a reward of blessing (for his "cleanness of . . . hands"). Yet in Psalm 103, David praises God for withholding a reward of punishment (for his sin). So God, in His grace, both gives positive rewards for our faithfulness and withholds negative reward when we confess our sin. God has "compassion on those who fear Him." He knows we are but "dust."*

    *Here, juxtaposed in these two passages and in the life of the man who wrote them, is a glorious display of God's grace. Either way, in our faithfulness and in our transgression, God indeed does not treat us as is deserved! Instead, because of His great mercy, He both forgives our sins and (as if His forgiveness was not enough to warrant praise forever and ever) He rewards our faithful service and obedience! What a glorious and gracious God we serve!*

[3] *This and other verses cited in this section are understood by some to teach the requirement of perseverance to gain the "prize" of heaven itself. While I agree that some teaching in the Bible seems to speak of a need for perseverance for salvation (e.g., Rom. 8:22), I do not believe these verses do so. But as I point out at greater length in Appendix 2: Common Emotional and Theological Objections, <u>as far as rewards are concerned,</u> perseverance for salvation versus perseverance for reward is a distinction without a difference. In the view of the "perseverance" camp, heaven is at stake. In the opinion of the "rewards' camp," the riches of heaven are at stake. So long as both camps believe there is reward in heaven to be had, this verse supports both arguments because perseverance is a necessary condition for reward in heaven: one must be <u>in heaven</u> if one is to enjoy <u>reward in heaven</u>.*

# Chapter 16  Rewards for Loving Our Neighbor

*And the second is like it: "Love your neighbor as yourself."*
(Matt. 22:39)

Jesus said the Second Great Commandment is like the first. In what sense are they alike? Our love of our neighbor is an expression of our love for God. We declare our love to God when we share in His love for people.

Suppose a man marries a widow with children. And suppose the man often expresses his love to his wife but is indifferent toward her children whom she greatly loves. Wouldn't his indifference toward her children call into question the man's love for his wife? Conversely, if the man loves her children, adopts them, and cares for them, wouldn't his wife feel more greatly loved by her husband? In the same way, when we love and serve God's children, we love and serve the God who loves them.

This point is made by Jesus in what, for me, is one of the most poignant passages in the Bible. When those whom the King praised asked when they had served Him, he replies, *"I tell you the truth, whatever you did for one of the least of these brothers of mine, you did for me"* (Matt. 25:34-40). Jesus was teaching us that to serve others is to serve Him. The message is reiterated by the author of Hebrews, who assures us that *"God is not unjust; he will not forget your work and the love you have shown him as you have helped his people and continue to help them"* (Heb. 6:10).

As I say in appendix 2, Jesus isn't a dispassionate clinical therapist. He cares deeply for people. How does He communicate His love? Through us. We are His ears to listen, His voice to speak, His hand to touch the lives of people He loves. And while I'm at it, let me remind you of something else I said about love in chapter 3: love and rewards are mutually reinforcing incentives, since the more we experience God's generous love for people, the more love we have to give. As I said, you can't give what you don't

185

already have. Our hope of rewards only increases our desire to share with others the riches of God.

In the verses with conditional promises, we find that to *"love your neighbor as yourself"* entails 1) loving your enemies, 2) treating people justly, 3) doing good deeds, and 4) using money in ways that helps people.

## Love Your Enemies

God has a way of asking for the unexpected. For example, He asks you to give food and drink to your enemy. (See Prov. 25:21-22, expanded upon by Jesus and repeated by Paul in Rom. 12:20.) Anyone can love a friend, Jesus said. Even sinners do that! But, we are called to . . .

> *Love your enemies, do good to those who hate you, bless those who curse you, pray for those who mistreat you. If someone strikes you on one cheek, turn to him the other also. If someone takes your cloak, do not stop him from taking your tunic. Give to everyone who asks you, and if anyone takes what belongs to you, do not demand it back. Do to others as you would have them do to you . . . Love your enemies, do good to them, and lend to them without expecting to get anything back. Then your reward will be great, and you will be sons of the Most High, because he is kind to the ungrateful and wicked.* (Luke 6:27-33, 35)

Jesus didn't ask anything of us that he did not do Himself, for He died for us while we were yet sinners {Rom. 5:8}.

Consider for a moment who are your "enemies." Think beyond the obvious: the competitive colleague, someone hostile to your faith, the antagonistic family member. Reflect on all your relationships. Are you often suspicious of people's motives and assume they might hurt you if you are not defensively and offensively armored? Does your heart feel unsafe, so you hide behind protective emotional walls? Do you approach people like my dog approaches other canines: cautious, sniffing, and with the hair up on your neck?

I encourage you to let down your guard. Love your perceived enemies. Don't be afraid of what they may do to you. Let Jesus be your defender. Your reward may be the discovery that they mean you no harm or that they, too, need God's healing. Maybe they have their own insecurities that prompt them to be mistrustful or defensive. For loving them by allowing yourself to be vulnerable, you may earn for yourself a friend in this life, and perhaps a friend for eternity.

## Do What Is Just

God is just, and He loves justice. As we discussed earlier, God is not only just in all He does, but also He is the Great Judge, and it is His command that we treat people fairly. Some of God's harshest punishments on His people in the Old Testament came upon them because they had failed to act justly.

But even as God promises judgment of injustice, He also promises rewards for . . .

. . . doing what is just and right:

*Good will come to him . . . who conducts his affairs with justice.* (Ps. 112:5)

. . . refraining from what is unjust:

*For I, the LORD... hate robbery and iniquity.* (Isa. 61:8)

... standing against injustice:

*Is not this the kind of fasting I have chosen:*
*to loose the chains of injustice*
*and untie the cords of the yoke,*
*to set the oppressed free*
*and break every yoke?*
(Isa. 58:6)

## Do Good Deeds

The first step in doing "good" is to see the need for the deed. We most often spot these needs and opportunities in the context and relationships of our life. Our opportunities to do good will come most often among those with whom we live and work: listening, encouraging, demonstrating patience, offering a kind word, serving, assisting. You know what that means in your dealings with the chatty coworker, the demanding customer, the impatient boss, the disrespectful teenager, the frustrated spouse. Love the people around you and see if you don't learn of struggles in their lives, of which you were completely unaware.

Also, God may call you to step outside your usual circle of acquaintances in search of needs. The local rescue mission needs mentors; Little Brothers need Big Brothers; children need someone to read to them; single mothers need help repairing the house; the sick need visiting; the poor need help with housing and tax returns; the elderly need transport to doctors and to the grocery store. There are agencies in every city in which you could have regular contact with people in need. These agencies, some of them secular, are always looking for help, and few nonsectarian agencies would reject your help for offering it in the name of Jesus.

As we discussed earlier, a condition for being rewarded with honor and glory by the Father is, like Jesus, making oneself "last" by becoming a servant to Christ and to people {1 Cor. 7:22}. Actually, a form of the Greek word *"douloō"* often translated "servant" can be—and sometimes is—translated "slave." The dual meaning of the term is useful since there are times when we are called merely to make ourselves available to people on a limited basis; and there are other times when we are called to brand ourselves—in a manner of speaking—someone's slave for God's sake, wholly relinquishing our rights and prerogatives. Such service involves a sacrifice of time and effort—large or small. Jesus said that doing something as trivial as offering a cup of cold water in His name will be greatly rewarded (Matt. 10:42).

## Use Money to Help People

Followers of Jesus are also called to a sacrifice of money and possessions. It is a demanding mandate, made easier by the Bible's promise to richly reward those who answer it.[1] Just as your belief in the profit potential of an investment compels you to write a check for the purchase of a stock, your belief in God's promise of eternal profit convinces you to invest in God's Kingdom.

Indeed, that is the best way to think of biblical stewardship: as an investment. There is no more *sacrifice* in giving to God's Kingdom purposes than there is a *sacrifice* in worldly investing. When you invest money, you aren't giving up anything that you don't expect to get back, plus earnings. The difference between earthly (in)securities and heavenly securities is that the investment you make in God's business is a sure thing!

Furthermore, your earthly venture is not likely (to say the least) to earn the 10,000 percent return your investment in the Kingdom of God will produce. Of course, that hundredfold return Jesus promised (in Matt. 13:8, 18, 19:29; Mark 10:28) is only an allegory for the immeasurable size of our expected heavenly dividend. Our investment in God's business is more like an annuity that never expires. (I call it an "eternity.") The PV (Present Value) of, and the ROI (Return on Investment) on, money invested in God's Kingdom is—literally—infinitely large. (And, as my Christian financial advisor points out, there is no inflation or taxes to worry about!)

So, choose your investments wisely. Instead of being *heavily* invested in that which will not last, be *heavenly* invested in that which will produce an eternal dividend. To repeat this book's touchstone passage,

*Do not store up for yourselves **treasures** on earth,*
*where moth and rust destroy, and where thieves break in and steal.*
*But store up for yourselves **treasures** in heaven,*
*where moth and rust do not destroy,*
*and where thieves do not break in and steal.*
(Matthew 6:19-20)

"So, how can I get a piece of the action!?" you ask. Well, you already have what it takes to start your eternal investment program. If, by God's grace, you have put your faith in Jesus, you already have assets to invest that are beyond measure. You have access to the *"boundless riches of Christ"* (Eph. 3:8). And He will give you anything for which you ask—if that for which you ask is in accordance with His will and purposes (John 16:23-24).

What is more, He has given you His investment strategy manual, His Word, and His investment Counselor, the Holy Spirit, by whose wisdom and power we have *"everything we need for life and godliness"* (2 Pet. 1:3). (If this were an earthly investment, you would be charged with trading on insider information!)

You already have an education, connections, friendships, abilities, and (hopefully) health and a job. And you probably have financial means. Those means may or may not be significant as compared to others. You may have been given only five mina, while others have been given ten

(Luke 19:11-27). But how much you have doesn't matter as far as your opportunity is concerned; what is essential is what you do with what you have.

### *A sacrifice that is no sacrifice is no sacrifice.*

Consider what Jesus said to the rich man when he asked Jesus what he must do to be rich in heaven (Matt. 19 and elsewhere).[2] The man must have at first sighed with relief when Jesus inquired about his fealty to the Law. He'd done that! But then Jesus said there was something he still lacked. Jesus told him that he had to forsake his position of authority on earth, sell everything he owned, and give it to the poor. Only then would he have the wealth and status in heaven he sought. Upon hearing the condition, the man walked away sad because he loved his money and the worldly honor it afforded more than he loved Jesus. He could not bring himself to pay the price required to gain the treasure in heaven that Jesus offered him.

You may be thinking that Jesus's command is only to rich people. Why would you assume that? After all, Jesus praised the poor widow for giving everything she had—even that on which she had to live (Mark 12:41-44; Luke 21:1-4). Sell *all* you have and give it *all* away, whether you have much or little, and you too will be praised by God.

Besides, you are likely richer than you think. Do you have a reasonably comfortable life? Do you have good health, a house, a reliable car, a decent and secure job, regular vacations? Yes? Then you are probably in the top ten percent—maybe even the top five percent—of the *wealthiest* people in the world. Perhaps most of my readers are among "The one percent" of wealthiest people who ever lived.

Indeed, all things considered, you and I probably have more wealth than the rich man of Jesus's story. And you may have an even higher position of influence or authority than he did. What do you have that Jesus wants you to give? What does surrender of everything mean for you?

Only God knows . . .

. . . until you ask.

I dare you to ask Him.

## The embedded promise

As you consider what Jesus is calling you to do, don't forget the promise embedded in Jesus's reply to the rich man. Most people overlook it. They remember *"sell all you have and give it to the poor"* and skip right over to this: *"Then come, follow me."* But, sandwiched, like sweet peanut butter and jelly between the bread of commands, is the great promise of what we will receive for doing so. Jesus told the rich man that when he sells everything and gives it to the poor, he *"will have treasure in heaven!"*[3]

Later, encouraged by Jesus's earlier reply to the rich man, James and John asked a similar question of Jesus. Having already left everything to follow Jesus, they were emboldened to ask for authority in heaven: the seats to the right and left of the throne of Jesus!

He gave them essentially the same answer He had given the rich man: give everything and you will have authority in heaven. But James and John (and later the rest of the disciples) were asked to sacrifice far more than mere money and status. They were asked to give their very lives. It was a price they were willing to pay to gain authority in His Kingdom. (The exception was their fellow disciple, Judas, who *betrayed* Jesus in exchange for a paltry thirty pieces of silver! "I would never do that!" you may think. But do we not often betray Jesus in our own subtle ways?) As a result, the disciples now enjoy the seats of honor for which James and John had asked. And so will we, if we follow their example.

Clearly, Jesus isn't interested only in our getting into heaven. He wants us to have both a *rich* life and to be *rich* in heaven. *"I am come,"* Jesus tells us elsewhere, *"that they might have life, and have it to the full"* (John 10:10)! I like the King James translation: *". . . that they might have it more abundantly."*

## Give everything?

You may be thinking: "But I can only give so much! Where do I draw the line in giving?" The great news is that there is no need to fuss with drawing a line. You can still invest *everything*—by making yourself a *"slave to God"* (Rom. 6:19-23; Eph. 6:6). A slave has nothing that is "his." He has no possessions. He does not even use the possessive when referring to things at his disposal: he never speaks of "my car," "my house," or "my bed" because, as I said, the slave owns nothing. Everything belongs to the master, and its best and highest use is for the master's purposes {1 Cor. 7:31, 9:19-23}. Even personal necessities like the slave's cloak or sandals do not belong to him: they are the master's, given to the slave that he might be warm and thus healthy and able to serve the master.

Likewise, in considering ourselves slaves to God, we live our lives as if every ability, every opportunity, every dollar, literally every breath, and every heartbeat belongs to God and thus is most profitably invested in the Kingdom. We do so with the confident expectation of an eventual and boundless return.

Conversely, every dollar (even those used for essential food, clothing, and shelter) not spent to advance the Kingdom of the Master is a wasted opportunity to invest in eternity. Since God has limitless resources, there is no loss to God for the squandered funds—but the servant's forfeiture of reward is immeasurable.[4]

Can one be rich in heaven for giving less than everything—for, say, giving only a tithe when one could afford to give far more? Yes. However, that person won't be *as rich* as he could have been. You see, as with any good investment, the more one puts into it, the more one will gain in return.

As Paul told the Corinthians,

> *Remember this: Whoever sows sparingly will also reap sparingly, and whoever sows generously will also reap generously.* (2 Cor. 9:6)

Jonathan Edwards commented on that verse.

> 'Tis revealed to us that there are different degrees of glory to that end that we might seek after the higher degrees. God offered high degrees of glory to that end, that we might seek them by eminent holiness and good works. (*Selected Sermons of Jonathan Edwards*)

Jesus told his disciples,

> *No one who has left home or brothers or sisters or mother or father or children or fields for me and the gospel will fail to receive—in this life and, more importantly, in the life to come—a hundred times as many homes, brothers,*

*sisters, mothers, children and fields.* (Mark 10:29-31, author's translation)[5]

So, the answer to your question about how much to give is *your* answer to *this* question: How rich do you want to be in heaven?

Once again, unfortunately, many of our churches and pastors have missed a great opportunity in neglecting the teaching of rewards. They tell their congregations that they should give financially to God's work. They quote Paul: *"God loves a cheerful giver!"* (1 Cor. 9:7). But they fail to explain *why* God's people can be cheerful in giving. (The congregation is left to think, "Great . . . I am supposed to give and be *happy* about it.") We are not reminded that we can be happy in our giving because a great reward awaits those who are faithful in doing so. It is not pointed out that God will repay everything that is given, with a big (and I mean *huge*) dividend. (To repeat, there is no guarantee in Scripture that the return will be material and in this life. See appendix 1.)

## Encourage with God's Promises

Loving our neighbor includes encouraging people to look beyond merely getting into heaven. Like Jesus, we must tell people how to be rich when they get there. Faith that acts on God's promise to reward in heaven is a continuation and an expansion of saving faith that draws us into a closer and closer relationship with Jesus. Saving faith that is exercised by faith in God's promise of reward becomes a stronger faith. It is a faith that propels us to *"run in such a way as to win the prize"* (1 Cor. 9:24). That is the definition of eternal life that Jesus cares most about. He wants us not only to go to heaven, but to enter the Kingdom of God in the fullest and richest sense.

As your spiritual, financial advisor, I suggest you heavily weight your portfolio with investments in *people*. God would approve because people are His favorite investment: His *"treasured possession"* (Mal. 3:17 and elsewhere). Furthermore, *"you will be welcomed into the eternal dwellings"* by the very people you served for Christ's sake (Luke 16:9). Much of your reward, your *"joy and crown,"* as Paul put it, will be the people in whom you invested (Phil. 4:1; 1 Thess. 2:19).

I will put those promised returns up against any this world has to offer! No investment in this life beats God's reward.

**Notes and Asides:**

[1]  *I highly recommend Randy Alcorn's excellent book on financial stewardship, <u>Money, Possession and Eternity</u>. Alcorn condensed that more extensive work into the book entitled <u>The Treasure Principle</u>, which can be summarized succinctly: "You can't take it with you, but you can send it on ahead."*

[2]  *The presence of the story of the rich man in all three of the synoptic gospels (in Matt. 19; Mark 10; and Luke 18) reminds us to carefully consider what it teaches.*

*The rich man came—he ran!—to ask Jesus a question about eternal life. But precisely what was he so eager to know? It seems unlikely, as is generally supposed, that his interest was in attaining a place in heaven. As if he—like a student asking the teacher for a term paper's minimum required length—had come to Jesus to ask, "What is the <u>least</u> I must do to get into heaven?"*

*It seems more likely that he came to Jesus holding the presumption that he was already bound for heaven. First, he was a faithful, law-abiding son of Abraham. Why would he doubt his place in heaven? Moreover, he was rich and (we know from Luke's account) that he was a ruler among his people. Both likely convinced him, as they convinced the disciples and his culture, that he already enjoyed God's special favor. Furthermore, his words (related to us in Greek) support that understanding. "Zōēn aiōnion," translated "eternal life," has far weightier meaning than simply "heaven," the eternal place and time.*

*The word "eternal" ("<u>aiōnios</u>") does not speak only of the future. And "life" is translated from the Greek word "<u>zóēn</u>," which is both a physical (present) and a spiritual (future) existence. Thus, believers live "eternal life" right now; they experience this quality of God's life now, as a present possession. The Greek for "eternal life" is also in the present tense in John 3:36, 5:24, 6:47; and Romans 6:23. Therefore, it is reasonable to suppose the man's interest in coming to Jesus was in maintaining and augmenting his wealth and position in heaven, not in the qualifications for entry into heaven. He was asking, "What must I do to have riches and authority in heaven?"*

*And that was the question Jesus answered (whether or not the rich man was asking about entry into heaven). After confirming the man's fealty to the Law, Jesus prefaced his answer to the man's question with*

194

*this: "If you want to be 'teleios,' perfectly, completely, 100 percent obedient to the Law . . . if you are in earnest about being entirely faithful to God's Law, then demonstrate that desire by releasing your hold on all that is dear to you, including your money and the position it affords. In return, God will reward you with true riches in heaven."*

*There is a similar story in Luke 10, beginning at verse 28. An expert in the Law stood up to test Jesus. "Teacher," he asked, "what must I do to inherit eternal life?" "What is written in the Law?" Jesus asked. "How do you read it?" The man answered, "'Love the Lord your God with all your heart and with all your soul and with all your strength and with all your mind'; and, 'Love your neighbor as yourself.'" "You have answered correctly," Jesus replied. "Do this and you will live."*

*Jesus did not say that the man must fully obey the First and Second Great Commandments to go to heaven. (Who of us loves God with all his or her heart, soul, and strength?) But he said, truly, that if the man were to do so, he would live—in heaven. Jesus didn't give a minimum requirement for entry into heaven because Jesus isn't interested only in us going to heaven, He wants us to have riches in heaven. And if we have riches in heaven, we will be in heaven to enjoy them. So, even if my understanding of the rich man's intended question is incorrect— and he was actually asking about how he could go to heaven—Jesus's answer concerning riches in heaven still applies.*

*That distinction between heaven and riches in heaven helps us to understand the meaning of these often misinterpreted passages. Jesus is neither teaching that one will go to heaven (the place) for giving everything nor that one will not go to heaven (the place) because one did not sacrifice everything. Either understanding would be inconsistent with the rest of the Bible, which teaches that heaven itself is an unmerited gift of God's grace received in faith, not by works (Eph. 2:8-9).*

*There is a caution to observe in this story, as well. We should be careful in the assurances of heaven we give to people. While it is clear to God who is His child and who is not, it is not so clear to us. We cannot always discern when saving grace has been applied to a given individual. I'm thinking, for example, of a professed Christian who committed adultery and divorced her husband. She commented afterward (and without repenting of her sin), "God's grace covers me." Is she truly a follower of Jesus? I don't know. I shouldn't say she is, merely because she claims it.*

*Indeed, if one's only interest is in gaining heaven without investing in God's Kingdom, then that person has reason to consider whether he is even bound for heaven. "Let not any slothful one say, if I get to heaven at all, I will be content!" Surely John Wesley was right, despite what he infers in his next sentence about the possibility of losing one's salvation: "Such a one may let heaven go altogether" (706). For, as James tells us, faith without works is a dead faith {James 2:14-24}. And as Paul wrote to the Corinthians, "Examine yourselves to see whether you are in the faith; test yourselves. Do you not realize that Christ Jesus is in you—unless, of course, you fail the test?" {2 Cor. 13:5}. Therefore, a belief that one is bound for heaven based upon a profession of faith that has brought forth no fruit is not saving faith. Some will be surprised to hear Jesus someday ask, "Why do you call me Lord, Lord, but do not the things that I say?" (Luke 6:46).*

*To repeat, works do not save. But our <u>assurance</u> of salvation (the conviction that heaven is our destination, Heb. 11:1) is bolstered by ongoing evidence of obedience to—and empowerment by—the Spirit within us. "The things that accompany salvation" convince our hearts of the future that awaits us (Heb. 6:9-12). One who anticipates the riches in heaven that genuine service to Jesus produces will be all the more confident of heaven—and all the more diligent to secure those additional blessings.*

*(See more on this topic in Appendix 2: Common Emotional and Theological Objections.)*

[3] *My interpretation of the conversation between Jesus and the rich man is consistent with two other occasions in which Jesus tells us to sell everything. In Luke 12:33-34, Jesus says, "Sell your possessions and give to the poor. Provide purses for yourselves that will not wear out, a treasure in heaven that will not be exhausted, where no thief comes near and no moth destroys. For where your treasure is, there your heart will be also." In Matthew 13:44, He says, "The kingdom of heaven is like treasure hidden in a field. When a man found it, he hid it again, and then in his joy went and sold all he had and bought that field." In both cases, Jesus speaks of the "treasure" one will have for doing so. If Jesus is saying that selling **everything** is required for the*

196

*attainment of heaven, rather than for the realization of riches therein, then few of us will be there.*

*Having themselves left everything for Jesus, Peter pipes up and asks, "What then will there be for us?" (Matt. 19:27). Can you believe his chutzpah? But, far from scolding him ('There is nothing in it for you!'), Jesus said that the condition for sharing the fullest rights and privileges of His Kingdom is placing oneself unreservedly and wholly under the authority of its King! (vv. 28-30; Mark 10:29-31; Luke 18:29-30). It is a difficult calling to a life of sacrifice, made all the more difficult when there is much to relinquish. Thus, "how hard it is for the rich in this life to fully enter into the Kingdom of God" (Matt. 19:23). The Kingdom of God is much more than our preferred eternal retirement community. Jesus desires that we share the bounties of that Kingdom.*

*I have often asked Christians what Jesus replied to the rich man. Not one in ten recites the phrase, ". . . and you will have treasure in heaven." They, like the rich man, are so shocked by the condition (sell all and give it all away—to the poor no less!) that they aren't even listening when Jesus tells them what they will have for doing so. Unlike the rich man, we should ask Jesus a follow-up question: "Treasure, you say? Tell me more about it!"*

[4] *One reason not to take that which the Master has not given is that, in doing so, we rob God and ourselves of the joy of having God unexpectedly give it to us. Sometimes He does that: He hands us a generous material gift of what we might have been tempted to, but didn't, take for ourselves. It is a sweet experience of God's love when that happens.*

*Sandy and I once had such an experience on a business trip to a conference in historic Williamsburg, Virginia. Simultaneous to our arrival at the Williamsburg Inn, a college friend and his dear parents arrived for their own unrelated stay. Delighted to see each other after many years, we agreed to meet up later.*

*Having checked in, we were taken to our room, which was one of the least expensive available. As we owned the business, expenses were ours to pay. We could have afforded more expensive accommodation, but it was our desire to be faithful stewards of God's resources, so we didn't allow ourselves the extravagance.*

*However, when the porter opened the door to our room, he saw that it was already occupied. It had been double-booked. Having excused himself to the room's surprised occupants, he closed the door, thought for a moment, spun around, and said, "Follow me." After leading us (he on a bike and we in our car) this way and that through the quaint streets of Colonial Williamsburg, he stopped. "You can stay here—at no extra cost," he said. From where he stood on the sidewalk he pointed over a wooden gate—to a historic home.*

*The wood-framed, two-story house sat in a garden surrounded by a picket fence. It was lovely. And it would have cost many times what we would have paid, had we booked it for ourselves. What's more, God had confirmed that this was His doing—and not just a happy accident—and further amplified our enjoyment of it by bringing my friends and us together at the same moment. We were now able to invite them over to "our house" that evening for wine and cheese by a warm fire in the fireplace, while our infant daughter soundly slumbered upstairs.*

*It was perfect! And our enjoyment of such luxury and fellowship was many times what it would have been, had we presumed to take it for ourselves. It was a gift from God. But He could not have given it to us if we had first taken it.*

5  *Jesus prefaced this statement with "I tell you the truth." It was His way of emphasizing what He was about to say. It was like a boss calling out, "OK, people! Listen up!" We do well to pay attention.*

*It is unambiguous that Jesus first said that, for leaving one's home, family, and possessions in this life, one then gains more homes, family, and possessions—of a different and better sort—in this life. But the English translation (in this and most all English versions) of what follows ("in the age to come, eternal life") does not clearly extend those benefits to the life to come.*

*That is in part because many of us read "the age to come" and "eternal life" as synonymous expressions of a place and time called "heaven." (See note 2 above.) "In the age to come" (Gk. "aiōni") indeed does speak of an eternity of time, in a place and in the future. It is a future destination. But Jesus expands our understanding with a second use of a form of that word, "aiōnion," which speaks of all time, present, and future. Likewise, the Greek word "zóén," translated "life," is both a physical (present) and a spiritual (future) existence. Furthermore, that present and future life ("aiōnion") is of better* quality. So not only will one have blessings in this life, but one also will have those blessings in the life to come—for having given all to Jesus.

English translations obscure that meaning in yet another way. The "this life" part of the sentence and the "life to come" part are connected with the vague English word, "and." It isn't clear whether the "and" indicates a **change** from one state to another state or a **continuation** of the previous state into what follows. That ambiguity lends itself to the misunderstanding that our faithfulness results in reward in this life—and then we all go to heaven! End of story. But the Greek word "καί" is better translated "and moreover, indeed, or more importantly." Better than the word "and," such words infinitely extend the rewards for sacrifice in **this life** to the **eternity of life to come**.

Are you unconvinced? Then ask yourself: If Jesus wasn't conditionally promising a better quality of existence in **both** this life and the next, then why the redundant use of "aiōn?" It would be as if in the concluding phrase, "in the age to come, eternal life," Jesus was saying, nonsensically, "and then in heaven, you'll be in heaven."

More pointedly: What in the Bible would lead us to believe that Jesus will bestow benefits in this life—and then withhold them in the next? Do you expect God to bless the faithful in this life and then give **everyone**, including the less faithful, the same blessings in heaven? If so, then you have a radically different understanding of the Bible and of God's character than I do.

If you understand that the conditional promise of blessing is of heaven itself and not of additional blessing in heaven, then consider the next verse.

"Many who are now first will be last, and many who are now last will be first." (Matt. 19:31)

Some of the "first" who will be "last" are those discussed in footnote 2 above: those who, appearances aside, are not true believers. Such are not bound for heaven. Only God fully knows who those people are.

But Jesus also says, "the last will be first." If He is saying that giving everything, always placing ourselves as "last," is required for **entry** into heaven, Jesus would have been setting an impossible, works-based standard for entry into heaven. We'd none of us make it! And if instead, He was saying that we must—to at least some, undefined extent—place ourselves "last" in order to go to heaven, our eternal destiny would still be dependent upon our own efforts. Such is offensive to the doctrine of salvation by grace alone.

So, then, in what sense will "the last be first?" The _degree_ to which a given, authentic follower of Christ makes himself "last" will be the degree to which that follower will be made "first." He or she will experience heaven's glory to the extent of faithfulness to his or her call. (See "according to" in index 1.) Those who yield more to Jesus in this life will have more. And, per the above understanding of verses 29-30, they will have more of those spiritual blessings both in this life _and_ in the life to come than will those who commit less to Jesus in this life. (See also Rom. 2:6-7.)

To whom is the most glorious future promised? Who will be the "first"? The one who is willing to forsake all that is dear in this life—even all that is dearest—for the sake of God's Kingdom. The one who is ready to "drink of the cup Jesus drinks" (Matt. 19:38). The one who does so will have "a hundred times as much."

It is a prize worth running to win!

# Final Words: While It Is Still Called Today

After selling my business of twenty-seven years, I went through files to box up those I wished to keep and throw away those I didn't need. What a mix of emotions I felt as I rummaged through those records! It was like looking through old photos, but with an added poignancy: pictures are usually taken to capture happy moments, but these documents were snapshots of both the good and the ugly, the happiness and the pain in the life of a business owner. With this document, I fondly remembered people or circumstances; with that file, I was reminded of something hard and painful.

There were records of projects—some successful and of utility—and ventures that either failed outright or came to be of no particular consequence. There were records of dealings with customers, vendors, bankers, and employees. I recalled the faces of those with whom I had worked. "What do they think of me and how I dealt with them?" I wondered.

I wondered, too, what files God keeps of my life. At the Judgment Seat of Christ (2 Cor. 5:10), the Bema, will we go through those files together? Will we discuss my motives and my actions? Will I feel the sting of regret for wasted opportunity?

That which is worthy of praise *will* be remembered, and that which is not—like my unwanted files—will be "*burned up*" (1 Cor. 3:15). How much of what I have done will survive the fire of God's scrutiny? What gold, silver, and precious stones will I find amid the ashes of my wood, hay, and stubble? Quite sincerely, I shudder to think how little.

In fact, while researching and writing *Investing in Eternity* has been my life's most exciting project, it also has been one of its most challenging tasks. As I examined and pondered the promise of rewards in Scripture, I was always mindful of how far short of the prize I am. So much of my life's opportunities have been missed. Even now, with my heightened awareness

201

of what is at stake in this life, I fall short far too often. It would be easy to become discouraged by my failures.

Maybe you have had the same feelings while reading *Investing in Eternity* and God's Word about rewards. That is why you were reluctant to even consider the subject. So, let me tell you how God has encouraged me at such times.

First, He assured me that I will be held most responsible for that which I understood of His purposes, not for that which I did not understand. To the extent I had not been taught of God's rewards, I am less culpable than if I had ignored sound instruction. That's why I've directed many of my remarks at those who teach the Bible. They have a greater responsibility to know and teach the truth of God's Word {see James 3:1}. However, after having read *Investing in Eternity* and God's Word on the matter, you now no longer have the excuse of ignorance. As Jesus said, "*To whom much was given, of him much will be required*" (Luke 12:48 ESV).

Second, God reminded me that, while I can't change the past, I can learn from it. God "*makes all things work together for good*," even our mistakes and failings. All of us have struggled in one way or another in this life. God knows the obstacles you have faced. He will be gracious and loving when you stand before Him. Remember Paul's words of encouragement, "*Forget what is behind*" (Phil. 3:13).

Finally (and to finish Paul's thought), God encouraged me to "*strain toward what lies ahead!*" Your race is not yet done! The end of your story is not yet written! Whether for another seventy days or seventy years, you still can earn the hearty "Well done!" you hope to hear. Trust God's promises to inspire you to finish strong—to make up the lost ground in your race. You can do it because, as Paul said in Ephesians 3:16, God can give you His glorious, unlimited resources to empower you with inner strength through His Spirit.

I want nothing more than for *Investing in Eternity* to thus motivate followers of Jesus. I've written it to herald that final judgment of Christians, to provoke "Bema-focused living," to remind us that we will all stand before Jesus at His Judgment Seat. What you do in this life *does* matter! Solomon's muse was wrong! Life isn't meaningless! All that you do to advance God's purposes will be remembered—by God—for all of eternity.

Consider the athlete competing in a game of no importance: a nonconference match. The competition isn't all that tough. He is confident he and his team will win without a great effort. The athlete is doing his part but with no great enthusiasm or energy.

Then someone points out a scout sitting in the crowd, from a college to which the athlete hopes to receive an athletic scholarship. The scout has a clipboard. He is taking notes. Suddenly our athlete's indifference is transformed into focus. He is now driven to gain something far more significant than the win of a single, unimportant game. He works harder than he ever has before. He is determined to impress that scout and earn that scholarship!

Jesus is the "scout" sitting in the crowd. He is watching closely. He doesn't miss a thing; he can tell how hard you have practiced, trained your body, and prepared your mind. He can see by your performance whether your heart is in the game. He is taking notes. If you perform well, He will see, and He will reward.

There is a significant difference between the college scout and Jesus, of course. The scout merely observes, but Jesus delights in your performance! Jesus is not only evaluating you: He is rooting for you, just as we root for our kids and our friends' kids. Even more, He empowers you to do His will.

Anyone who has been to a school sports event with me knows I have (how to say it politely . . .) a large voice. I have embarrassed my wife and annoyed those around me with spirited cheering for my son at his swim meets. I watch closely to catch the rhythm of his breathing. And at the moment he turns his head to take a breath, causing his ear to come out of the water for just an instant, I yell, "GO ANDREW!!!"

While I sheepishly apologize to the spectators in front of me for yelling so loudly, I can't help myself! I want Andrew to know that I am watching and rooting for him. Of course, I love him no matter how well he performs, but *I want him to win*!! If there is any chance that he can hear me, and be inspired by my encouragement, I'm going to shout!

That sort of enthusiastic encouragement is undoubtedly what the writer of Hebrews had in mind when he said, *"consider how we might spur one another toward love and good deeds"* (Heb. 10:24). And that is what I have in mind as I write *Investing in Eternity*: "Go! Go! There is a prize to be won! Don't just jog to the finish line! Give it all you have! Make it hurt! It will be worth it! You will receive a crown of victory!"

I have told my kids, "If, as is the usual order of things, I die before you do, I want you to know this: when I get to heaven, I am going to ask Jesus to let me know when you are about to complete your race so I can be present when you cross the finish line. I want to hear Jesus tell you, with enthusiasm, *'Well done, good and faithful servant!'* I want to see Him give you a big, welcoming hug. I want to see Him beam! Not only will that welcome be a reward for you, my child, but also it will be a glory of endless delight for me to see and to hear. Please, don't disappoint me. Finish well. Finish strong!"

Other people will be standing at the finish line waiting for you, too. Your mom and dad, perhaps. The friend who introduced you to Jesus. The Sunday school teacher who taught you to better know and love Jesus. Your spouse. Your children. Your pastor. People who had a significant influence on your life. People who love you dearly. *You* will be a part of *their* reward! I urge you: don't disappoint that *"great cloud of witnesses"* who will be standing at the finish line, waiting for your homecoming (Heb. 12:1).

I will be among those witnesses, scanning the crowd of runners for those who have read this book and studied and trusted the promises of God it reviews. It is my fondest hope that many will run up to me after their lavish welcome from Jesus and say, "I was inspired by your book. I wanted to have the riches you described. I ran my race to gain God's reward!"

It is one thing to agree that Scripture often speaks of rewards. It is quite another to fully grasp its significance for your life. For my part, it has taken years of God's reminders amid life's struggles to learn how to trust those promises. The move from the head to the heart has been, for me, a slow migration. It began as a trickle—like the one the Little Dutch Boy spotted. But don't put your finger in the hole of the dike! Allow the erosion of your old ways of thinking! It will eventually produce a flood of hope, peace, and joy![1]

Don't delay living this truth! Like another pop song from the '70s reminded us, "Time keeps on slippin', slippin', slippin' into the future" (Miller). Every tick of the clock takes us closer to that moment—the outcome of which lasts forever—when we stand before Christ at His Bema.

As I wrote the above paragraph, an image appeared on one of my computer screens: one of the photos in Chromecast's rotation. Most of the pictures it displays are stunningly beautiful, but this one was uncharacteristically boring. Taken from a satellite, it showed a largely featureless terrestrial landscape. In the center of the gray-scale photo was a snake-shaped squiggle. At the bottom was a body of water.

But this picture instantly caught my attention. The words "Kauai, Hawaii" at the bottom confirmed my initial impression: it is of the long, uphill, and switchback road through Waimea Canyon. Sandy and I had traversed that dark, vegetation-enshrouded road just a few weeks earlier. At its end—and from the height of nearly a mile—we emerged from the shadows to one of the most beautiful vistas we had ever seen—of the vast and blue Pacific Ocean.

I can scarcely believe God put that image before my eyes at this moment—because it perfectly captures what my heart wants to portray in *Investing in Eternity*: a heavenly perspective of what lies ahead in Paradise at the end of the winding and challenging road of life. We now can only see it from afar—as if from a satellite. Someday, however, faithful followers of Jesus will stand on the heights, marveling at His beauty, surveying with awe and amazement His great and glorious work.

> Lord, *"open my eyes to see the wonderful truths in your instructions."* Psalm 118:18 (NLT)

And as you travel your sometimes arduous road in pursuit of God's reward, remember: to the extent you are faithful with the conduct of your life, when you finally arrive, you will be Jesus's reward, too! You will be His crown! After all, He loves you so much that He died for you. You are the *"joy that was set before Him"* {Heb. 12:2} when He endured the cross. He wants to lavish praise upon you. He wants to reward you forever with the riches of His grace. Please, don't disappoint Jesus.

> Press on, to take hold of that for which Christ Jesus took hold of you. (Phil. 3:12)

Please Him. Serve Him. *"Throw off everything that hinders."* (Heb. 12:1) It will be worth any cost, because . . .

**God promises to reward!**

## Notes and Asides

1 *Here is a suggestion that might help your heart's understanding: watch The Bema, a dramatization of what awaits all followers of Jesus when we stand before Christ on His throne, an even that is described for us by Paul in 2 Corinthians 5:10. (I found this dramatization on YouTube.) You will get a glimpse of what it will be like to stand before Jesus—and all of God's people—on that Day. You will see that it is true: nothing else matters but that Day and what it will portent for the eternity of days that follow it.*

# Indexes

# Index of the Nature of Rewards

*Rewards are conditional.*

The following references contain if-then words and phrases that support the premise: rewards are conditional, based upon our faithfulness. Some verses have both an "if" and "then." Many have either an "if," with the "then" implied, or a "then," with the "if" implied. Often both the "if" and "then" are implied in the Bible; but this book only references such verses when they are in proximity to expressly conditional promises.

I have counted **585** total instances of "if" and "then" conditions for rewards in the verses selected for Investing in Eternity. (My tally is certainly understated; but, as Paul said, "No matter how many promises God has made, they are "Yes" in Christ.") I record enough references here that the reader should have no doubt that many of God's blessings accrue only to those who meet the condition.

And keep in mind that there are many more if-then conditional promises of negative rewards than there are conditional promises of positive reward. Clearly, this is one of the most ubiquitous doctrine in all of Scripture.

*The "If" conditions.*

Every "if" condition is followed by the act(s) of faithfulness required to meet the condition, listed in index 3. There are no fewer than 416 "if" conditions in the verses.

The word "if" is used in 141 instances:

If you... Ex. 15:26; Lev. 25:18; Deut. 4:28 (twice), 7:12, 11:22, 27, 28, 22:13, 22, 27, 28: 1, 2, 9, 13, 28:2, 9, 13, 30:10, 17; 2, 1 Sam.

7:3, 12:14, 21:14; 1 Kings 9:4; 1 Chron. 15:2, 7:17; 22:12, 15:2;
Prov. 1, 3, 4; Isa. 1;9, 58:12 (2x), 10, 13 (3x); Zech. 3:6; Luke
6:35, 16:11-12; John 9:10, 15:5; 1 Cor. 3:14; 1 Pet. 3:13, 4:14, 16
If anyone ... Matt. 16:24-25; John 12:24; 2 Tim. 2:5, 12
If my people... 2 Chron. 7:14
If only... Deut. 15:5
If the righteous... Prov. 11:31
If we ... Rom. 8:17; Gal. 6:9
If we are careful... Deut. 7:12, 11:12
If you do these things... 2 Pt. 1:10
If you do not... Deut. 28:15 (twice)
If you find it.... Prov. 11:3, 24:14,
If you follow ... Lev. 26:3
If you fully... Deut. 28:1
If you obey ... Deut. 11:26, 30:15, 19
If you want... Matt. 19:21

There are approximately two hundred and fourteen (214) uses of "those,
those who, those whose, whoever, everyone who, the man or woman who,
they whose, who are, you who, etc." that indicate an "if" condition must be
met to receive the promised blessing. Here are some examples:

2 Chron. 16:9: Job 15-16, Ps. 1:1, 2, 24:3-5, (4x) 24:3, 31:19, 34:5, 7,
10, 12 18; 35:27, 40:16, 70:4, 84:11, 91:1, 112:2-5, 119:1-2; Prov.
3:12, 11:18, 13:13, 14:14, 19:17, 22, 21:1, 27:18 (twice), 28:10;
Eccl. 2:26; Dan. 12:3, 3; Ez. 18:5, 9: Mal. 3:16; Matt. 5:19, 7:8
(3 times), 10:31, 32, 39, 40, 12:50, 13:9, 12, 16:25; 19:28. 25"21.
23; Mark 4:25, 10:43, 44; Luke 6:18, 8:18, 9:46, 48, 12:8, 13:9,
10, 16:10; John 12:26; John 12:25, 26: Rom. 2:7, 10; 1 Cor. 3:12;
2 Cor. 9:6; Gal. 6:8; Heb. 12:11; 1 Pet. 3:10; James 1:12; Rev.
2:7, 11, 26, 29, 3:5, 6, 12, 21:7.

There are sixty-one (61) other words also used to indicate the "if"
conditionality of a promise.

Everyone who... 2 Chron. 30:18; Ezra 9:22; Matt. 19:29, 25:29;
Luke 19:26
All who... Judges 5:31; Ps. 40:16, 70:4, 128:1; Matt. 11:28; 2 Tim. 4:6

Anyone who ... Matt. 5:19, 10:41, 42, 11:6
As long as... 2 Chron. 26:5 2:26
As we... 1 Cor. 1:5
As you... Rom. 15:13
Be careful ... Josh. 1:7, 8
Be careful to do... Deut. 5:32;
But as for you... 2 Chron. 15:7
But if your heart... Deut. 30:7
But if... 1 John 1:7 (twice)
Chose... Deut. 30:19
Each will... 1 Cor. 4:5
Each man... 1 Sam. 26:23
Each one ... 1 Cor. 3:10, 2 Cor. 5:10
For all I have done... Neh. 5:19
In as much as you participate... 1 Pet. 4:13
In keeping ... Ps. 19:11
Just as you... Matt. 8:13
Many ... Matt. 19:30;
Now... Jer. 17:13
Of the remnant... Micah 7:18
Of the righteous... Prov. 13:21
Provided that... Rom. 11:22
Remember me for this... Neh. 13:14, 22
Since ... Col. 3:22
That person is... Ps. 1:3, 112:5
That which produces ... Heb. 6:7
That you may... Deut. 30:20
The good man... Prov. 14:14
The good soil... Matt. 13:8
The upright ....
These were... Heb. 11:39
They ... 2 Chron. 15:15; Ps. 119:1
This man... Luke 18:14
Your ... Psalm 34:7; Prov. 3:6; Jer. 7:3, 17:13; Matt. 9:22
You must ... Gen. 17:9
When... Neh. 9:27

## The "then" indicator of consequence

There are at least 169 total "then"—there will be a consequence—indicators of positive reward in the Bible. Satisfied "then" conditions are followed by a reward.
The word "then" is used in sixty-seven (67) instances:

> "Then"... Lev. 25:19; Deut. 7:1, 12, 11:13, 23, 15:10, 28:10, 30:16; Josh. 1:8; 1 Sam. 12:11; 1 Chron. 22:13; 2 Chron. 6:31, 7:14; 15:7, 15:2; Ps. 58:10; Prov. 3:4, 6, 10; Isa. 58:8 (twice), 9, 10, 14; Jer. 17:13, 29:12; Joel 2:27; Amos 5:4; Zech. 3:7; Mal. 3:12; 16; Matt. 6:4, 6, 8:13, 9:29, 13:44, 16:27, 20:16, Luke 6:35, 14:10, 1 Cor. 12:10, Rev. 2:23, 14:13"So that" ... Lev. 9:6, 20:22; Deut.5:16, 32; 6:18, 24, 8:1, 11:8, 9, 13,21, 14:29, 28:13, 29:9, 30:6, 14; Josh. 1:8: 1 Kings 2:3; 1 Chron. 22:12; 15:15; Ez. 18:9; John 4:36, 9:10: 1 Cor. 4:10-11, 9:22, 27; Phil. 2:15; 1 Tim. 6:19; Heb. 10:36, 11:3; James 1:4; 1 John 1:2; Rev. 3:11

There are also one hundred two (102) other words used to indicate the conditionality of a promise.

> "Because" (Heb. *yaan*, "as a consequence") ... Gen. 22:16, 18; 26:5; 2 Kings 10:30, 22:19; 2 Chron. 1:11, (There are nearly seven times as many instances—most of them in Ezekiel and the Prophets—when the described consequence is negative.)
> "Because" (Gk. *ki*, "that, for, when") ... Gen. 7:1; 32:28; Ex. 33:17; Deut. 15:10, 2 Chron. 14:7, 27:6; Ps. 16:8
> "Because" (Gk. *hoti*, expressing a causal connection) ... Matt. 5:2-12 (9 times), 13:11, 16 (twice); Mark 9:41; Luke 19:17; Acts 5:41; 1 Cor. 3:13, 15:58; Eph. 6:8; James 1:3, 12
> "Because, for" (Gk. *gar,* used to express cause) ... Matt. 12:33; Luke 6:23: Rom. 5:10; Heb. 10:34, 11:6, 26, 27; 1 Pet. 2:19
> "Because" (Gk. *epei,* since, of cause) ... Heb. 11:11
> "You will" ["then", implied]... Gen. 6:18, 12:2, Lev. 20:24, 25:18, 19, 26:5, 6, 7, 8; Deut. 4:28, 32, 11:23, 28:13, 30:16; Joshua 1:6, 8; 1 Chron. 22:13; Ps. 16:11, 62:11, 128:2; Prov. 3:4, 25:22; Isa. 54:17 (twice), 58:9 (twice), 11, 12, 14; Jer. 29:12, 13; Isa. 3:10; Hosea 3:5; Joel 2:26 (twice); 27, Zech. 3:7 (twice); Mal. 3:10, 18;

Matt. 7:7; 11:29, 12:37, 19:21; Mark 10:21, 35; Luke 6:21 (twice), 13:9, 14:10, 14 (twice), 16:9, 18:22; John 9:10, 13:17, 15:5, 16:24; Col. 3:24; Heb. 10:36; 1 Pet. 5:4; 2 Pt. 1:10, 11 (Often the same passage says there will be no blessing if there is disobedience.)

"Because" [implied] ... Lev. 26:4, 6 (twice), 9 (twice), 11, 12; Judges 10:16; 1 Sam. 7:3, 9; 2 Sam. 22:22; 2 Chron. 30:20; Isa. 49:4, 10-12, 58:11-13; Ez. 18:9; Neh. 9:27; Ps. 16:11, 24:5, 31:19, 37:4-6; Mal. 3:18, Matt. 5:2-12, 6:33, 7:7 (3 times), 11:28; Mark 10:21; Luke 6:23, 12:31, 14:14, John 9:11, 15:5; Rev. 2:10

"They will" [as a result] ... Prov. 3:2, Isa. 3:10, 61:7 (twice); Jer. 31:16; Hosea 3:5; Mal. 3:17; Matt. 5:3-12. 13:8: 1 Tim. 6:19; Rev. 3:3, 14:13; "You will" ... Isa. 61:7: Jer. 31:16; "This will" ... Prov. 3:8; "In this way" ... 1 Tim. 6:19: "And I will" ... Jer. 29:12: "That he may" ... 1 Pet. 5:6

"But" [nevertheless]... Judges 5:31; Prov. 12:12, 13:21; James 6:6

"Therefore" ... 2 Kings 22:20 (*ken*); Ps. 16:9, 18:21, 22; Heb. 11:16

"When" ... Lam. 3:57; Jonah 3:10, Matt. 5:3-10, 12, 12:37, 24:46; Mark 10:39; Luke, 12:34, 16:9; 19:17

"He" or his (12 times) ... Ps. 112:2-9

Note: The density of conditional promises in the New Testament is approximately 8 percent greater than that in the Old Testament.

Note: I have listed only the if-then statements of positive rewards. The Bible speaks far more often of negative rewards (which are punishments for sin.)

### *Rewards are a repayment.*

Rewards are a repayment, wage, salary, compensation, fare, price paid for services, payment on contract, recompensation; etc. There are 107 references to wages etc. using 21 different Hebrew and Greek roots. Several times the writer uses two different words in close proximity to emphasize his point.

## In Hebrew

Compensation, fare, fee for hire, reward, wage *sakar*, et al. Gen 15:1, 30:18; 2 Chron. 15:7; Prov. 11:18; Isa. 40:10, 62:11 (twice); Jer. 31:16

To return *shub*, et al. 1 Sam. 26:23, 2 Sam. 22:21, 25; Ps. 18:20, 24; Prov. 24:12

As a consequence, because of *eqeb*, et al. Ps. 19:11; Prov. 22:4

To bestow on, deal bountifully, do good, recompense, requite, reward *gamal,* et al. Ps. 18:20, 103:10, 116:7; Prov. 11:17; Isa. 35:4, 61:8

To give, put *nathan* 1 Kings 8:39; 2 Chron. 6:30; Jer. 32:19

A judgment that is due *mishpat* Isa. 49:4

Filled, sated, satisfied or surfeited *saba* Prov. 14:14

To make amends, make an end, finish, and full, give again, make good, repay again *shalam,* et al. Ruth 2:12, 1 Sam. 24:19; 2 Sam. 22:21; Job 34:11; Ps 62:12; Prov. 11:31, 13:13, 21; 19:17, 25:22; Joel 2:25

Recompense, reward, wages *peullah*, et al. Isa. 40:10, 49:4, 61:8, 62:11

Repay *maskoreth* Ruth 2:12

Heritage *nachalah Isa.* 54:17

First fruit, earnings, reward *peri*, et al. Ps 58:11, Prov. 12:14, Jer. 17:10

To take possession of or inherit *yarash* Isa. 61:8

## In Greek

To deliver again, give up, give back, return, restore *apodidómi,* et al. Matt. 6:4, 6, 18, 16:27, 20:8; Luke 10:35; Rom. 2:6; 2 Tim. 4:8, Heb. 12:11, Rev. 2:23 To requite (good or evil), recompense, render, repay *antapodidómi,* et al. Luke 14:14; Col. 3:24;

Wages, reward, payment for hire *misthos*, et al. Matt. 5:12, 46, 6:1, 10:41 (twice), 42, 20:8; Mark 9:41; Luke 6:23, 35, 10:7; John 4:36; 1 Cor. 3:8, 14, 9:17; 1 Tim. 5:18; Heb. 11:6, 26; 2 John 8; Rev. 11:18, 22:12; requital (good or bad), recompense of reward Heb. 10:35, 11:26

Take care of, recompensate, receive back *komizo*, et al. 2 Cor. 5:10;
   Eph. 6:8; 1 Pet. 5:4; Heb. 10:36
A prize, goal *brabeion*, et al. 1 Cor. 9:24; Phil. 3:14
To reap *therizó*, et al. 2 Cor. 9:6; Gal. 6:7-9 (three times)
To reach, seize, attain, lay hold of *katantaó*, et al. Phil. 3:11, 12
To obtain *epitugchanó* Heb. 6:15, 11:33

Wages (etc.) for sin (or rewards forfeited for improper motives.) I focus my attention on positive rewards. This list of negative rewards (punishments)—all are in proximity and in juxtaposition to positive rewards. There are many more such conditional promises of negative rewards in the rest of the Bible.

To return *shub* Judges 9:56
To recompense, requite, reward *gamal* Ps. 28:4, 103:10; Isa. 3:9, 11,
   59:18; Lam. 3:64
To give, put, *nathan* Ez. 23:49
To make amends, make an end, finish, full, give again, make good,
   repay again *shalam* et al Deut. 32:35, 41; Ps. 31:23, Jer. 25:14,
   51:24
To deliver again, give up, give back, return, restore; requite *apodidómi*
   et al. Matt. 12:36, 21:41; Rom. 12:19; Heb. 12:16; 2 Tim. 4:14 To
   requite (good or evil), recompense, render, repay *antapodidómi*
   Luke 14:12: 2 Thess. 1:6; Heb. 10:30
Wages, reward, payment for hire *misthos*, et al. Matt. 5:46; 6:1, 2,
   5, 16; Acts 1:18; 2 Pt. 2:13, 15, Jude 1:11 requital (good or bad),
   recompense of reward Heb. 2:2
To receive back *komizo*, et al. Col. 3:25
Wages *opsónion* Rom. 6:23

### *Rewards flow from God's holiness.*

*The Judge* is standing at the door! James 5:9
According to the *law of the Lord* (Ps. 119:1)
God *judges* the earth and rewards the righteous Ps. 7:8, 11, 58:11
God will *judge* us by our own words Luke 19:22
It is God who *judges* Ps. 75:7
Reward and recompense is *with Him* Isa. 40:10

Each will receive what is *due* Isa. 49:4

According to what *we have done* Rev. 12-13

According to one's *righteousness* and *cleanness* of hands Ps. 18:19-20

According to conduct and as deeds *deserve* Jer. 32:19

*Acquitted* by our words Matt. 12:37

*Nothing is hidden* that will not be disclosed Luke 8:16-17

Standing before the *judgment* seat Romans 14:10; 2 Cor. 5:10

Each will give *an account* Romans 14:12

The Lord *judges* 1 Cor. 4:4

We labor *not in vain* 1 Cor. 15:58

Each will receive *what is due* 2 Cor. 5:10

The righteous *judge* awards 2 Tim. 4:8

*He will not forget* your work Heb. 6:10

God *judges* each man's work impartially 1 Peter 1:17

According to the *rules* 2 Tim. 2:5

### Rewards are certain because God has promised them.

In My faithfulness... an everlasting covenant Isa. 61:8

A scroll of remembrance Mal. 3:16

For those for whom it is prepared Mark 10:40

Since the creation of the world Matt. 25:34

Inheritance from the Lord Col. 3:24

You will receive what he has promised Heb. 10:36

None had [yet] received what was promised Heb. 11:39

Promise for life and the life to come 1 Tim. 4:8

### Rewards (both negative and positive) are proportional to deeds.

According to what is done 1 Kings 8:39; 2 Chron. 6:30; Ps. 62:12; Prov. 24:12; Matt 16:27; Mark 8:34-35; Luke 0:23-24; John 12:25; Rom. 2:6; Rev. 20:12-13, 22:12

According to my righteousness Ps. 18:20, 23-24; 2 Sam. 22:21, 25; {Ps. 7:8}; Ps. 18:20, 24

According to the cleanness of my hands 2 Sam. 22:21; Ps. 18:20, 25

According to my cleanness in His sight 2 Sam. 22:25

According to conduct Jer. 17:10, 32:19

According to what his deeds deserve Jer. 17:10, 32:19
According to his own ways {Ez. 33:20, also, 7:27; 18:30, 24:14}
According to his own labor 1 Cor. 3:8
According to your deeds Rev. 2:23
According to my integrity {Ps. 7:8}
According to the law of the Lord Ps. 119:1
According to your faith Matt. 9:29
An accounting will be made Matt. 12:36
It will be measured to you as you measured Mark 4:24
What is due is paid Isa. 49:4; 2 Cor. 5:10
Our deeds will follow us Rev. 14:13

### *Rewards are many times greater than what was given*

In abundance Matt. 25:29; Luke 6:35;
A hundred times as much Matt. 19:29; Mark 10:30
Many times as much Luke 18:30
According to His glorious riches Phil. 4:19; Col. 1:11

### *Rewards are inexhaustible / eternal / undiminished*

Works of our hands will be "established." Ps. 90:17
Remembered forever Ps. 112:6
Will not wear out Luke 12:33
No thief will take, or moth will destroy Luke. 12:33
Eternal 2 Cor. 4:18
An inheritance that can never perish 1 Pet. 1:4
Being blessed by the Father Matt 25:34; Luke 14:1

# Index of Descriptions of Rewards

I count seven hundred seventy-seven (777) descriptions of God's rewards in the verses referenced in *Investing in Eternity*.

### *God is our Reward*

> To know Christ and gain Christ Phil. 3:7, 8, 10
> To be found in Him Phil. 3:9
> To have the fellowship of His suffering Acts 5:41: Phil. 3:10; Phil. 1:29: Col. 3:24
> To have closeness to God Ez. 45:4; James 4:8
> To experience the glory of God Lev. 9:6
> To find God Deut. 4:8
> To know Christ Phil. 3:10

### *Rewards are a wage, salary, recompense, etc.*

> (Refer to the 107 rewards listed in Index of the Nature of Rewards.)

### *Godly Pleasures*

> An end to misery Judges 11:16
> Comfort Ps. 5:11, 16:8, 35:27, 40:16, Job 36:16; Isa. 51:3; Matt. 5:4; 2 Cor. 1:3-5 (5x)
> Confidence Isa. 31:17; Heb. 4:13, 6:9; 1 John 2:28, 5:14
> Fellowship with God Phil. 3:10
> Gladness Ps. 16:9, 40:16, 58:10, 70:4; Prov. 29:6; Isa. 51:3; Matt. 5:12; John 4:36; Rev. 19:7
> Glory from God Isa. 62:2; Rom. 2:7,10, 8:17, 18; 1 Pet. 5:10; 2 Cor. 4:17; II Thess. 2:14; 19, 20

Happiness Eccl. 2:26; Matt. 25:22, 23

Heard by God Ex. 2:24; 2 Chron. 7:14; Lam. 3:56

Hope Prov. 24:14; Jer. 29:11; Rom. 5:10, 15:4 (3x); Eph. 1:18; 2 Thess. 2:19; 1 Pet. 1:3

Joy / Enjoyment Ps. 5:11, 16:11, 19, 19:8; 35:27, 37:3, 11, 97:10, 126:5, 6, 149:5; Prov. 12:20, 28:16, 29:6; Isa. 3:10, 51:3, 58:14; 61:7, 65:13; Matt. 13:44; Luke 6:23; John 9:10 (twice), 16:24; Acts 5:41; Rom. 15:13; Gal. 5:22; Col. 1:12; 2 Thess. 2:19, 20; 1 Tim. 6:17; Heb. 10:34, 11:25, 16:17; James 1:2; 1 Pet. 1:6, 8, 4:8; 1 John 1:4

Love and faithfulness Prov. 14:22

Mercy from God Neh. 13:22; Ps. 4:1; Prov. 28:13; Is. 55:7; Matt. 5:7; Luke 18:13; Heb. 4:16;

Nearness of God Lam. 3:57

No fear Lev. 26:6; Ps. 112:8

Peace Lev. 26:6; Ps. 37:11, 112:7; Prov. 3:17; 29:6; Isa. 26:3, 32:17, 57:2; Rom. 2:5, 15:13; Gal. 5:22; Phil. 4:6; Heb. 12:11

Pleasure and delight Ps. 16:11: Prov. 3:17; Mal. 3:12; 2 Tim. 2:5

Rejoicing 1 Chron. 16:10; Ps. 5:11, 16:8, 33:21, 40:16, 64:10, 70:4, 89:16, 97:10, 105:3, 107:42, 149:4; Isa. 41:16, 61:7, 62:5 (twice), 65:13; Matt. 4:12; Luke 6:23; 2 Cor. 13:11; Col. 1:24; 1 Pet. 1:6, 4:13; Rev. 19:7

Renewal 2 Cor. 4:16; 1 Pet. 5:10

Rest 2 Chron. 14:7, 15:15; Ps. 16:9, 90:17, 91:1, 116:7; Isa. 57:2; Matt. 11:28, 29; Rev. 14:13

Revival of the soul Ps. 19:7

Satisfaction Eccl. 2:24; Luke 6:21; Isa. 58:11

Security Lev. 26:6; 2 Kings 23:20; Ps. 16:9, 112:8 Prov. 10:9, 14:26; Isa. 32:18; Jer. 17:13; 1 Sam. 21:8

Steadfastness Ps. 112:7; Isa. 26:3; 1 Pt. 5:10

Strength 1 Cor. 12:10

Thanksgiving Isa. 51:1; 2 Cor. 4:15

## *Approval from God*

Being declared good and faithful Matt. 25:21, 23; Luke 19:17

Being declared worthy of the Lord Matt. 10:37, 38; Rev. 3:4

Being dressed in white Rev. 3:4

Being known by God Ex. 33:17

Receiving a rich welcome into heaven 2 Pt. 1:11

Receiving commendation from God Luke 16:8: 2 Cor. 10:18, Heb. 11 (4 x), 1 Pet. 2:18-19

Receiving praise from God 1 Cor 4:5

Receiving praise, glory, and honor 1 Pet. 1:7

Receiving the kindness of God Rom. 11:22

Receiving the favor of God Lev. 26:9; Ps. 90:17

## *Honor before others*

All the nations will call you blessed Mal. 3:12

Called great in the kingdom Matt. 5:19

Called sons of God Matt. 5:9; Luke 6:35

Double honor 1 Tim. 5:17

Double portion Isa. 61:7

Exaltation Ps. 75:7, Luke 14:11; Luke 18:14; James 4:10

Favor and good name with God and man Gen. 35:10; 2 Chron. 33:12; Prov. 3:4, 13:15; Matt. 6:2; Luke 14:10; Col. 3:22;

Favor Lev. 26:9; Neh. 5:19; Ps. 5:12; 84:11, 90:17; Prov 3:34, 8:35, 11:2, 12:2, 16:15; Isa. 62:2

First (as opposed to last) Deut. 28:12-13; Matt. 19:30, 20:16; Mark 10:44

Glory and honor Rom. 2:7, 10; 1 Pet. 1:7

Head and not the tail Deut. 28:13

Honor 1 Sam. 2:3; Ps. 15:3; 84:1, 89:17, 91:15, 112:9, 149:5; Prov. 3:16, 35, 4:8, 11:16. 21:11; 22:4; 27:18, 29:23; Zeph. 3:12; Mal. 3:16; John 12:26; 1 Pet. 1:33

Honored before angels by Jesus Luke 12:8

Horn lifted high in honor Ps. 89:17, 112:9

In the sight of men Ps. 31:19; Prov. 3:4

Lifted up (in due time) Ps. 75:10; Ps. 112:9, 146:5; 1 Pet. 5:6; Rev. 20:12

Made great among others Matt. 5:3, 10, 19; Mark 10:43; Luke 9:46, 22:7

Made the head and not the tail Deut. 28:13

More than others Matt. 13:12, 25:29; Mark 4: 25; Luke 8:18, 11:9, 19:26

Remembered Neh. 5:19, 13:14; Ps. 112:6
Set high above all the nations of earth Deut. 28:1

## *Sharing in the suffering of Christ*

Job 36:15-16, Romans 5:10, 8:17, 1 Cor. 4:10-11, 2 Cor. 1:5; Phil. 3:10: Col. 1:24: 2 Tim. 2:3

## *Vindication*

Ps. 7:8, 17:2, 24:5, 35:27, 57:2, 58:10-11, 112:2-9, 135:14; Isa. 54:17, 62:1-2; Jer. 51:10; Matt. 10:26-27, 12:37; Luke 8:16-17, 12:2 (See also Ps. 43:1-3, 54:1-3, 135:14, Isa. 50:7-9)
Acquitted Matt. 12:37
Never again shamed Joel 2:27
No longer scorned Joel 2:19
Your enemies will fall Lev. 26:7

## *Authority and Responsibility*

A throne 1 King 9:5; 2 Chron. 7:18; Prov. 29:14
Authority over the nations Rev. 2:26
Given the kingdom of heaven / God Matt. 5:3; 10; Matt. 25:34; Luke 6:20
Power 2 Chron. 27:6
Put in charge of the master's possessions Matt. 24:47; 25:21, 23
Put in charge of cities Luke 19:19
The right to sit with Jesus on His throne Rev. 3:21

## *A Harvest*

A harvest Gal. 6:9
A hundred, sixty, or thirty-fold increase Matt. 13:8
A share of the crops 2 Tim. 2:6
Fruit Prov. 27:18; Isa. 3:10; John 15:5
Increased store of seed and enlarged harvest 2 Cor. 9:10
Productive "land" receives the blessing of God Heb. 6:7

### Children (mortal and spiritual)

Children will be mighty in the land Lev. 26:9; Deut. 11:21; Ps. 112:2
Descendants Gen. 22:17-18
God will love you and increase your numbers Deut. 7:13
You will increase in number Duet. 8:1, 11:21

### A Treasure

Hidden treasure Prov. 15:6, 24:4; Matt 13:44
Riches through Christ's poverty 1 Cor. 8:9
Treasure in heaven Matt. 6:19, 19:21; Mark 10:21; Luke 12:33; Luke
    18:22; Col. 2:3; 1 Tim. 6:19
True riches Luke 16:11; Eph. 11:17

### A Crown

A crown to hold forever Rev. 3:11
Of glory that will not fade away 1 Peter 5:4
Of life James 1:12; Rev. 2:10
Of people Phil. 4:1; 1 Thess. 2:19
Of righteousness 2 Tim 4:8
Of victory Ps. 149:4; 2 Tim 2:5, Rev. 2:10
That lasts forever 1 Cor. 9:25

### Righteousness

A righteousness that comes from God Phil. 3:9
A righteousness that shines like the dawn Ps. 37:6
Enduring righteousness Ps. 112:3
Filled with righteousness Matt. 5:6
God will be our righteousness Duet 6:25
Harvest of righteousness Heb. 12:11
Heir of righteousness Heb. 11:7
His righteousness Matt. 6:33
Showers of righteousness Hosea 10:12

## Wisdom and Understanding

Discretion and understanding 1 Chron. 22:12
Guidance Prov. 3:5
Light to the eyes Ps. 19:8
Maturity, completeness, lacking nothing James 1:3
Shrewdness 2 Sam. 22:27
Wisdom Ps. 19:7
Wisdom and knowledge 2 Chron. 1:11; Eccl. 2:26
Wisdom that is better than gold Prov. 3:14-15

## Spiritual Bounty and Success

A great gain 1 Tim 6:6
A land flowing with milk and honey; fruit, food Lev. 20:24; 25:19;
     Lev. 26:4-5; Deut. 6:18, 11:9, 13
Abounding grace 2 Cor. 9:8
Abounding in good works 2 Cor. 9:8
All that you need 2 Cor 9:8; Joel 2:19
An inheritance Lev. 20:24; Prov. 28:10; Isa. 58:14; Matt. 25:34;
     Heb. 11:7
Dwell in the land forever Ps. 37:27
Floodgates of blessing Mal. 3:10
Life Amos 5:14; Prov. 22:4
Like a tree planted by streams of water Ps. 13
Long life and prosperity Duet. 6:24
Plenty to eat Joel 2:26
Possession of the land Num. 33:53; Deut. 8:1, 11:8; 2 Chron. 14:7
Success 1 Chron. 14:7, 22:13: 2 Chron. 26:5
Success in whatever is undertaken 2 Kings 18:7

## A New Identity

A name of the city of God Rev. 3:12
Labeled as God's Rev. 3:12
New name Gen. 17:5, 32:27; Rev. 3:12

## Steadfastness

God will establish you as his holy people Deut. 28:9
God will establish your throne 1 King 9:5; 2 Chron. 7:18
God will establish the work of your hands Ps. 90:17
You will not (never) be shaken Ps. 16:8, 112:6, 9
You will never fall 2 Pet. 1:10
You will have perseverance James 1:2

## Blessing

Gen. 12:2 (twice), 3 (twice), 22:17, 18, 26:4 (twice), 26:3-4, 32:26, 35:9-10; Ex. 20:24, 23:25, 32:29; Num. 6:27; Deut. 2:7, 7:13, 14, 11:13, 26, 27, 14:29, 15:4, 10, 18, 23:20, 24:19, 28:2-8, 12, 30:16, 19, 40:4, 41:1; 2 Sam. 6:12;1 Chon. 4:9; Ps. 1:1, 2:12, 5:12, 24:5, 34:8, 37:26, 40:4, 41:1-2, 84:4-5, 12, 89:15, 106:3, 112: 1-2, 106:3, 112:2 (twice), 115:13, 119:1-2, 128:1, 4, 146:5; Prov. 3:13, 18, 33, 8:32, 33, 10:6, 11:26, 14:21, 16:20, 20:7, 22:9, 24:25, 28:20, 29:18; Isa. 30:18, 32: 20, 56:2; Jer. 17:7; Hosea 3:5; Mal. 3:10, 12; Matt 5:3-11, 27, 11:6, 13:16, 25:34; Luke 6:20-22, 22 14:14; John 13:17; 1 Cor. 9:23; Heb. 6:7, 14; James 1:12, 25, 5:11; 1 Peter 3:9, 14, 4:14; Rev. 1:3, 22:7, 14

## Material blessings in this life

(See appendix 1 for a discussion of material rewards)

A storehouse of bounty Deut. 28:11-12
Children and descendants Deut. 28:11; Ps. 112:2
Health and healing Ex. 15:26; 2 Chron. 30:20; Prov. 3:8; Isa. 58:8; 11; Matt. 8:13, 9:22
Prolonged life Prov. 3:2; Prov. 3:16
Prosper in everything you do Deut. 29:9; 1 Kings 2:3: 2 Chron. 31:21
Prosperity Prov. 3:2; Jer. 29:11; Luke 16:12
Protection Isa. 58:8
Sight restored Matt. 9:30
Wealth and riches Ps. 112:3; Prov. 3:9, 3:16, 13:21, 22:4

## *Other Descriptions of Rewards*

A better resurrection Heb. 11:35

A country of their own, a better country Heb. 11:14, 16

A firm foundation for the age to come 1 Tim. 6:19

A prize for running well 1 Cor. 9:24, 27

A prophet's reward Matt. 10:41

A righteous man's reward Matt. 10:41

An answer from God 1 Sam. 7:9

Deliverance 1 Sam. 7:3, 21:11, 2 Sam. 22:17-18; 2 Kings 17:39; Ps. 119:153

Established throne 1 Kings 9:5, 2 Kings 11:4; 2 Chron. 7:18

Eternal life Gal. 6:8; 1 Tim.6:12

Excellent and profitable Titus 3:8

Faith, genuine and of greater worth than gold 1 Pet. 1:7

Forgiveness 1 Chron. 7:14; Amos 7:2; 1 John 1:9

God revealing Himself pure and blameless 2 Sam. 22:26

God will keep His covenant of love Duet. 7:12

God's compassion Neh. 9:27; Joel 2:18

Godly character Rom. 5:10

Good Ps. 84: 11; 112:5; Matt. 24:46; Zech. 8:15

Good gifts Matt. 7:11

Goodness Lam. 3:25

Healing of sin Hosea 14:4

Heirs and coheirs with Christ Rom. 8:17

It will be well Isa. 3:10

Light that dawns / shines Ps. 112:4; Isa. 58:8; 10

Like the sun when it rises in its strength Judges 5:31

People Luke 16:9; Phil. 4:1

Pillar in the temple of God Rev. 3:12

Promise for this life and the next 1 Tim. 4:8

Redemption of life Lam. 3:58

Remembered by God Neh. 5:19; Neh. 13:14, 22

Restored, made strong, firm and steadfast I Pt 5:10

Revelation of what is hidden Matt. 11:25

Seeing God Matt. 5:8

Spared of judgment Ex. 15:26; Amos 7:2, 6; Jonah 3:10; Micah 7:18

That for which he asks Matt. 7:7-8

The City Heb. 11:10; 16
The earth as an inheritance Matt. 5:5
The gracious hand of the Lord Ezra 9:22
The Lord God Almighty will be with you Amos 5:14
The water of life Rev. 21:6
To be his son Rev 21:7
To shine like stars for ever and ever Dan. 12:3
Unfailing love Hosea 10:12
Value for all things 1 Tim. 4:8
Victory Ps. 149:4
Walk with God Lev. 26:12; Rev. 3: 4

# Index of How Rewards Are Earned

The following index of means by which rewards are earned is drawn exclusively from the verses of reward in *Investing in Eternity*. I have focused on these verses because of their close proximity to, and the conditionality of, the rewards that are promised. Of course, properly understood, much of the rest of the Bible gives instruction and encouragement to live in such a way as to receive rewards.

## *Rewards For Loving God With All Your Heart, Mind and Soul*

### *Be Holy*

Be godly 1 Tim. 4:8; 6:6; 1 Tim. 6:11
Be holy 1 Pet. 1:15-16
Be patient Heb. 6:12; Rev. 14:12
Be pure in heart Ps. 24:4; Matt. 5:8; James 4:8
Be righteous / desire righteousness Gen. 7:1; 1 Sam. 26:23; 2 Sam. 22:25; Ps. 18:20, 24; Prov. 4:33,11:17; Isa. 58:8; Ez. 18:5; Matt. 5:6; 1 Tim. 6:10
Be self-controlled 1 Pet. 1:13; 2 Pt. 1:5
Be strong 2 Chron. 15:7
Confess your sins 1 John 1:9
Consecrate yourself Lev. 20:7-8
Do not worship idols Duet 11:6; Judges 11:16; 2 Kings 17:35; Ex. 18:6
Do what is right Duet 6:18; Ez. 18:5
Exhibit the fruit of the Spirit 2 Pt. 1:5-7; (Gal. 5:22)
Have clean hands James 4:8
Honor your father and mother Duet 5:16

Keep from sin 2 Sam. 22:21; Ps. 58:11, 84:11; 1 Tim. 6:11

Keep God's commands 2 Chron. 7:17; Ex. 25:26; 27:3; Deut 11:27: Ez. 18:9

Meditate on God's Word Josh. 1:8; Ps. 1:2

Plan for what is good Prov 14:22

Shun earthly desires 1 Pet. 1:14

Speak truth Ps. 24:4

Speak wholesomely Matt. 12: 33-37

Walk in integrity 1 Kings 9:4; Ps 1:1

Walk in the light 1 John 1:7

## Be of Pure Motives

Be earnest 2 Cor. 8:7

Be humble 2 Chron. 7:14; Ps. 149:4; Prov. 4:34; Joel 2:12; Luke 14:7-14; Luke 18:9-14; 1 Pet. 5:6; James 4:3, 6, 9-10; 2 Kings 23:19

Be steadfast before the Lord 2 Chron. 27:6

Commit yourselves to the Lord 2 Chron. 16:9

God weighs the heart Prov. 24:12

Have pure motives Jer. 17:10; James 4:2-3

Love God Judges 5:31: 2 Chron. 15:15; 1 Cor. 2:9

Love God, not money Luke 16:13

Pursue and take hold of eternal life 1 Tim. 6:11-12

Seek good, not evil Amos 5:14, 15

Seek the Lord Deut. 4:28; 2 Chron. 14:7, 15:2,15, 26:5; 30:18; Jer. 29:12; Hosea 3:5,10:12

Seek to please God (not people) Lev 9:6: Eccl. 2: 24-26; 2 Cor. 5:9; Col. 3:23; 2 Tim. 2:4; 1 Cor. 4:5

Serve without recognition from people Matt. 6: 1-18

Walk steadfastly before the Lord 2 Chron. 27:6

Want the things of God Matt. 19:17, 21; Mark 10:35, 41, 44; Phil. 3:10; 2 Tim. 2:4

## Be Trusting of God

Acknowledge God Prov. 3:5

Ask God Ex 33:17; 2 Chron. 30:18

Be "weak" 1 Cor. 12:10

Be knowledgeable of the things of God 2 Cor. 8:7

Be meek Matt. 5:5

Believe, have faith, in God Matt. 8:13, 9:22, 11:28

Cry out to God Ex. 2:23; 2 Sam 22:4,7: Ezra 9:22; Neh 9:27; Neh. 12:14, 22; Lam. 3:55-57; Joel 2:32

Do not trust in idols Ps. 24:4

Don't be afraid; trust God's promise to reward Gen 15:1

Fear the Lord Ps. 31:19; Prov. 3:5; Mal. 3:16;

Give your finances to God Deut 14:28; Duet 15:5, 10

Have eyes fixed on what is unseen 2 Cor. 4:18

Have faith in God 2 Cor. 8:7; 1 Tim. 6:11-12; Heb. 6:12; Heb. 11 (entire chapter); 1 Pet. 1:5

Listen to God 2 Chron. 15: 2

Put your hope in God Lam. 3:25; 1 Tim. 6:17

Remain in God's love John 9:10; 15:5

Set your hope on the grace to be revealed 1 Pet. 1:13

Submit to God James 4:7; Matt. 11:29; James 4:10

Trust in the Lord Ps. 37:3; Prov. 3:5; Luke 12:22-32

Wrestle with God Gen 32:28

## Serve and Obey God

Be faithful 1 Sam. 26:23; Prov. 3:3; 1 Cor. 4:2: 2 Chron. 31:20-21

Be fully committed to God 2 Chron. 16:9

Be productive Matt. 13:8, 24; Heb. 6:7

Become a slave to Christ Rom. 6:19-23

Compete to win 2 Tim. 2:5

Do everything God commands you Gen 6:22; Num. 33:50-53; Duet 4:32: Deut 7:12; 8:1, 11: 11:8, 13, 22; 28:1-2; 9. 13; 29: 9; 1 Kings 2:2-3; 2 Kings 11:4; 37; I Chron 22:12-13; Ps. 119:153; Jer. 17:13; John 9:10

Do good Ps. 37:3

Forsake everything for Christ Matt. 13:44, 46; Luke 21:4; Phil. 3:7-8

Having a heart committed to God 2 Chron. 16:9

Keep God's covenant Gen 17:9

Keep the law of the Lord Deut. 30: 11-20; Ps. 19:11; Prov. 3:1; 2 Sam. 22:22-23; Isa. 58:13

Leave your family Gen 12:1; 22:16

Listen to, see and hear God Lev 20:22: 25:18; Ezra 9:22; Matt. 13:16

Make every effort Luke 13:24; John 5:44; Rom. 14:19; Eph. 4:3; Heb. 4:11; Heb. 12:14; 2 Pt. 1:5, 15, 3:14

Serve God 1 Cor. 3:8-15; 2 Chron. 31:21

Work for the Lord 1 Cor. 15:58; 2 Tim. 2:6; Col. 3:23; Heb. 6:10

Worship the Lord 2 Kings 17:36, 39; 18:6

## Endure trials

Be poor in spirit Matt. 5:3; Luke 6:20

Endure trouble and persecution Job 36:15-16, Ps. 119:153, Matt. 5:10, 11; Luke 6:22; Luke 12:8; John 12:23-26; Rom. 5:10, 8:17; 1 Cor. 4:10-11,15:58; 2 Cor. 4:17; Col 3:24; 2 Tim. 2:3; Heb. 10:35; James 1:2, 12; 1 Pet. 1:6-7, 22, 3:14, 4:13-16; 5:10

Hungry Luke 6:21

Mourn Matt. 5:4; Luke 6:21

Thirst for the water of life Rev. 21:6

## Persevere until the end

Gen. 32:26; 2 Tim. 4:7; Heb. 10:36; Heb. 6:11: 1 John 2:28; 2 John 3; Rev. 2:7, 10-11, 25-26, 3:5, 11, 21; Rev. 21:7

## Rewards for Loving Your Neighbor as Yourself

## Love

Love 1 Tim. 6:11; Heb. 6:10

Love people 1 Thess. 2:17-20; 1 Tim. 6:11

Love even your enemies Matt. 5:43-48; Luke 6:27-36; Prov. 25:21

## Do what is just

Act justly Ps. 112:4, 5; Isa. 58:6, 7, 10; 61:8; Amos 5:15: Zech. 8:16

Be merciful Matt. 5:7

Be a peacemaker Matt. 5:9; Phil. 2:14

*Do good deeds*

   Ps. 62:12; Ps. 90:17; Isa. 3:10; Isa. 58:7; Hosea 10:12; Matt. 10:42;
      25:35-36; Mark 9:41; Rom. 2:7, 10; Eph. 6:8; Heb. 6:10
   Be a servant Prov. 25:21, Mark 10:43-44; John 13: 14-17; 1 Cor 9:22
   Hold out the word of life Phil. 2:15
   Obey those in authority over you Eph. 6:5; Col. 3:22
   Shine Phil. 2:15
   Speak truth to each other Zech. 8:16
   Turn from evil Jonah 3:10

*Use money to help people*

   Be a faithful steward Luke 16:11; Luke 19:11-27
   Be generous with money Ps. 112:5; Prov. 3:9, 19:17; Mal. 3:10; 1
      Tim. 6:18; Matt. 13:44-45; Matt. 19:21; Mark 10:21; Luke 18:18-
      30; 2 Cor. 8:7-8; Phil. 4:17; 2 Cor. 9:6-7
   Forsake a hope in wealth 1 Tim. 6:6, 17
   Use wealth to win people to God Luke 16:9; Luke 12:33

*Be a good shepherd of people*

   Be a good shepherd 1 Pet. 5:2-3
   Lead well Dan 12:3; Matt. 24:45-46
   Preach and teach 1 Tim. 5:17-18
   Teach God's commands to your children Deut 11:19, 20
   Tend to God's charge Prov. 27:18; Matt. 25:14-23

# Index of Scripture Used

| Book | Verse(s) | Page(s) | Book | Verse(s) | Page(s) |
|------|----------|---------|------|----------|---------|
| Gen. | 3:18 | 16 | Deut. | 26:18 | 131 |
| Gen. | 12:2 | 49 | Deut. | 30:15 | 34 |
| Gen. | 17:5 | 47 | Deut. | 30:19 | 34, 159 |
| Gen. | 22:2 | 49 | Joshua | 23:15-16 | 35 |
| Gen. | 22:9-10 | 49 | Joshua | 23:14 | 34 |
| Gen. | 22:11-12 | 49 | Judges | Ch.6-8 | 71 |
| Gen. | 22:16-18 | 50 | 1 Sam. | 6:6-7 | 181 |
| Gen. | 32:21-22 | 275 | 1 Sam. | 26:23 | 84, 98 |
| Gen. | 32:26 | 275 | 2 Sam. | 6:14-15 | 89 |
| Gen. | 32:27-28 | 173 | 2 Sam. | 22:21-25 | 84 |
| Exodus | 2:23 | 169 | 2 Kings | 18:5-6 | 51 |
| Exodus | 7:5 | 124 | 1 Chron. | 16:34 | 10 |
| Exodus | 14:2 | 131 | Isaiah | 58:8, 11 | 257 |
| Exodus | 17:8-13 | 167 | Isaiah | 58:9 | 46, 169 |
| Exodus | 19:5 | 131 | Isaiah | 61:7 | 92 |
| Exodus | 19:18 | xxxviii | Isaiah | 61:8 | 187 |
| Lev. | 11:44, 45 | 84, 164 | Isaiah | 62:5 | 83 |
| Num. | 10:11-12 | 180 | Jer. | 12:1 | 258 |
| Num. | 11:1 | xxxiii | Jer. | 17:10 | 69 |
| Num. | 16:35 | xxxiii | Jer. | 20:5 | 258 |
| Deut. | 4:8 | 176 | Jer. | 29:10 | 169 |
| Deut. | 7:6 | 131 | Jer. | 29:12-13 | 168 |
| Deut. | 8:18 | 260 | Jer. | 32:19 | 98 |
| Deut. | 11:1-7 | 127 | Ezekiel | 7:27 | 70, 123 |

| Book | Verse(s) | Page(s) | Book | Verse(s) | Page(s) |
|------|----------|---------|------|----------|---------|
| 2 Cor. | 4:17 | 178 | Phil. | 1:12 | 144 |
| 2 Cor. | 4:18 | 12, 170 | James | 2:17 | 92 |
| 2 Cor. | 5:9 | 80 | James | 4:2-3 | 78, 171 |
| 2 Cor. | 5:10 | 8, 93, 201 | James | 4:7-8 | 135 |
| 2 Cor. | 5:21 | 48 | James | 4:10 | 91 |
| 2 Cor. | 9:6 | 192 | James | 5:11 | 129 |
| 2 Cor. | 10:4-5 | 134 | 1 Peter | 1:6-7 | 108, 142, 178 |
| 2 Cor. | 10:18 | 91 | | | |
| 2 Cor. | 13:5 | 144, 196 | 1 Peter | 1:8 | 65 |
| Gal. | 4:4-5 | 265 | 1 Peter | 1:13 | 164, 170 |
| Gal. | 5:22-23 | 84 | 1 Peter | 1:15-16 | 164 |
| Gal. | 5:22 | 164 | 1 Peter | 1:15 | 161, 164 |
| Gal. | 6:7-10 | 9 | 1 Peter | 1:16 | 84 |
| Gal. | 6:7-8 | 99 | 1 Peter | 1:17 | 98, 158 |
| Gal. | 6:7 | 181 | 1 Peter | 1:22 | 145 |
| Gal. | 6:8 | 177 | 1 Peter | 2:9 | 131 |
| Gal. | 6:9 | 163 | 1 Peter | 3:8-9 | 45 |
| Eph. | 1:18-19 | 137 | 1 Peter | 3:14 | 179 |
| Eph. | 1:19-21 | 135 | 1 Peter | 4:10 | 132 |
| Eph. | 1:20-21 | 37 | 1 Peter | 4:13 | 141 |
| Eph. | 2:8-9 | 92, 195 | 1 Peter | 4:13-14 | 142 |
| Eph. | 2:10 | 78, 92 | 1 Peter | 5:1-6 | 68, 109 |
| Eph. | 3:8 | 189 | 1 Peter | 5:6 | 126, 164 |
| Eph. | 3:17-19 | 53 | 1 Peter | 5:8 | 134 |
| Eph. | 3:20 | 156 | 1 Peter | 5:10 | 179 |
| Eph. | 4:3 | 156 | 2 Peter | 1:3 | 189 |
| Eph. | 5:15-17 | xxxi | 2 Peter | 1:5-11 | 90, 156, 159 |
| Eph. | 6:5-8 | 147 | | | |
| Eph. | 6:6 | 191 | 2 Peter | 1:5-7 | 164 |
| Eph. | 6:7 | 9 | 2 Peter | 1:10-11 | 21, 299 |
| Eph. | 6:8 | 125 | 2 Peter | 1:15 | 156 |
| Eph. | 6:12 | 52, 146, 156 | 2 Peter | 3:7 | 26 |
| | | | 2 Peter | 3:7-13 | 53 |

241

# Bibliography

Abrose, S. (Undated). *The Sacred Writings of St. Ambrose*. North Charleson: Createspace.

Albert Einstein, L. I. (1938). *The Evolution of Physics: The Growth of Ideas from Early Concepts to Relativity and Quanta*. Cambridge: Cambridge University Press.

Alcorn, R. (1989). *Money, Possessions and Eternity*. Carol Stream, Illinois, USA: Tyndale House Publishers.

Alcorn, R. (2001). *The Treasure Principle*. MultnomahPress.Alcorn, R. (2010, March 2). *Questions to Randy Alcorn About Eternal Rewards*. Retrieved from Eternal Perspectives Ministry: https://www.epm.org/resources/2010/Mar/2/questions-randy-alcorn-about-eternal-rewards/

Alexandria, C. o. (1867). *The Writings of Clement of Alexandria*. (W. Wilson, Trans.) Edinburgh: T. & T. Clark.

Associated Press. (2010). NKorean killed for spreading the Gospel. Seoul: AP Press. Retrieved from http://archive.boston.com/news/world/asia/articles/2010/07/05/ap_exclusive_nkorean_killed_for_spreading_gospel/

Atwood, R. (2013). *Masters of Preaching* (Vol. II). Lamham: Hamilton Books.

Augustine, S. (2009). *The City of God*. (M. Dods, Trans.) Peabody, MA: Hendrickson Publishers.

Barklay, W. (1975, 2003). *The New Daily Study Bible: The Letters of James and Peter*. Louisville, Kentucky: Westminster John Knox Press.

Billheimer, P. E. (1975). *Destined for the Throne.* Minneapolis MN and Fort Washington PA: Bethany House Publishers and Christian Literature Crusade.

Blanchard, R. (1959). Fill My Cup, Lord, No. 641. The United Methodist Hymnal.

Bonhoeffer, D. (2001). *Dietrich Bonhoeffer Works* (Vol. 4). Augsburg Fortress.

Bonhoeffer, D. (2003). *Discipleship.* Minneapolis: Fortress.

Bonhoeffer, D. (2015). *The Cost of Discipleship.* London: SCM Press.

Bunyan, J. (Undated). *The Works of John Bunyan.* London: Blackie and Son.

Calvin, J. (1960). *The Institutes of the Christian Religion* (Vol. II). (J. McNeill, Ed., & F. L. Battles, Trans.) Louisville, KY: Westminster John Knox Press.

Calvin, J. (2016). *Institutes of Christian Religion.* (A. Uyl, Ed., & H. Beveridge, Trans.) Woodstock, Ontario, Canada: Devoted Publishing .

Chesterton, G. K. (1936). *The Autobiography of G. K. Chesterton* (Vols. Collected Works, Vol. 16). Ignatius.

Clairvaux, B. o. (2005). *Bernard of Clairvaux: Selected Works.* (G. R. (translator), Ed.) New York, New York: HarperCollins.

Clairvaux, B. o. (2016). *Commentary on the Song of Solomon.* Altenmunster, Germany: Jazzy Verlag Jurgen Beck.

Clark, T. (2011). *Nerve: Poise Under Pressure, Serenity Under Stress, and the Brave New Science of Brave and Cool.* New York: Little, Brown and Company.

Cranmer, F. (July 9, 2019). The Independent Review of FCO support for Persecuted Christians. Retrieved from https://christianpersecutionreview.org.uk/interim-report/

Dante, Alighieri. (2004, August 2). *The Vision of Paradise*. Retrieved from The Gutenberg Project: https://www.gutenberg.org/files/8799/8799-h/8799-h.htm

Dickens, C. (1843). *A Christmas Carol*. London: Chapman & Hall.

Dillow, J. (2015). *Final Destiny: The Future Reign of the Servant Kings* (Kindle Edition ed.). Grace Theological Press.

Eberstadt, M. (2019). *Primal Screams, How the Sexual Revolution Created Identity Politics* (Kindle Edition ed.). West Conshohocken, PA: Templeton Press.

Edwards, J. (1834). *Jonathan Edwards, The Works of* (Vol. 2). Edinburgh: Banner of Truth Trust.

Edwards, J. (1904). *Selected Sermons of Jonathan Edwards*. Norwood, Massachusetts: Norwood Press.

Edwards, J. (2018). *Sinners in the Hands of an Angry God*. e-book: Musaicum Books.

Esposito. (2009). *The Conditional Promises of God*. Mustang, OK: Tate Publishing.

Finney, C. (1839). Lecture 18: Affections and Emotions of God. *The Oberlin Evangelist, Vol 1*(22).

Finney, C. G. (1844). Blessed Are the Poor in Spirit. *The Oberlin Evangelist, Vol. 6*, p. 194.

Finney, C. G. (2001). *Principles of Prayer* (2 ed.). (L. G. Parkhurst, Ed.) Grand Rapids, Michigan, USA: Bethany House Publishers.

Gaga with Andrew Wyatt, A. R. (2018). Shallow, from the movie "A Star is Born" [Recorded by Gaga].

Gonzáles, J. L. (2010). *The Story of Christianity* (Vol. Volume 1: The Early Church at the Dawn of the Reformation). New York: HarperCollins Publishers.

Hafemann, S. (2001). *The God of Promise and the Life of Faith.* Wheaton, Illinois : Crossway Books (div. of Good News Publishers).

Henry, M. (1839). *The Life of the Rev. Philip Henry.* London: William Ball.

Henry, M. (1850). *The Miscellaneous Works of the Rev. Matthew Henry.* R. Carter & brothers.

Hill, J. (2019). *Peter's Epistles.* Self-published.

Hudson, H. (Director). (1981). *Chariots of Fire* [Motion Picture].

Hunt, P. H. (Director). (1972). *1776* [Motion Picture].

Jerome, S. (1945). *The Principle Works of St. Jerome* (Vol. VI). (H. a. Wace, Ed.) New York, NY: Charles Scribner's Sons.

Keller, T. (2011). *Jesus the King* (2016 ed.). New York, New York, USA: Penguin Random House.

Kimmett, J. (2018). Prize Worth Fighting For. [Song]

Kossak, R. a. (2017). *Simplicity: Ideals of Practice in Mathematics and the Arts.* Cham, Switzerland: Springer International Publishing .

Kroll, W. (2008). *Facing Your Final Job Review.* Wheaton, Illinois: Crossway Books, div. of Good News Publishers.

Kroll, W. M. (1977). *Tested by Fire.* Neptune, NJ: Loieaux Brothers.

Lewis, C. (2016). The Last Battle. Hong Kong: Enrich Spot, Ltd.

Lewis, C. (1977). *Mere Christianity.* New York: Macmillan.

Lewis, C. S. (1958). *Version Vernacular.* The Christian Century, 1515.

Lewis, C. S. (1991). *The Four Loves.* New York: Harcourt Brace.

Lewis, C. S. (2009). *The Weight of Glory.* New York: HarperOne.

Livingston, D. F. (2007). *The Pursuit of Pleasure in the Pleasure of Another.* Zulon Press.

Luther, M. (1904). *The Precious and Sacred Writings of Martin Luther.* (J. N. Lenker, Ed.) Minneapolis, MN: Lutherans In All Lands Co.

Luther, M. (n.d.). *Sermons Of Martin Luther.* Retrieved from, http://www. godrules.net/library/luther/129luther_d21.htm (accessed December 02, 2018).

Lutzer, E. (2015). Your Eternal Reward. Chicago, Illinois, USA: Moody Publishers.

Macartney, S. (Director). (2017). *Call the Midwife* [Motion Picture].

Martyr, J. (1970). First Apology. In W. Jurgens, *The Faith of the Early Fathers: Pre-Nicene and Nicene Eras.* Collegeville, MN: the Liturgical Press.

Maslow, A. (2016, original publication in 1943). *A Theory of Human Motivation.* Midwest Journal Press.

Mcguire, J. (2019, April 11). A runner who was left paralysed trying to escape attacker completes second New York Marathon. Retrieved from Runner's World: https://www.runnersworld.com/uk/news/a776547/ paralysed-runner-completes-new-york-marathon-on-crutches/

Melanchthon, P. (1921). *Augsburg Confession (Concordia Triglotta).* St. Louis, MO: Concordia Publishing House.

Miller, S. (1976). Fly Like an Eagle [Recorded by SMB].

Milne, A. A. (1928). *The House at Pooh Corner.* London: Methuen & Co. Ltd..

Online Etymology Dictionary. (n.d.). Retrieved from Online Etymology Dictionary: https://www.etymonline.com/word/mercy

Origen. (1926). *The Ante-Nicene Fathers: The Writings of the Fathers Down to A.D. 325* (Vol. Vol. IV). (. J. Alexander Roberts, & n. b. Coxe, Eds.) New York, NY: Charles Scribner's Sons.

Packer, J. I. (1993). *The Institutes of the Christian Religion.* Wheaton, Illinois, USA: Tyndale House Pub., Inc.

Parker, J. H. (1848). *The Homilies of St. John Chrysostom on the Epistle of St. Paul to the Romans.* Oxford: Oxford Press.

Pascal, B. (2003). *Pensees.* (W. F. Trotter, Trans.) Mineola, NY: Dover Publications, Inc.

Phipps, W. (2012, April 6). *Wintley Phipps - It Is Well With My Soul [Live].* Retrieved October 5, 2019, from YouTube: https://www.youtube.com/watch?v=E8HffdyLd0c&list=RDi60rIMmPrq0&index=22

Piper, J. (2011). *Desiring God, Meditations of a Christian Hedonist, Revised Edition* (Revised ed.). Colorado Springs, Colorado: Multnomah Books.

Plantenga, C. (2002). *Engaging God's World: A Christian Vision of Faith, Learning, and Living.* Grand Rapids: Wm. B. Eerdmans Publishing Co.

*Power Can Chill the Mind's Capacity for Empathy, Researchers Find.* (2017, December 4).

Reeves, K. (2019, May 11). The Late Show With Stephen Colbert. (S. Colbert, Interviewer) Retrieved from https://www.youtube.com/watch?v=oNu6NyMkp8k

Retrieved from Association for Psychological Science: https://www.
psychologicalscience.org/uncategorized/power-can-chill-the-minds-
capacity-for-empathy-researchers-find.html

Richards, K. (1965). (I Can' t Get No) Satisfaction [Recorded by M. Jagger].

Rolling Stone Magazine. (2011, April 7). *500 Greatest Songs of All
Time*. Retrieved from Rolling Stone: https://www.rollingstone.com/
music/music-lists/500-greatest-songs-of-all-time-151127/the-everly
-brothers-cathys-clown-63263/

Sciolist", ". (n.d.). *Online Etymology Dictionary*. Retrieved from Online
Etymology Dictionary: https://www.etymonline.com/

Smithsonian Institution. (2019). *The Hope Diamond*. Retrieved from
Smithsonian: https://www.si.edu/spotlight/hope-diamond

Sorge, B. (2001). *Secrets of the Secret Place*. Grandview: Oasis House.

Sproul, R. C. (1992). *Essential Truth of the Christian Faith*. Tyndale House.

Sproul, R. C. (1996). *Now That's a Good Question*. Carol Stream, Illinois:
Tyndale House Publishers.

Sproul, R. C. (1997). *What is Reformed Theology?* (Vol. Kindle Edition).
Grand Rapids, MI: Baker Books

Melanchthon. (1959). *Apology for the Augsburg Confession* (quarto edition
ed., Vol. Apol. 4:194; Book of Concord). Philadelphia: Fortress.

Spurgeon, C. (1902). In A. P. Fitt, & W. R. Series edited by Alexander
McConnell (Ed.), *Record of Christian Work* (Vol. 21). New York, New
York, USA: F.H. Revell Company.

Tertullian. (1903). *The Ante-Nicene Fathers: Latin Christianity: its
founder, Tertullian* (Vol. 3). (A. a. Roberts, Ed.) New York, New York:
Charles Scribner's Sons.

The Sun News Site. (2019, August 1). *Millennial Melancholy*. Retrieved from The Sun.

Tolkien, J. (1965). *The Lord of the Rings: The Two Towers*. London: Ballantine Books.

Traherne, T. (2007). *Centuries of Meditations*. (B. Dobell, Ed.) New York, NY: Cosimo Classics.

U.S. Army. (2015, January 20). *All We Could Be: How an Advertising Campaign Helped Remake the Army*. Retrieved from National Museum of the U.S. Army : https://armyhistory.org

Van Der Kolk, B. (2015). *The Body Keeps the Score*. New York: Penguin Books.

Walsh, M. (2012). *Witness of the Saints*. San Francisco: Ignatius.

Walsh, M. (2012). *Witness of the Saints: Patristic Readings in the Liturgy of the Hours*. Ignatius Press. Retrieved from Documenta Catholica Omnia: http://www.documentacatholicaomnia.eu/03d/0345-0407,_Iohannes_Chrysostomus,_Homilies_on_The_Epistle_To_The_Romans,_EN.pdf

*When Americans Say They Believe in God, What Do They Mean?* (2018, April 25). Retrieved from Pew Research: https://www.pewforum.org/2018/04/25/when-americans-say-they-believe-in-god-what-do-they-mean/

Wesley, J. (1818). *Explanatory Notes Upon the New Testament*. New York, New York, USA: J. Soule and T. Mason.

Wikipedia. (n.d.). *(I Can't Get No) Satisfaction*. Retrieved from Wikipedia: https://en.wikipedia.org/wiki/(I_Can%27t_Get_No)_Satisfaction

Wilkin, R. (2013). Four Views on the Role of Works at the Final Judgment. In T. S. Robert Wilken, & A. P. Stanley (Ed.). Grand Rapids, Michigan: Zondervan.

Wilkinson, B. (2002). *A Life God Rewards*. Colorado Springs: Multnomah Books.

Wright, N. T. (2002). *Matthew for Everyone*. London, Great Britain: Society for Promoting Christian Knowledge.

# Appendices

# Appendix 1  Rewards and Material Blessings

God *__does not__* promise an abundance of *__material__* blessings in this life.

The teaching referred to sometimes as the "prosperity gospel" or "health and wealth gospel" is common and dangerous enough that I must explicitly disavow any association with it. The New Testament speaks little of material benefits for faithfulness to God. In fact, Jesus and the New Testament writers warn us to expect just the opposite: A life of following Jesus is apt to be a life of suffering and persecution. Jesus told us that anyone who would follow Jesus must *"deny himself and take up his cross and follow me."* (Matt. 16:24; Mark. 8:34; Luke 9:23, 14:27)

On the other hand, the Bible does speak of material blessings for faithfulness in the Old Testament. God often promised to bless through visible means: wealth and riches (Ps. 112:2-9; Prov. 3:9; Prov. 3:16), health and healing (Prov. 3:8; Isa. 58:8, 11), children and descendants (Ps. 112:2-9); prolonged life and prosperity (Prov. 3:2; 16). God often blessed His faithful materially as a sign of His favor.

Such blessings were not shared by all of the faithful in the Old Testament, however. For example, speaking of those before Christ who trusted God's promises, the writer of Hebrews tells us some. . .

> *. . . were tortured and refused to be released, so that they might gain a better resurrection. Some faced jeers and flogging, while still others were chained and put in prison. They were stoned; they were sawed in two; they were put to death by the sword. They went about in sheepskins and goatskins, destitute, persecuted and mistreated . . . They wandered in deserts and mountains, and in caves and holes in the ground. These were all commended for their*

257

*faith, yet none of them received what had been promised.*
(Heb. 11:36-39)

So, worldly blessings for faith and faithfulness are not guaranteed as an indication of God's favor, even in the Old Testament. To think otherwise is to join Job's "friends," who, on the supposed evidence of his troubles, accused Job of sin.

Furthermore, people who generally live moral lives apart from God often prosper materially, even as do some who obviously live sinful lives. Jeremiah complained to God about such people. *"I would speak with you about your justice: Why does the way of the wicked prosper? Why do all the faithless live at ease?"* (Jer. 12:1) God assured Jeremiah that He was aware of, and would deal with, their greed. *"I will hand over to their enemies all the wealth of this city—all its products, all its valuables and all the treasures of the kings of Judah."* (Jer. 20:5)

Jeremiah's prophecy soon came true; yet, the righteous suffered too. All the people of Israel (the faithful and evil alike) were hauled off to Babylon. So, again, we see that material prosperity is not always an indicator of God's blessing in the Old Testament.

On this matter of material blessings, some make the mistake of Jesus's disciples, who thought that the riches of the young man who came to Jesus was a sign of his righteous standing before God. Astonished at Jesus's teaching, they asked if it is hard for the rich to be saved, "Who then can be saved?" (Matt. 19 and elsewhere).

The disciples came to grasp that the material blessings promised in the Old Testament, like much else in the Old Testament, pointed to greater truth as revealed at Christ's coming. While Jesus healed as a sign of his Messiahship, none of the material benefits promised in the Old Testament are reiterated in the New Testament as rewards to be expected in this lifetime. When Jesus came, he fulfilled the promises foreshadowed in the material blessing found in the Old Testament.

Jesus sent His Holy Spirit to teach us a deeper understanding of His rewards. In the Old Testament, God sometimes delivered temporal, material blessings by way of demonstrating His approval in tangible ways. The people of the Old Testament could not enjoy God's spiritual blessings as fully as we can today, for God had not yet fully revealed Himself. His Holy Spirit did not yet dwell within the people of the Old Testament. We now have the witness of the Holy Spirit to confirm in us, and to give us a foretaste of God's reward.

As I repeatedly say in the body of the book, God calls us—not to a life of wealth and ease—but to a life of sacrifice and, sometimes, to pain and deprivation. Nevertheless, most of us suffer very little materially. We avoid hardship, often by making security and comfort our first priority. Millions of followers of Jesus, however, *have* suffered and *are* suffering for Christ. It is obscene to think that rich and comfy Christians are more blessed of God than those faithful saints.

None of this means that God never blesses materially in response to our faithfulness. Earlier this week, for example, a friend told me about how he and his wife had decided to be obedient to God in the area of financial stewardship. They cut up their credit cards and determined to be faithful in their giving and by living within their means. The very next day, their daughter told them that she needed tennis shoes for a camp she was planning to attend. The shoes were not in the budget; so, though the shoes were not a burdensome expense, my friends committed the need to God. Later that same day, the wife came across an acquaintance with a bag in her arms, who said to her, "This is probably crazy to ask, but could you use any of these?" She opened the bag to reveal several pairs of shoes, three of which were the daughter's size. God had not just provided a needed pair of shoes; He provided three pairs!

You may have stories of God's material blessing, too. God can and often does provide for our needs in ways that are proximate to our faithfulness. There are times that God rewards with tangible blessings because we have been faithful. Indeed, I suspect He longs for us to give financially to the point of abject dependence upon Him; thereby allowing Him to demonstrate His provision in miraculous and tangible ways. Instead, like a two-year-old, we tell God, "I do myself!" I think God longs to have us more dependent upon Him for our needs.

Among the perks frequent flyers or hotel rewards program participants enjoy is the "free upgrade." Well, one of the reasons not to presumptively take that which God has not given is that, in doing so, we rob ourselves of the joy of experiencing a "free upgrade" from God. Sometimes He does that: He gives a generous material gift of something we might have been tempted to take for ourselves. It is a rich experience of God's love when that happens.

Sandy and I have had such an experience. We had checked into a reasonably priced room at the Williamsburg Inn on the occasion of a business conference. But when the porter took us to our room, it was already occupied. So, he turned to us and said, "Follow me." After leading us through the quaint streets of Colonial Williamsburg, he stopped—in front of a *house*! "You can stay here—at no extra cost," he said." He had taken us to a reconstruction of a historic home, complete with a fireplace and a second floor on which we could let our baby daughter sleep.

What's more, I had run into an old college friend as we checked in, so we invited him over to "our house" for wine and cheese. It was perfect! And our enjoyment of such a luxury was many times what it would have been, had we booked the house for ourselves rather than allow God to give it to us as a gift.

But I speak as if God does not already shower most of us with blessings—every day. We, in the West, are among the richest the world has ever known. So wealthy are we that we often take God's everyday provisions for granted. When, for example, did you last miss a meal for lack of money? When was the last time you had to sleep in the street for lack of shelter? Most of us (in the United States, anyway) are quite well taken care of by God, aren't we? His provision is so consistent and bountiful that we forget it is all from God's hands. He blesses us, and He urges us, *"Remember the LORD your God, for it is he who gives you the ability to produce wealth."* (Deut. 8:18)

Jesus encouraged us to trust God for basic needs. *"Seek first his kingdom and his righteousness, and all these things will be given to you as well* (Matt. 6:33). Yet, God does not always provide His children even with the most basic of needs. Many of our brothers and sisters in the Lord are hungry at this very moment. They lack many of the basic necessities of life. Many of them die for lack of provision.

I do not understand (and I do not explore here) why God allows many of His children to be in need. (No doubt God will someday point a finger of judgment at our indifference toward the plight of the poor and especially the poor in His family.) God does not always provide materially, even for people who love and trust Him. Many millions of Christians have not been spared their lives as they suffered martyrdom for the sake of Christ.

The "prosperity gospel" is, therefore, an affront to God and to all who have faithfully served God over the centuries. It is all the more odious when such a "gospel" is used as an excuse for extravagant consumption of resources that could have been used to further the Gospel and to aid the poor. God gives us all material things as a stewardship. It is an obscenity to wallow in our wealth and to justify our indulgences on the supposition that we have God's special favor because we deserve it.

Excessive consumption is not only immoral; it is simply stupid. It is a wasted investment opportunity. What is your first question to a stockbroker when he suggests an investment opportunity? *"What sort of return should I expect?"* His answer will be, at best, an educated guess as to the potential for profit. But we don't have to guess about what our return in heaven will be. Jesus says it will be *"one hundred times"* as much. (Matt 19:29, Mark 10:30) Of course, He was speaking metaphorically: The return on investment in God's Kingdom is immeasurable because it is eternal.

If everything you give back to God earns you *"one hundred times"* as much in the life to come (Matt. 19:29), why would you not invest every dime you could spare into Kingdom purposes? If God rewards your faithfulness with even more material blessings, then why would you not take the opportunity to be even more faithful by investing those additional resources as well, to earn (you guessed it) even more reward in heaven. Jesus said, *"For everyone who has will be given more, and he will have an abundance"* (Matt. 25:29).

Hear this: If God has blessed you materially, He has done so that you might put it to Kingdom purposes and thereby earn an even greater reward in heaven. Consume it now, and you will *"have received [your] reward in full"* (Matt. 6:5). Invest it back into the Kingdom of God, and you will enjoy the riches of His reward forever.

So, is there a sense in which we can expect to enjoy blessing in the here and now? Yes, some rewards are experienced in the here and now. As you read His Word on the subject, you will see that those rewards are mostly great benefits to the soul. These rewards for faithful service can be experienced in two ways. First, God's Spirit sometimes speaks directly to our hearts with words of commendation for our faithfulness. He often fills us with rapture and joy as we worship or serve Him. Second, more regularly and increasingly, we experience the joy of anticipating our reward in heaven. As our faith grows, we will glory in the hope that our efforts and sacrifices are duly noted and that, ultimately, God will reward.

# Appendix 2  Common Emotional and Theological Objections

Most of the content of this section is addressed more thoroughly in the body of the book. I include this appendix, however, for those who are especially skeptical of this teaching. These answers are not intended to address all objections but to provide an opening to the discussion. If the doubtful reader begins here, I hope he or she will then move to the collection of verses (following suggestions in appendix 3 for how to study them) and then eventually to what I have to say in the body of the book.

**The Promise of Reward Provokes . . .**

My insightful daughter Rachel suggested a reason some are uncomfortable with the idea of God's rewards. Their qualms aren't theological. They are personal.

*Shame*

Some feel utterly unworthy and incapable of gaining God's reward. Mostly what they feel when reminded of God's promises is shame and the inevitability of failure.

I understand that feeling, though perhaps not as profoundly as many. For some of you, there is a keen sense of embarrassment and unworthiness deep within. Tragically, these feelings are often the product of trauma such as abuse or neglect as a child. The love of Jesus is hard to feel because you have never palpably experienced love. You've known mostly hatred or anger or betrayal. Others of you feel guilt and shame for your own past or present behavior. You feel dirty: "How could a holy God love me? How much less likely is it that He would ever reward me for service to Him?"

263

Most of you, I hope, have no such obvious reason for your shame. You only know that you struggle with believing you have value. You swim into a current that relentlessly pushes downstream against you. You have trouble enough believing Jesus would die for you—much less that He would ever someday praise you. As far as you are concerned, your heavenly bank account is already in the red, and your checks are bouncing: "How could I ever lay up treasure in heaven?" You are as discouraged as someone on the cusp of retirement without a penny to your name and no plausible means of acquiring it.

You will see how you can fill heaven's accounts in section 3, after you first glimpse the treasure that awaits you for doing so in section 2. But for now, let me assure you of one important truth: while your bank account was overdrawn indeed when you first came to Jesus, he has fully paid all your debts. He simultaneously offered you the riches of Christ to have and to enjoy both in this life and the life to come. God contributes to your heavenly 401(k) in vast disproportion to your contribution; nevertheless, you must work to earn it.

Jesus cares deeply for you. He is not some dispassionate therapist, listening and nodding thoughtfully as you talk out your problems in spiritual, cognitive behavioral therapy. You *are* worthy of the love of Jesus because He considers you worthy of it. He loves you *exactly* as you are. His passion for you is endless and unconditional.

But as with human relationships, you must accept the love of Jesus to experience it. You can only feel His devotion to the extent you embrace it. And for that loving relationship to be fully satisfying, you must return it by giving your whole heart to Jesus, even as a bride gives herself to her betrothed on their wedding day. God's Word is brimming with expressions of His love. Spend time in them and ask His Spirit to reveal their truth to your heart. The love of Jesus is before you like an ocean. Come on in! The water is fine!

### Discouragement

*"I'm too far behind in my race. I can't catch up."*

Maybe you feel that if you agree that God rewards, you will be admitting to yourself that you have failed thus far in your Christian life. Let me encourage you in that too.

First, there is a dimension to God's assessment of our individual qualifications for a reward that we are utterly incapable of anticipating: God knows our hearts and our experiences in a way that we can not—and will not—know until He reveals it to us. That means that you and I cannot examine ourselves and foretell the extent to which we will be judged worthy of God's reward. The full impact of circumstances and influences upon our lives is impossible for us to comprehend.

Even more impossible—if that is possible—is the comparison of one person to another. My race may be across a level field, which is to say that I may have had a godly upbringing relatively free of the effects of evil and temptations to participate in it. Your race, on the other hand, may be up a steep mountain, which is to say that you have had experiences that make it hard for you to trust anyone, even God. Just remember:

> *The Lord does not look at the things people look at. People look at the outward appearance, but the Lord looks at the heart.* {1 Sam. 16:7}

He knows what you are up against. Besides, consider this question: For whom is it easier to trust God, the confident and self-sufficient person who has their life "together"—or someone like you who struggles? Might it not be easier for you to ask God for help than the person who has no apparent need? So "*judge no one*" (John 8:15), not even yourself. Don't worry about the past. Look toward the future: "*Forget what lies behind and press on to what lies ahead*" (Phil. 3:13). Heed Paul's encouragement:

> *Each one should test their own actions. Then they can take pride in themselves alone, without comparing themselves to someone else, for each one should carry their own load.* (Gal. 4:4-5)

Furthermore, God has a way of turning all things (even our mistakes) into good when we love and serve Him. He can leverage the lessons you have learned through your confessed shortcomings to catapult you far beyond where you thought you were in your race. Your legs have been made strong by your uphill climb, so you can now sprint to the finish! If you are swimming upstream against a fast current, God will give you swim fins to better overcome it. Jesus turned water into wine! He can just as easily transform your weaknesses into strengths. Trust Him to make the most of *all* that you are and have done. He wants you to win!

Remember the people in the Bible who failed God and came humbly to Him for forgiveness: David, the Prodigal Son, Peter, the indebted man in Matthew 18. Remember the many displays of God's desire for restoration: in Hosea's marriage to an adulterous woman, the parables of the lost sheep (Matt. 18:12-14; Luke 15:3-7) and the lost coin (Luke 15:8-10), the entire history of the Jewish people. How often is God willing to forgive you? *"Seventy times seven,"* which is to say, as many times as it takes (Matt. 18:22).

Please don't spurn God's offer of reward because you have felt yourself a failure in the past. Just do what all of us must do to earn God's reward: ask God's forgiveness, trust Him, serve Him, love Him. He will sweep you across the finish line! Spend time reading God's many promises to bless you. Listen to His Spirit speak through them. Give it time. It's a prize worth fighting for.

Does the promise of reward seem to make your burden heavier? Then, consider a comparison between a rewards-oriented view of our service to God to the non-rewards view you now hold. You know what you should be doing for God and—like all of us—you have often failed and felt guilty for that failure. However, on those occasions that you have been obedient, you don't allow yourself to feel a deep satisfaction for having done so. While service to God may produce pleasant emotions, you may be restrained in your enjoyment of them; you don't turn to your heavenly Father and say, "Look what I did for you, Daddy!" because you don't expect to hear His praise. You only feel that you have done your duty. So, your motivation is a small "carrot" and a large "stick."

God would rather that those motivations were inverted. It is my earnest desire that you will do what you already know to do and that you will then—as a result—experience God's pleasure in doing it. Far from adding to your to-do list, the expectation of God's reward in this life and the next will give you a renewed vigor in tackling the duties you already have before you to do.

Hannah Gavois finished last at the 2019 New York City Marathon—on crutches. Three years beforehand, she was told that she would never again walk, having fallen one-hundred-fifty feet off a cliff while escaping an attacker. *That* is what it means to finish the race. You may not cross the line first, but you will be a winner—if you persist to the end (Mcguire).

## Theological Misgivings about Rewards

Rachel also asked a telling question of me as I worked on *Investing in Eternity*. "Dad," she said, "can't you use a word other than . . . 'reward'?" Her question perfectly betrayed her—and perhaps your—general discomfort with the word—and even the concept of rewards. I have been tempted to allay that discomfort and change every use of the word "reward" to "blessing." After all, properly understood, they mean the same thing, don't they? We all believe that God blesses. We even say, "God bless you!" when strangers sneeze! Surely the use of the word "blessing" would make the argument more palatable than the use of the word "reward."

The problem in doing so is that the word "blessing" connotes something wholly out of our control. It carries little or no element of the conditionality inherent to the word "reward." And conditionality (the if-then relationship between our faithfulness and many of God's blessings) is essential to this teaching. And therein, we glimpse an underlying misunderstanding that the word "reward" exposes.

### *The definition of reward*

The word "reward" is unambiguous in its conditionality. Rewards are a repayment, wage, salary, compensation, fare, price paid for services, payment on contract, recompensation, etc. There are 107 references to wages, etc. using 21 different Hebrew and Greek roots. Several times the writer uses two different words in close proximity to emphasize his point. (Find these and other descriptions of rewards in the Index of the Nature of Rewards.)

Anyone who considers the Bible to be God's Word could not deny that God responds to our obedience with rewards. But the word "reward" is ambiguous; by itself it does not describe well what those rewards actually are. Those promises of God's loving intent are fleshed out in the if-then conditional promises of Scripture. With those many descriptions, we have a far greater understanding of the nature and character of the rewards that await the faithful.

### God's sovereignty and our will

The doctrine of rewards produces a seeming discordance between God's sovereignty and our free will. We wince at the cognitive dissonance of those two realities. How can both be true? As with a penultimate, dissonant musical cord or the suspenseful plot of a novel, we yearn for resolution.

Rather than wait for the Conductor to signal the final, resolving cord, we draw our bows prematurely. Rather than wait for the Author of the book to show us the final chapter—which is the Revelation of Jesus—we write our own ending. Uncomfortable with our understanding of an incomprehensible choice God made in eternity past based upon what He knows about us (Rom. 8:28-30), we unilaterally end our discomfort by resolving to one or the other of seemingly contradictory ideas.

Ironically, one of the results is discordance of a different sort which is tragically contrary to Jesus's great desire expressed in John 17: a church universal often bitterly divided along theological fault lines. The other ill effect is to the individual's understanding of God, His purposes, and our place in it. This book calls people to relish the anticipation of God's final resolution of the God-created, mysterious coexistence of His sovereignty and our free will—to hold our collective breath as we expectantly wait for the understanding God will someday bring to our hearts and minds {1 Cor. 13:12}.

### The relationship of grace and works

There is a parallel discomfort with the relationship of God's grace and the works of God's people. For five hundred years, Reformed Protestants have (correctly) defended the soteriology of grace alone. It is a foreign concept to all other religions, including much of what passes itself off as Christianity. But while focusing attention on an essential doctrine of our faith, another manifestation of God's grace has been neglected or actively avoided: that grace of God which offers us a rewarding part in God's Kingdom. Even those who assent to the doctrine speak little of it, for fear of confusion or a perceived conflation of the grace that provides salvation and that which promises reward. *Investing in Eternity* addresses those concerns with evidence from God's Word. (See especially chapters 4 and 13.)

## Transaction versus relationship

Some are uncomfortable with the word "rewards" because—improperly understood—they seem transactional rather than relational. The word evokes Pavlov holding out a treat and commanding a dog, "Sit, boy! Sit!" We imagine that God is like my brother, who tests his dog's obedience by putting a treat on its nose and saying, "Staaaay. Staaaay . . ." until finally he says, "OK!" and the compliant canine scarfs down the treat. God does indeed entice us to obedience with promises of blessing, but obedience isn't the ultimate goal. It is the means by which we enter more deeply into *relationship* with Him. And He entices us into that trusting relationship by giving us a myriad of promises of tasty treats.

## Conditions for rewards and conditions of grace

Some of the verses I use to support my argument are understood by some to speak of a condition of grace necessary for heaven itself, rather than of reward in heaven. For example:

> You need to persevere so that when you have done the will of God, you will receive what he has promised. (Heb. 10:36)

But God has *"promised"* hundreds of blessings. Why would we assume the writer of Hebrews is talking about (or only about) salvation?

Or take James 1:12:

> Blessed is the man who perseveres under trial, because when he has stood the test, he will receive the crown of life that God has promised to those who love him.

But what does it mean, precisely, to *"persevere under trial"*? God's work will be evident in all real followers of Christ {James 2:14-29}. (See also chapter 16, note 2.) But, do any of us unwaveringly persevere to the end—without sin—in utter and unwavering faith in God?

Jesus said,

269

*Be faithful, even to the point of death, and I will give you
the crown of life.* (Rev. 2:10).

What is the *"crown of life"* that James and Jesus say is at stake?
Heaven? Well, suppose your wife and children are threatened with rape,
torture, and death unless you verbally recant your faith in Jesus. Then—
having recanted—you are killed. Would you have forfeited your eternal
salvation for denying Jesus in your final moment of life? I hardly think so.

More likely, the *"crown of life"* at stake is described a few verses earlier
in James's letter:

*Perseverance must finish its work so that you may be
mature and complete, not lacking anything.* (James 1:4)

James did not say that we will go to heaven if we persevere in trails.
He says that if we unwaveringly persevere in trials we will be *"mature and
complete, not lacking anything."*

Nevertheless, if I've errantly cited verses that speak of faith (or faith/
obedience) unto salvation rather than of faith/obedience unto reward,
my thesis still holds true, *because the former is a necessary condition
for the latter.* Without faith that saves, one cannot have faith that God
rewards (Heb. 11). So, *with regard to the doctrine of rewards,* to speak of a
condition of grace or of salvation as different from a reward for obedience
is to make a distinction without a practical difference. Either way, an
eternity of blessing is at stake.

If an accomplished broad jumper attempts to beat the world record—
which currently stands at 12 feet, 2¾ inches—it would be of no concern to
him if the first foot or two—or even the first eight or ten feet—over which
he jumped was a mile-deep chasm: his attention would be on sailing well
over the gap to break the record.

Likewise, this book encourages training oneself to trust God to propel
the vault over the deadly chasm—and beyond: to break the record, to win
the prize. If the jumper underestimates the demands of faith and if he has
not prepared himself for the jump, he might fall short. But that is not his
concern because he is focused on *rewards* in heaven. For he will be *in
heaven* as he enjoys them.

Here is a look at the matter via graph:

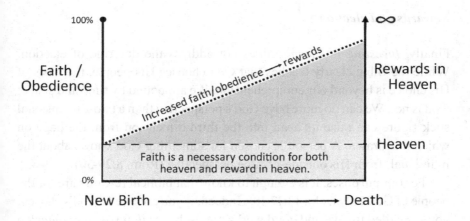

Faith that saves and faith that earns God's reward are made of the same stuff. The difference is one of the depth, not of kind. The former is foundational (1 Cor. 3:11) and the latter spurs us to win the prize (1 Cor. 9:24). If we read every conditional promise as if it speaks only of salvation, we miss the entire point: God wants us to enjoy the riches of heaven, not only to "get into" heaven.

Nevertheless, I have avoided the use of verses that most clearly speak (to me anyway) of a condition of salvation as opposed to a condition for a reward. One such verse—which I have not included in my list of conditional promises—is Matthew 24:13, *"But the one who stands firm to the end will be saved."* That verse arguably supports the doctrine of perseverance for salvation. If my reader believes that some of the verses I have cited speak about conditions of grace or of perseverance to salvation rather than of rewards—and if they distract you from the thesis—I invite you to ignore my use of them: plenty of verses will remain that are less given to that interpretation. (And I would be delighted if you emailed me your thoughts at kevin.w.kaufman@gmail.com.)

However, if you are about to lay aside some of the verses, I suggest that you first apply the principle of "Scripture interprets Scripture" to the contended verses in light of those which unambiguously speak of God's reward. You may come to see that Scripture you believe speaks of salvation actually—or also—speaks of reward.

## Rewards and election

Finally, *Investing in Eternity* does not address the doctrine of election. While the Bible clearly teaches that God chooses His people, the basis of His choice is beyond our comprehension. We are bound by time and space; God is not. We can no more have God's perspective than a two-dimensional stick figure can raise its head into the third dimension from the page on which it is drawn. A person is chosen for something God knows about the individual, from His outside-of-time perspective (Rom. 8:29-30).

For our purposes, it is enough to know that biblical rewards are for the people of God only (John 13:17-18). Indeed, if you are one of God's chosen, you are called to love and good works precisely "*so that you may inherit a blessing*" (1 Pet. 3:8-9) and "that *you might share in the glory of our Lord Jesus Christ*" (2 Thess. 2:14).

## Other Misgivings That May You May Have

### *"We are unable to earn anything. Jesus does it all."*

We are saved by God's grace, not by our works. That is unquestionably true: "*So too, at the present time, there is a remnant chosen by grace. And if by grace, then it is no longer by works; if it were, grace would no longer be grace*" (Rom. 11:5-6). Ephesians 2:8-9 is so often quoted because it is so evident in its teaching: "*For it is by grace you have been saved, through faith—and this not from yourselves, it is the gift of God—not by works, so that no one can boast.*" (If you have yet to become a child of God, please go now to appendix 5.)

However, the doctrine of rewards is not about how we come to be saved. Rewards are about that which Paul tells us in the next verse of Ephesians 2: "*For we are God's workmanship, created in Christ Jesus to do good works, which God prepared in advance for us to do.*" It is for cooperating in the doing of those works that we will be rewarded (Eph. 2:10).

### *"I am motivated by love (giving) rather than by rewards (getting)."*

Jesus said, "*It is more blessed to give than to receive*" (quoted by Paul in Acts 20:35). Who is "*more blessed*" in giving? *The giver.* The recipient is blessed by the gift, but the giver gets more than he gives. Why would it be wrong to act upon that promise by Jesus?

Besides, the motivation of rewards is not a substitute for the motive of love. Instead, love and rewards are complementary motivations. That is because loving God and loving people both produce the reward of joy and true happiness. You might even say that loving God and people is its own reward. It is profoundly satisfying to love God and love people. That is no surprise since it is to love and be loved that we were created.

Second, our love for God is enhanced by the experience and the anticipation of God's rewards (which are an expression of His love) in return for our love and faithfulness to Him.

Third, the more we appreciate the love of God as expressed in His rewards for love and obedience, the higher our capacity to love others. After all, you can't give what you don't already have. You can only love to the extent that you experience love. Since we are unable by our own power to love people the way God loves them, the more we grasp the love of God (as seen, among other ways, in His gracious promise to reward us), the more we can love others.

So love and rewards produce a reinforcing cycle: when God rewards, the recipient feels God's love and approval. The more that love and approval are experienced, the more one wants it for others and wants to give it to others. That desire produces a love that spills over onto those around us like water out of a cup that is already full.

Therefore, love and obey God—not merely because you *should* do so but because in doing so you will *experience the blessings* of God's love which you can then *share* with others—which will produce more rewards for you and give you more motivation to love . . . repeat ad infinitum.

### *"God has done so much for me already. How could I expect more?"*

"If I were to serve God for my entire lifetime, I would not even begin to make up to Him what He has already given me. *'In view of God's mercies'* (Rom. 12:1), how could I expect more?" It is true, as far as it goes: In His grace, God has already done immeasurably more for us than we deserve. We could never pay him back. We will spend an eternity praising Him for His gift of salvation.

However, some will have even more reason to praise God's grace in heaven, for they will have received from God's gracious hands their promised rewards for faithful service to God. These promises and their rewards are—like Jesus's sacrifice on the cross—the gifts of God's grace. Our sovereign God, who is free to act for His good pleasure, has decreed that in exchange for our small service that is nonetheless significant to Him, He will give even more. We deserve this kindness no more than we deserve the kindness of His salvation. Nevertheless, in His boundless grace and generosity, God offers these conditional blessings to us.

We presume nothing of Him when we claim His promises of reward. Our gratitude is enhanced, not diminished, by the expectation of a reward we do not deserve but will nevertheless receive by God's grace. Gratitude and hope of reward are not mutually exclusive. The latter enhances the former.

Here is an illustration: A wealthy man gives you $1 million and says, "This money is for you to spend as you wish. It is yours." (This represents our salvation in the illustration.) You would be very grateful, I'm sure. But suppose he added, "However, I will reimburse you $100 for every dollar of this money you spend to promote my good name, to serve my interests, and to invite others to share in your bounty." What would be your response? "Oh, that is too generous of an offer! I cannot accept it!" I think you would not be so foolish. You would accept the proposition and be grateful beyond expression for the man's initial, unconditional generosity (the $1 million) *and* for his conditional generosity (the potential of an additional $100 million).

Isn't that the essential message of the parables of the talents and the minas? Isn't that what Jesus meant when he said to his disciples that everyone who leaves family and investments and security will receive one hundred times as much in return? Do you or I deserve that? No! Will those who leave behind all that is dear to them be grateful when they receive the hundredfold reward? Of course, they will. Would their sacrifice of everything to obtain the promised reward be selfish? No, not if it was done to advance the interests of the Kingdom and to gain that which God wants to give.

Why would we *not* work for those promised rewards? Unlike the Hebrews, we don't adequately believe that God rewards those who diligently seek Him (Heb. 11:6). Maybe we simply do not believe—or know to believe—that God will reward. I urge you, therefore, to read His Word on this subject in the verses I've collected. Study them, for in them you will see that God promises to reward.

### *"What about Romans 11:35!"*

*"Who has first given to Him that it might be paid back to Him?"* (NASB). Unfortunately, some translations leave out the word "first" (προδίδωμι) in that question. That verse paraphrases Job 41:11, in which God says, *"Who has preceded Me* [יְנָמִיתְקָה] *that I should pay him."* In other words, God is saying that He is the first cause of everything. Clearly, we did not initiate rewards. We cannot demand payment of Sovereign God. But we can trust God, who took the first step—in eternity past—when He purposed to create us, to send Jesus to save us, and then, ultimately, to reward us for our faithfulness {2 Tim. 1:9}.

### *"We are not worthy of anything from God!"*

This both is and is not true. We are indeed like Jacob, who prayed, *"I am unworthy of all the kindness and faithfulness you have shown your servant"* {Gen. 32:10}. Nevertheless, Jacob—in the very next verse—reminded God of His promises, given first to his grandfather Abraham, *"But you have said, 'I will surely make you prosper and will make your descendants like the sand of the sea, which cannot be counted'"* (Gen. 32:21-22). Jacob claimed God's promise of blessing in spite of his own unworthiness.

Jesus indeed taught that our *attitude* should be that of feeling unworthy.

> *Suppose one of you had a servant plowing or looking after the sheep. Would he say to the servant when he comes in from the field, "Come along now and sit down to eat"? Would he not rather say, "Prepare my supper, get yourself ready and wait on me while I eat and drink; after that you may eat and drink"? Would he thank the servant because he did what he was told to do? So you also, when you have done everything you were told to do, should say, "We are unworthy servants; we have only done our duty."* (Luke 17:7-10)

This passage speaks of God's rights as Master and of the servant's obligations. God has the right to demand service. We have a duty to obey. Our attitude should be: *"We are unworthy servants; we have only* [to do] *our duty."*

However, this passage does not tell us how God <u>will</u> treat His servants.

> *He who tends a fig tree will eat its fruit, and he who looks*
> *after his master will be honored.* (Prov. 27:18)

*"Unworthy servants"* though we are, He will give the faithful a seat of honor. He prepares for us a table in the presence of our enemies (Ps. 23:5). He will invite us to the marriage supper of the Lamb (Rev. 19:9). We will be worthy because God will have declared us worthy—if we tend the fig tree.

When Jesus begins His story, *"Suppose one of you had a servant…,"* Jesus was contrasting the disciples' expectation to His unanticipated intention. The lesson is the same as that of the Prodigal Son in Luke 15. The wayward son returned to his father in humility. He hoped only that his father would make him a servant. Was he in for a surprise! The father joyfully embraced his son and restored the broken relationship. (Meanwhile, the Prodigal Son's brother, who proudly felt entitled to his father's blessings, was bitter with his brother and with his father.) Our attitude is to be one of unworthiness, but God honors that humility with praise and restoration.

> *Humility is the fear of the LORD; its wages are riches and*
> *honor and life.* (Prov. 22:4)

Humility is a repeated theme in Luke's gospel. In Luke 8 we find the story of the centurion. The centurion's servant, whom his master valued highly, was sick and about to die.

> *The centurion heard of Jesus and sent some elders of the*
> *Jews to him, asking him to come and heal his servant.*
> *When they came to Jesus, they* [the Jewish elders] *pleaded*
> *earnestly with him, "This man deserves to have you*
> *do this, because he loves our nation and has built our*
> *synagogue." So Jesus went with them.* (Luke 8:3-6)

Jesus started toward the house of the centurion because He had been told of the man's love and good works. Jesus altered His plans to go to the centurion's house because of what the Jewish elders had told Him—that the centurion was worthy of the attention of Jesus.

The story continues,

> [Jesus] *was not far from the house when the centurion sent friends to say to him: "Lord, don't trouble yourself, for I do not deserve to have you come under my roof. That is why I did not even consider myself worthy to come to you. But say the word, and my servant will be healed. For I myself am a man under authority, with soldiers under me. I tell this one, 'Go,' and he goes; and that one, 'Come,' and he comes. I say to my servant, 'Do this,' and he does it." When Jesus heard this, he was amazed at him, and turning to the crowd following him, he said, "I tell you, I have not found such great faith even in Israel." Then the men who had been sent returned to the house and found the servant well.* (vv. 7-10)

When Jesus is amazed at someone, we do well to consider what so struck Him, especially if we want Jesus to similarly marvel at us. What was it that took Jesus aback? The man's humble faith. The centurion humbly recognized that he was not worthy of Jesus's time and trouble; nevertheless, his confidence in Jesus's ability to heal compelled him first to send for Jesus and then to dispatch friends to ask Jesus to spare Himself the trouble of coming and to just heal the servant from afar.

Like the servant in Luke 17, the centurion rightly considered himself unworthy. However, (and this is the point) Jesus *did* consider him worthy! Jesus considered him worthy precisely because of the centurion's actions and his faith. Jesus was amazed at the strength of the centurion's faith and was impressed with how that faith found expression, both in his support of the Jewish community and in seeking Jesus's healing for his servant. The centurion's righteous humility notwithstanding, Jesus considered the centurion worthy of His attention and help.

There is story about a different centurion that has parallels to that story. Again, the author is Luke, who writes in Acts 10 of Cornelius: *"He and all his family were devout and God-fearing; he gave generously to those in need and prayed to God regularly"* (Acts 10:2). Later in the story, Cornelius was described as *"a righteous and God-fearing man, who is respected by all the Jewish people."* The clear implication in Luke's affirmation and reaffirmation of Cornelius's good character is it was *because* he was devout and God-fearing that God miraculously arranged for Cornelius and Peter to meet. Still, if not for the vision God gave him, Peter would not have considered Cornelius worthy of his time and effort. But God did.

If, as Jesus said in Matthew 10:38, *"anyone who **does not** take up his cross and follow me is not worthy of me,"* does it not follow that anyone who *does* take up his cross and follows *is* worthy of Jesus? In taking up our cross, we will have *"lived a life worthy of the Lord"* (Col. 1:10). Jesus taught us, *"My Father will honor the one who serves me"* (John 12:26b). We are not worthy in and of ourselves; but, by the grace and gift of God through Jesus, we are made worthy of our reward!

As John Wesley wrote,

> *Happy is he who judges himself an unprofitable servant; miserable is he whom God pronounces such. But though we are unprofitable to him, our serving him is not unprofitable to us; for he is pleased to give by his grace a value to our good works which, in consequence of his promise, entitles us to an eternal reward.* (193)

## *"We cannot obligate God."*

That is true! God is the sovereign Lord. (See the above discussion of Romans 11:35.) Almost 300 times in the Bible (NIV) the Lord is referred to as the *"Sovereign Lord."* God does as he wishes. Isaiah says it beautifully in chapter 40.

> *Do you not know?*
> *Have you not heard?*
> *Has it not been told you from the beginning?*
> *Have you not understood since the earth was founded?*
> *He sits enthroned above the circle of the earth,*
> *and its people are like grasshoppers.*
> *He stretches out the heavens like a canopy,*
> *and spreads them out like a tent to live in.*
> *To whom will you compare me?*
> *Or who is my equal? says the Holy One.*

Since God is sovereign, He can act in whatever way He pleases. And our sovereign God is pleased to obligate Himself. ***These obligations are***

**commonly referred to as promises.** To cite the most striking example of God binding His own actions: *"before the beginning of time,"* God obligated Himself to send His Son to save the world from its sins and to demonstrate His love {2 Tim. 1:9}. Jesus was crucified *"by God's deliberate plan and foreknowledge"* {Acts 2:23}. No man obligated God to sacrifice His Son, but generations of God's people trusted His promise to send the Messiah.

Likewise, God has obligated Himself to reward faithfulness. God's people in Hebrews 11 were commended by God for their faith in God and His promises. It delighted God that they should do so. Indeed, it is impossible to fully please God without believing that *"God rewards those who earnestly seek Him"* (Heb. 11:6). God's promises preceded my faith in them. My faith did not produce the promises, but my faith activates them.

> The reward is given, not because the works themselves, due to their intrinsic value, impose an obligation on God to reward them, but because God, in His grace, offered such a reward as part of an agreement. (Sproul, *What is Reformed Theology?*, 111)

(Note: Though, as I argue in *Investing in Eternity*, the prospect of eternal reward has vast implications for followers of Christ, this is the only reference to rewards found in the index of Sproul's book. There is likewise only one reference to rewards in the index of a popular 2,000-page commentary of the Bible. Why this would be so is utterly incomprehensible to me.)

### *"Rewards feel so mercenary . . . so transactional."*

I will answer this objection with an extended quote from G. K. Chesterton's autobiography.

> The [modern cynic] always imagines that there is an element of corruption, in his own cynical manner, about the idea of reward, about the position of the child who can say, as in Stevenson's verses, "Every day when I've been good, I get an orange after food." To the man made ignorant by experience this always appears as a vulgar bribe to the child . . . But it does not seem like that to

the child. It would not seem like that to the child, if the Fairy Queen said to the Prince, "You will receive the golden apple from the magic tree when you have fought the dragon." For the child is not a Manichee. He does not think that good things are in their nature separate from being good . . . He has the ordinary selfish obstacles and misunderstandings; but he does not, in his heart, regard it as odd that his parents would be good to him, to the extent of an orange, or that he should be good to them, to the extent of some elementary experiments in good behavior. He has no sense of being corrupted. It is only we, who have eaten the forbidden apple (or orange) who think of pleasure as a bribe. (52–53)

Chesterton gets to the heart of rewards in an analogy between parent and child. Our problem is in our habit of thinking in crass, commercial terms. The rewards we receive and will receive from God are as natural as that which a child expects to receive from his or her parent. There is no thought of obligation either on the part of the parent or the child because the love in the relationship motivates both parties to act in a manner that pleases and honors the other.

(See chapter 4 for further explanation.)

### *"It is God who works in us to will and to act in order to fulfill his good purpose." (Phil. 2:13)*

That is true; however, that statement does not preclude the requirement of our voluntary cooperation with God's purposes. As Paul explains later in the letter, after we come to know Jesus, we *"are **empowered** to do all things through Christ who strengthens me"* (Phil. 4:13). Before Christ, we were powerless to do God's will. But once we have God's Spirit living within us, we can do *"all things."*

Given Paul's many reminders of what God requires of His people, Paul knows we will not *inevitably* obey. (The Corinthian Christians amply proved that point.) But then, do any of us fully obey? Which raises the question: If we have no choice in our obedience (after we come to Jesus), why would God not always *make us* obey? Is that to be our understanding of sanctification: God occasionally makes us, against our stubborn will, conform to His will? If so, could He not sanctify us immediately?

Of course, He could. But He does not because this—painfully slow—process of transformation advances God's ultimate goal of a more excellent relationship with us. 'Relationship' is something one willingly enters into. One cannot be forced against his or her will into a loving relationship. God always does His part, but we have to respond if the relationship is to thrive. (See chapters 3 and 4.) So:

*By God's will and design, our cooperation is generally a necessary, though infinitely insufficient, condition for doing God's will.*

It is true that, in any given instance, we do not know whether our God-honoring actions are of God's unilateral doing or of our volitional cooperation with Him. I can only leave it to God to tell me at the Bema on which occasions He worked *despite* me and on which occasions I voluntarily *cooperated* in His work. Paul said,

> *Therefore judge nothing before the appointed time; wait till the Lord comes. He will bring to light what is hidden in darkness and will expose the motives of men's hearts. At that time each will receive his praise from God.* (1 Cor. 4:3-5)

So, in the meantime, given our intrinsically limited perspective—and the enormity of what is at stake—that uncertainty is all the more reason to *proceed* in every situation as if we have been given a choice by God. For as Peter warned Christians, *"Since you call on a Father who judges each man's work impartially, live your lives as strangers here in reverent fear"* (1 Pet. 1:17). Do I really want to risk standing before Jesus someday as He reviews my life and have Him ask me, for example, why I did not publicly claim Him as my Lord that day at the office, when He had given me the perfect opportunity to do so? Am I going to say, "Well, gee, I was waiting on You to make me do it!"

*"Jesus taught we will all receive the same wages in heaven."*

Some point to the parable of the workers in Matt. 20:1-16 in support of this understanding. In the story, groups of laborers are hired at different times of the day yet are given the same wage at the end of the day. Those hired first complained that they were not paid more than those who were hired later.

If this passage is referring to rewards (and I'll explain in a moment why I think it is not), then it is actually supportive of the doctrine. Each of the workers was equally faithful to his call to work. The only difference was the timing of his call to work, which was wholly at the discretion of the master. Once hired, each did the job to which he was called and thus was compensated by the master for that faithfulness. Likewise, none of us has control when (or to precisely what) we are called; but, having been called, we are responsible to be faithful workers in the Kingdom.

But, as I said, I don't believe this passage is talking about rewards. Like so many other parables, Jesus's remarks are directed at the religious leaders who considered themselves superior to others. They thought they were more faithful—and deserving—because they had obeyed the Law their entire lives. Their hearts were prideful. Their attitudes negated their obedience to the Law. Jesus told them, *"The first* [you, who think you are so righteous] *will be last, and the last* [the humble and repentant, like the tax collectors and the prostitutes in Matt. 21:31] *will be first"* (Matt. 20:16). Jesus was telling them, as he so often did, that they were not the obedient servants they thought they were.

Either way, this is a cautionary tale. While God rewards faithful service, we must not presume the "size" (for lack of a better word) of the reward we will receive. That is for God to determine.

*"It is selfish to seek rewards."*

It would be selfish to seek rewards if they are earned at the expense of others. But others don't lose when we win. In fact, just the opposite is true: Rewards are earned as we seek the *benefit* of others. Therefore, rewards are a win-win proposition: we win rewards as others—by our faithfulness—come to know God's grace through our love and actions.

God's infinite storehouse is undiminished when He rewards His faithful, so our receipt of reward from God does not diminish the reward others might receive. (As if God digs through His bag of goodies: "Hum, now let's see what is left for you.") We are competing not against individuals, but—as it were—against the clock. We compete not to win something that someone else will lose as a consequence of our winning; we compete to gain a part of God's infinite bounty. There is more than enough of God's blessing to go around!

It is true: our desire to gain something of value is self-seeking and self-interested. Is that wrong? Are we not created as dependent creatures, with what C. S. Lewis in *The Four Loves* calls *"need-loves"*? (11). Are we not all beggars, really? Besides, is there anything wrong with wanting the most and best of that which God wants for us? What is wrong with desiring and working for the very things for which God created us?

Is it selfish to seek something that God promises to give? On the contrary, is God not glorified when we take him at His Word, and we trust Him to make good on those promises? As earthly parents, are we not delighted when our child accepts our promise of ice cream—after she has done her homework? *"If we as human parents know how to give good gifts to our children, how much more will our heavenly Father give good gifts to those who ask him?"* (Matt. 7:11; Luke 11:13).

If God did not want us to seek our own good in striving for rewards, then why did He so often speak of rewards in His Word? Why are we encouraged to consider the *"credit"* that we receive for loving our enemies (Luke 6:27-35)? Why did he tell the rich young ruler about the treasure he would receive for giving all he had to the poor (Matt. 19; Mark 10; Luke 18)? Why are we told that we will receive *"what is due"* (2 Cor. 5:10)? Why did Paul tell us to *"run in such a way as to get the prize"* (1 Cor. 9:24)? Read all of the verses in *Investing in Eternity* and ask yourself: Why would God tell us all of this if he did not want us to be motivated to trust Him to fulfill His promises?

Is it selfish to seek rewards, or is it arrogant to claim that we don't need them as motivation for faithful service? Is it not boastful to declare, "I don't need an incentive; my own virtue motivates me! I am completely void of self-seeking"? Are you a Stoic, or are you a Christian?

Only God is self-sufficient. He alone needs nothing. He alone is good. We, on the other hand, were created dependent upon Him, His kindness, and His beneficence. We are needy, and God offers to fill those needs, on His terms and in a way that is consistent with His character and our design: by rewarding us for love and trust in Him.

Does it not disrespect God to spurn what He wants to give—what He promises to deliver? God is a Giver. He did not just give Jesus; He continues to provide—endlessly. It is in His nature to give. He delights in giving. We highly honor Him when we look expectantly for God's reward.

## May I Now Ask You a Few Questions?

If you are unsatisfied with my answers to your theological objections, would you entertain a few questions from me?

1) If God does not reward (repay, give a wage to compensate, give back to) all who faithfully serve Him, why then did His Spirit inspire the use of those very words in the writing of Scripture to describe that which the faithful alone will receive? In using those words, what did God intend to communicate, if not His intent to reward?

2) If God did not mean for His people to be motivated by the prospect of rewards, why did He so often speak of them? If it is sinful to work to earn an award, why did God tell us of them?

3) Is it wrong to do that which God commands to gain that which He promises? Why?

4) If we believe that we are saved by grace (and I do so believe), then what does the Bible mean when it repeatedly says that *"God will give to each person according to what he has done"*? (Rom. 2:6, etc.)

5) Paul says, *"Do not be deceived: God cannot be mocked. A man reaps what he sows"* (Gal. 6:7). Does this principle apply to Christians as well as to the lost? If not, then why did Paul write those words to Christians?

6) a. Does the Christian who is saved *"only as one escaping through the flames"* (1 Cor. 3:15) reap the same harvest as does the one who faithfully endures *"in all kinds of trials"*(1 Peter 1:6)?

   b. If those two Christians face the *same* eternal future, then what does Paul mean when he says that *"you know that the Lord will reward everyone for whatever good he does"* (Eph. 6:8)?

   c. If those two Christians do indeed face *different* futures in heaven, then is it not merciful to warn the slacker and disobedient about their forfeiture of rewards and to encourage the faithful who might otherwise grow weary in doing good?

7) If there is no reward to gain (or lose), then why does John warn us to "*watch out that you do not lose what you have worked for*" (2 John 8)? If you believe this is a warning about losing one's salvation, then you think even more is at stake in our obedience than I do!

8) How well considered is your opinion on the doctrine of rewards? Have you spent time studying God's Word and seeking God's wisdom on the matter? Are you prepared (especially as a shepherd of the flock) to stand before God and defend your understanding?

If your honest answer to that last question is "No," I urge you to give attention to God's Word on the matter, using the suggestions for study provided in appendix 3. God probably won't ask you someday if you studied my book. He might, however, ask why you did not consider His Word on the subject, especially when it is so plainly laid before you.

Whether or not you agree with my conclusions or have remaining questions, I invite you to write to me at www.facebook.com/InvestinginEternity. Please give me your feedback.

# Appendix 3  How to Study the Verses on Reward

I am delighted that you have come to this appendix, for if you follow the suggestions for study given below, you will retrace what was for me an exciting journey through Scripture. If you have not yet read what I've written in the body of the book and you instead spend time in the Scripture (using the simple ideas below), you may never get to what I wrote. That would be fine with me, for you will have been taught by the best Teacher using His primary text. You can do no better than that!

I suggest that you go through the verses several times, each time looking for something different. This will take some time to do thoroughly. Since this is not a mere academic exercise, you might do this study as part of your devotions over a period of weeks. Take your time; there is no rush. This approach also works well as a subject for a Bible study group.

**Here are some suggestions for how to study the verses listed in appendix 7:**

Pray before you begin, with something like this: "Lord, open my heart and my mind to the truth of Your Word. Teach me by Your Holy Spirit to understand Your intent to reward faithfulness." If you are not yet convinced of the truth of this teaching, simply add, "if such is Your intent." If you find yourself especially wary of this teaching, then you may also pray, such as this, "I admit the *possibility* that I am unaware of or ill-informed concerning important teaching of Scripture." In all love, I encourage you not to let pride stop you from exploring God's Word—never mind my words—on this subject. God resists the proud, but He gives grace to the humble. (Prov. 3:34; James 4:6; 1 Pet. 5:5)

*First read-through*: Scan for the verses with words in bold and read their context. Most often, the bolded word is "reward"; but many times it is another word with similar meaning. (You will find the several original Greek and Hebrew words, along with their meanings, in Index 1, under The Nature of God's Rewards.) Ask yourself as you read these verses, "Do these passages teach that there is something that God intends to be "earned" (properly understood) by Christians?" If you believe that the verses do not teach of something that is earned, and since you take God's Word seriously, then ask yourself (and God, in prayer) what these words are intended to communicate? One way or another, these many uses of the word "reward" et al. must be taken seriously if you take the Bible as inspired by God.

*Second read-through*: With a highlighter in hand, find each word or phrase that describes the rewards. Make notes on what you find. See if there are any patterns in the descriptions. What do these verses promise? Underline words and phrases that indicate that God's rewards are proportional to our sacrifice and service. "According to" is a common phrase. You will also find "whatever measure," "quality," "what is due," "rich," "great," "one hundredfold," "many times," and the like. Let it soak in that what you do in this life has a direct effect upon you for all of eternity.

*Third read-through*: With yet another color, highlight those parts of the verses that give, implicitly or explicitly, the "if" *condition* for receiving your reward. What actions and attitudes does God promise to bless? What do these verses teach about how rewards are earned?

*Fourth read-through*: Now that you have begun to understand the doctrine of rewards, ask yourself as you reread the verses, "What are the implications for how I live my life? How will the awareness of the eternal consequences of my attitudes and actions affect the decisions I make in life?" Hopefully, a sense of the enormity of the implications has been growing in you ever since you started reading the verses. How you live this life matters. It matters to you, to your family, to your friends, to those you shepherd, and to God.

What these verses teach will matter to you for all of eternity, because God promises to reward.

# Appendix 4  How to Teach the Doctrine of Reward

No doubt many of you are familiar with the blessings described in *Investing in Eternity*, though you may not think of them as "rewards" for your faithfulness and trust in God. You may not know that God wants you to *want them* and to *work to receive more of them*. You may not know that these blessings for service to God will accrue to your benefit for all of eternity. Nevertheless, in receiving them, you are being rewarded. So, even if you can't bring yourself to call them rewards, be all the more obedient—that you may experience more and more of *"the unsearchable riches of Christ."* (Eph. 3:8)

However, I ask you to consider using the biblical language of rewards, especially if you are a pastor or teacher. Its use will help your flock realign their thinking and expectations. The sheer ubiquity in Scripture of this teaching should give you reason enough to speak of it.

There is no particular virtue; no one is godlier, for doing their duty without thought of what God will give them for it. Be sure that your aversion to this doctrine is not a manifestation of pride. You may be one of Lewis's "bold and silly creatures" that boasts, "I'm no beggar. I love you disinterestedly."

You must speak frankly in terms of "rewards" because, in doing so, you will encourage others to search for those great riches. Is it your practice to "encourage" people to do what they *"should"* do? Or do you encourage them with the *promises of God?* (The words "should" and "ought" appear only eighteen times in the verses I've listed. Each one contains a promise of blessing for doing what one ought.)

Why not be like Jonathan, who came to David at Horesh and *"helped him find strength in God."* Jonathan did not merely exhort David, "Don't be afraid!" He said, *"You will be king over Israel"* (1 Sam. 23:16-17). Jonathan was reminding David of God's promise to someday make David king of Israel. We, too, do well to remind each other of God's promise to *crown us*. Don't just tell your fellow Christians what they *should* do . . . Tell them *why* to do it!

> ***Tell the righteous*** *it will be well with them,* ***for they will enjoy*** *the* ***fruit of their deeds.*** (Isa. 3:10)

The Bible is full of the hope of such reward. I have focused in *Investing in Eternity* upon those verses that make the cause and effect connection between service to God and His reward. However, there are thousands of other passages of Scripture which, when read from the perspective of God's intent to reward, take on new significance. For example, the word "joy" is found hundreds of times in the Bible. Likewise, "delight" is a recurring theme, as is "hope," "rejoicing" and "peace." God says throughout His Word: This is what I want to give you! Trust me, seek me, and these delights will be yours forever!

> *Glory in his holy name; let the hearts* ***of those*** *who seek the LORD rejoice.* (1 Chron. 16:10; Ps. 105:3)

> *May* <u>all who</u> *seek you rejoice and be glad in you; may* ***those who*** *love your salvation always say, "The LORD be exalted!"* (Ps. 40:16; 70:4)

> This is Good News! We should teach it. And you will be rewarded if you do! (Matt. 5:19)

Appendix 3 suggests one method for teaching this doctrine: by inductive Bible study, perhaps with a small group. One might also, of course, explain the doctrine of rewards as one would teach any other doctrine: With a sermon series or a Sunday school class. Indeed, such teaching will be helpful, especially by way of introducing rewards to people unfamiliar with or resistant to the doctrine.

But it seems to me that such instruction will have little lasting effect unless it is integrated into that which is ***regularly*** taught and preached. This approach is consistent with the way the Bible presents God's promise to reward. In practically every instance, the biblical writer or speaker is either expressing hope in the prospect of God's rewards or is encouraging his readers with that prospect *in the context of life*. This doctrine isn't something you just know. Its power is in *living it*!

So, I propose that you, the pastor or teacher, follow the biblical example and often speak of God's intent to reward in the context of your ongoing instruction and counsel. Don't be afraid to use the very word "reward," which God so often uses in His Word.

**Finish the sentence . . .**

The striking feature of the verses on reward I cite is the (explicit or implicit) "if this – then that" construction of the promises. The "if" statement or clause contains the condition of obedience. The "then" statement or clause contains the promised reward for obedience. Often we tell people what they *should* do without giving the encouragement of the (God-given) *reason* to do it. The one is incomplete without the other.

Below are examples of passages that clearly promise that, <u>if</u> you are faithful, <u>then</u> you will be rewarded. So, telling both <u>*how*</u> to please God and <u>*why*</u> to do so may be as easy as finishing the verse or passage.

| <u>If</u> you serve God... | <u>Then</u> God will reward. |
|---|---|
| So when you give to the needy, do not announce it with trumpets... to be honored by men. | Then your Father, who sees what is done in secret, will reward you. (Matt. 6:2-4) |
| What good will it be for a man if he gains the whole world, yet forfeits his soul? Or what can a man give in exchange for his soul? | For the Son of Man is going to come ... and then he will reward each person according to what he has done. (Matt. 16:26-27) |
| [G]o, sell your possessions and give to the poor. . . | ...and you will have treasure in heaven. (Matt. 18:21 et al.) |
| You have been faithful with a few things... | Well done, good and faithful servant! I will put you in charge of many things. Come and share your master's happiness! (Matt. 25:21) |

| | |
|---|---|
| Blessed are you when men hate you… exclude you… insult you and reject your name as evil, because of the Son of Man. Rejoice . . . and leap for joy. . . | . . .because great is your reward in heaven. (Luke 6:22-23) |
| But love your enemies, do good to them, and lend to them without expecting to get anything back. | Then your reward will be great… (Luke 6:35) |
| [H]e who humbles himself. . . | . . . will be exalted. (Luke 14:11, 18:14) |
| [W]hen you give a banquet, invite the poor, the crippled, the lame, the blind. . . | . . .you will be… repaid at the resurrection of the righteous." (Luke 14:13-14) |
| Whoever serves me must follow me . . . | My Father will honor the one who serves me. (John 12:26) |
| There will be trouble and distress for every human being who does evil . . . | . . . but glory, honor, and peace for everyone who does good. (Rom. 2:8-9) |
| [The Lord] will bring to light what is hidden in darkness and will expose the motives of men's hearts. | At that time each will receive his praise from God. (1 Cor. 4:5) |
| I have become all things to all men so that by all possible means I might save some. | I do all this for the sake of the gospel, that I may share in its blessings. Do you not know that in a race . . . only one gets the prize? (1 Cor. 9:22-24) |
| So we make it our goal to please him . . . For we must all appear before the judgment seat of Christ. . . | . . . that each one may receive what is due him for the things done while in the body, whether good or bad. (2 Cor. 5:9-10) |
| Serve wholeheartedly, as if you were serving the Lord, not men . . . | . . . because you know the Lord will reward everyone for whatever good he does…. (Eph. 6:7-8) |

| | |
|---|---|
| Whatever you do, work at it with all your heart, as working for the Lord, not for men. . . | . . . since you know that you will receive an inheritance from the Lord as a reward. (Col. 3:23-24) |
| Command [the rich] to do good, to be rich in good deeds, and to be generous and willing to share. | In this way they will lay up treasure for themselves as a firm foundation for the coming age, so that they may take hold of the life that is truly life. (1 Tim. 6:18-19) |
| I have fought the good fight, I have finished the race, I have kept the faith. | Now there is in store for me the crown of right-eousness, which the Lord... will award to me on that day- and not only to me, but also to all who have longed for his appearing. (2 Tim. 4:7-8) |
| So do not throw away your confidence. . . | . . .it will be richly rewarded. (Heb. 10:35) |
| [P]ersevere. . . | . . . so when you have done the will of God you will receive what he has promised. (Heb. 10:36) |
| [M]ake every effort to add to your faith goodness . . . knowledge . . . self-control . . . perseverance . . . godliness . . . brotherly kindness . . . and love. . . | For if you do these things . . . you will receive a rich welcome into the eternal kingdom of our Lord and Savior Jesus Christ. (2 Pet. 1:5-10) |
| [C]ontinue in Him . . . | . . . so that when He appears we may be confident and unashamed before Him at His coming. (1 John 2:28) |
| Be faithful, even to the point of death . . . | . . . and I will give you the crown of life. (Rev. 2:10) |
| I am He who searches hearts and minds . . . | . . . and I will repay each of you according to your deeds. (Rev. 2:23) |

## By all means, exhort—but also encourage!

We are great at telling people what to do. We are less practiced at encouraging one another. We seldom tell people what awaits those who are faithful. I give examples below for spurring one another to love and good works (Heb. 10:24) using Scripture on reward, cited whole or in part. The examples are in the form of a response to a statement. They might also be formed as a question for someone with whom I am speaking. (E.g., as with the first statement below, the question could be asked, "Are you afraid?")

These are merely examples; there are as many ways to insert this doctrine into your current teaching as there are Spirit-led people of God. My purpose here is to illustrate how easily the doctrine of rewards can be taught and how it can be practically applied. I hope that you discover how naturally and effortlessly you can *tell the righteous that it will be well with them, for they will enjoy the fruit of their deeds."* (Isa. 3:10)

### *"I am afraid."*

The Bible is full of people just like you: People facing scary, even terrifying, circumstances. Moses was fearful when he went back to Egypt to confront Pharaoh. David was afraid of Saul. Even Jesus sweat drops of blood at the prospect of the cross. He asked the Father if there was any way the cross could be avoided.

Each looked past the frightening circumstances to God's promise to reward them for their faithfulness. Moses looked forward to the reward of God's approval. (Heb. 11: 26) David was convinced that God would make good on His promise to give him the throne. Jesus went to the cross because He believed God would raise Him from the dead and that the Father would reward Him with, among other things, the very people for whom He died.

Jesus taught that whatever frightening circumstance of life or threat of man, we only need fear that which will come at the end of time: The Judgment before Christ at the Bema (Matt. 10:28). A *"scroll of remembrance"* is being kept by God. He will not forget your trust in Him (Mal. 3:16).

*"I am in pain."*

When humbly accepted as from the hand of God, pain and suffering will someday produce for you a *"harvest of righteousness and peace"* (Heb. 12:11). That is why you can rejoice even in the middle of painful circumstances, knowing that this pain is not *merely* to be endured until it ends; the pain is a *means* to a glorious end. Jesus said that, when you suffer in faith, *"Great is your reward in heaven."* (Matt. 5:1-12)

*"I am falsely accused.*

Job understood how you feel, for he too was wrongly accused. But—unwittingly—his accuser, Elihu, was right: *"It is unthinkable that God would do wrong, that the Almighty would pervert justice."* God indeed *"repays a man for what he has done."* (Job 34:11, 12) That repayment comes in God's time, not ours. Sometimes it is in this life, as—eventually—it was for Job, and other times it comes in the life to come.

   Likewise, David looked forward to his vindication, when God would deal with him, *"according to* [his] *righteousness"* and reward him according to the cleanness of his hands. (Ps. 18:20) Jesus said you are actually *blessed* for being falsely accused or misunderstood; for if you trust God to ultimately vindicate you, you can rejoice, even leap for joy, in your persecution. It is a means by which you will eventually receive a great reward from God. (Matt. 5:1-12) The question isn't whether God rewards, but when and how He will reward. So don't despair. God will vindicate you before your accusers (Job 42).

*"I am tired of serving God and others."*

Don't I sometimes know how you feel! That is why I am so encouraged by Paul's words to the Galatians. He doesn't only tell them to not grow weary in doing good; he tells them why they should not give up: "[F]*or at the proper time we will reap a harvest. . ..*" (Gal. 6:9) Serve wholeheartedly, he says, *"because you know that the Lord will reward everyone for whatever good he does. . .."* (Eph. 6:8)

### *"I don't understand why God allows bad things to happen to me."*

God makes all things—not just *some* things—work to the good of those who love Him. (Rom. 8:28) In this life, we cannot see all that He will accomplish through our pain and suffering; but, we do know—by faith in His promises—that faithfulness for those who love God *will* produce a *"harvest of righteousness."* (Heb. 12:11) Your perseverance and confidence in God's essential goodness will be richly rewarded. (Heb. 10:35-36)

### *"I already give financially. I could give more; but, why should I?"*

Jesus said that when we give in His name something even as small as a cup of water, we earn a reward. (Matt. 10:42; Mark 9:41) He promised that God will give in abundance to his most loyal servants. (Matt. 25:29) He said their *"reward will be great."* (Luke 6:35) Jesus promises that anyone who leaves family, security, or comfort will receive *"a hundred times as much"* in return (Matt. 19:29; Mark 10:30; see also Mark 4:8, 20; Luke 8:8)

Using Jesus's formula, you can calculate that an investment in God's work of $1,000 will earn credit to *your* account of $100,000 worth of heaven's currency. What a great return on investment! Of course, your *"treasure in heaven"* (as Jesus called it) will not be monetary. *It will be far better than that!* So, giving more isn't really a sacrifice; it is an *investment* that will never be depleted or fade away. Your reward for faithful stewardship (of whatever resources God has given you) will be immeasurable.

*(By the way, this is the one area in which some pastors are less shy to speak of rewards. It would be greeted with less cynicism if this appeal was applied more broadly and regularly, as it is in Scripture, to "whole-life stewardship," not just to financial stewardship.)*

### *"Why should I do what God tells me to do?"*

*(That is a question you seldom hear expressed. Nevertheless, it is in the heart, which, like a two-year-old, always asks, "Why?" We must always address the unasked "Why?")*

You are asking if there is *anything in it for you* in your obedience to God. This answer may surprise you; but, Yes, there is something in it for you! You might think that you are called to obey without a self-seeking motive. That is not wholly true, for there *is* a sense in which you can and should seek your own profit in genuine service to God.

God promises to repay all our acts of faithfulness to Him. Scripture teaches that a man reaps what he sows. (Prov. 11:18; 2 Cor. 9:6; Gal. 6:7) And since what you gain for service is proportional to what you give, then *it is in your eternal best interest* to be fully obedient to God and to serve Him wholeheartedly. In doing so, you will gain a lasting benefit from God.

No doubt, you will find or anticipate other questions in the minds of the people you shepherd. Always be on the lookout for ways to answer those questions by incorporating God's promise to reward into your teaching. If you do, someday *you* will be called *"great in the kingdom of heaven"* (Matt. 5:19).

## Regularly find occasion to speak of God's rewards

I understand that not every sermon can say everything. But if your teaching draws heavily upon God's Word (as I hope it does), then you need not always *create* an occasion for teaching this doctrine. Scripture so often speaks of God's promise to reward that, if you have eyes to see the teaching as you prepare your instruction, you will talk about this doctrine as a matter of course.

However, even if a mention of God's intent to reward is not in your immediate purview, I strongly urge you to speak, explicitly, intentionally, and often of God's promise to do so. Let no call to duty and obedience be without a reminder to His people of God's obligation (His promise) to repay the faithful. I submit that every Sunday's message and every Bible study taught should have some reference, at least in passing, to God's promise to reward faithfulness. Every Sunday, and at every weekday Bible study, our brothers and sisters must be reminded: If they do that which you have admonished them to do from Scripture, they *"will receive a rich welcome into the eternal Kingdom of God"* (2 Pet. 1:10-11).

This is most likely to happen when the teacher has fully engaged the implications and power of those promises; so, I again urge you to spend time in God's Word on the subject. Let the clear and repeated language of Scripture and the promptings of the Spirit convince you of the vital importance of God's promise to reward those whom you shepherd.

Encourage and motivate your flock to godliness and service with the promise of God's reward.

# Appendix 5  The Gift of God

First the "Bad News": The Bible clearly teaches that there is nothing we can do to earn our salvation or entry into heaven. Biblical rewards are decidedly not about how one gets to heaven.

Now the "Good News": God offers salvation as a gift! He offers it freely to all who come to Jesus for the forgiveness of their sins. Jesus said, *"I am the way, the truth, and the life. No one comes to the Father except through Me"* (John 14:6). The Apostle Paul further explains, *"For the wages of sin is death; but the gift of God is eternal life, through Jesus Christ our Lord."* (Romans 6:23) Elsewhere, he says, *"For there is one God and one mediator between God and men, the man Christ Jesus, who gave himself as a ransom for all men."* {1 Tim. 2:5}

Here is my own experience of that truth. One summer, when I was between the first and second grade, Father and Mother had our house remodeled and expanded to accommodate our growing family. (I am the middle of five children.) As a helpful child (so says my mom), I did everything I could to contribute to the effort. I swept and picked up after the workers, helped them carry building materials, brought them water, and the like. One day as I worked, everything I did went wrong. I scuffed a wall with a roll of tar paper. I ran into something with the tractor-loader I was driving. (Why I was allowed to drive a tractor-loader at that age, I do not know!) And, the final straw, which turned out to be the coup de grâce: when I picked up a long board to move it, I raised one end too high. The tip of the board touched a newly plastered ceiling—one into which had been brushed an intricate pattern—and tore a two-foot-long gash into it.

I had been scolded for each of my mistakes that day, but for this last blunder, I was severely chastised by my father. He wasn't physically harsh (he never was), but his words were. I protested that my intentions had been

301

honorable! I was trying to be helpful! "I'm only seven years old, Dad! I make mistakes!" But my protestations didn't move my father. I had done something stupid and irresponsible. My spirit was crushed. I felt shame and anger.

But, as I said, it was a coup de grâce—a "blow of mercy"—from God, because that was when the Lord spoke to me. He said, "You know, Kevin, you could go through your entire life trying to do good, and it still won't be good enough." That may sound like a cruel thing for God to say, but I knew He was right. I could never—on my own—be "good" enough to merit God's grace. No matter how hard I tried or, for that matter, how good I actually lived my life, I would inevitably fall short. I had trouble enough meeting my own father's expectations; I knew I could never meet the standards of my holy, heavenly Father.

So, I went to my mom and told her I wanted to accept Jesus as my Lord and Savior. I wanted Him to make me clean and to take away my sin. I wanted Him to help me to live a life pleasing to Him.

We knelt by a sawhorse—in what was to be my room, at a spot which was later to be at the end of my bed— and I prayed the simple prayer, "Lord, I know I am a sinner. I know that I can never be good enough. Please save me and make me your child."

I never tell that story without tearing up. The peace and happiness and *release* that flooded my soul at that moment was indescribable. I will praise God forever for bringing me to that point of humility before Him. Oh, how I wish everyone in the world could experience such joy!

Why did Jesus die on the cross as our ransom? The answer is a beautiful story of God's love. People are separated from relationship with a holy God by their sin; so, God sent his Son to become one of us, thereby subjecting Jesus to the curse of death that all mankind is under. He lived among us, taught of God's love and purposes, and then allowed Himself to be crucified by jealous people. In this way, *"God demonstrated his own love for us in this: While we were still sinners, Christ died for us."* {Rom. 5:8}

But Jesus didn't stay dead and in the grave. God the Father raised Jesus from the dead three days later. (We celebrate that day as Easter Sunday.) By raising Jesus up, God declared and demonstrated that Jesus, the sinless sacrifice for sins, had conquered sin and death. Jesus had paid the penalty for the sins of all who claim Jesus as their Savior. All who put their faith in Jesus can now share in His life.

If you have yet to trust Jesus for your salvation from sin and spiritual death, then I urge you to give your heart to the Lord. Believe in Messiah Jesus, and you will be saved! He loves you and wants you to share a glorious life with Him forever. Just pray a simple prayer:

*Heavenly Father, I know that I am separated from You by my sin. I believe in Jesus, who died for me so I could be forgiven and brought into fellowship with You. So, please, forgive me and make me Your child.*

*Thank you, Father, for your love for me and for hearing and answering my prayer.*

If you prayed that prayer and sincerely put your faith in Jesus, then God has begun a great work in you! Please tell someone you know to be a follower of Jesus of your step of faith. Find a church family that teaches God's Word and get involved. Nurture your newfound faith in Jesus. Spend time in His Word—including in the Word of God that is the subject of *Investing in Eternity*! Begin right away to seek to please the God of your salvation. He wants you to grow in faith and in relationship with Jesus.

God loves you! *Love Him back,* and He will give you all the more abundantly the great blessings He promises.

# Appendix 6  Quotes in Support
## the Doctrine of Reward

## Early Church Fathers

### St. John Chrysostom

Speaking as if the words of Jesus, "You are bound to me by innumerable favors, and now I ask you to make some return. Not that I demand it as my due. I reward you as though you were acting out of generosity. For your trifling gestures, I am giving you a kingdom." (Walsh, from 559)

Has anyone reviled thee and abused thee, whether truly or falsely, he weaves for thee a very great crown if thou bearest meekly his contumely; since he too, who calumniated, provides for us an abundant reward. (Parker, 162)

### Augustine of Hippo

But who can conceive, not to say describe, what degrees of honor and glory shall be awarded to the various degrees of merit? Yet it cannot be doubted that there shall be degrees. And in that blessed city there shall be this great blessing, that no inferior shall envy any superior, as now the archangels are not envied by the angels, because no one will wish to be what he has not received, though bound in strictest concord with him who has received; as in the body the finger does not seek to be the eye, though both members are harmoniously included in the complete structure of the body. And thus, along with his gift, greater or less, each shall receive this further gift of contentment to desire no more than he has. (Augustine, *City of God, 779*)

305

## Clement of Alexandria

And you know that, of all truths, this is the truest, that the good and godly shall obtain the good reward inasmuch as they held goodness in high esteem; while, on the other hand, the wicked shall receive meet punishment." (*The Writings of Clement of Alexandra*, 86)

## Ambrose

But it is fitting for God that those whom He has invited by grace He should lead on by increase of that grace. And so He first bestows on us a gift by baptism, and afterwards gives more abundantly to those who serve Him faithfully. So, then, the benefits of Christ are both incentives and rewards of virtue. (Ambrose, 463)

## Justin Martyr

We have learned from the prophets and we hold it as true that punishments and chastisements and good rewards are distributed according to the merit of each man's actions. (53)

## Cyril of Jerusalem

Wash yourself clean, so that you may hold a richer store of grace. Sins are forgiven equally for all, but communion in the Holy Spirit is given in the measure of each one's faith. If you have done little work, you will receive little; if you have achieved a great deal, great will be your reward. The race you are running is for your own advantage; look after your own interests. (Atwood, 113)

## Jerome

It is our task, according to our different virtues, to prepare for ourselves different rewards. . . . If we were all going to be equal in heaven it would be useless for us to humble ourselves here in order to have a greater place there. . . . Why should virgins persevere? Why should widows toil? Why should married women be content? Let us all sin, and after we repent we shall be the same as the apostles are! (200)

The fourth proposition of Jovinianus, that all who are saved will have equal reward, is refuted by the various yields of thirty, sixty, and a hundredfold in the parable of the sower, by the "stars differing in glory" of 1 Cor. xv. 41. It is strange to find the advocate of self-indulgence now claiming equality to the saints. But as there were differences in Ezekiel between cattle and cattle, so in St. Paul between those who built gold or stubble on the one foundation. The differences of gifts, of punishments, of guilt, as in Pilate and the Chief Priests, of the produce of the good seed, of the mansions promised in heaven, of the judgment upon sins both in the church and in Scripture, of those called at different times to the vineyard are arguments for the diversity of rewards. The parable of the talents holds out as rewards differences of station, and so does the church in its different orders. (387)

## Origen

Let all men, therefore. . . rest assured that punishment shall be inflicted on the wicked, and rewards shall be bestowed upon the righteous, by Him who deals with every one as he deserves, and who will proportion His rewards to the good that each has done, and to the account of himself that he is able to give. (*The Ante-Nicene Fathers*, 659)

## Tertullian

A good deed has God for its debtor [cf. Prov. 19:17], just as also an Evil One; for a judge is the rewarder in every case. [cf. Rom. 13:3–4] (658)

## Medieval Period

## Bernard of Clairvaux

For our deeds do not pass away as they seem to. On the contrary, every deed done in this life is the seed of a harvest to be reaped in eternity. The fool will be amazed when he sees the huge yield of the few seeds he has sown, good or bad, according to the quality of the seed. He who bears this in mind will never think sin a trifle, because he will look to the future harvest rather than what he sows. Men sow unknowingly; they sow, hiding the mysteries of iniquity, and disguise the notes of vanity; the business of darkness is done in the dark. (*Bernard of Clairvaux: Selected Works*, 21)

Dearest indeed, who are intoxicated with love. Intoxicated indeed, who deserve to be present at the wedding feast of the Lord, eating and drinking at his table in his kingdom, when he takes his Church to him in glory, without blemish or wrinkle or any defect. Then will he intoxicate his dearest ones with the torrent of his delight, for in the most passionate and most chaste embrace of Bridegroom and Bride, the rush of the river makes glad the city of God. I think this is no other than what the Son of God, who waits on us as he goes, promised . . . Here is fullness without disgust, insatiable curiosity that is not restless, an eternal and endless desire that knows no lack, and last, that sober intoxication that does not come from drinking too much, that is no reeking of wine but a burning of God." (199)

## Reformation and Post-Reformation

### *John Calvin*

We should regard as above all controversy the teaching of Scripture that, just as God, variously distributing his gifts to the saints in this world, beams upon them unequally, so there will not be an equal measure of glory in heaven, where God shall crown his own gifts. (*Calvin: The Institutes of the Christian Religion*, Volume 2, 1005)

"Nothing is clearer than that a reward is promised to good works, in order to support the weakness of our flesh by some comfort; but not to inflate our minds with vain glory." (362)

### *Melanchthon*

We teach that good works are meritorious - not for the forgiveness of sins, grace, or justification (for we obtain these only by faith) but for other physical and spiritual rewards in this life and in that which is to come. (*Augsburg Confession,* 175)

### *Martin Luther*

Now when Christ says: make to yourselves friends, lay up for yourselves treasures, and the like, you see that He means: do good, and it will follow of itself without your seeking, that you will have friends, find treasures in heaven, and receive a reward. (310-11)

## *John Bunyan*

Whatever good thing you do for Him, if done according to the Word, is laid for you as treasure in chests and coffers, to be brought out to be rewarded before both men and angels, to your eternal comfort. (737)

## *Traherne, Thomas*

I am sure nothing is more acceptable to Him, than to love others so as to be willing to imperil even one's own soul for their benefit and welfare. Nevertheless it is infinitely rewarded, though it seemeth difficult. For by this love do we become heirs of all men's joys, and co-heirs with Christ. For, what is the reason of your own joys, when you are blessed with benefits? Is it not self-love? Did you love others as you love yourself, you would be as much affected with their joys. Did you love them more, more. For according to the measure of your love to others will you be happy in them. For, according thereto you will be delightful to them, and delighted in your felicity. The more you love men, the more delightful you will be to God, and the more delight you will take in God, and the more you will enjoy Him. So that the more like you are to Him in goodness, the more abundantly you will enjoy His goodness. By loving others you live in others to receive it. (267)

## *Blaise Pascal*

All men seek happiness. This is without exception. Whatever different means they employ, they all tend to this end. The cause of some going to war, and of others avoiding it, is the same desire in both, attended with different views. The will never takes the least step but to this object. This is the motive of every action of every man, even of those who hang themselves. . . .. What then does this craving and inability cry to us, if not that there once was a true happiness in man, of which there now remains only the mark and empty trace? He tries vainly to fill it with everything around him, seeking from things absent the help he does not receive from things present. But they are all inadequate, because only an infinite and immutable object – that is, God himself – can fill this infinite abyss. (Pascal, 113)

## Matthew Henry

Now it is here demonstrated by Eternal Truth itself, that it is our interest to be religious; and therefore *religion* deserves to be called *wisdom,* because it teaches us to do well for ourselves. And it is certain, that the way to be *happy,* that is, perfectly *holy,* hereafter, is to be *holy,* that is, truly *happy,* now. It is laid down for a principle here, *Happy is the man that finds wisdom, (v.* 13.) that finds the principles and habits of it planted in his own soul by divine grace; that, having diligently sought, has, at length, found that *Pearl of great price:* the man that getteth understanding, reckons himself therein a true gainer. The man—*quiprofert intelligentiam—that draws out understanding,* so the original word signifies; that *produces* it, and *brings it forth;* and so the Chaldee reads it.—Happy is the man, that, having a good principle in him, makes use of it both for his own and others' benefit; that, having laid up, lays out. (*Miscellaneous Works*, 226)

You have got a notion it may be and are confirmed in it by the common cry of the multitude that religion is a sour melancholy thing that it is to bid farewell to all pleasure and delight and to spend your days in grief and your years in sighing . . . (233)

Now sum up the whole, and then tell me, whether religion be not a pleasant thing, indeed, when even the *duties* of it themselves are so much the delights of it: and whether we do not serve a good master, who has thus made our work its own wages, and has graciously provided *two* heavens for those that never deserved *one.* (240)

True piety has true pleasure in it. (255)

It is an unspeakable comfort to industrious Christians, that they are working together with God, and he with them; that their Master's eye is upon them, and a witness to their sincerity: he sees in secret, and will reward openly, Matt. 6:6. God now accepts their works, smiles upon them, and his Spirit speaks to them good words and comfortable words, (Zech. 1:13) witnessing to their adoption. And this is very encouraging to God's servants.... The prospect of the recompense of reward, is in a special manner encouraging to us in our work, and makes it pleasant, and the little difficulties we meet with in it to be as nothing. (257)

Depend upon God to make up to you what you lay out in good works, and to recompense it abundantly in the resurrection of the just; nay, and you are encouraged to wait upon him, for a return of it even in this life; it is bread cast upon the waters, which you shall find again after many days. (449)

## Jonathan Edwards

There are different degrees of happiness and glory in heaven. . .. The glory of the saints above will be in some proportion to their eminency in holiness and good works here. Christ will reward all according to their works. . .. Christ tells us that he who gives a cup of cold water unto a disciple in the name of a disciple, shall in no wise lose his reward. But this could not be true, if a person should have no greater reward for doing many good works than if he did but few. (*The Works of Jonathan Edwards*, 342)

There are many mansions in God's house because heaven is intended for various degrees of honor and blessedness. Some are designed to sit in higher places there than others; some are designed to be advanced to higher degrees of honor and glory than others are; and, therefore, there are various mansions and seats, in heaven than others. Though they are all seats of exceeding honor and blessedness yet some more so than others. (*Selected Sermons*, 70)

The second exhortation that I would offer from what has been said is to seek a high place in heaven. Seeing there are many mansions of different degrees of honor and dignity in heaven, let us seek to obtain a mansion of distinguished glory. 'Tis revealed to us that there are different degrees of glory to that end that we might seek after the higher degrees. God offered high degrees of glory to that end, that we might seek them by eminent holiness and good works: 2 Corinthians 9:6, "He that sows sparingly [shall reap also sparingly; and he that soweth bountifully shall reap also bountifully]." It is not becoming persons to be over anxious about an high seat in God's house in this world, for that is the honor that is of men; but we can't too earnestly seek after an high seat in God's house above, by seeking eminent holiness, for that is the honor that is of God.

But the mansions in God's house above are everlasting mansions. Those that have seats allotted 'em there, whether of greater or lesser dignity, whether nearer or further from the throne, will hold 'em to all eternity. This is promised, Revelation 3:12: "Him that overcometh I will make him a pillar in the temple [of my God, and he shall go no more out]." . . . It will

311

be of infinite and everlasting concern to you where your seat is in another world. Let your great concern be while in this world so to improve your opportunities in God's house in this world, whether you sit high or low, as that you may have a distinguished and glorious mansion in God's house in heaven, where you may be fixed in your place in that glorious assembly in an everlasting rest. (*Many Mansions*, 101)

## John Wesley

Let not any slothful one say, If I get to heaven at all, I will be content! Such a one may let heaven go altogether. In worldly things, men are ambitious to get as high as they can. Christians have a far more noble ambition. The difference between the very highest and the lowest state in the world is nothing to the smallest difference between the degrees of glory. *Explanatory Notes Upon the New Testament*, 193)

Happy is he who judges himself an unprofitable servant; miserable is he whom God pronounces such. But though we are unprofitable to him, our serving him is not unprofitable to us; for he is pleased to give by his grace a value to our good works which, in consequence of his promise, entitles us to an eternal reward. (706)

## Modern

### Charles H. Spurgeon

Seek secrecy for your good deeds. Do not even see your own virtue. Hide from yourself that which you yourself have done that is commendable; for the proud contemplation of your own generosity may tarnish all your alms. Keep the thing so secret that even you yourself are hardly aware that you are doing anything at all praiseworthy. He will reward you, reward you openly, reward you as a Father rewards a child, reward you as one who saw what you did, and knew that you did it wholly unto him." (72)

### G. K. Chesterton

The [modern cynic] always imagines that there is an element of corruption, in his own cynical manner, about the idea of reward, about the position of the child who can say, as in Stevenson's verses, "Every day when I've been good, I get an orange after food." To the man made ignorant by experience this always appears as a vulgar *bribe* to the child. The modern philosopher knows that it would require a very large bribe indeed to induce *him* to be good. It therefore seems to the modern philosopher what it would seem to the modern politician to say, "I will give you fifty thousand pounds when you have, on some one definite and demonstrated occasion, kept your word." The solid price seems something quite distinct from the rare and reluctant labour. But it does not seem like that to the child. It would not seem like that to the child, if the Fairy Queen said to the Prince, "You will receive the golden apple from the magic tree when you have fought the dragon." For the child is not a Manichee. He does not think that good things are in their nature separate from being good. In other words, he does not, like the reluctant realist, regard goodness as a bad thing. To him the goodness of the gift and the golden apple, that is called an orange, is all part of one substantial paradise and naturally goes together. In other words, he regards himself as normally on amiable terms with the natural authorities; not normally as quarrelling or bargaining with them. He has the ordinary selfish obstacles and understandings; but he does not, in his heart, regard it as odd that his parents would be good to him, to the extent of an orange, or that he should be good to them, to the extent of some elementary experiments in good behavior. He has no sense of being corrupted. It is only we, who have eaten the forbidden apple (or orange) who think of pleasure as a bribe. (52– 53)

## Dietrich Bonhoeffer

There is nothing hidden which will not be revealed. That is how God made things to be, before whom everything hidden is already revealed. God wants to show us what is hidden. God will make it visible. Being revealed in public is the reward ordained by God for hiddenness. The question is only where and from whom people receive this reward of public recognition. If they long for it to be in sight of other people, then they will have had their reward as soon as they get such publicity. There is no difference whether they seek it in the cruder form, in the presence of others, or in the more subtle form, in the presence of themselves. Whenever the left hand knows what the right is doing, whenever I myself become aware of my own hidden goodness, whenever I want to know about my own goodness, then I have already prepared for myself the public reward which God intended to store up for me. I am the one who revealed my own hiddenness to myself. I do not wait for God to show it to me. So I have gotten my reward. But those who remain hidden even from themselves until the end will receive from God the reward of being revealed. But who can live in such a way as to do the extraordinary in secret? Who can prevent the left hand form knowing what the right hand is doing? What sort of love is that which does not know itself, but can remain hidden from itself until the last day? It is clear that because it is hidden love, it cannot be a visible virtue, a human hubris (attitude). Beware – it says – that you do not mistake genuine love for the virtue of kindness or for a human "quality"! (*Discipleship*, 151)

Thus hiddenness has a counterpart in manifestation. For there is nothing hidden that shall not be revealed. For our God is a God unto whom all hearts are open, and from whom no secrets are hid. God will show us the hidden and make it visible. Manifestation is the appointed reward for hiddenness, and the only question is where we shall receive it and who will give it us. (*Cost of Discipleship*, 160)

The curse, the deadly persecution and evil slander confirm the blessed state of the disciples in their fellowship with Jesus. It could not be otherwise, for these meek strangers are bound to provoke the world to insult, violence and slander.... This is fatal, and so, while Jesus calls them blessed, the world cries: "Away with them, away with them!" Yes, but whither? To the kingdom of heaven. "Rejoice and be exceeding glad: for great is your reward in heaven." There shall the poor be seen in halls of joy. With his own hand God wipes away the tears from the eyes of those who had mourned upon earth. He feeds the hungry at his Banquet. There stand the scarred bodies of the martyrs, now glorified and clothed in the white robes of eternal righteousness instead of the rags of sin and repentance. The echoes of this joy reach the little flock below as it stands beneath the cross, and they hear Jesus saying: "Blessed are ye!" (266)

## C. S. Lewis

The New Testament has lots to say about self-denial, but not about self-denial as an end in itself. We are told to deny ourselves and to take up our crosses in order that we may follow Christ; and nearly every description of what we shall ultimately find if we do so contains an appeal to desire. If there lurks in most modern minds the notion that to desire our own good and earnestly to hope for the enjoyment of it is a bad thing, I submit

314

that this notion has crept in from Kant and the Stoics and is no part of the Christian faith. Indeed, if we consider the unblushing promises of reward and the staggering nature of the rewards promised in the Gospels, it would seem that Our Lord finds our desires, not too strong, but too weak. We are half-hearted creatures, fooling about with drink and sex and ambition when infinite joy is offered us, like an ignorant child who wants to go on making mud pies in a slum because he cannot imagine what is meant by the offer of a holiday at the sea. We are far too easily pleased." (*Weight of Glory*, 25–26)

We walk every day on the razor edge between these two incredible possibilities." (41)

Divine love is Gift-love. (*The Four Loves*, 1)

It would be a bold and silly creature that came before its Creator with the boast, "I'm no beggar. I love you disinterestedly." (4)

### Randy Alcorn

It is common to believe God is glorified only when we think of him alone and that any motive besides love for God is inferior or unacceptable. Yet it is God in his Word who gives us other motives—love for people, fear of disobedience and hope of reward among them. These are not mixed motives, but multiple motives—all God-given. ("Eternal Perspectives Ministry website")

### N. T. Wright

Many people imagine that [Jesus] is asking us to do everything with no thought of reward, and are then rather shocked when he repeats, three times [in Matthew 6], his belief that our heavenly father will repay us (verses 4, 6, 18). Clearly, Jesus is not so bothered about the notion of disinterested behavior or 'altruism', as we sometimes are. (53)

### R.C. Sproul

. . . Christians are shocked when I say there are various levels of heaven as well as gradations of severity of punishment in hell. We owe much of this confusion to the Protestant emphasis on the doctrine of justification by faith alone. We hammer away at that doctrine, teaching emphatically

315

that a person does not get to heaven through his good works . . . We emphasis this doctrine to the extent that people conclude good works are insignificant and have no bearing at all upon the Christian's future life. ... but we are promised rewards in heaven *according to our works*. (Emphasis in original) .... Everybody's cup in heaven is full; but not everybody in heaven has the same size cup." (*Now That's a Good Question*, 287)

### Charles Stanley

The kingdom of God will not be the same for all believers . . . Some believers will have rewards for their earthly faithfulness. Others will not. Some will reign with Christ. Others will not. Some will be rich in the kingdom of God. Others will be poor. Some will be given true riches. Others will not. Some will be given heavenly treasures of their own. Others will not. (Quoted by Wilkinson, 123)

### J. I. Packer

There will be different degrees of blessedness and reward in heaven. All will be blessed up to the limit of what they can receive, but capacities will vary just as they do in this world. As for rewards (an area in which present irresponsibility can bring permanent future loss: 1 Cor. 3:10-15), two points must be grasped. The first is that when God rewards our works he is crowning his own gifts, for it was only by grace that those works were done. The second is that essence of the reward in each case will be more of what the Christian desires most, namely, a deepening of his or her love-relationship with the Savior, which is the reality to which all the biblical imagery of honorific crowns and robes and feasts is pointing. The reward is parallel to the reward of courtship, which is the enriching of the love-relationship itself through marriage. (264

### Scott Hafemann

Whatever we hope for inevitably determines how we live. The object of our hope determines the contours of our conduct. This is a universal principle of human nature. Even at the trivial level, hope is what motivates us. (168)

Our treasure becomes our *hope*. In turn, our hope determines how we act, since we always spend our lives on whatever we think will make us happy. As a result, life is one long "treasure hunt" in search of the things we hope will meet our needs. (169)

At its most fundamental level, therefore, serving or loving God means transforming *where* we place our hopes. Notice that Jesus does not say that we should give up wanting treasure. The issue is what that treasure is – God or the world." (171)

Our obedience is not something we do for God, as if he needed us to obey him, but the redeemed way of life God grants to us "for our good. (172)

### *John Piper*

When I was in college I had a vague, pervasive notion that if I did something good because it would make me happy, I would ruin its goodness. I figured that the goodness of my moral action was lessened to the degree I was motivated by a desire for my own pleasure. At the time, buying ice cream in the Student Center just for pleasure didn't bother me, because the moral consequences of that action seemed so insignificant. But to be motivated by a desire for happiness or pleasure when I volunteered for Christian service or went to church — that seemed selfish, utilitarian, mercenary. (18)

If you come to God dutifully offering Him the reward of your fellowship instead of thirsting after the reward of His fellowship, then you exalt yourself above God as His benefactor and belittle Him as a needy beneficiary - and that is evil. (111)

# Appendix 7  God's Word on the Subject of Reward

## Investing in Eternity
### Abridged Collection of Verses

Find the complete collection at Investing-in-Eternity.org.

*Tell the righteous it will be well with them,*
*for they will enjoy the fruit of their deeds.*
Isaiah 3:10

### Preface to this collection of verses

All verses are from the New International Version

**Verse selection criteria**

The following passages were chosen for their conditional—"if-then—statements of God's promises. The rewards and conditions for gaining them are summarized in Indexes 1 - 3. The "'If-Then' Summary" column restates the passage's essence as conditional statements—to orient the reader to its conditionality. The summary is does not purport to interpret the passage or to reiterate every point therein.

I mostly cite verses containing promises of positive rewards. Verses that speak of negative rewards (punishments) are included only when negative and positive rewards are proximate to one another. Many other verses in the Bible speak of negative rewards but are not quoted here. Some of the verses cited express benefits God bestows upon all He loves.

However, the *fullness* of God's blessing is conditioned by the deeds and motives described in these verses.

Some of the verses concern—or arguably concern—conditions for entry into heaven, rather than to the rewards earned for enjoyment therein. I have included, for example, Romans 6:23 only because it is part of a passage that also speaks of reward. But, clearly, the vast majority of these verses are not talking about salvation or salvation only. They speak of something more—to be gained through obedience. If they only address salvation, then eternal salvation is earned.

If you judge some of the verses I cite as not contributory to my method, simply ignore them for purposes of my thesis. There will be plenty of other verses less ambiguous to your understanding. (See appendix 5 of *Investing in Eternity* for more on this point.)

**Consider this question as you read:**

Why does God so often repeat such conditional promises of blessing in Scripture?

**Suggested Read-Throughs:**

| | |
|---|---|
| First: | Scan the verses for **bolded** references to **reward, recompense, wage**, et al. |
| Second: | Highlight with a marker the conditions that must be met to gain the rewards. |
| Third: | Highlight with a different marker the descriptions of the promised rewards. |
| Fourth: | Ask yourself, "How does this inform the conduct of my life?" |

| Passages with Conditional Promises | "If/Then" Summary |
|---|---|
| **Genesis 7**:1 "Go into the ark, you and our whole family, because I have found you righteous in this generation." | If you are found to be righteous, then you will be spared judgment. |
| **Genesis 12**:1 The Lord had said to Abram, "Go from your country, your people and your father's household to the land I will show you. 2 "I will make you into a great nation, and I will bless you; I will make your name great, and you will be a blessing. 3 I will bless those who bless you and whoever curses you I will curse; and all peoples on earth will be blessed through you." 4 So Abram went, as the Lord had told him... | If you leave your people, then God will bless you, and people through you. |
| **Genesis 15**:1 After this, the word of the LORD came to Abram in a vision: "Do not be afraid, Abram. I am your shield, your very great **reward**." . . . 6 Abram believed the Lord, and he credited it to him as righteousness. | If you trust God, then He will protect you and will reward you with Himself. |
| **Genesis 17**:3... God said to him, 4 As for me, this is my covenant with you: You will be the father of many nations. 5 No longer will you be called Abram; your name will be Abraham, for I have made you a father of many nations. 5 I will make you very fruitful; I will make nations happy of you, and kings will come from you.... 9 As for you, you must keep my covenant, you and your descendants after you for the generations to come. | If you and your descendants keep God's covenant, then He will fulfill his covenant with you and make you fruitful. |
| **Genesis 22**:15 The angel of the Lord called to Abraham from heaven a second time 16 and said, "I swear by myself, declares the Lord, that because you have done this and have not withheld your son, your only son, 17 I will surely bless you and make your descendants as numerous as the stars in the sky and as the sand on the seashore. Your descendants will take possession of the cities of their enemies, 18 | If you obey and withhold nothing from God, then He will bless you and give you many descendants and God will bless many people. |

| | |
|---|---|
| and through your offspring all nations on earth will be blessed, because you have obeyed me." | |
| **Genesis 35**:1 Then God said to Jacob, "Arise, go up to Bethel and live there, and make an altar there to God. 2 So Jacob said to his household and to all who were with him, "Put away the foreign gods which are among you, and purify yourselves and change your garments; 3 and let us arise and go up to Bethel, and I will make an altar there to God. . .. 9 After Jacob returned from Paddan Aram, God appeared to him again and blessed him. 10 God said to him, "Your name is Jacob, but you will no longer be called Jacob; your name will be Israel." So he named him Israel. | If you obey and worship God, and go where He tells you to go, then He will bless you. |
| **Exodus 17**:11 As long as Moses held up his hands, the Israelites were winning, but whenever he lowered his hands, the Amalekites were winning. 12 When Moses' hands grew tired, they took a stone and put it under him and he sat on it. Aaron and Hur held his hands up—one on one side, one on the other—so that his hands remained steady till sunset. 13 So Joshua overcame the Amalekite army with the sword. | If you continuely look to God for help and strength, then He will give you victory. |
| **Exodus 33**:17 And the Lord said to Moses, "I will do the very thing you have asked, because I am pleased with you and I know you by name." | If you please God, then He will give that for which you asked. |
| **Leviticus 9**:6 Then Moses said, "This is what the Lord has commanded you to do, so that the glory of the Lord may appear to you." | If you do what the Lord has commanded you to do, then you will see His glory. |
| **Leviticus 25**:18 Follow my decrees and be careful to obey my laws, and you will live safely in the land. 19 Then the land will yield its fruit, and you will eat your fill and live there in safety. | If you follow God's decrees and obey His laws, then you will live and be safe in a fruitful land. |

| | |
|---|---|
| **Deuteronomy** 2: 40 Keep his decrees and commands, which I am giving you today, so that it may go well with you and your children after you and that you may live long in the land the Lord your God gives you for all time. | If you do as the Lord commands, then you will be blessed. |
| **Deuteronomy 5**:32 So be careful to do what the Lord your God has commanded you; do not turn aside to the right or to the left. 33 Walk in obedience to all that the Lord your God has commanded you, so that you may live and prosper and prolong your days in the land that you will possess. | If you do what God commands, then you will prosper. |
| **Deuteronomy 6**:18 Do what is right and good in the Lord's sight, so that it may go well with you and you may go in and take over the good land the Lord promised on oath to your ancestors.... 24 The Lord commanded us to obey all these decrees and to fear the Lord our God, so that we might always prosper and be kept alive, as is the case today. 25 And if we are careful to obey all this law before the Lord our God, as he has commanded us that will be our righteousness. | If you do what is right and good in God's sight, then life will go well for you. If you are careful to obey all God's commands, then you will prosper and be kept safe and alive. |
| **Deuteronomy 7**:12 If you pay attention to these laws and are careful to follow them, then the Lord your God will keep his covenant of love with you, as he swore to your ancestors. 13 He will love you and bless you and increase your numbers. | If you follow God's law, then He will keep His covenant of love with you; He will love you, bless you, and increase your numbers. |
| **Deuteronomy 14**:28 ...bring all the tithes of that year's produce... 29 ... so that the Lord your God may bless you in all the work of your hands. | If you give of your wealth, then the Lord will bless you and your work. |

| | |
|---|---|
| **Deuteronomy 15**:4 …He will richly bless you, 5 if only you fully obey the Lord your God and are careful to follow all these commands I am giving you today. 10 Give generously to them and do so without a grudging heart; then because of this the Lord your God will bless you in all your work and in everything you put your hand to. . .. | If you fully obey the Lord and if you give willingly and generously, then He will richly bless you. |
| **Deuteronomy 28**:1 If you fully obey the Lord your God and carefully follow all his commands I give you today, the Lord your God will set you high above all the nations on earth. 2 All these blessings will come on you and accompany you if you obey the Lord your God. | If you fully obey the Lord your God, then the He will exalt you above others. |
| **Deuteronomy 29**:9 Carefully follow the terms of this covenant, so that you may prosper in everything you do. | If you carefully follow the covenant, then you will prosper. |
| **Joshua 1**:7 Be careful to obey all the law my servant Moses gave you; do not turn from it to the right or to the left, that you may be successful wherever you go. 8 Do not let this Book of the Law depart from your mouth; meditate on it day and night, so that you may be careful to do everything written in it. Then you will be prosperous and successful. | If you carefully do all that the Book of the Law requires, then you will be strong and courageous; you will prosper and succeed. |
| **Judges 5**:31 But may all who love you be like the sun when it rises in its strength. | If you love God, then you will shine like the sun. |
| **1 Samuel 2**:30 But now the Lord declares: …Those who honor me I will honor, but those who despise me will be disdained. | If you honor God, then He will honor you. |
| **1 Samuel 26**:23 The LORD will **repay** each man for his righteousness and his faithfulness. | If you are righteous and faithful, then God will repay you. |

| | |
|---|---|
| **2 Samuel 22**:21 The LORD has dealt with me according to my righteousness; according to the cleanness of my hands he has **rewarded** me. 22 For I have kept the ways of the LORD; I have not done evil by turning from my God. All his laws are before me; I have not turned away from his decrees. I have been blameless before him and have kept myself from sin.<br><br>    25 The LORD has **rewarded** me according to my righteousness, according to my cleanness in his sight. 26 To the faithful you show yourself faithful, to the blameless you show yourself blameless, 27 to the pure you show yourself pure, but to the devious you show yourself shrewd. 28 You save the humble, but your eyes are on the haughty to bring them low. | If you are righteous and keep yourself from sin, then the Lord will reward you accordingly.<br><br>If you live a righteous life, then God will reward you.<br><br>If you are humble before God, then you will be saved. |
| **1 Kings 2**:2 So be strong, act like a man, 3 and observe what the Lord your God requires: Walk in obedience to him, and keep his decrees and commands, his laws and regulations, as written in the Law of Moses. Do this so that you may prosper in all you do and wherever you go 4 and that the Lord may keep his promise to me … | If you keep God's decrees and commands, then you will prosper in all you do and wherever you go and God will keep his promise. |
| **1 Kings 8**:39 Now Lord … forgive and act; **deal with** each man according to all he does, since you know his heart (for you alone know the hearts of all men). | If your heart is acceptable to God, then you will be rewarded. |
| **2 Kings 18**:5 Hezekiah trusted in the Lord, the God of Israel…, 6 He held fast to the Lord and did not stop following him; he kept the commands the Lord had given Moses. 7 And the Lord was with him; he was successful in whatever he undertook. | If you trust in God, then you will succeed in life. |

| | |
|---|---|
| **2 Chronicles 1**:11 God said to Solomon, "Because you had this in mind, and did not ask for riches, wealth or honor, or the life of those who hate you, nor have you even asked for long life, but you have asked for yourself wisdom and knowledge that you may rule My people over whom I have made you king, 12 wisdom and knowledge have been granted to you. | If you seek wisdom rather than things of this world, then you will be wise. |
| **2 Chronicles 6**:30 Forgive, and **deal with** each man according to all he does, since you know his heart (for you alone know the hearts of men), 31 so that they will fear you and walk in your ways all the time they live in the land you gave our fathers. | If you fear and walk in God's ways, then you will be rewarded according to what you have done. |
| **2 Chronicles 7**:14 …if my people, who are called by my name, will humble themselves and pray and seek my face and turn from their wicked ways, then I will hear from heaven, and I will forgive their sin and will heal their land. 15 Now my eyes will be open and my ears attentive to the prayers offered in this place. | If you humble yourself before God and turn from sin, then God will attend to your prayers. |
| **2 Chronicles 14**:7 [Asa] said to Judah… "The land is still ours, because we have sought the Lord our God; we sought him and he has given us rest on every side." So they built and prospered. | If you seek the Lord, then you will have rest and prosperity. |
| **2 Chronicles 15**: 7 But as for you, be strong and do not give up, for your work will be **rewarded**.…15 They sought God eagerly, and he was found by them. So the Lord gave them rest on every side. | If you are persistent and strong, then you will be rewarded. |
| **2 Chronicles 16**:9 For the eyes of the Lord range throughout the earth to strengthen those whose hearts are fully committed to him. | If your heart is committed to God, then He will give strength. |
| **Ezra 9**:22 The gracious hand of our God is on everyone who looks to him, but his great anger is against all who forsake him. | If you look to God, then His gracious hand will be upon you. |

| | |
|---|---|
| **Job 34:**<br>10 So listen to me, you men of understanding.<br><br>Far be it from God to do evil,<br>from the Almighty to do wrong.<br>11 He **repays** a man for what he has done;<br>he brings upon him what his conduct deserves.<br>12 It is unthinkable that God would do wrong,<br>that the Almighty would pervert justice. | If your conduct is deserving, then God will reward you.<br><br>(*The message of the book is summed in this passage, even though it is spoken as an accusation against Job.*) |
| **Psalm 1:**1 Blessed is the one who does not walk in step with the wicked or stand in the way that sinners take or sit in the company of mockers, 2 but whose delight is in the law of the Lord, and who meditates on his law day and night. 3 That person is like a tree planted by streams of water, which yields its fruit in season and whose leaf does not wither – whatever they do prospers. | If you walk with God rather than with sinners, then you will flourish. |
| **Psalm 2:**8 Ask me, and I will make the nations your inheritance, the ends of the earth your possession.... 12 Blessed are all who take refuge in him. | If you ask God, then He will give you an inheritance and keep you safe. |
| **Psalm 3:**4 I call out to the Lord, and he answers me from his holy mountain. | If you call out to God, then He will answer you. |
| **Psalm 5:**12 Surely, Lord, you bless the righteous; you surround them with your favor as with a shield. | If you are righteous, then you will have God's favor. |
| **Psalm 11:**7 For the Lord is righteous, he loves justice; the upright will see his face. | If you are upright, then you will see God's face. |

| | |
|---|---|
| **Psalm 18**: 20 The LORD has dealt with me according to my righteousness; according to the cleanness of my hands he has **rewarded** me. 21 For I have kept the ways of the LORD; I have not done evil by turning from my God. All his laws are before me; I have not turned away from his decrees. I have been blameless before him and have kept myself from sin. 24 The LORD has **rewarded** me according to my righteousness, according to the cleanness of my hands in his sight. | If you call out to the Lord; keep the ways of the Lord; are blameless, and have not turned from God, then the He will rescue you and reward you according to your righteousness. |
| **Psalm 19**<br>7    The law of the LORD is perfect, reviving the soul.<br>      The statutes of the LORD are trustworthy, making wise the simple.<br>8    The precepts of the LORD are right, giving joy to the heart.<br>      The commands of the LORD are radiant, giving light to the eyes.<br>9    The fear of the LORD is pure, enduring forever.<br>      The ordinances of the LORD are sure and altogether righteous.<br>10  They are more precious than gold, than much pure gold;<br>      they are sweeter than honey, than honey from the comb.<br>11  By them is your servant warned; in keeping them there is great **reward**. | If you follow God's law, then you will have wisdom, joy, radiance, and riches greater than gold and sweeter than honey. |
| **Psalms 24**:3 Who may ascend the hill of the LORD? Who may stand in his holy place? 4 He who has clean hands and a pure heart, who does not lift up his soul to an idol or swear by what is false. 5 He will receive blessing from the LORD and vindication from God his Savior. | If you have clean hands and a pure heart, then you will be vindicated and blessed to stand in God's holiest place. |

| | |
|---|---|
| **Psalm 25**:3 No one who hopes in you will ever be put to shame, but shame will come on those who are treacherous without cause. 9 He guides the humble in what is right and teaches them his way. 10 All the ways of the Lord are loving and faithful toward those who keep the demands of his covenant… 12 Who, then, are those who fear the Lord? He will instruct them in the ways they should choose. 13 They will spend their days in prosperity, and their descendants will inherit the land. 14 The Lord confides in those who fear him; he makes his covenant known to them. | If you hope in God; fear him; humble yourself before Him, and keep His commands, then you will never be put to shame, and you will prosper; you will inherit the land. |
| **Psalm 31**:19 How great is your goodness, which you have stored up for those who fear you, which you bestow in the sight of men on those who take refuge in you. . .. 23 Love the Lord, all his faithful people! The Lord preserves those who are true to him, but the proud he pays back in full. | If you fear God and are faithful to Him, then you know the greatness of God's goodness. |
| **Psalm 33**:18 But the eyes of the Lord are on those who fear him, on those whose hope is in his unfailing love, 19 to deliver them from death and keep them alive in famine. | If you trust in the Lord, then He will deliver from death and your heart will rejoice. |
| **Psalm 40**:4 Blessed is the one who trusts in the Lord. | If you seek God, then you will blessed |
| **Psalm 41**:1 Blessed are those who have regard for the weak; the Lord delivers them in times of trouble. 2 The Lord protects and preserves them— they are counted among the blessed in the land— he does not give them over to the desire of their foes. | If you have regard for the weak, then the Lord will preserve and protect you. |
| **Psalm 55**: 22 Cast your cares on the Lord and he will sustain you; he will never let the righteous be shaken. | If you cast your cares upon God, then He will answer your prayers. |

| | |
|---|---|
| **Psalm 58**:10 The righteous will be glad when they are avenged... 11 Then men will say, "Surely the righteous still are **rewarded**; surely there is a God who judges the earth." | If you are righteous, then you will be rewarded. |
| **Psalm 62**:11 One thing God has spoken, two things have I heard: that you, O God, are strong, 12 and that you, O Lord, are loving. Surely you will **reward** each person according to what he has done. | If you are deserving, then God will reward you to the extent of your deservedness. |
| **Psalm 64**:10 The righteous will rejoice in the LORD and take refuge in him; all the upright in heart will glory in him! | If you are upright and righteous, then you will rejoice in the Lord. |
| **Psalm 73**:1 Surely God is good to Israel, to those who are pure in heart. | If you are pure of heart, then God will be good to you. |
| **Psalm 81**:10 Open wide your mouth and I will fill it. | If you ask, then God will give. |
| **Psalm 84**: 4 Blessed are those who dwell in your house. . . Blessed are those whose strength is in you. . . 11 For the LORD God is a sun and shield; the LORD bestows favor and honor; no good thing does he withhold from those whose walk is blameless. 12 LORD Almighty, blessed is the one who trusts in you. | If your walk is blameless, then God will bestow favor and honor. |
| **Psalm 89**:15 Blessed are those who have learned to acclaim you, who walk in the light of your presence, LORD. 16 They rejoice in your name all day long; they celebrate your righteousness. 17 For you are their glory and strength, and by your favor you exalt our horn. | If you proclaim God's greatness, then you will walk with God and He will exalt you. |

| | |
|---|---|
| **Psalm 91**:1 Whoever dwells in the shelter of the Most High will rest in the shadow of the Almighty. . . 9 If you say, "The LORD is my refuge," and you make the Most High your dwelling, 10 no harm will overtake you, no disaster will come near your tent. . . 14 Because he loves me," says the LORD, "I will rescue him; I will protect him, for he acknowledges my name. 15 He will call on me, and I will answer him; I will be with him in trouble, I will deliver him and honor him. | If you take shelter in God, then you will have rest. If you call on the Lord, then He will answer you. If you love God, then He will rescue, protect, deliver, and honor you. |
| **Psalm 92**:12 The righteous will flourish like a palm tree, they will grow like a cedar of Lebanon;13 planted in the house of the LORD, they will flourish in the courts of our God. | If you are righteous, then you will flourish. |
| **Psalm 103**:17 But from everlasting to everlasting the LORD's love is with those who fear him, and his righteousness with their children's children—18 with those who keep his covenant and remember to obey his precepts. | If you fear God and keep His covenant and obey His precepts, then you the Lord's love will be with you forever. |
| **Psalm 106**:3 Blessed are those who act justly, who always do what is right. | If you act justly and do what is right, then you will be blessed. |
| **Psalm 107**:42 The upright see and rejoice. | If you are upright, then you will rejoice. |
| **Psalm 111**:10 The fear of the LORD is the beginning of wisdom; all who follow his precepts have good understanding. | If you fear the Lord, then you will know wisdom. |

| | |
|---|---|
| **Psalm 112**:2 Blessed is the man who fears the LORD, who finds great delight in his commands.... 6 Surely he will never be shaken; a righteous man will be remembered forever. 7 He will have no fear of bad news; his heart is steadfast, trusting in the LORD. 8 His heart is secure, he will have no fear; in the end he will look in triumph on his foes. 9 He has scattered abroad his gifts to the poor, his righteousness endures forever; his horn will be lifted high in honor. | If you fear God and are gracious, compassionate and righteous, then you will have delights, children, righteousness, riches, security, and honor. |
| **Psalm 115**:13 He will bless those who fear the LORD, the small together with the great. | If you fear the Lord, then He will bless you. |
| **Psalm 116**:6 The LORD protects the simplehearted; when I was in great need, he saved me. 7 Be at rest once more, O my soul, for the LORD has been **good** to you. | If you are open to His instruction, then God will meet your needs. |
| **Psalm 119**:1 Blessed are they whose ways are blameless, who walk according to the law of the LORD. 2 Blessed are those who keep his statutes and seek him with all their heart . . .. 165 Great peace have those who love your law, and nothing can make them stumble. | If you walk blamelessly according to God's law, you will be blessed and delivered from your suffering. |
| **Psalm 128**:1 Blessed are all who fear the Lord, who walk in obedience to him. 2 You will eat the fruit of your labor; blessings and prosperity will be yours. | If you fear God and walk in obedience to Him, then you will be fruitful and blessed. |
| **Psalm 135**:14 For the LORD will vindicate his people and have compassion on his servants. | If you serve God, then He will vindicate you. |
| **Psalm 145**:18 The LORD is near to all who call on him, to all who call on him in truth. 19 He fulfills the desires of those who fear him; he hears their cry and saves them. 20 The LORD watches over all who love him.... | If you call on the Lord and fear Him, then He will fulfill your desires. |

| | |
|---|---|
| **Psalm 147**:6 The LORD sustains the humble. . . . 11 the LORD delights in those who fear him, who put their hope in his unfailing love. | If you are humble, then God will delight in you. |
| **Psalm 149**:4 For the LORD takes delight in his people; he crowns the humble with victory. 5 Let his faithful people rejoice in this honor and sing for joy on their beds. | If you humbly serve God, then He will give you a crown of victory. |
| **Proverbs 1**:7 The fear of the LORD is the beginning of knowledge but fools despise wisdom and instruction. 8 Listen, my son, to your father's instruction and do not forsake your mother's teaching. 9 They are a garland to grace your head and a chain to adorn your neck. . . 23 Repent at my rebuke! Then I will pour out my thoughts to you, I will make known to you my teachings. . . 33 whoever listens to me will live in safety and be at ease, without fear of harm. | If you fear the Lord, listen to instruction and repent, then you will have the wisdom of God and you will be safe from harm. |
| **Proverbs 2**:1 My son, if you accept my words and store up my commands within you, 2 turning your ear to wisdom and applying your heart to understanding; 3 Indeed, if you call out for insight and cry aloud for understanding, 4 and if you look for it as for silver and search for it as for hidden treasure, 5 then you will understand the fear of the Lord and find the knowledge of God. . .7 He holds success in store for the upright, he is a shield to those whose walk is blameless, 8 for he guards the course of the just and protects the way of his faithful ones. . .20 Thus you will walk in the ways of the good and keep to the paths of the righteous. 21 For the upright will live in the land, and the blameless will remain in it. | *The if-then construction is explicit in verses 1-5.*<br><br>If you are one of the faithful who whose walk is blameless, then God will guard and protect you. |

| | |
|---|---|
| **Proverbs 8**:32 Now then, my children, listen to me; blessed are those who keep my ways. 33 Listen to my instruction and be wise; do not disregard it. 34 Blessed are those who listen to me, watching daily at my doors, waiting at my doorway. 35 For those who find me find life and receive favor from the LORD. | If you listen to and choose God's instruction, then you will have wisdom that is more precious than rubies. |
| **Proverbs 9**:10 The fear of the LORD is the beginning of wisdom, and knowledge of the Holy One is understanding. 11 For through wisdom your days will be many, and years will be added to your life. 12 If you are wise, your wisdom will **reward** you; if you are a mocker, you alone will suffer. | If you fear the Lord and if you are wise, you will be rewarded. |
| **Proverbs 10**:6 Blessings crown the head of the righteous, but violence overwhelms the mouth of the wicked. . . 30 The righteous will never be uprooted, but the wicked will not remain in the land. | *The entire chapter is a contrast of implicit if-then conditions and consequences for both righteousness and for sin.* |
| **Proverbs 11**: 8 The righteous person is rescued from trouble, and it falls on the wicked instead. . . .. 16 A kindhearted woman gains honor, but ruthless men gain only wealth. 17 A kind man benefits himself, but a cruel man brings trouble on himself. 18 The wicked man earns deceptive **wages**, but he who sows righteousness reaps a sure **reward**. . .. 25 A generous person will prosper; whoever refreshes others will be refreshed. 26 People curse the one who hoards grain, but they pray God's blessing on the one who is willing to sell. . .. 30 The fruit of the righteous is a tree of life, and the one who is wise saves lives. 31 If the righteous receive their **due** on earth, how much more the ungodly and the sinner! | If you are honest, then God will favor you.

If you sow righteousness, then you will reap what is your due, a wage, a reward. |

| | |
|---|---|
| **Proverbs 12**:2 Good people obtain favor from the Lord, but he condemns those who devise wicked schemes. . ..14 From the fruit of his lips a man is filled with good things as surely as the work of his hands **rewards** him. 19 Truthful lips endure forever, but a lying tongue lasts only a moment. 20 Deceit is in the hearts of those who plot evil, but those who promote peace have joy. 21 No harm overtakes the righteous, but the wicked have their fill of trouble. | If you are good, righteous, and truthful, then you will find favor with the Lord, you will flourish, you will escape trouble, and you will be rewarded. |
| **Proverbs 13**:6 Righteousness guards the person of integrity, but wickedness overthrows the sinner. 13 He who scorns instruction will pay for it, but he who respects a command is **rewarded**. . .. 15 Good judgment wins favor, but the way of the unfaithful leads to their destruction. 21 Misfortune pursues the sinner, but prosperity is the **reward** of the righteous. | If you respect God's commands and are righteous, then He will reward you. |
| **Proverbs 14**:11 The house of the wicked will be destroyed, but the tent of the upright will flourish. . ..14 The faithless will be fully repaid for their ways, and the good man **rewarded** for his. . .. 18 The simple inherit folly, but the prudent are crowned with knowledge. 22 Do not those who plot evil go astray? But those who plan what is good find love and faithfulness. . .. 26 Whoever fears the Lord has a secure fortress, and for their children it will be a refuge. 27 The fear of the Lord is a fountain of life, turning a person from the snares of death. . .. 14 It is a sin to despise one's neighbor but blessed is the one who is kind to the needy. | If you are a good man and make good plans; if you fear the Lord, then you will be secure, flourish and find love.

If you are kind to the needy, then you will be blessed. |
| **Proverbs 15**:6 The house of the righteous contains great treasure, but the income of the wicked brings ruin. | If you are righteous, then you will have riches (in heaven). |

| | |
|---|---|
| **Proverbs 16**:3 Commit to the Lord whatever you do, and he will establish your plans. . .. 20 Whoever gives heed to instruction prospers, and blessed is the one who trusts in the LORD. | If you commit what you do to the Lord and heed instruction, then he will establish your plans. |
| **Proverbs 19**:8 The one who gets wisdom loves life; the one who cherishes understanding will soon prosper. . .. 17 He who is kind to the poor lends to the LORD, and he will **reward** him for what he has done. . .. 23 The fear of the LORD leads to life; then one rests content, untouched by trouble. | If you love wisdom and accept advice, then you will prosper.<br><br>If you lend to the poor, then God will reward you. |
| **Proverbs 22**:4 Humility is the fear of the LORD; its wages are riches and honor and life. . .. 9 The generous will themselves be blessed, for they share their food with the poor. . .. 11 One who loves a pure heart and who speaks with grace will have the king for a friend. | If you humbly fear God, then you will be rewarded with pleasure, riches, honor, life, and friendship with the King. |
| **Proverbs 24**:3 By wisdom a house is built, and through understanding it is established; 4 through knowledge its rooms are filled with rare and beautiful treasures. . .. 12 If you say, "But we knew nothing about this," does not he who weighs the heart perceive it? Does not he who guards your life know it? Will he not **repay** each person according to what he has done? 13 Eat honey, my son, for it is good; honey from the comb is sweet to your taste. 14 Know also that wisdom is sweet to your soul; if you find it, there is a future hope for you, and your hope will not be cut off. . .. 25 But it will go well with those who convict the guilty, and rich blessing will come on them. | If you are wise, then you will have beautiful treasures.<br><br>If you are deserving, then you will be rewarded according to what you have done.<br><br>If you seek wisdom, then you will have a future hope. |
| **Proverbs 25**:21 If your enemy is hungry, give him food to eat; if he is thirsty, give him water to drink. 22 In doing this, you will heap burning coals on his head, and the LORD will **reward** you. | If you humble yourself, whether before kings or enemies, then God will reward you. |

| | |
|---|---|
| **Proverbs 27**:18 He who tends a fig tree will eat its fruit, and he who looks after his master will be honored. | If you serve God's purposes, then He will honor you. |
| **Proverbs 28**:18 The one whose walk is blameless is kept safe. . .. 19 Those who work their land will have abundant food. . .. 20 A faithful person will be richly blessed. . .; 25 those who trust in the LORD will prosper. . .; 26 those who walk in wisdom are kept safe. 27 Those who give to the poor will lack nothing. . .. | If you live blamelessly, then you will receive a large inheritance.<br><br>If you trust the Lord, then you will prosper. |
| **Proverbs 29**:18 Blessed is the one who heeds wisdom's instruction. . .. 23 Pride brings a person low, but the lowly in spirit gain honor. . .. 25 Fear of man will prove to be a snare, but whoever trusts in the LORD is kept safe. | If you are righteous, then you will shout for joy and be glad and you throne will last forever. |
| **Proverbs 30**:5 "Every word of God is flawless; he is a shield to those who take refuge in him. | If you take refuge in God, then He will be your shield. |
| **Proverbs 31**:30 Charm is deceptive, and beauty is fleeting; but a woman who fears the LORD is to be praised. | If you fear the Lord, then you will be praised. |
| **Ecclesiastes 2**:26 To the man who pleases him, God gives wisdom, knowledge and happiness . . .. | If you please God, then He will give you wisdom, knowledge and happiness. |
| **Song of Songs** | (*The entire book describes the rewards of a loving relationship.*) |
| **Isaiah 1**:19 If you are willing and obedient, you will eat the good things of the land. 20 but if you resist and rebel, you will be devoured by the sword. | If you are willing and obedient, then you will benefit. |

| | |
|---|---|
| **Isaiah 3**:10 Tell the righteous it will be well with them, for they will enjoy the **fruit of their deeds**. 11 Woe to the wicked! Disaster is upon them! They will be **paid back** for what their hands have done. | If you are righteous, then you will be reimbursed by God, and you will enjoy the fruit of your deeds. |
| **Isaiah 26**:3 You will keep in perfect peace those whose minds are steadfast, because they trust in you. Trust in the LORD forever, for the LORD, the LORD himself, is the Rock eternal. | If you trust in the Lord, then you will be at peace. |
| **Isaiah 30**:18 Yet the LORD longs to be gracious to you; therefore he will rise up to show you compassion. For the LORD is a God of justice. Blessed are all who wait for him! . . . 19 How gracious he will be when you cry for help! As soon as he hears, he will answer you. | If you wait on the Lord, then he will be gracious to you and show you compassion. If you cry out to Him, then He will answer. |
| **Isaiah 35**:4 Say to those with fearful hearts, "Be strong, do not fear; your God will come, he will come with vengeance; with **divine retribution** he will come to save you." | If you trust in God, then he will repay you. |
| **Isaiah 40**:10 See, the Sovereign LORD comes with power, and his arm rules for him. See, his **reward** is with him, and his **recompense** accompanies him. | If you are worthy, then God will reward; then He will pay back what you gave to Him. |
| **Isaiah 49**:4 But I said, "I have labored to no purpose; I have spent my strength in vain and for nothing. Yet what is **due** me is in the LORD's hand, and my **reward** is with my God." | If you have labored for God, then God will repay you as your due. |
| **Isaiah 54**:17 No weapon forged against you will prevail, and you will refute every tongue that accuses you. This is the **heritage** of the servants of the LORD, and this is their vindication from me." declares the LORD. | If you are a servant of the Lord, then you will have a heritage and God's vindication. |

| | |
|---|---|
| **Isaiah 55**:1 Come, all you who are thirsty, come to the waters; and you who have no money, come, buy and eat! Come, buy wine and milk without money and without cost. . .. 7 Let them turn to the LORD, and he will have mercy on them, and to our God, for he will freely pardon. | If come thirsty for God, then He will quench your thirst and you will be pardoned. |
| **Isaiah 56**:2 Blessed is the one who does this—the person who holds it fast, who keeps the Sabbath without desecrating it, and keeps their hands from doing any evil. . .. 5 to them I will give within my temple and its walls a memorial and a name better than sons and daughters; I will give them an everlasting name that will endure forever. | If you hold fast to the commandments and keep from evil, then you will be blessed and you will be given a name that will last forever. |
| **Isaiah 57**:2 Those who walk uprightly enter into peace; they find rest as they lie in death. . .. 13 Whoever takes refuge in me will inherit the land and possess my holy mountain. | If you walk uprightly, then you will find rest at your death and have an inheritance. |
| **Isaiah 61**:8 For I, the LORD, love justice; I hate robbery and iniquity. In my faithfulness I will **reward** them and make an everlasting covenant with them. | If you are just and hate sin, then God will reward you. |
| **Isaiah 62**:11 The LORD has made proclamation to the ends of the earth: "Say to the Daughter of Zion, "See, your Savior comes! See, his **reward** is with him, and his **recompense** accompanies him." | If you expectantly wait for God your Savior then you will receive a reward; a recompense. |
| **Isaiah 64**:4 Since ancient times no one has heard, no ear has perceived, no eye has seen any God besides you, who acts on behalf of those who wait for him. 5 You come to the help of those who gladly do right, who remember your ways. | If you wait on the Lord, help other do what is right and remember God's ways, then He will act on your behalf. |
| **Isaiah 66**:2 These are the ones I look on with favor: those who are humble and contrite in spirit, and who tremble at my word. | If you are humble and contrite before God, then He will look upon you with favor. |

| | |
|---|---|
| **Jeremiah 17**:7 But blessed is the one who trusts in the LORD, whose confidence is in him. . ... 10 "I the LORD search the heart and examine the mind, to **reward** a man according to his conduct, according to what his deeds deserve." | If you trust in the Lord, then you will be rewarded according to what your deeds deserve. |
| **Jeremiah 32**:18 O great and powerful God, whose name is the LORD Almighty, 19 great are your purposes and mighty are your deeds. Your eyes are open to all the ways of men; you **reward** everyone according to his conduct and as his deeds deserve. | If God looks at your deeds and approves of what He sees, then He will reward you accordingly. |
| **Jeremiah 33**:3 Call to me and I will answer you and tell you great and unsearchable things you do not know. | If you call on the Lord, then he will tell you great things. |
| **Lamenations 4**:25 The LORD is good to those whose hope is in him, to the one who seeks him; 26 it is good to wait quietly for the salvation of the LORD. | If you hope in the Lord and seek Him, then He will be good to you. |
| **Ezekiel 18**:5 Suppose there is a righteous man who does what is just and right. 6 He does not eat at the mountain shrines or look to the idols of Israel. 7 He does not.... 8 He does not... [do what is wicked] 9 He follows my decrees and faithfully keeps my laws. That man is righteous; he will surely live, declares the Sovereign Lord. | If you are righteous and follow God's laws, then you will life. *(Most of the book speaks of negative rewards/ punishments.)* |
| **Daniel 12**:3 Those who are wise will shine like the brightness of the heavens, and those who lead many to righteousness, like the stars for ever and ever. | If you are wise and lead others into righteousness, then you will shine like the stars of heaven. |
| **Hosea 10**:12 Sow for yourselves righteousness, reap the fruit of unfailing love, and break up your unplowed ground; for it is time to seek the Lord, until he comes and showers righteousness on you. | If you sow righteousness, then God will shower you with righteousness. |

| | |
|---|---|
| **Joel 2**:12 "Even now," declares the Lord, "return to me with all your heart, with fasting and weeping and mourning.". . . 25 I will **repay** you for the years the locusts have eaten…. | If you repent, then God will reward you. |
| **Nahum 1**:7 The Lord is good, a refuge in times of trouble. He cares for those who trust in him. | If you trust God, then He will take care of you. |
| **Zechariah 3**:7 This is what the LORD Almighty says: "If you will walk in my ways and keep my requirements, then you will govern my house and have charge of my courts, and I will give you a place among these standing here." | *The construction of the promise is conditional.* |
| **Malachi 4**:2 But for you who revere my name, the sun of righteousness will rise with healing in its rays. And you will go out and frolic like well-fed calves. | If you revere God, then you will be healed and joyful. |
| **Matthew 5**<br><br>3   Blessed are the poor in spirit, [because] theirs is the kingdom of heaven.<br>4   Blessed are those who mourn, [because] they will be comforted.<br>5   Blessed are the meek, [because] they will inherit the earth.<br>6   Blessed are those who hunger and thirst for righteousness, [because] for they will be filled.<br>7   Blessed are the merciful, [because] they will be shown mercy.<br>8   Blessed are the pure in heart, [because] they will see God.<br>9   Blessed are the peacemakers, [because] they will be called sons of God.<br>10   Blessed are those who are persecuted because of righteousness, for [because] theirs is the kingdom of heaven.<br>11   Blessed are you when people insult you, persecute you and falsely say all kinds of evil against you because of me. | If you are (see verses 1-11), then you will be blessed of God.<br><br>If are persecuted, then you will receive a reward in heaven.<br><br>If you teach and practice God's commands, then you will be called great in the Kingdom.<br><br>If you love your neighbor, then you will be rewarded. |

| | |
|---|---|
| 12  Rejoice and be glad, because great is your **reward** in heaven, for in the same way they persecuted the prophets who were before you... <br> 19  Anyone who breaks one of the least of these commandments and teaches others to do the same will be called least in the kingdom of heaven, but whoever practices and teaches these commands will be called great in the kingdom of heaven. <br> 43 You have heard that it was said, 'Love your neighbor and hate your enemy.' 44 But tell you: Love your enemies and pray for those who persecute you, 45 that you may be sons of your Father in heaven.... 46 If you love those who love you, what **reward** will you get? | |
| **Matthew 6**:1 Be careful not to do your acts of righteousness before men, to be seen by them. . . . 3 But when you give to the needy, do not let your left hand know what your right hand is doing, 4 so that your giving may be in secret. Then your Father, who sees what is done in secret, will **reward** you. <br><br> 5 And when you pray, do not be like the hypocrites, for they love to pray standing in the synagogues and on the street corners to be seen by men. I tell you the truth; they have received their **reward** in full. 6 But when you pray, go into your room, close the door and pray to your Father, who is unseen. Then your Father, who sees what is done in secret, will **reward** you.... <br><br> 16 When you fast, do not look somber as the hypocrites do, for they disfigure their faces to show men they are fasting. I tell you the truth, they have received their **reward** in full. 17 But when you fast, put oil on your head and wash your face, 18 so that it will not be obvious to men that you are fasting, but only to your Father, who is unseen; and your Father, who sees what is done in secret, will **reward** you. | If you live your life only for the approval of God and not for the approval of men, then God will reward you. <br><br> If everything you do in life is for the sake of God's Kingdom, then you will have a great treasure in heaven. <br><br> If you seek God's Kingdom and His righteousness in this life, then you will have everything you truly need. |

| | |
|---|---|
| 19 Do not store up for yourselves treasures on earth, where moth and rust destroy, and where thieves break in and steal. 20 But store up for yourselves treasures in heaven, where moth and rust do not destroy, and where thieves do not break in and steal. 21 For where your treasure is, there your heart will be also. . . ..33 But seek first his kingdom and his righteousness, and all these things will be given to you as well. | |
| **Matthew 7**:7 Ask and it will be given to you; seek and you will find; knock and the door will be opened to you. 8 For everyone who asks receives; the one who seeks finds; and to the one who knocks, the door will be opened. 9 Which of you, if your son asks for bread, will give him a stone? 10 Or if he asks for a fish, will give him a snake? 11 If you, then, though you are evil, know how to give good gifts to your children, how much more will your Father in heaven give good gifts to those who ask him! | If you persist in seeking something good from God, then He will give it to you. |
| **Matthew 10**:26 "So do not be afraid of them, for there is nothing concealed that will not be disclosed, or hidden that will not be made known. 27 What I tell you in the dark, speak in the daylight; what is whispered in your ear, proclaim from the roofs. . . .. <br><br> 37 Anyone who loves his father or mother more than me is not worthy of me; anyone who loves his son or daughter more than me is not worthy of me; 38 and anyone who does not take his cross and follow me is not worthy of me. 39 Whoever finds his life will lose it, and whoever loses his life for my sake will find [his life]. <br><br> 40 He who receives you receives me, and he who receives me receives the one who sent me. 41 Anyone who receives a prophet because he is a prophet will receive a prophet's **reward**, and | If you give up family, or hospitality, or even a cup of water, then you will earn a reward from God. |

| | |
|---|---|
| anyone who receives a righteous man because he is a righteous man will receive a righteous man's **reward**. 42 And if anyone gives even a cup of cold water to one of these little ones because he is my disciple, I tell you the truth, he will certainly not lose his **reward**. | |
| **Matthew 12**:50 For whoever does the will of my Father in heaven is my brother and sister and mother. | If you do God's will, then you are His child. |
| **Matthew 16**:24 Then Jesus said to his disciples, "If anyone would come after me, he must deny himself and take up his cross and follow me. 25 For whoever wants to save his life will lose it, but whoever loses his life for me will find it. 26 What good will it be for a man if he gains the whole world, yet forfeits his soul? Or what can a man give in exchange for his soul? 27 For the Son of Man is going to come in his Father's glory with his angels, and then he will **reward** each person according to what he has done." (*See also Mark 8:34-35; Luke 9:23-24; John 12:25*) | If you deny your own interests, then God will reward you to the extent you have done so. |
| **Matthew 17**:20 Truly I tell you, if you have faith as small as a mustard seed, you can say to this mountain, 'Move from here to there,' and it will move. Nothing will be impossible for you. | If you have faith as a mustard seed, then you will be able to do anything. |
| **Matthew 19**<br>16 Now a man came up to Jesus and asked, "Teacher, what good thing must I do to get eternal life?"<br>21 Jesus answered, "If you want to be perfect, go, sell your possessions and give to the poor, and you will have treasure in heaven. Then come, follow me."<br>27 Peter answered him, "We have left everything to follow you! What then will there be for us?" | If it is your desire to perfectly please God and if you act upon that desire by giving up everything else in your life, then you will have treasure in heaven. |

| | |
|---|---|
| 28 Jesus said to them, "I tell you the truth, at the renewal of all things, when the Son of Man sits on his glorious throne, you who have followed me will also sit on twelve thrones, judging the twelve tribes of Israel. 29 And everyone who has left houses or brothers or sisters or father or mother or children or fields for my sake will receive a hundred times as much and will inherit eternal life. 30 But many who are first will be last, and many who are last will be first." | If you leave everything of value in your life for the sake of Jesus, then God will return to you many times what you sacrificed.<br><br>(*See also Mark 10; Luke 18*) |
| **Matthew 20**:16 But many who are first will be last, and many who are last will be first. 25 You know that the rulers of the Gentiles lord it over them, and their high officials exercise authority over them. 26 Not so with you. Instead, whoever wants to become great among you must be your servant, 27 and whoever wants to be first must be your slave—28 just as the Son of Man did not come to be served, but to serve, and to give his life as a ransom for many. | If you make yourself last, then God will make you first.<br><br>If you sacrifice your life like Jesus sacrificed Himself, then you will be great. |
| **Matthew 23**:11 The greatest among you will be your servant. 12 For those who exalt themselves will be humbled, and those who humble themselves will be exalted. | If you humble yourself, then God will exalt you. |
| *Matthew 25:14 Again, it will be like a man going on a journey, who called his servants and entrusted his property to them. 15 To one he gave five talents of money, to another two talents, and to another one talent, each according to his ability. Then he went on his journey. 16 The man who had received the five talents went at once and put his money to work and gained five more. 17 So also, the one with the two talents gained two more. 18 But the man who had received the one talent went off, dug a hole in the ground and hid his master's money.* | If you are a faithful steward of what God has put in your charge, then you will be rewarded with much more than what you gave, and you will be invited to share in the master's happiness. |

| | |
|---|---|
| 19 After a long time the master of those servants returned and settled accounts with them. 20 The man who had received the five talents brought the other five. "Master," he said, "you entrusted me with five talents. See, I have gained five more." | If you serve King Jesus, then you will inherit the His Kingdom. |
| 21 His master replied, "Well done, good and faithful servant! You have been faithful with a few things; I will put you in charge of many things. Come and share your master's happiness!" | |
| 22 The man with the two talents also came. "Master," he said, "you entrusted me with two talents; see, I have gained two more." | |
| 23 His master replied, "Well done, good and faithful servant! You have been faithful with a few things; *I will* put you in charge of many things. Come and share your master's happiness!" | |
| 34 Then the King will say to those on his right, `Come, you who are blessed by my Father; take your inheritance, the kingdom prepared for you since the creation of the world. 35 For I was hungry and you gave me something to eat, I was thirsty and you gave me something to drink, I was a stranger and you invited me in, 36 I needed clothes and you clothed me, I was sick and you looked after me, I was in prison and you came to visit me. | |
| **Mark 4**:20 Others, like seed sown on good soil, hear the word, accept it, and produce a crop—some thirty, some sixty, some a hundred times what was sown. . .. 24 "Consider carefully what you hear," he continued. "With the measure you use, it will be measured to you—and even more. 25 Whoever has will be given more; whoever does not have, even what he has will be taken from him." | If you listen to God, then He will give back to you according to your obedience. |

| | |
|---|---|
| **Mark 8**:34 Whoever wants to be my disciple must deny themselves and take up their cross and follow me. 35 For whoever wants to save their life will lose it, but whoever loses their life for me and for the gospel will save it. 36 What good is it for someone to gain the whole world, yet forfeit their soul? 37 Or what can anyone give in exchange for their soul? 38 If anyone is ashamed of me and my words in this adulterous and sinful generation, the Son of Man will be ashamed of them when he comes in his Father's glory with the holy angels. | If you are a disciple of Jesus to the point of losing your life, then God will not be ashamed of you when you stand before Christ in heaven. |
| **Mark 9**:41 I tell you the truth, anyone who gives you a cup of water in my name because you belong to Christ will certainly not lose his **reward**. | If you give even a cup of water to someone in the name of Jesus, then you will be rewarded. |
| **Mark 10**:35 Then James and John, the sons of Zebedee, came to him. "Teacher," they said, "we want you to do for us whatever we ask." 36 "What do you want me to do for you?" he asked. 37 They replied, "Let one of us sit at your right and the other at your left in your glory." 38 "You don't know what you are asking," Jesus said. "Can you drink the cup I drink or be baptized with the baptism I am baptized with?" 39 "We can," they answered. Jesus said to them, "You will drink the cup I drink and be baptized with the baptism I am baptized with, 40 but to sit at my right or left is not for me to grant. These places belong to those for whom they have been prepared." | If you give everything away for God's sake, then you will have treasure in heaven.<br><br>If you leave your family to serve God, then you will receive an even greater family in return.<br><br>*(See Matt. 19:16-30)* |

| | |
|---|---|
| 41 When the ten heard about this, they became indignant with James and John. 42 Jesus called them together and said, "You know that those who are regarded as rulers of the Gentiles lord it over them, and their high officials exercise authority over them. 43 Not so with you. Instead, whoever wants to become great among you must be your servant, 44 and whoever wants to be first must be slave of all. 45 For even the Son of Man did not come to be served, but to serve, and to give his life as a ransom for many." | |
| **Luke 6**:20 Looking at his disciples, he said:<br>　Blessed are you who are poor, for yours is the kingdom of God.<br><br>21　Blessed are you who hunger now, for you will be satisfied.<br>　Blessed are you who weep now, for you will laugh.<br>22　Blessed are you when men hate you, when they exclude you and insult you and reject your name as evil, because of the Son of Man.<br>23　"Rejoice in that day and leap for joy, because great is your **reward** in heaven. For that is how their fathers treated the prophets. 35 But love your enemies, do good to them, and lend to them without expecting to get anything back. Then your **reward** will be great, and you will be sons of the Most High, because he is kind to the ungrateful and wicked. 36 Be merciful, just as your Father is merciful. 37 Do not judge, and you will not be judged. Do not condemn, and you will not be condemned. Forgive, and you will be forgiven. 38 Give, and it will be given to you. A good measure, pressed down, shaken together and running over, will be poured into your lap. For with the measure you use, it will be measured to you. | If you are poor, hungry, sorrowful, and hated for the sake of Jesus, then you will be rewarded with joy and happiness.<br><br>If you love people, then you will be greatly rewarded.<br><br>If you give, then it will be given to you. |

| | |
|---|---|
| **Luke 8**:8 Still other seed fell on good soil. It came up and yielded a crop, a hundred times more than was sown. . .. 15 But the seed on good soil stands for those with a noble and good heart, who hear the word, retain it, and by persevering produce a crop. 16 No one lights a lamp and hides it in a jar or puts it under a bed. Instead, he puts it on a stand, so that those who come in can see the light. 17 For there is nothing hidden that will not be disclosed, and nothing concealed that will not be known or brought out into the open. 18 Therefore consider carefully how you listen. Whoever has will be given more; whoever does not have, even what he thinks he has will be taken from him. . .. 21 My mother and brothers are those who hear God's word and put it into practice. | If you are good soil, then you will produce a hundred times what was sown.<br><br>If you have, then you will be given even more.<br><br>If you put God's word into practice then you will be children of God. |
| **Luke 9**:23 Then he said to them all: "Whoever wants to be my disciple must deny themselves and take up their cross daily and follow me. 24 For whoever wants to save their life will lose it, but whoever loses their life for me will save it. . .. 46 An argument started among the disciples as to which of them would be the greatest. 47 Jesus, knowing their thoughts, took a little child and had him stand beside him. 48 Then he said to them, Whoever welcomes this little child in my name welcomes me; and whoever welcomes me welcomes the one who sent me. For he who is least among you all—he is the greatest. | If you lose your life, then you will save it.<br><br>If you make yourself as the least, then God will make you the greatest. |

**Luke 12**:2 There is nothing concealed that will not be disclosed or hidden that will not be made known. 3 What you have said in the dark will be heard in the daylight, and what you have whispered in the ear in the inner rooms will be proclaimed from the roofs.

8 I tell you, whoever acknowledges me before men, the Son of Man will also acknowledge him before the angels of God. 9 But he who disowns me before men will be disowned before the angels of God.

31 But seek his kingdom, and these things will be given to you as well. . .. 32 Do not be afraid, little flock, for your Father has been pleased to give you the kingdom. 33 Sell your possessions and give to the poor. Provide purses for yourselves that will not wear out, a treasure in heaven that will not be exhausted, where no thief comes near and no moth destroys. 34 For where your treasure is, thereqq your heart will be also.

37 It will be good for those servants whose master finds them watching when he comes. Truly I tell you, he will dress himself to serve, will have them recline at the table and will come and wait on them. 38 It will be good for those servants whose master finds them ready, even if he comes in the middle of the night or toward daybreak. . ..

42 Who then is the faithful and wise manager, whom the master puts in charge of his servants to give them their food allowance at the proper time? 43 It will be good for that servant whom the master finds doing so when he returns. 44 Truly I tell you, he will put him in charge of all his possessions. . ..
48 From everyone who has been given much, much will be demanded; and from the one who has been entrusted with much, much more will be asked.

If you give your concerns about life to God, then God will provide all that you need, and far, far more in return.

If you sell your possessions and give to the poor, they you will be given the Kingdom; a treasure in heaven that will never be exhausted.

If your Master finds you watching for His coming, then it will be good for you.

If you to see to the needs of others, then you will be put in charge of all the Master's possessions.

| | |
|---|---|
| **Luke 13**:9 So I say to you: Ask and it will be given to you; seek and you will find; knock and the door will be opened to you. 10 For everyone who asks receives; he who seeks finds; and to him who knocks, the door will be opened. 11 Which of you fathers, if your son asks for a fish, will give him a snake instead? 12 Or if he asks for an egg, will give him a scorpion? 13 If you then, though you are evil, know how to give good gifts to your children, how much more will your Father in heaven give the Holy Spirit to those who ask him! . . . 30 Indeed there are those who are last who will be first, and first who will be last. | If you persistently entreat God for your needs, then God will provide.<br><br>If you make yourself last, God will place you as first. |
| **Luke 14**:10 But when you are invited, take the lowest place, so that when your host comes, he will say to you, `Friend, move up to a better place.' Then you will be honored in the presence of all your fellow guests. 11 For everyone who exalts himself will be humbled, and he who humbles himself will be exalted."<br><br>12 Then Jesus said to his host, "you give a luncheon or dinner, do not invite your friends, your brothers or relatives, or your rich neighbors; if you do, they may invite you back and so you will be repaid. 13 But when you give a banquet, invite the poor, the crippled, the lame, the blind, 14 and you will be blessed. Although they cannot repay you, you will be **repaid** at the resurrection of the righteous."<br><br>26 "If anyone comes to me and does not hate father and mother, wife and children, brothers and sisters—yes, even their own life—such a person cannot be my disciple. 27 And whoever does not carry their cross and follow me cannot be my disciple. | If you humble yourself, then God will humble you.<br><br>If you care for the poor and disabled, then you will be rewarded.<br><br>If you forsake your father, mother, wife and children for Christ's sake, then you will be His disciple. |

| | |
|---|---|
| **Luke 18**:13 "But the tax collector stood at a distance. He would not even look up to heaven, but beat his breast and said, 'God, have mercy on me, a sinner.' 14 "I tell you that this man, rather than the other, went home justified before God. For everyone who exalts himself will be humbled, and he who humbles himself will be exalted."<br><br>22 When Jesus heard this, he said to him, "You still lack one thing. Sell everything you have and give to the poor, and you will have treasure in heaven. Then come, follow me."<br><br>28 Peter said to him, "We have left all we had to follow you!" 29 I tell you the truth," Jesus said to them, "no one who has left home or wife or brothers or parents or children for the sake of the kingdom of God 30 will fail to receive many times as much in this age and, in the age to come, eternal life." | If you are humble before God, then God will exalt you.<br><br>If you give everything of value to God's purposes, then you will have treasure in heaven.<br><br>*(See Matt. 19:16-30 for the conversation with the rich ruler.)* |
| **Luke 21**:3 "Truly I tell you," he said, "this poor widow has put in more than all the others. 4 All these people gave their gifts out of their wealth; but she out of her poverty put in all she had to live on." | If you give everything you have to God, then Jesus will praise you. |
| **Luke 22**:24 A dispute also arose among them as to which of them was considered to be greatest. 25 Jesus said to them, "The kings of the Gentiles lord it over them; and those who exercise authority over them call themselves Benefactors. 26 But you are not to be like that. Instead, the greatest among you should be like the youngest, and the one who rules like the one who serves. 27 For who is greater, the one who is at the table or the one who serves? Is it not the one who is at the table? But I am among you as one who serves. 28 You are those who have stood by me in my trials. 29 And I confer on you a kingdom, just as my Father conferred one on me, 30 so that you may eat and drink at my table in my kingdom and sit on thrones, judging the twelve tribes of Israel. | If you make yourself a servant to others, then you will be given the Kingdom where you will eat and drink at Jesus' table and you will sit on throne of judgment. |

| | |
|---|---|
| **John 4**:36 Even now the reaper draws his **wages**, even now he harvests the crop for eternal life, so that the sower and the reaper may be glad together. 37 Thus the saying 'One sows and another reaps' is true. | If you work for Jesus, then you will be rewarded. |
| **John 8**:31 To the Jews who had believed him, Jesus said, "If you hold to my teaching, you are really my disciples. 32 Then you will know the truth, and the truth will set you free. | *The conditionality of the statement is explicit as written.* |
| **John 12**: 25 The man who loves his life will lose it, while the man who hates his life in this world will keep it for eternal life. 26 Whoever serves me must follow me; and where I am, my servant also will be. My Father will honor the one who serves me. | If you die to self and serve Jesus, then you will be fruitful and God will honor you. |
| **John 13**:14 Now that I, your Lord and Teacher, have washed your feet, you also should wash one another's feet. 15 I have set you an example that you should do as I have done for you. 16 Very truly I tell you, no servant is greater than his master, nor is a messenger greater than the one who sent him. 17 Now that you know these things, you will be blessed if you do them. | If you follow Jesus' example and serve others, then God will bless you. |
| **John 15**:5 If you remain in me and I in you, you will bear much fruit; apart from me you can do nothing. 6 If you do not remain in me, you are like a branch that is thrown away and withers; such branches are picked up, thrown into the fire and burned. 7 If you remain in me and my words remain in you, ask whatever you wish, and it will be done for you. 8 This is to my Father's glory, that you bear much fruit, showing yourselves to be my disciples. . .. 11 I have told you this so that my joy may be in you and that your joy may be complete. . ... 14 You are my friends if you do what I command. | If you remain in Jesus, then you will bear fruit.<br><br>If you do what Jesus commands, then your joy will complete. |

| | |
|---|---|
| **John 16**:23 Very truly I tell you, my Father will give you whatever you ask in my name. 24 Until now you have not asked for anything in my name. Ask and you will receive, and your joy will be complete. | If you pray in the name of Jesus, then you will joyfully receive that for which you asked. |
| **Acts 5**:41 The apostles left the Sanhedrin, rejoicing because they had been counted worthy of suffering disgrace for the Name. | If you suffer for Jesus, then you will rejoice in that suffering. |
| **Romans 2**:5 But because of your stubbornness and your unrepentant heart, you are storing up wrath against yourself for the day of God's wrath, when his righteous judgment will be revealed. 6 God "will **give** to each person according to what he has done." 7 To those who by persistence in doing good seek glory, honor and immortality, he will give eternal life. 8 But for those who are self-seeking and who reject the truth and follow evil, there will be wrath and anger. 9 There will be trouble and distress for every human being who does evil: first for the Jew, then for the Gentile; 10 but glory, honor and peace for everyone who does good: first for the Jew, then for the Gentile. 11 For God does not show favoritism. | If you persist in doing good, then you will be rewarded with glory, honor and immortality to the extent you have so lived. |
| **Romans 5**:10 Not only so, but we also glory in our sufferings, because we know that suffering produces perseverance; perseverance, character; and character, hope. | If you suffer for Christ, then God will give you a glorious hope. |
| **Romans 14**:10 You, then, why do you judge your brother? Or why do you look down on your brother? For we will all stand before God's judgment seat. 11 It is written: "'As surely as I live,' says the Lord, 'every knee will bow before me; tongue will confess to God.'" 12 So then, each of us will give an account of himself to God. | If you humble yourself before the Lord, then you will stand unashamed before His judgment seat. |

| | |
|---|---|
| **1 Corinthians 2**:9 What no eye has seen, what no ear has heard, and what no human mind has conceived - the things God has prepared for those who love him - 10 these are the things God has revealed to us by his Spirit. The Spirit searches all things, even the deep things of God. | If you love God, then He will reveal what He has prepared for you. |
| **1 Corinthians 3**:8 The man who plants and the man who waters have one purpose, and each will be **rewarded** according to his own labor. 9 For we are God's fellow workers; you are God's field, God's building. 10 By the grace God has given me, I laid a foundation as an expert builder, and someone else is building on it. But each one should be careful how he builds. 11 For no one can lay any foundation other than the one already laid, which is Jesus Christ. 12 If any man builds on this foundation using gold, silver, costly stones, wood, hay or straw, 13 his work will be shown for what it is, because the Day will bring it to light. It will be revealed with fire, and the fire will test the quality of each man's work. 14 If what he has built survives, he will receive his **reward**. 15 If it is burned up, he will suffer loss; he himself will be saved, but only as one escaping through the flames. | If you work for the Lord to advance His purposes, then you will be rewarded.

If you a fool for Christ, then you will be wise. |
| **1 Corinthians 4**:1 So then, men ought to regard us as servants of Christ and as those entrusted with the secret things of God. 2 Now it is required that those who have been given a trust must prove faithful. 3 I care very little if I am judged by you or by any human court; indeed, I do not even judge myself. 4 My conscience is clear, but that does not make me innocent. It is the Lord who judges me. 5 Therefore judge nothing before the appointed time; wait till the Lord comes. He will bring to light what is hidden in darkness and will expose the motives of men's hearts. At that time each will receive his praise from God. | If you are faithful with what God has given you, then you will be praised by God. |

| | |
|---|---|
| 10 We always carry around in our body the death of Jesus, so that the life of Jesus may also be revealed in our body. 11 For we who are alive are always being given over to death for Jesus' sake, so that his life may also be revealed in our mortal body. | |
| **1 Corinthians 8**:3 But whoever loves God is known by God. | If you love God, then you are known by God. |
| **1 Corinthians 9**:22 I have become all things to all men so that by all possible means I might save some. 23 I do all this for the sake of the gospel, that I may share in its blessings. 24 Do you not know that in a race all the runners run, but only one gets the **prize**? Run in such a way as to get the **prize**. 25 Everyone who competes in the games goes into strict training. They do it to get a crown that will not last; but we do it to get a crown that will last forever. 26 Therefore I do not run like a man running aimlessly; I do not fight like a man beating the air. 27 No, I beat my body and make it my slave so that after I have preached to others, I myself will not be disqualified for the prize. | If you sacrifice something for Christ, then part of your reward is the opportunity to preach the gospel that sacrifice affords.<br><br>If you persist in living your life for Jesus, then you will win a prize, a crown, from God. |
| **1 Corinthians 12**:10 Therefore I am well content with weaknesses, with insults, with distresses, with persecutions, with difficulties, for Christ's sake; for when I am weak, then I am strong. | If in your weakness you endure insults and persecution, then you will be strong. |
| **1 Corinthians 15**:58 Therefore, my dear brothers, stand firm. Let nothing move you. Always give yourselves fully to the work of the Lord, because you know that your labor in the Lord is not in vain. | If you give yourself to the work of the Lord, then your labor will not be in vain. |

| | |
|---|---|
| 2 **Corinthians 1**:3 Praise be to the God and Father of our Lord Jesus Christ, the Father of compassion and the God of all comfort, 4 who comforts us in all our troubles, so that we can comfort those in any trouble with the comfort we ourselves receive from God. 5 For just as we share abundantly in the sufferings of Christ, so also our comfort abounds through Christ. | If you share in Christ's suffering, then you will be comforted and will be better able to comfort others. |
| 2 **Corinthians 3**:16 But whenever anyone turns to the Lord, the veil is taken away. 17 Now the Lord is the Spirit, and where the Spirit of the Lord is, there is freedom. 18 And we all, who with unveiled faces contemplate the Lord's glory, are being transformed into his image with ever-increasing glory, which comes from the Lord, who is the Spirit. | If you turn to the Lord to contemplate His glory, then you will be transformed into Christ's image with ever-increasing glory. |
| 2 **Corinthians 4**:17 For our light and momentary troubles are achieving for us an eternal glory that far outweighs them all. 18 So we fix our eyes not on what is seen, but on what is unseen. For what is seen is temporary; but what is unseen is eternal. | If you endure suffering for the sake of Christ, you will achieve eternal glory that far outweighs them all. |
| 2 **Corinthians 5**:9 So we make it our goal to please him, whether we are at home in the body or away from it. 10 For we must all appear before the judgment seat of Christ, that each one may receive **what is due** him for the things done while in the body, whether good or bad. | If we please Jesus, then we will be rewarded. |
| 2 **Corinthians 9**:6 Remember this: Whoever sows sparingly will also reap sparingly, and whoever sows generously will also **reap** generously. | If you give generously to God, then you will be rewarded with God's generosity. |
| 2 **Corinthians 10**:17 But, "Let him who boasts boast in the Lord." 18 For it is not the one who commends himself who is approved, but the one whom the Lord commends. | If you wait for God's commendation, then you will be commended by God. |

| | |
|---|---|
| **2 Corinthians 12**:9 But he said to me, "My grace is sufficient for you, for my power is made perfect in weakness." Therefore I will boast all the more gladly about my weaknesses, so that Christ's power may rest on me. 10 That is why, for Christ's sake, I delight in weaknesses, in insults, in hardships, in persecutions, in difficulties. For when I am weak, then I am strong. | If you are weak, then you will be strong. |
| **2 Corinthians 13**:11 Finally, brothers and sisters, rejoice! Strive for full restoration, encourage one another, be of one mind, live in peace. And the God of love and peace will be with you. | If you strive for full restoration, then the God of love and peace will be with you. |
| **Galatians 6**:7 Do not be deceived: God cannot be mocked. A man **reaps** what he sows. 8 The one who sows to please his sinful nature, from that nature will reap destruction; the one who sows to please the Spirit, from the Spirit will **reap** eternal life. 9 Let us not become weary in doing good, for at the proper time we will **reap** a harvest if we do not give up. 10 Therefore, as we have opportunity, let us do good to all people, especially to those who belong to the family of believers. | If you live your life to please God, then you will reap (3x) a reward. |
| **Ephesians 5**:13 But everything exposed by the light becomes visible—and everything that is illuminated becomes a light. 14 This is why it is said:<br>    "Wake up, sleeper,<br>    rise from the dead,<br>    and Christ will shine on you." | If you live wisely, make the most of every opportunity, are filled with the Spirit, sing and make music from your heart, and always |

| | |
|---|---|
| 15 Be very careful, then, how you live—not as unwise but as wise, 16 making the most of every opportunity, because the days are evil. 17 Therefore do not be foolish, but understand what the Lord's will is. 18 Do not get drunk on wine, which leads to debauchery. Instead, be filled with the Spirit, 19 speaking to one another with psalms, hymns, and songs from the Spirit. Sing and make music from your heart to the Lord, 20 always giving thanks to God the Father for everything, in the name of our Lord Jesus Christ. | give thanks to God for everything, then your works will be seen for what they are when your life is illuminated by Christ. |
| **Ephesians 6**:7 Serve wholeheartedly, as if you were serving the Lord, not men, 8 because you know that the Lord will **reward** everyone for whatever good he does, whether he is slave or free. . . .. 10 Finally, be strong in the Lord and in his mighty power. 11 Put on the full armor of God, so that you can take your stand against the devil's schemes. 12 For our struggle is not against flesh and blood, but against the rulers, against the authorities, against the powers of this dark world and against the spiritual forces of evil in the heavenly realms. 13 Therefore put on the full armor of God, so that when the day of evil comes, you may be able to stand your ground, and after you have done everything, to stand. | If you serve God wholeheartedly, then He will reward you for the good you do.<br><br>If you put on the full armor of God, then you will withstand the attacks of the devil. |
| **Philippians 2**:14 Do everything without grumbling or arguing, 15 so that you may become blameless and pure, "children of God without fault in a warped and crooked generation." Then you will shine among them like stars in the sky 16 as you hold firmly to the word of life. And then I will be able to boast on the day of Christ that I did not run or labor in vain. | If you live without complaining or arguing, are pure and blameless, and if you hold firmly to God's word, then you will shine like stars. |

| | |
|---|---|
| **Philippians 3**:7 But whatever was to my profit I now consider loss for the sake of Christ. 8 What is more, I consider everything a loss compared to the surpassing greatness of knowing Christ Jesus my Lord, for whose sake I have lost all things. I consider them rubbish, that I may gain Christ 9 and be found in him, not having a righteousness of my own that comes from the law, but that which is through faith in Christ—the righteousness that comes from God and is by faith. 10 I want to know Christ and the power of his resurrection and the fellowship of sharing in his sufferings, becoming like him in his death, 11 [so that by every means possible be so dead to sin that I attain a resurrection from the dead that is like that of Jesus.] 12 Not that I have already obtained all this, or have already been made perfect, but I press on to **take hold** of that for which Christ Jesus took hold of me. 13 Brothers, I do not consider myself yet to have taken hold of it. But one thing I do: Forgetting what is behind and straining toward what is ahead, 14 I press on toward the goal to win the prize for which God has called me heavenward in Christ Jesus. 15 All of us who are mature should take such a view of things. And if on some point you think differently, that too God will make clear to you. | If you do everything for the sake of Christ; if you are found in the end to be in Him; if you want to know Christ above everything; if you share in his suffering; if you become like Him in his death, then you will be rewarded. |
| **Philippians 4**:6 Do not be anxious about anything, but in every situation, by prayer and petition, with thanksgiving, present your requests to God. 7 And the peace of God, which transcends all understanding, will guard your hearts and your minds in Christ Jesus. | If you bring you concerns to Him, then God will give you peace. |

| | |
|---|---|
| **Colossians 3**:20 Children, obey your parents in everything, for this pleases the Lord. . ... 22 Slaves obey your earthly masters in everything; and do it, not only when their eye is on you and to win their favor, but with sincerity of heart and reverence for the Lord. 23 Whatever you do, work at it with all your heart, as working for the Lord, not for men, 24 since you know that you will receive an inheritance from the Lord as a **reward**. It is the Lord Christ you are serving. 25 Anyone who does wrong will be repaid for his wrong, and there is no favoritism. | If children obey their parents, then they please God.<br><br>If you serve the Lord with all your heart, then you will be rewarded. |
| **1 Thessalonians 1**:6 God is just: He will pay back trouble to those who trouble you 7 and give relief to you who are troubled, and to us as well. | If you endure persecution, then God, who is just, will give you relief. |
| **2 Thessalonians 2**:14 He called you to this through our gospel, that you might share in the glory of our Lord Jesus Christ. 15 So then, brothers, stand firm and hold to the teaching we passed on to you, whether by word of mouth or by letter. . ... 19 For what is our hope, our joy, or the crown in which we will glory in the presence of our Lord Jesus when he comes? Is it not you? 20 Indeed, you are our glory and joy. | If you stand firm and hold to God's teaching, then you will share in the glory of Christ. |
| **I Timothy 4**:7 Have nothing to do with godless myths and old wives' tales; rather, train yourself to be godly. 8 For physical training is of some value, but godliness has value for all things, holding promise for both the present life and the life to come. | If you are godly, then you will have what God promises. |
| **I Timothy 5**:17 The elders who direct the affairs of the church well are worthy of double honor, especially those whose work is preaching and teaching. 18 For the Scripture says, "Do not muzzle the ox while it is treading out the grain, "and "The worker deserves his **wages**." | If you work for God, then you will earn God's wage. |

| | |
|---|---|
| **I Timothy 6**:6 But godliness with contentment is great gain.... 11 But you, man of God, flee from [the love of money], and pursue righteousness, godliness, faith, love, endurance and gentleness. 12 Fight the good fight of the faith. Take hold of the eternal life to which you were called... 17 Command those who are rich in this present world not to be arrogant nor to put their hope in wealth, which is so uncertain, but to put their hope in God, who richly provides us with everything for our enjoyment. 18 Command them to do good, to be rich in good deeds, and to be generous and willing to share. 19 In this way they will lay up treasure for themselves as a firm foundation for the coming age, so that they may take hold of the life that is truly life. | If you give your wealth to God, then you will have a treasure in heaven; you will have life that is truly life. |
| **2 Timothy 2**:3 Endure hardship with us like a good soldier of Christ Jesus. 4 No one serving as a soldier gets involved in civilian affairs—he wants to please his commanding officer. 5 Similarly, if anyone competes as an athlete, he does not receive the victor's crown unless he competes according to the rules. 6 The hardworking farmer should be the first to receive a share of the crops.<br><br>7 Reflect on what I am saying, for the Lord will give you insight into all this. . ..<br><br>9 Therefore I endure everything for the sake of the elect, that they too may obtain the salvation that is in Christ Jesus, with eternal glory. 10 Here is a trustworthy saying: If we died with him, we will also live with him; if we endure, we will also reign with him. . ..<br><br>14 Keep reminding God's people of these things. Warn them before God against quarreling about words; it is of no value, and only ruins those who listen. . .. | If you endure hardship and if you work hard for the Lord, then you will earn a crown; you will share in the harvest; you will have eternal glory; you will reign with Christ.<br><br>If we endure, then we will reign with Him.<br><br>If you cleanse yourself from sin, then you will be an instrument of special purposes, made holy and useful to the Master to do any good work. |

| | |
|---|---|
| 20 In a large house there are articles not only of gold and silver, but also of wood and clay; some are for special purposes and some for common use. 21 Those who cleanse themselves from the latter will be instruments for special purposes, made holy, useful to the Master and prepared to do any good work. | |
| **2 Timothy 4**:6 For I am already being poured out like a drink offering, and the time has come for my departure. 7 I have fought the good fight, I have finished the race, I have kept the faith. 8 Now there is in store for me the crown of righteousness, which the Lord, the righteous Judge, will **award** to me on that day—and not only to me, but also to all who have longed for his appearing. | If you give your all to Jesus until the end of your life, then He will award you at the great judgment. |
| **Hebrews 4**:13 Nothing in all creation is hidden from God's sight. Everything is uncovered and laid bare before the eyes of him to whom we must give account. . .16 Let us then approach God's throne of grace with confidence, so that we may receive mercy and find grace to help us in our time of need. | If God is pleased with your life, then you can be confident that you will find mercy and grace. |
| **Hebrews 6**:7 Land that drinks in the rain often falling on it and that produces a crop useful to those for whom it is farmed receives the blessing of God. 8 But land that produces thorns and thistles is worthless and is in danger of being cursed. In the end it will be burned. 9 Even though we speak like this, dear friends, we are confident of better things in your case—things that accompany salvation. 10 God is not unjust; he will not forget your work and the love you have shown him as you have helped his people and continue to help them. 11 We want each of you to show this same diligence to the very end, in order to make your hope sure. 12 We do not want you to become lazy, but to imitate those who through faith and patience inherit what has been promised. | If you produce a crop for God, then He will bless you.<br><br>If you love and help people, then God will remember you.<br><br>If you wait upon God's timing, as Abraham did, then you will receive God's promised blessings. |

| | |
|---|---|
| 13 When God made his promise to Abraham, since there was no one greater for him to swear by, he swore by himself, 14 saying, "I will surely bless you and give you many descendants." 15 And so after waiting patiently, Abraham **received** what was promised. | |
| **Hebrews 10**:35 So do not throw away your confidence; it will be richly **rewarded**. 36 You need to persevere so that when you have done the will of God, you will **receive** what he has promised. | If you endure persecution, then you will be richly rewarded. |
| **Hebrews 11**:1 Now faith is being sure of what we hope for and certain of what we do not see. 2 This is what the ancients were commended for. 3 By faith we understand that the universe was formed at God's command, so that what is seen was not made out of what was visible. 4 By faith Abel . . . 5 By faith Enoch . . . was commended as one who pleased God. 6 And without faith it is impossible to please God, because anyone who comes to him must believe that he exists and that he **rewards** those who earnestly seek him.<br><br>7 By faith Noah . . .. 8 By faith Abraham, when called to go to a place he would later receive as his inheritance, obeyed and went, even though he did not know where he was going. 9 By faith he made his home in the promised land like a stranger in a foreign country; he lived in tents, as did Isaac and Jacob, who were heirs with him of the same promise. 10 For he was looking forward to the city with foundations, whose architect and builder is God. . .. 12 And so from this one man, and he as good as dead, came descendants as numerous as the stars in the sky and as countless as the sand on the seashore. | If you, like the people of the Bible, believe that God rewards faithfulness to Him and if you act upon that belief, then you will be rewarded. |

39 All these people were still living by faith when they died. They did not receive the things promised; they only saw them and welcomed them from a distance. And they admitted that they were aliens and strangers on earth. 14 People who say such things show that they are looking for a country of their own. . ..16 Instead, they were longing for a better country—a heavenly one. Therefore, God is not ashamed to be called their God, for he has prepared a city for them.

17 By faith Abraham, when God tested him, offered Isaac as a sacrifice. He who had received the promises was about to sacrifice his one and only son, 18 even though God had said to him, "It is through Isaac that your offspring will be reckoned." 19 Abraham reasoned that God could raise the dead, and figuratively speaking, he did receive Isaac back from death.

By faith Isaac... By faith Jacob... By faith Joseph... faith Moses' parents... 24 By faith Moses, when he had grown up, refused to be known as the son of Pharaoh's daughter. 25 He chose to be mistreated along with the people of God rather than to enjoy the pleasures of sin for a short time. 26 He regarded disgrace for the sake of Christ as of greater value than the treasures of Egypt, because he was looking ahead to his **reward**. 27 By faith he left Egypt, not fearing the king's anger; he persevered because he saw him who is invisible....

By faith the people... 31 By faith the prostitute Rahab... And what more shall I say? I do not have time to tell about Gideon, Barak, Samson, Jephthah, David, Samuel and the prophets, 33 who through faith conquered kingdoms, administered justice, and **gained** what was promised; who shut the mouths of lions, 34 quenched the fury of the flames, and escaped the edge of the sword; whose weakness was turned to strength; and who became

| | |
|---|---|
| powerful in battle and routed foreign armies. 35 Women received back their dead, raised to life again. Others were tortured and refused to be released, so that they might gain a better resurrection. 36 Some faced jeers and flogging, while still others were chained and put in prison. 37 They were stoned; they were sawed in two; they were put to death by the sword. They went about in sheepskins and goatskins, destitute, persecuted and mistreated— 38 the world was not worthy of them. They wandered in deserts and mountains, and in caves and holes in the ground.<br><br>39 These were all commended for their faith, yet none of them received what had been promised. 40 God had planned something better for us so that only together with us would they be made perfect. | |
| **Hebrews 12**:1 Therefore, since we are surrounded by such a great cloud of witnesses, let us throw off everything that hinders and the sin that so easily entangles. 7 Endure hardship as discipline; God is treating you as sons. For what son is not disciplined by his father? . . . 11 No discipline seems pleasant at the time, but painful. Later on, however, it **produces** a harvest of righteousness and peace for those who have been trained by it. | If you endure hardships in life, then you will share in God's holiness and be rewarded with a harvest of righteousness and peace. |
| **James 1**:2 Consider it pure joy, my brothers, whenever you face trials of many kinds, 3 because you know that the testing of your faith develops perseverance. 4 Perseverance must finish its work so that you may be mature and complete, not lacking anything. 5 If any of you lacks wisdom, you should ask God, who gives generously to all without finding fault, and it will be given to you. 12 Blessed is the man who perseveres under trial, because when he has stood the test, he will receive the crown of life that God has promised to those who love him. | If you persevere through trials for the sake of Christ, then God give you the crown of life that He has promised to all who love Him. |

366

**1 Peter 1**:3 Praise be to the God and Father of our Lord Jesus Christ! In his great mercy he has given us new birth into a living hope through the resurrection of Jesus Christ from the dead, 4 and into an inheritance that can never perish, spoil or fade—kept in heaven for you, 5 who through faith are shielded by God's power until the coming of the salvation that is ready to be revealed in the last time.

6 In this you greatly rejoice, though now for a little while you may have had to suffer grief in all kinds of trials. 7 These have come so that your faith—of greater worth than gold, which perishes even though refined by fire—may be proved genuine and may result in praise, glory and honor when Jesus Christ is revealed. 8 Though you have not seen him, you love him; and even though you do not see him now, you believe in him and are filled with an inexpressible and glorious joy, 9 for you are receiving the goal of your faith, the salvation of your souls.

13 Therefore, prepare your minds for action; be self-controlled; set your hope fully on the grace to be given you when Jesus Christ is revealed. 14 As obedient children do not conform to the evil desires you had when you lived in ignorance. 15 But just as he who called you is holy, so be holy in all you do; 16 for it is written: "Be holy, because I am holy." 17 Since you call on a Father who judges each man's work impartially, live your lives as strangers here in reverent fear.

If you walk in faith, then you will have a glorious inheritance.

If you have faith, then you will rejoice in God's protection.

If you suffer trials; if you are holy in all you do, if you set your hope fully in the Lord, then you will be judged worthy by God. then you will be praised, glorified, and honored by Jesus.

| | |
|---|---|
| **1 Peter 2**:2 Like newborn babies, crave pure spiritual milk, so that by it you may grow up in your salvation, 3 now that you have tasted that the Lord is good. 4 As you come to him, the living Stone—rejected by humans but chosen by God and precious to him— 5 you… are being built into a spiritual house to be a holy priesthood, offering spiritual sacrifices acceptable to God through Jesus Christ. | If you crave spiritual food, then you will thrive. |
| **1 Peter 3**:10 For, "Whoever would love life and see good days must keep their tongue from evil and their lips from deceitful speech. 11 They must turn from evil and do good; they must seek peace and pursue it. 12 For the eyes of the Lord are on the righteous and his ears are attentive to their prayer, but the face of the Lord is against those who do evil." | If you do good and turn from evil, then God will hear and answer your prayers and you will be blessed. |
| **2 Peter 1**:5 For this very reason, make every effort to add to your faith goodness; and to goodness, knowledge; 6 and to knowledge, self-control; and to self-control, perseverance; and to perseverance, godliness; 7 and to godliness, brotherly kindness; and to brotherly kindness, love. … 10b For if you do these things, you will never fall, 11 and you will receive a rich welcome into the eternal kingdom of our Lord and Savior Jesus Christ. | If you live by faith, goodness, godly understanding, self-control, godliness, brotherly kindness and love, then you will receive a rich welcome into Christ's Kingdom. |
| 1 John **1**:7 But if we walk in the light, as he is in the light, we have fellowship with one another, and the blood of Jesus his Son cleanses us from all sin…. 9 If we confess our sins, he is faithful and just to forgive us our sins and to cleanse us from all unrighteousness. | If you walk with Christ, then you will have fellowship with one another. |
| **1 John 2**:28 And now, dear children, continue in him, so that when he appears we may be confident and unashamed before him at his coming. | If you continue in Christ, then you will be confident when He returns. |

| | |
|---|---|
| **2 John** 8 Watch out that you do not lose what we have worked for, but that you may be **rewarded** fully. | If you persist, then God will reward you. |
| **Revelation 2**:7 To the one who is victorious, I will give the right to eat from the tree of life, which is in the paradise of God. . . .. 10 Be faithful, even to the point of death, and I will give you life as your victor's crown. 11 Whoever has ears, let them hear what the Spirit says to the churches. The one who is victorious will not be hurt at all by the second death. . . .. 17 Whoever has ears, let them hear what the Spirit says to the churches. To the one who is victorious, I will give some of the hidden manna. I will also give that person a white stone with a new name written on it, known only to the one who receives it. . . .. 26 To the one who is victorious and does my will to the end, I will give authority over the nations— 27 that one 'will rule them with an iron scepter and will dash them to pieces like pottery'—just as I have received authority from my Father. 28 I will also give that one the morning star. 29 Whoever has ears, let them hear what the Spirit says to the churches. | If you hear and obey the Spirit, then you will victorious and you will be given authority. |
| **Revelation 3**:11 I am coming soon. Hold on to what you have, so that no one will take your crown. 12 Him who overcomes I will make a pillar in the temple of my God. Never again will he leave it. I will write on him the name of my God and the name of the city of my God, the new Jerusalem, which is coming down out of heaven from my God; and I will also write on him my new name. . . .. 18 I counsel you to buy from me gold refined in the fire, so you can become rich; and white clothes to wear, so you can cover your shameful nakedness; and salve to put on your eyes, | If you walk in a manner worthy of the Lord and if you overcome, then Jesus will acknowledge you before God and angels.

If you overcome, then you will sit at the right hand of Jesus on His throne. |

| | |
|---|---|
| so you can see. 19 Those whom I love I rebuke and discipline. So be earnest, and repent. 20 Here I am! I stand at the door and knock. If anyone hears my voice and opens the door, I will come in and eat with him, and he with me. 21 To him who overcomes, I will give the right to sit with me on my throne, just as I overcame and sat down with my Father on his throne. | |
| **Revelation 11**:18b The time has come for judging the dead, and for **rewarding** your servants the prophets and your saints and those who reverence your name, both small and great— and for destroying those who destroy the earth. | If you are God's servant in this life, then God will reward you. |
| **Revelation 19**:7 Let us rejoice and be glad and give him glory! For the wedding of the Lamb has come, and his bride has made herself ready. 8 Fine linen, bright and clean, was given her to wear; for fine linen stands for the righteous acts of the saints. | If you make yourself ready for your marriage with Jesus, then you will wear your righteousness in heaven. |
| **Revelation 21**:6 To he who is thirsty I will give to drink without cost from the spring of the water of life. 7 He who overcomes will inherit all this, and I will be his God and he will be my son. | If you overcome, then you will inherit God's blessing. |

Printed in the United States
By Bookmasters